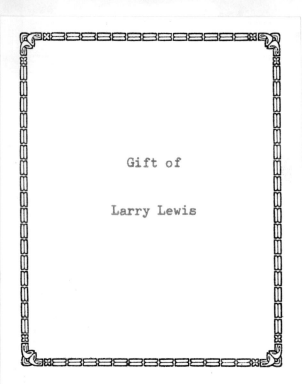

Gift of

Larry Lewis

Hon. Charles E. Whittaker: U.S. Supreme Court Justice 1957-62 (resigned), in a letter 1964:
"I have found it thoughtful, responsible, well-written and very interesting."

Dr. C. Perry Patterson: University of Texas, Professor 1925-57 (American History, specialist on Jefferson's writings):
"Never in my forty years of teaching, researching, and writing [in this field] . . . has such an important and well done piece of work passed over my desk . . . There is nothing like it in our political literature or any publication that approaches it in scope, character, organization, and fundamental nature . . . I regard it as more fundamental and realistic than Alexis de Toqueville's *Democracy in America* or James Bryce's *The American Commonwealth*. It should be used in the classrooms of American High Schools, Colleges and Universities . . . and read by every American . . ."

Dr. Harley L. Lutz: Princeton University, Professor 1928-47 (Economics):
". . . timely exposition . . . reveals prodigious effort . . . [best use] . . . in schools and colleges . . . could contribute much to the revival of that pride in our institutions and heritage . . . The definition of Equality . . . should be required reading . . . emphasis on self-discipline and the absence of coercion . . . discussion . . . of taxation is sound and illuminating . . . section on individual enterprise . . . especially important . . . the book is a scholarly treatment . . ."

Dr. Ralph C. Hutchison: President Lafayette College 1945-57; also President of Washington & Jefferson College 1931-45:
". . . [seeks] to recover for society the basic principles of political thought . . . a service profoundly needed at this time . . . courageous definition of principles is scholarly, unique and stimulating . . . the most remarkable culling-out and collection of the statements of these principles . . . [by The Founders] . . . set forth vividly . . . useful to young people . . . lay readers . . . one of the finest, most pertinent, and usable anthologies . . . clear and unequivocal statement of principles] . . . [Part II, Background Discussion] . . . invaluable reference for young people and laymen, even political historians . . . [Part IV] . . . reprinting of the great documents . . . inspire the intelligent reading of them . . . in full text, is a little touch of genius . . ."

Dr. Richard B. Morris: Columbia University, Professor 1959-76—a leading authority on early American History:

"I think that you have put together in a very ingenious way a series of appropriate quotations on basic American principles. It is important in these times that Americans should be reminded about their heritage, and to that end you have made a useful and suggestive contribution."

Dr. William Yandell Elliott: Harvard University, Professor 1923-63, (Government):

"It is indeed an impressive effort to supply a textbook that goes to the heart of the problems, that a school ought to be interested in affording to its students . . . its wealth of quotations and its well organized selection of American principles will prove useful as much to the teachers as to the students. I congratulate the Boston School Committee on getting this book into general use as a textbook . . . fills a real need for a basic and simple student text on the bases of American constitutional principles and their functions for the protection of our true liberties."

Dr. James Washington Bell: Northwestern University, Professor 1922-55 (Economics):

". . . carefully prepared and objective treatment . . . makes clear the spirit and meaning of the product of centuries of human experience . . . instructive and illuminating . . . The author obviously has the training and scholarship qualifications to do a successful research job and to write an authoritative work on the subject . . . Form and organization . . . sound . . . the most thorough and accurate analysis, in short compass, of the political, moral and legal principles . . ."

Dr. Walter E. Spahr: New York University, Professor 1923-56 (Economics):

". . . marked by mature and careful scholarship and deserves the widest possible reading . . . most helpful to younger people . . . badly needed by the present college generation and by all who wish to understand . . . the great verities . . . a helpful and sobering document . . . outlines the best thought and principles of behavior in this nation when . . . in accordance with the highminded philosophy . . . [of The Founders]."

Boston (Mass.) School Committee [Board of Education]: October 1967 Resolution adopting this book as a textbook (with approval of Board of Superintendents):

"Ordered, that the following textbook is hereby authorized for use . . . [grades 7-12]."

COMMENDATIONS

AUTHOR'S FORENOTE

to

1976 Bicentennial Reprinting

This reprinting reproduces photographically the text originally published in 1963, defining the whole of the traditional American philosophy: the fundamental Principles of 1776. It does not represent a revision of that text.

The book reflects the essence of The Founders' convictions as to these Principles, based on their writings—most notably those of the signers of the Declaration of Independence and the Constitution. Their writings will never change. The 1963 text, therefore, does not need revision. It will be as valid and useful in 2076 as it is in this 1976. The Principles are timeless in value to all generations, indeed to Mankind; so the book is enduring in worth.

Being the only book in existence which defines *the indivisible whole* of the 1776 philosophy, it fills a grave need of all Americans today as well as of Posterity.

The preceding commendations by eminent authorities certify the book's soundness as a scholarly report, definition, of this philosophy. No scholar has faulted a word in it since publication.

The original title: *Your American Yardstick*—descriptive of the book's usefulness to readers—has been changed so as to denote the nature of its contents:

THE AMERICAN IDEAL OF 1776

*   *   *   *   *   *

The Twelve Basic American Principles

May 3, 1976
Independence Square   HAMILTON ABERT LONG
Philadelphia, Pa.

THE AMERICAN IDEAL OF 1776

The Twelve Basic American Principles

by

HAMILTON ABERT LONG
(A member of the New York Bar, ret.)

1976
Your Heritage Books, Inc.
Philadelphia

1963 Printing 20,000 copies
1965 Printing 30,000 copies
1976 Bicentennial Printing 25,000 copies
(former title: *Your American Yardstick*)

Library of Congress Catalog Card No. 76-16597
ISBN 0-911668-02-0

Manufactured in the United States of America

> History, by apprising them of the past, will enable them to judge of the future . . .
> Thomas Jefferson (1782)

TO
YOUNG AMERICA
TODAY AND TOMORROW

> "Our country is in danger, but not to be despaired of . . . On you depend the fortunes of America. You are to decide the important question, on which rest the happiness and liberty of millions yet unborn. Act worthy of yourselves."
> Dr. Joseph Warren (1775)

The Spirit of '76

1776 BATTLE-FLAG

Culpeper (Va.) County Militia unit combining two popular slogans with popular emblem of rattlesnake symbolizing vigilance, striking-power and fair warning.

(Reproduced by permission; see page 322, *post.*)

AN AMERICAN

> There ought to be no New England men, no New Yorker, &c.,
> known on the Continent, but all of us Americans . . .
> Christopher Gadsden
> (Letter to Chas. Garth, after attending the
> Stamp Act Congress representing S.C., 1765)

> The distinctions between Virginians, Pennsylvanians, New York-
> ers, and New Englanders, are no more. I am not a Virginian,
> but an American.
> Patrick Henry
> (In Continental Congress, 1774)

THE NAME OF AMERICAN

> The name of AMERICAN, which belongs to you, in your national
> capacity, must always exalt the just pride of Patriotism, more
> than any appellation derived from local discriminations.
> President George Washington, *Farewell Address*

TRULY AMERICAN PRINCIPLES

> We are laboring hard to establish in this country principles more and
> more *national* and free from all foreign ingredients, so that we may be
> neither "Greeks nor Trojans," but truly Americans.
> (Emphasis per the original.)
> Alexander Hamilton
> (Letter to Rufus King, 1796)

WHAT IS AN AMERICAN?

> What then is the American, this new man? . . . *He* is an American, who
> leaving behind him all his ancient prejudices and manners, receives new
> ones from the new mode of life he has embraced, the new government he
> obeys, and the new rank he holds . . . The American is a new man, who
> acts upon new principles; he must therefore entertain new ideas, and form
> new opinions. From involuntary idleness, servile dependence, penury, and
> useless labour, he has passed to toils of a very different nature, rewarded
> by ample subsistence.—This is an American.
> (Emphasis per the original.)
> J. Hector St. John de Crévecoeur
> (A French immigrant become a New York farmer;
> essays, 1782—*Letters From An American Farmer*)

PATRIOTISM

Patriotism . . . This noble affection which impels us to sacrifice every thing dear, even life itself, to our country . . .

John Hancock
(Oration, Boston, March 5, 1774)

The only [worthy] principles of public conduct . . . are to sacrifice estate, ease, health, and applause, and even life, to the sacred calls of his country. These manly sentiments, in private life, make the good citizen; in public life, the patriot and the hero.

James Otis
(Statement in Court opposing "Writs of Assistance," 1761)

To a generous mind, the public good, as it is the end of government, so it is also such a noble and excellent one, that the prospect of attaining it will animate the pursuit, and being attained, it will reward the pains. The very name of patriotism is indeed become a jest with some men; which would be much stranger than it is, had not so many others made a jest of the thing, serving their own base and wicked ends, under the pretext and colour of it. But there will be hypocrites in politicks, as well as in religion. Nor ought so sacred a name to fall into contempt, however it may have been prostituted & profaned, to varnish over crimes. And those times are *perilous* indeed, wherein *men shall be* only *lovers of their own selves*, having no concern for the good of the public. Shall we go to the pagans to learn this god-like virtue? Even they can teach it . . . [A Christian lacking patriotism] . . . would be a reproach not only to his religion, a religion of charity and beneficence, but even to our own common nature, as corrupt and depraved as it is. But how much more infamous were this, in persons of public character? in those, on whom the welfare of their country, under providence, immediately depends?
(Emphasis per original.)

Rev. Jonathan Mayhew
(Election Sermon, 1754)

PATRIOTISM

Patriotism is as much a virtue as justice, and is as necessary for the support of societies as natural affection is for the support of families. The *Amor Patriae* is both a moral and a religious duty. It comprehends not only the love of our neighbors but of millions of our fellow creatures, not only of the present but of future generations. This virtue we find constitutes a part of the first characters of history.

Dr. Benjamin Rush
(An essay, 1773)

The *true patriot* therefore, will enquire into the causes of the *fears* and *jealousies* of his countrymen; and if he finds they are not *groundless*, he will be far from endeavoring to allay or stifle them: On the contrary, constrain'd by the *Amor Patriæ*, and from *public* views, he will by all proper means in his power *foment* and *cherish* them: He will, as far as he is able, keep the attention of his fellow citizens awake to their grievances; and not suffer them to be at rest, till the causes of their just complaints are removed.—At such a time *Philanthrop's* Patriot [a King's man] may be "very cautious of charging the want of *ability* or *integrity* to those with whom any of the powers of government are entrusted": But the *true* patriot, will constantly be jealous of those very men: Knowing that power, especially in times of corruption, makes men wanton; that it intoxicates the mind; and unless those with whom it is entrusted, are carefully watched, such is the weakness or the perverseness of human nature, they will be apt to *domineer* over the people, instead of governing them, according to the known laws of the state, to which *alone* they have submitted. If he finds, upon the best enquiry, the want of ability or integrity; that is, an ignorance of, or a disposition to depart from, the constitution, which is the measure and rule of government & submission, he will point them out, and *loudly proclaim* them: He will stir up the people, *incessantly* to complain of *such men*, till they are either reform'd, or remov'd from that sacred trust, which it is dangerous for them any longer to hold.—
(Emphasis per original.)

Samuel Adams
(Essay in Boston Gazette, 1771)

CONTENTS

PART II

SOME ASPECTS OF THE TRADITIONAL
AMERICAN PHILOSOPHY

BACKGROUND DISCUSSION

PART III

ALL HONOR TO THE FOUNDERS

PART IV

APPENDIX

Be it remembered, however, that liberty must at all hazards be supported . . . cannot be preserved without a general knowledge among the people . . . And the preservation of the means of knowledge among the lowest ranks, is of more importance to the public than all the property of all the rich men in the country.   John Adams
("A Dissertation on the Canon and Feudal Law," 1765)

I know no safe depository of the ultimate powers of the society but the people themselves; and if we think them not enlightened enough to exercise their control with a wholesome discretion, the remedy is not to take it from them, but to inform their discretion by education.
Thomas Jefferson
(Letter to Wm. C. Jarvis, 1820)

A popular Government, without popular information, or the means of acquiring it, is but a Prologue to a Farce or a Tragedy; or, perhaps both. Knowledge will forever govern ignorance: And a people who mean to be their own Governors, must arm themselves with the power which knowledge gives.   James Madison
(Letter to W. T. Barry, 1822)

Knowledge is in every country the surest basis of public happiness. In one in which the measures of Government receive their impression so immediately from the sense of the Community as in ours it is proportionably essential. To the security of a free Constitution it contributes in various ways: By convincing those who are intrusted with the public administration, that every valuable end of Government is best answered by the enlightened confidence of the people: and by teaching the people themselves to know and to value their own rights; to discern and provide against invasions of them; to distinguish between oppression and the necessary exercise of lawful authority; between burthens proceeding from a disregard to their convenience and those resulting from the inevitable exigencies of Society; to discriminate the spirit of Liberty from that of licentiousness, cherishing the first, avoiding the last, and uniting a speedy, but temperate vigilance against encroachments, with an inviolable respect to the Laws.   President George Washington
(First Annual Message to Congress, 1790)

LIBERTY'S SECURITY DEPENDS MAINLY UPON THE PEOPLE'S KNOWING THEIR RIGHTS AND UPON THEIR SPIRIT—THEIR WILLINGNESS TO DEFEND THEM

> If a nation expects to be ignorant and free, in a state of civilization, it expects what never was and never will be.
>
> Thomas Jefferson
> (Letter to Chas. Yancey, 1816)

> It [education] is favourable to liberty. Freedom can exist only in the society of knowledge. Without learning, men are incapable of knowing their rights, and where learning is confined to a few people, liberty can be neither equal nor universal.
>
> Dr. Benjamin Rush
> (Essay, 1786)

> Although all men are born free, and all nations might be so, yet too true it is, that slavery has been the general lot of the human race. Ignorant —they have been cheated; asleep—they have been surprized; divided— the yoke has been forced upon them. But what is the lesson? that because the people *may* betray themselves, they ought to give themselves up, blindfold, to those who have an interest in betraying them? Rather conclude that the people ought to be enlightened, to be awakened, to be united, that after establishing a government they should watch over it, as well as obey it.
> (Emphasis per original.)
>
> James Madison
> (Essay: "Who Are the Best Keepers of the People's Liberties?" 1792)

> [Effective resistance to usurpers possible only] provided the citizens understand their rights and are disposed to defend them.*
>
> _____
>
> [Safeguards of Liberty are just and constitutional laws] and above all the vigilant and manly spirit which actuates the people of America, a spirit which nourishes freedom, and in return is nourished by it.**
>
> *The Federalist*
> (*No. 28 by Alexander Hamilton;
> **No. 57 by James Madison)

LIBERTY SECURE
UNDER THE CONSTITUTION, UNLESS AND UNTIL
A CORRUPTED PEOPLE NEED, INVITE, BEING RULED

Though, when a people shall have become incapable of governing themselves and fit for a master, it is of little consequence from what quarter
he comes.

George Washington
(Letter to Lafayette, 1788)

. . . the powers reserved by the people [under the Constitution] render
them secure, and, until they themselves become corrupt, they will always
have upright and able rulers. I give my assent to the Constitution. . . .

John Hancock
(Massachusetts Ratifying Convention, 1788)

[I] . . . believe farther that this [new government under the Constitution]
is likely to be well administered for a course of years, and can only end
in Despotism, as other forms have done before it, when the people shall
become so corrupted as to need despotic Government, being incapable of
any other.

Benjamin Franklin
(In the Framing Convention, 1787)

*With money we will get men, said Caesar, and with men we will get
money.* Nor should our assembly [the Virginia Legislature] be deluded by
the integrity of their own purposes, and conclude that these unlimited
powers will never be abused, because themselves are not disposed to abuse
them. They *should look forward to a time, and that not a distant one,
when a corruption* in this, as in the country from which we derive our
origin [Great Britain], *will have seized the heads of government, and be
spread by them through the body of the people; when they will purchase
the voices of the people, and make them pay the price. Human nature is
the same on every side of the Atlantic,* and will be alike influenced by the
same causes. *The time to guard against corruption and tyranny, is before
they shall have gotten hold on us.* It is better to keep the wolf out of the
fold, than to trust to drawing his teeth and talons after he shall have
entered.
(Emphasis added.)

Thomas Jefferson
("Notes on the State of Virginia," 1782)

EXPERIENCE A SOUND GUIDE

Foresight through hindsight conduces insight.

To fail to learn from history is to be doomed to repeat the mistakes of the past.   A maxim

Experience keeps a dear School, but Fools will learn in no other, and scarce in that . . .   Benjamin Franklin
(Poor Richard in "The Way to Wealth")
(Note: "dear" meaning costly.)

Experience is the oracle of truth; and where its responses are unequivocal, they ought to be conclusive and sacred.   *The Federalist*
(No. 20, by Madison)

I have but one lamp by which my feet are guided; and that is the lamp of experience. I know of no way of judging of the future but by the past.
Patrick Henry
(Address in the second Virginia Convention, 1775)

. . . forty years of experience in government is worth a century of book-reading. . . .   Thomas Jefferson
(Letter to Samuel Kercheval, 1816)

Experience is a severe preceptor, but it teaches useful truths, and however harsh, is always honest.—Be calm and dispassionate, and listen to what it tells us.   Chief Justice of New York John Jay
(Address to People of N.Y. State, 1788)

. . . experience is the surest standard, by which to test the real tendency of the existing Constitution of a country; that facility in changes upon the credit of mere hypotheses and opinion exposes to perpetual change, from the endless variety of hypotheses and opinion . . .
President George Washington, *Farewell Address*

xxi

KNOWLEDGE AND FREEDOM

> To be free, Man must have and exercise freedom of choice
> Based on knowledge, understanding, of the alternatives,
> Which he must be at liberty to help conceive, create,
> In order to make freedom of choice most beneficial.

FREEDOM FOR TRUTH TO PREVAIL OVER ERROR

> . . . truth is great and will prevail if left to herself, that she is the proper and sufficient antagonist to error, and has nothing to fear from the conflict, unless by human interposition disarmed of her natural weapons, free argument and debate, errors ceasing to be dangerous when it is permitted freely to contradict them.
>
> Virginia Statute of Religious Liberty, 1786

THE FATEFUL ROLE OF SELF-GOVERNING AMERICANS

> It has been frequently remarked, that it seems to have been reserved to the people of this country, by their conduct and example, to decide the important question, whether societies of men are really capable or not, of establishing good government from reflection and choice, or whether they are forever destined to depend, for their political constitutions, on accident and force.
>
> *The Federalist*
> (No. 1, by Alexander Hamilton)

ONLY THE PEOPLE'S VIRTUE
CAN GUARANTEE LIBERTY'S SAFETY

> But I go on this great republican principle, that the people will have virtue and intelligence to select men of virtue and wisdom. Is there no virtue among us? If there be not, we are in a wretched situation. No theoretical checks—no form of government can render us secure. To suppose that any form of government will secure liberty or happiness without any virtue in the people, is a chimerical idea. If there be sufficient virtue and intelligence in the community, it will be exercised in the selection of these men. So that we do not depend on their virtue, or put confidence in our rulers, but in the people who are to choose them.
>
> James Madison
> (Virginia Ratifying Convention, 1788)
> ("republican" means: of a republic)

A PEOPLE AND THEIR ROOTS

A people must, from time to time, refresh themselves at the well-springs of their origin, lest they perish.

(An adage)

THE LOFTY STANDARD

Let us raise a standard to which the wise and the honest can repair. The event is in the hand of God.

George Washington
(In the Framing Convention, 1787)

A RETURN TO FUNDAMENTAL PRINCIPLES

That no free government, or the blessings of liberty, can be preserved to any people, but by a firm adherence to justice, moderation, temperance, frugality and virtue, and by frequent recurrence to fundamental principles.

Virginia Declaration of Rights, 1776

A frequent recurrence to the fundamental principles of the constitution, and a constant adherence to those of piety, justice, moderation, temperance, industry and frugality, are absolutely necessary to preserve the advantages of liberty, and to maintain a free government.

Massachusetts Bill of Rights, 1780

Our conflict is not likely to cease so soon as every good Man would wish. The measure of iniquity is not yet filled; and unless we can return a little more to first principles, and act a little more upon patriotic ground, I do not know when it will, or, what may be the Issue of the contest. . . . many melancholy proofs of the decay of public virtue . . . [are evident; the British boast] . . . that we shall be our own conquerers. Cannot our common Country Am. [America], possess virtue enough to disappoint them? . . . Our cause is noble, it is the cause of Mankind! and the danger to it, is to be apprehended from ourselves.

George Washington
(Letter to James Warren, 1779)

INTRODUCTION

This study-guide fills a long-felt and grave need. It presents in brief but reasonably comprehensive and simple form the definitions of the fundamental principles underlying America's traditional, governmental philosophy. This is the philosophy of Man-over-Government. It stems from the uniquely American concept of Man's possessing God-given, unalienable rights and creating governments as his tools, or instruments, primarily to make and keep these rights secure, as proclaimed in 1776 in the Declaration of Independence. This philosophy is an indivisible whole and must be accepted, or rejected, as such.

These traditional American principles were well understood and faithfully supported governmentally by all generations of Americans from the birth of the Republic in 1789 through the first third of the present century. Since then, however, the present generation has allowed itself to become confused and to lose its way; in practice, it has betrayed and abandoned these traditional principles. This is widely recognized in America as well as by some in informed circles abroad. Earlier generations in America may have made mistakes, to be sure, but nothing comparable to this betrayal and abandonment.

This confusion, betrayal and abandonment in practice—despite lip-service at times by many—have produced a condition which may soundly be defined in the form of a "confession," or self-appraisal, by the present generation in America (especially those of middle-age or older) as follows:

We Americans of the mid-twentieth century have in our traditional, governmental philosophy unique and invaluable beliefs and principles about The Individual and his unalienable rights, in relation to God as his Creator and the giver of these rights—about the consequently limited role of government as the creature and tool, or instrument, of the sovereign and self-governing people, as well as about history and human destiny; but we do not duly honor in practice these beliefs and principles. With woefully few exceptions, we do not even seem to know, much less adequately comprehend and appreciate, the infinitely great values which constitute the foundation of our heritage and civilization. We do not believe in them with requisite conviction and fervor. Our default, as the temporary trustees of the just heritage of Young America of today and tomorrow, is all the more complete due to our failure for decades to train the children in schools and colleges, as well as in homes and churches, to understand, to respect, and to honor this heritage of beliefs, principles and values which add up to the essence of traditional America. Thus sinning, we are in truth guilty of the most heinous of sins: the lost consciousness of sin.

The guilt is personal and individual, of course; so it is the problem and duty, in good conscience and in the light of the trust reposed by the helpless little children of today, of each adult American to decide for himself or herself the measure of his or her own guilt.

Such sentiments would be heartily endorsed, it is believed, by the Founding Fathers and their fellow-American leaders—indeed, by the American people and their leaders of every generation in America prior to the present one—could they return today and pass judgment upon the performance of this generation as the temporary trustees of the American heritage of Individual Liberty, the just heritage of American Posterity.

This study-guide is unique; nothing like it exists, according to the author's many years of research in this field. There has never been prepared, it seems, any presentation of such a set of definitions of the fundamental American principles. Not even a comparable listing, brief but comprehensive, of the basic principles themselves could be found, much less their adequate definition. The core-concepts of the American philosophy are, of course, stated in the second to fourth sentences of the Declaration of Independence; and the Signers and their fellow leaders of that generation left voluminous writings of a general nature about the subject. It is on the basis of these writings that the present statement of American principles has been developed. Of these writings, the ones which have been relied upon for present purposes are numerous and some of the principal ones are identified later, in the "Background Discussion" (Part II).

The fresh approach offered by the definitions of these American principles, and the ready usefulness to the reader of the unusual form of presentation, induce the hope that this study-guide will be conducive to greater clarity of thought and to sound understanding among the American people and their leaders in all walks of life, particularly in the exercise of that most inclusive of all freedoms—freedom of choice—regarding America's course governmentally. It is designed to serve particularly as a useful tool for Young America, today and tomorrow. It will help to focus attention on the basic causes, not symptoms—on fundamentals, not things superficial.

Soundness of thinking and of the expression of thoughts depends upon accuracy of the definitions of words and terms used. It is especially noteworthy that the term "Individual Liberty"—or more fully stated: "Individual Liberty-Responsibility"—means primarily Man's Liberty against Government-over-Man; that is, Man's Freedom from Government-over-Man. This Liberty, or Freedom, is inclusive of all of Man's liberties, freedoms and rights, as well as of the duties underlying the inseparable factor of Responsibility. The word "Man," as used in this discussion, always connotes The Individual.

Of particular interest, perhaps, is "American Traditionist"—a term suggested as an accurate "label" for adherents, including the present writer, of the traditional American philosophy including the principles discussed in this study-guide. The term connotes one who is forward-looking in keeping with The American Vision and its high goals and ideals, sensibly judged in the light of recorded human experience, especially of America's own history. This term embraces, most importantly, the ideals proclaimed in the Declaration of Independence and in the Preamble to the United States Constitution, as well as the realism governmentally underlying the philosophy and system of constitutionally limited government defined in the body of the Constitution, and as further defined by the prohibitions, against the Federal government *only,* which were made express in the first eight (Bill of Rights) amendments in order to supplement and confirm the implied, over-all prohibition in the original instrument due to its denial of all powers not enumerated as being granted to this government. These amendments were induced by the people's great fear of the new central government as a potential threat to their hard-won liberties; while each of the States was left free from any restriction by these amendments so as to be able to continue to deal, as it should see fit, with the topics involved. The term "American Traditionist" contemplates sound progress through proper constitutional change by the people by amendment from time to time if, when and as they choose to amend the Constitution. This term embraces the concept of sound progress aided by foresight gained through hindsight. This means the American people's making sound progress toward their chosen goals on the basis of adequate understanding of their roots, of traditional American values, as the needed firm foundation for well-grounded growth. The term "American Traditionist" is useful especially because it is reasonably self-defining and not readily misunderstandable or open to easy misrepresentation.

Thomas Jefferson's writings are referred to so frequently in this study-guide, much more so than the writings of any other leader of his day, that a brief explanation is in order. He was considered by most as being second to none—by some as being pre-eminent—among the governmental philosophers of America. He continued to occupy the life-long role of one of the chief expositors of the American philosophy and system of government; that is, Man-over-Government. Moreover, his vastly varied and distinguished experience in government, matched by few and exceeded by none among his fellow leaders, added immensely to the practical significance of his writings. He was active in this role, in and out of office, throughout the entire half-century and more from the pre-1776 period to the time of his death in 1826. He was exceptional, even among the distinguished leaders of that day, because of his ability to write in easily quotable form—tersely but rich in meaning. The richness of his writings, for purposes of quotation on an infinitely varied list of subjects, is indicated by the fact that a volume of over nine thousand quotations (1,000 pages) was published in 1900: *The Jeffersonian Cyclopedia*. It is an excellent guide to his original writings. Furthermore, he was at least the equal, if not the peer, of even the more articulate leaders of his day in perceiving and expressing the enduring American principles in keeping with the "common sense" of the subject—with "the American mind"—which, as he wrote many years later (1825 letter to Henry Lee), was all that he tried to express in the Declaration of Independence. That this was true—that no ideas but those then well-known to the American people were expressed in it—was borne out for example by John Adams' contemporaneous statement (letter to Samuel Chase, July 1, 1776) about the debate in Congress over Jefferson's draft of the Declaration: ". . . nothing was said but what had been repeated and hackneyed in that room before, a hundred times, for six months past."

Because of John Adams' justifiable pride in his own profound knowledge and great skill as a writer as well as his seniority in service and leadership in the Congress, which fully entitled him to assume the major role among the members of the committee appointed by the Congress in June, 1776 to draft the Declaration, it is of special interest to note that he insisted that Jefferson do the primary work of actual drafting and that Adams wrote long afterward (1822 letter to Timothy Pickering) that Jefferson had come to the Congress in June, 1775 with "a reputation for literature, science, and a happy talent of composition. Writings of his were handed about, remarkable for the peculiar felicity of expression." The high and growing esteem in which Jefferson has been held by succeeding generations of Americans testifies to the reality of his eminence. This is illustrated by the fact that in the present generation he has seemingly been quoted more often by more people than any other leader of his day—perhaps more than all of the others combined. In the past quarter-century or so, leaders of both principal political parties have often sought to win popular following by claiming (often unsoundly) that he has been the inspiration of their policies and programs. He has been cited, but could not be correctly quoted, by many politicians as being a source of their ideas which he would have abhorred, judged by his writings and his record.

The considerable number of quotations presented in this study-guide, selected from the writings of various individuals and from official sources pertaining to the founding of the Republic, represent only a very small fraction of those available; and the ones used are merely illustrative of the great quantity of material to be found in pertinent, historical sources. The quotations used, moreover, which were selected mainly from the writings of well-known leaders of that period, truly reflect the sentiments of the people in general, as proved by the present writer's extensive researches. These quotations may be accepted as a sound sample of what is available in the records.

The fact that numerous references to *The Federalist* occur makes it desirable that the reader consult, at the outset, the discussion in Part II of this famous and great work. The authorship of some of the 85 essays comprising this book has long been disputed, as between Hamilton and Madison. Modern research proves this conclusion as to authorship, relied upon in this study-guide, is reasonable: Hamilton 51 essays—numbers 1, 6-9, 11-13, 15-17, 21-36, 59-61, 65-85; Madison 26 essays—10, 14, 37-58 and probably 62, 63; Madison (some data from Hamilton)—18-20; and Jay five—2-5, 64, chiefly on foreign affairs. (Jay was then, as he had been for some years past, in charge of foreign affairs for the Confederation government.) Authorship of a particular essay is in reality unimportant because this work was their joint report of the intent of the Framing Convention, expressed in the words of the Constitution; although each of these authors wrote separately.

Reference is made, in Part II, to discussions in Congress in the early years of the Republic, commencing in 1789. In this period, there were no official, complete reports of proceedings in Congress; its Journal was very brief and sketchy. Later, when the *Annals* of Congress were first prepared and published, including this early period, they were—and ever since have been—accepted officially as being reliable. For the early years, the *Annals* used, as one source, the contemporary reports of debates in Congress as published in newspapers at the seat of the Federal government. These published reports were therefore known to the members of Congress whose remarks were thus recorded, in substance. In the absence of any recorded challenge, of the accuracy of the contemporaneous reports, by such members—for instance, in the official Journal or in their writings—it is reasonable and sound to assume that the reports were accepted by them as accurate. This is one reason why the *Annals,* which rely in part upon these contemporaneous reports, have been accepted officially as being dependable in this regard.

Precise references for all quotations are listed in a special section in the Appendix, with appropriate comments about some sources of main interest. Where no source is indicated for a seeming quotation, the present writer is the author.

Permission to quote, in the following pages, copyrighted material from other writings is gratefully acknowledged; as indicated in detail in the pertinent Note in the Appendix (page 322).

Throughout the discussion, the use of the masculine (Man, he, his, him) should be read as including also the feminine. Woman's role now, of course, is the same as Man's with respect to all duties, as well as rights, of Individual Liberty-Responsibility, in the United States.

Sincere thanks are extended to those who have helped in various ways, during the years of work involved in the development of this study-guide, from its initial printed stage in embryonic form in 1952 —for private consideration only—to the present writing, chiefly by way of editorial criticism. Much other preparatory work—research, writing and lecturing—was done during the preceding two decades.

This study-guide is offered as the work solely of the undersigned as an individual—not connected in any way with any other person or with any group or organization. No other person has ever had any authority or responsibility regarding its conception, form, content, or production—involving a number of drafts over the years.

Hamilton Abert Long

October 31, 1963
Washington, D.C.

PREFATORY NOTE
(regarding the Principles)

It is basic that all statements made in the following pages about Man's rights—his liberties or freedoms—are to be considered as subject to the fact of the existence of the inseparable duty factor of Individual Liberty-Responsibility and especially this factor's primary aspect. This aspect is the duty to respect the equal rights of others. The term Individual Liberty always connotes Liberty-Responsibility because Liberty cannot exist separate and apart from Responsibility, nor Right from Duty.

The term "unalienable rights" should, in every instance of its use, be read as meaning *God*-given, unalienable rights, because the only basis for considering them to be unalienable is the fundamental and uniquely American concept of their Divine origin—that Man possesses them solely by reason of endowment by his Creator. Unless considered to be of Divine origin, these rights cannot properly be classified as being unalienable. They are then subject to being considered as mere conditional privileges granted by government. In such case, there can be no moral or constitutional basis for objecting to their violation, by government or by others, such as exists in the case of God-given rights as protected traditionally by the American constitutional system; such government-granted privileges are not comparable in dignity with God-given rights.

In the presentation of definitions and discussion of Principles, some overlapping and repetition have been unavoidable. The aim has been to make the definition and discussion of each Principle as self-sufficient as possible in order to permit quick reference to it alone, from time to time, with minimum risk of misunderstanding by any reader. This enhances greatly the usefulness, to the many, of the presentation as a frequently consulted study-guide, and especially to the Young and others not familiar with the subject.

For most convenient reference, the following definitions of the Principles are presented first, then followed by the supporting "Background Discussion." These definitions embody the present writer's own phrasing, in the light of his careful analysis based upon long and extensive research among original sources—some noted in the "Background Discussion." The definitions are unique; they are not to be found in any other writings—not even anything comparable; hence the great potential value and usefulness of this study-guide.

THE AUTHOR

xxxi

PART I
THE TWELVE BASIC AMERICAN PRINCIPLES

PRINCIPLE ONE

THE SPIRITUAL IS SUPREME

AMERICANS A RELIGIOUS PEOPLE

From the day of the Declaration . . . They [the American people] were bound by the laws of God, which they all, and by the laws of the Gospel, which they nearly all, acknowledged as the rules of their conduct.

John Quincy Adams, Secretary of State
(Oration celebrating July 4, 1821)

FAITH IN GOD SUFFICIENT, WITHOUT "PROOF"

The sceptical philosophers claim and exercise the privilege of assuming, without proof, the very first principles of their philosophy; and yet they require, from others, a proof of everything by reasoning. They are unreasonable in both points . . .

U.S. Supreme Court Justice James Wilson
(Lectures, 1790-1791)

RIGHT AND MORAL DUTY TO WORSHIP GOD

It is the right as well as the duty of all men in society, publicly, and at stated seasons, to worship the Supreme Being, the great Creator and Preserver of the universe.   Massachusetts Bill of Rights, 1780

RELIGION, MORALITY, LIBERTY

Of all the dispositions and habits which lead to political prosperity, Religion and morality are indispensable supports. In vain would that man claim the tribute of Patriotism, who should labour to subvert these great Pillars of human happiness, these firmest props of the duties of Men and citizens. The mere Politician, equally with the pious man ought to respect and to cherish them. A volume could not trace all their connections with private and public felicity. Let it simply be asked where is the security for property, for reputation, for life, if the sense of religious obligation *desert* the oaths, which are the instruments of investigation in Courts of Justice? And let us with caution indulge the supposition, that morality can be maintained without religion. Whatever may be conceded to the influence of refined education on minds of peculiar structure, reason and experience both forbid us to expect that National morality can prevail in exclusion of religious principle. 'Tis substantially true, that virtue or morality is a necessary spring of popular government. (Emphasis his)

President George Washington, *Farewell Address*

RELIGIOUS BELIEF (TYPICAL OF THE FOUNDERS) OF BENJAMIN FRANKLIN—FAMED AS A SCIENTIST—FALSELY CLAIMED BY SOME TO HAVE BEEN AN ATHEIST

I have lived, Sir, a long time, and the longer I live, the more convincing proofs I see of this truth—*that God governs in the affairs of men*. And if a sparrow cannot fall to the ground without his notice, is it probable that an empire can rise without his aid? . . . I also believe that without his concurring aid we shall succeed in this political building no better than the Builders of Babel . . .

In Federal [Framing] Convention, 1787, making a motion for Prayer

(Note: emphasis Franklin's; word "God" underscored twice in original.)

I never doubted, for instance, the existence of a Deity; that he made the world and governed it by his providence; that the most acceptable service of God was the doing good to man; that our souls are immortal; and that all crimes will be punished, and virtue rewarded, either here or hereafter.   "Autobiography"

. . . I can only shew my Gratitude for these mercies from God, by a readiness to help his other Children and my Brethren . . . Even the mix'd imperfect Pleasures we enjoy in this World, are rather from God's Goodness than our Merit; how much more such Happiness of Heaven. For my own part I have not the Vanity to think I deserve it, the Folly to expect it, nor the Ambition to desire it; but content myself in submitting to the Will and Disposal of that God who made me . . .

Letter to Joseph Huey, 1753

I BELIEVE there is one supreme, most perfect Being . . . Also, when I stretch my imagination through and beyond our system of planets, beyond the visible fixed stars themselves, into that space that is every way infinite, and conceive it filled with suns like ours, each with a chorus of worlds for ever moving round him; then this little ball on which we move, seems, even in my narrow imagination, to be almost nothing, and myself less than nothing, and of no sort of consequence. . . . That I may be preserved from atheism . . . Help me, O Father! . . . For all thy innumerable benefits; for life, and reason . . . My good God, I thank thee!

"Articles of Belief . . . ," 1728

(Note: written by Franklin when 22 years of age)

RELIGION MOST IMPORTANT OF ALL

. . . every encroachment upon *religion, of all things the most important,* ought to be considered as the greatest imposition. . . . By religion, I mean an inward habitual reverence for, and devotedness to the Deity, *with such external homage, either public or private, as the worshiper believes most acceptable to him.* According to this definition, it is impossible for human laws to regulate religion without destroying it; for they cannot compel *inward* religious reverence, that being altogether mental and of a spiritual nature; nor can they enforce *outward* religious homage, because all such homage is either a man's own choice, and then it is not compelled, or it is repugnant to it, and then it cannot be religious. . . . the *consciences of men are not the objects of human legislation.* . . . [any delegation of power over religion to public officials] . . . would be a mere nullity, and the compact by which it was ceded, altogether nugatory, *the rights of conscience being immutably personal and absolutely inalienable,* nor can the state or community as such have any concern in the matter.

(Attributed to) William Livingston, Governor of N.J., 1778

(Emphasis in first line added; all other emphasis per the original.)

THE INDIVIDUAL'S RELIGION AND VIRTUE
THE KEY TO PUBLIC HAPPINESS AND LIBERTY

. . . I fully agree in Opinion with a very celebrated Author, that "Freedom or Slavery will prevail in a (City or) Country according as the Disposition & Manners of the People render them fit for the one or the other"; and I have long been convincd that our Enemies have made it an Object, to eradicate from the Minds of the People in general a Sense of true Religion & Virtue, in hopes thereby the more easily to carry their Point of enslaving them. Indeed my Friend, this is a Subject so important in my Mind, that I know not how to leave it. Revelation assures us that "Righteousness exalteth a Nation"—Communities are dealt with in this World by the wise and just Ruler of the Universe. He rewards or punishes them according to their general Character. The diminution of publick Virtue is usually attended with that of publick Happiness, and the public Liberty will not long survive the total Extinction of Morals.

("convincd" in original.)

Samuel Adams
(Letter to John Scollay, 1776)

A Principle of The Traditional American Philosophy

1. THE SPIRITUAL IS SUPREME

"... all men are __created__ ... endowed by their __Creator__ ..."
(Declaration of Independence)

The Principle

1. The fundamental principle underlying the traditional American philosophy is that the Spiritual is supreme—that Man is of Divine origin and his spiritual, or religious, nature is of supreme value and importance compared with things material.

Religious Nature

2. This governmental philosophy is, therefore, essentially religious in nature. It is uniquely American; no other people in all history have ever made this principle the basis of their governmental philosophy. The spiritual brotherhood of men under the common fatherhood of God is a concept which is basic to this American philosophy. It expresses the spiritual relationship of God to Man and, in the light thereof, of Man to Man. To forget these truths is a most heinous offense against the spirit of traditional America because the greatest sin is the lost consciousness of sin.

The fundamentally religious basis of this philosophy is the foundation of its moral code, which contemplates The Individual's moral duty as being created by God's Law: the Natural Law. The Individual's duty requires obedience to this higher Law; while knowledge of this duty comes from conscience, which the religious-minded and morally-aware Individual feels duty-bound to heed. This philosophy asserts that there are moral absolutes: truths, such as those mentioned above, which are binding upon all Individuals at all times under all circumstances. This indicates some of the spiritual and moral values which are inherent in its concept of Individual Liberty-Responsibility.

An Indivisible Whole

3. The American philosophy, based upon this principle, is an indivisible whole and must be accepted or rejected as such. It cannot

7

be treated piece-meal. Its fundamentals and its implicit meanings and obligations must be accepted together with its benefits.

The Individual's Self-respect

4. The concept of Man's spiritual nature, and the resulting concept of the supreme dignity and value of each Individual, provide the fundamental basis for each Individual's self-respect and the consequent mutual respect among Individuals. This self-respect as well as this mutual respect are the outgrowth of, and evidenced by, The Individual's maintenance of his God-given, unalienable rights. They are maintained by requiring that government and other Individuals respect them, as well as by his dedication to his own unceasing growth toward realization of his highest potential—spiritually, morally, intellectually, in every aspect of life. This is in order that he may merit maximum respect by self and by others.

Some Things Excluded

5. This concept of Man's spiritual nature excludes any idea of intrusion by government into this Man-to-Man spiritual relationship. It excludes the anti-moral precept that the end justifies the means and the related idea that the means can be separated from the end when judging them morally. This concept therefore excludes necessarily any idea of attempting to do good by force—for instance, through coercion of Man by Government, whether or not claimed to be for his own good or for the so-called common good or general welfare.

It excludes disbelief in—even doubt as to the existence of—God as the Creator of Man: and therefore excludes all ideas, theories and schools of thought—however ethical and lofty in intentions—which reject affirmative and positive belief in God as Man's Creator.

The Truly American Concept

6. Only those ideas, programs and practices, regarding things governmental, which are consistent with the concept that "The Spiritual is supreme" can justly be claimed to be truly American traditionally. Anything and everything governmental, which is in conflict with this concept, is non-American—judged by traditional belief.

This applies particularly to that which is agnostic, or atheistic— neutral about, or hostile to, positive and affirmative belief in this con-

8

cept based upon belief in God as Man's Creator. There is no room for doubt, much less disbelief, in this regard from the standpoint of the traditional American philosophy. Its indivisible nature makes this inescapably true. This pertains, of course, to the realm of ideas and not to any person; it is the conflicting idea which is classified as non-American, according to this philosophy.

America a Haven For All Religions

7. The traditional American philosophy teaches that belief in God is the fundamental link which unites the adherents of all religions in a spiritual brotherhood. This philosophy allows for no differentiation between them in this unifying conviction: ". . . all men are created . . . endowed by their Creator . . ." This philosophy is all inclusive as to believers in God.. Although America was originally colonized predominantly by adherents of the Christian religion, and principally by Protestants, the Founding Fathers steadfastly conformed to this all-embracing character of the approach of the American philosophy to religion. This was expressly and affirmatively indicated in the proclamation in 1776 of the fundamental American philosophy, of its basic principles, in the Declaration of Independence. This was further indicated, negatively, in 1787-1788 by the Framers and Ratifiers of the Constitution—as a "blueprint" for the structure of the then proposed Federal government, with strictly limited powers—by not permitting it to possess any power with regard to religion. This implied prohibition against the Federal government was reinforced by the addition of the First Amendment expressly prohibiting it, through the Congress, from making any law "respecting an establishment of religion, or prohibiting the free exercise thereof . . ."—the words "an establishment of religion" being intended to mean, specifically and only, a church or religious *organization* which is established, supported and preferred by the government, like the Church of England establishments then existing in some of the States.

The Conclusion

8. Belief in Man's Divine origin is the foundation of the fundamental American principle which controls his relationship to government: that Man—The Individual—is of supreme dignity and value because of his spiritual nature.

PRINCIPLE TWO

FEAR OF GOVERNMENT-OVER-MAN

THE TRAP OF OVER-TRUSTFULNESS

But there is a Degree of Watchfulness over all Men possessed of Power or Influence upon which the Liberties of Mankind much depend. It is necessary to guard against the Infirmities of the best as well as the Wickedness of the worst of Men. Such is the Weakness of human Nature that Tyranny has oftener sprang from that than any other Source. It is this that unravels the Mystery of Millions being enslaved by a few. (Exactly per original.)

Samuel Adams
(Letter to Elbridge Gerry, 1784)

For it is a truth which the experience of all ages has attested, that the people are commonly most in danger, when the means of injuring their rights are in the possession of those of whom they entertain the least suspicion.*

They know from experience, that they sometimes err; and the wonder is, that they so seldom err as they do; beset as they continually are by the wiles of parasites and sycophants by the snares of the ambitious, the avaricious, the desperate; by the artifices of men, who possess their confidence more than they deserve it, and of those who seek to possess, rather than to deserve it.**

The Federalist
(*No. 25; **no. 71; by Alexander Hamilton)

History, by apprising them of the past, will enable them to judge of the future; it will avail them of the experience of other times and other nations; it will qualify them as judges of the actions and designs of men; it will enable them to know ambition under every guise it may assume; and knowing it, to defeat its views. *In every government on earth is some trace of human weakness, some germ of corruption and degeneracy, which cunning will discover, and wickedness insensibly open, cultivate and improve.* Every government degenerates when trusted to the rulers of the people alone. The people themselves therefore are its only safe depositories. And to render even them safe, their minds must be improved to a certain degree. . . . The influence over government must be shared among all the people. . . . [If all participate] the government will be safe; because the corrupting the whole mass will . . . [be difficult]. (Emphasis added.)

Thomas Jefferson
("Notes on the State of Virginia," 1782)

GOVERNMENT OF LAWS AND NOT OF MEN

[Division of powers between three separate Branches] to the end it may be a government of laws and not of men.

Massachusetts Bill of Rights, 1780

The government of the United States has been emphatically termed a government of laws, and not of men.

Chief Justice of U.S., John Marshall
(Speaking for the Court in 1803 *Marbury* case)

GOVERNMENT BY MILITARY FORCE
IS DESPOTISM—AND DESPISED

The use of the military power to enforce the execution of the laws, is, in the opinion of this House, inconsistent with the spirit of a free constitution, and the very nature of government.

House of Representatives of Mass., 1769
(A communication to the Governor)

Hence likewise they [the people] will avoid the necessity of those overgrown Military establishments, which under any form of Government are inauspicious to liberty, and which are to be regarded as particularly hostile to Republican Liberty [in a republic].

President George Washington, *Farewell Address*

Government is frequently and aptly classed under two descriptions—a government of FORCE, and a government of LAWS; the first is the definition of despotism—the last, of liberty . . .
(Emphasis per original.)   Alexander Hamilton
("Tully Papers," 1794)

But whatever may be the design of this military appearance; whatever use some persons may intend and expect to make of it: This we all know, and *every child in the street is taught to know it*; that while a people retain a just sense of Liberty, as blessed be God, this people yet do, the insolence of power will for ever be despised . . .
(Emphasis added.)   Samuel Adams
(About British forces in Boston; essay, Boston Gazette, 1768)

13

FEAR OF THE CENTRAL GOVERNMENT

. . . the good people of the U. States in their late generous contest, contended for free government in the fullest, clearest, and strongest sense. That they had no idea of being brought under despotic rule under the notion of "Strong Government," or in the form of *elective despotism*: Chains being still Chains, whether made of gold or iron. The corrupting nature of power, and its insatiable appetite for increase . . . [makes amendments necessary to safeguard natural rights]*

The greatness of the powers given, and the multitude of places [offices] to be created produce a coalition . . . [dangerous to Liberty and requiring] . . . such changes and securities as reason and experience prove to be necessary against the encroachments of power upon the indispensable rights of human nature.**

(Emphasis per the original)   Richard Henry Lee
(Letters to S. Adams* and Geo. Mason** Oct., 1787)

SOME PEACEABLE REMEDIES OF THE STATES
AGAINST THE FEDERAL GOVERNMENT

[In case of an unconstitutional, or an unpopular, measure by the Federal government] . . . the means of opposition to it [by the States] are powerful and at hand. The disquietude of the people, their repugnance and perhaps refusal to co-operate with the officers of the union, the frowns of the executive magistracy of the state, the embarrassments created by legislative devices, which would often be added on such occasions, would oppose in any state difficulties not to be despised; would form in a large state very serious impediments, and where the sentiments of several adjoining states happened to be in unison, would present obstructions which the federal government would hardly be willing to encounter.

The Federalist (no. 46, by Madison)
(Note: Nos. 28 and 46 discuss States' defense by force in last resort.)

Therefore Resolved, That it be and hereby is recommended to the legislatures of the several states represented in this Convention, to adopt all such measures as may be necessary effectually to protect the citizens of said states from the operation and effects of all acts which have been or may be passed by the Congress of the United States, which shall contain provisions, subjecting the militia or other citizens to forcible drafts, conscriptions, or impressments, not authorised by the constitution of the United States.

A Resolution of the Hartford Convention, 1815
(Note: a convention representing Mass., Conn., R.I., Vt., and N.H., protesting Federal usurpations, during War with Great Britain.)

14

A Principle of The Traditional American Philosophy

2. FEAR OF GOVERNMENT-OVER-MAN

"In questions of power, then, let no more be heard of confidence in man, but bind him down from mischief by the chains of the Constitution."

(Kentucky Resolutions, by Thomas Jefferson)

The Principle
1. A main principle of the traditional American philosophy is expressed in the phrase: fear of Government-over-Man.

Cause of Fear
2. This fear is due to the ever-present, never-changing weaknesses of human nature in government which are conducive to "love of power and proneness to abuse it," as Washington's *Farewell Address* warned. This means public officials' human weaknesses, especially as aggravated by the corresponding weaknesses among the self-governing people themselves. It is a truism that government's power needs only to exist to be feared—to be dominant, over the fear-ridden, without ever needing to be exercised aggressively.

Man—Good and Evil, Mixed
3. This philosophy asserts that human nature is a mixture of good and evil, of strength and weakness, and is not perfectible during life on earth. There is "a portion of virtue and honor among Mankind" and the better side of Man, The Individual, can be strengthened and made more dependable through spiritual growth. The resulting moral development is conducive to sound conduct, in keeping with conscience in the light of a personal moral code based upon religious-moral considerations. Yet history teaches that the previously mentioned weaknesses of human nature provide just cause for never-ceasing fear of Government-over-Man.

Government Like a Fire

4. Americans of the period 1776-1787 firmly believed in the soundness of the accepted maxim that "government is like a fire: a dangerous servant and a fearful master;" that, to be useful, it must be strictly controlled for safety against its getting out of hand and doing great harm. Through the generations, the people have considered that this maxim expresses one of history's most profoundly important lessons for Free Man. This maxim is based upon the knowledge that, in last analysis, government is force and must be feared and controlled accordingly. The great fear in 1787-1788 of the new, central government under the proposed Constitution was evidenced by the fact that the State Ratifying Conventions proposed scores of amendments, designed chiefly to keep under more rigid control what they considered to be this potential monster of power so dangerous to their liberties: the central, or Federal, government.

The Views of Jefferson and Madison
and the Kentucky and Virginia Resolutions

5. This fear was of abuse by government of power granted to it by the people, as well as of usurpation by it of power denied or prohibited to it by them, through the Constitution, to the injury if not doom of their liberties—of the God-given, unalienable rights of The Individual. Jefferson merely voiced the lesson of history—well known to, and accepted by, his fellow Americans—when he stated, in the "Diffusion of Knowledge" Bill in 1779, in the Virginia legislature:

". . . experience hath shewn, that even under the best forms [of government], those entrusted with power have, in time, and by slow operations, perverted it into tyranny . . ."

Jefferson also expressed this traditional, American viewpoint in his famous writing known as the Kentucky Resolutions, as adopted in 1798 by the Kentucky legislature, in these words in part:

". . . it would be a dangerous delusion were a confidence in the men of our choice to silence our fears for the safety of our rights: that confidence is everywhere the parent of despotism: free government is founded in jealousy and not in confidence; it is jealousy and not confidence which prescribes limited Constitutions to bind down those whom we are obliged to trust with power: that our Constitution has accordingly fixed the limits to which and no further our confidence may go; . . . In questions of power then let no more be heard of confidence in man, but bind him down from mischief by the chains of the Constitution."

These Kentucky Resolutions are closely akin to the contemporaneous Virginia Resolutions of 1798 adopted soon afterward by the Virginia legislature—written mainly by Madison who was, as usual, in close touch with Jefferson in this period. Both sets of resolutions were protests against what were considered and denounced as abuses and usurpations of power by the Federal government—chiefly through the Alien and Sedition Laws adopted by Congress in 1798. Such protests by a State legislature were in keeping with the remedies available to the States in such a situation—remedies contemplated by The Framers as being within the constitutional system—as discussed, for example, by Madison in 1788 in *The Federalist* number 46. The Sedition Act was designed to restrict freedom of speech and of the Press so as to stifle criticism of Federal officials and therefore grossly violated the Constitution; and it was opposed, for example, by John Marshall, as a member of Congress, and by Alexander Hamilton —the latter stating: "Let us not establish a tyranny." (These laws soon disappeared from the statute books, due to their widespread unpopularity which the above-mentioned 1798 resolutions had helped initially to foster.)

Precedents for Other States' Protests
Such As
The Hartford Convention Resolutions

6. These 1798 protests by the Kentucky and Virginia legislatures were not the first such development in the life of the Republic. A predecessor resolution of protest, for example, had been adopted by the Virginia legislature in 1790: the "Protest and Remonstrance" against the assumption by the Federal government of the war-incurred debts of the States, as being unconstitutional. This protest set a precedent for the above-mentioned 1798 resolutions. They, in turn, set precedents for similar resolutions of protest adopted by various States —in New England, the North, the Mid-west as well as in the South —during the following decades when they considered themselves to be victimized, potentially or actually, by either abuses or usurpations of power by the Federal government; such developments being the subject of comment, for example, by former President John Quincy Adams in his celebrated "Jubilee" address of April 30, 1839. (Some

17

of these later resolutions even relied on the *Virginia Resolutions* of 1798 as a precedent.) An example is the set of resolutions adopted in 1815, during the war with England, by the Hartford Convention—representing Massachusetts, Connecticut, Rhode Island, Vermont, and New Hampshire—protesting against what were considered to be Federal usurpations, potential or actual, regarding use of the States' Militia in war operations and other national defense matters.

The View of Patrick Henry

7. In the Virginia Ratifying Convention in 1788, Patrick Henry protested with vehemence against the proposed new Constitution's lack of adequate limits on the central government's power, lack of sufficient safeguards against governmental abuses due to human weaknesses among its officials, saying:

"Show me that age and country where the rights and liberties of the people were placed on the sole chance of their rulers being good men, without a consequent loss of liberty! I say that the loss of that dearest privilege has ever followed, with absolute certainty, every such mad attempt."

The American People's View
Also Expressed in the
Pittsfield Petition of 1776

8. These quoted sentiments were accepted as maxims by American leaders in general and by the American people as a whole in that generation of Free Men—free in spirit and willing to fight and die for their Freedom from Government-over-Man. This acceptance is illustrated by the below-quoted words of the Pittsfield, Massachusetts, town-meeting petition of a decade earlier, in May, 1776. It was penned by the Reverend Thomas Allen, ardent friend of American Independence and of Man's Liberty against Government-over-Man. It stated why Massachusetts needed a new, basic law of the people, a Constitution to be adopted by the people only, in part as follows:

"That, knowing the strong bias of human nature to tyranny and despotism, we have nothing else in view but to provide for posterity against the wanton exercise of power, which cannot otherwise be done than by the formation of a fundamental constitution."

This petition reflected the sentiments of the frontier, "backwoods" people of Berkshire County, led by this patriot as head of "The Berkshire Constitutionalists," over a decade before the 1787 Federal Convention framed the United States Constitution. These were truly the sentiments of the American people at large. They are in harmony with the later phrasing of this idea as follows in *The Federalist* (number 55, by Madison):

"As there is a degree of depravity in mankind which requires a certain degree of circumspection and distrust: So there are other qualities in human nature, which justify a certain portion of esteem and confidence."

Never-changing Weaknesses of Human Nature Create Never-changing Need for Safeguards

9. The never-changing need for, and value of, constitutional safeguards against abuse, or usurpation, of power by public servants—as contemplated, and as provided for, by The Framers and Adopters of the Constitution in 1787-1788 and by those who proposed, framed and adopted the first ten Amendments (including the Bill of Rights made applicable against the Federal, or central, government only)—are due to the never-changing weaknesses of human nature in government and among the self-governing people. These weaknesses never change; therefore the need for these safeguards can never change.

The Conclusion

10. Fear of Government-over-Man was the dominant fear in that day of uncompromisingly individualistic Americans—Free Men, ever jealous of the safety of Individual Liberty, of the security of their God-given, unalienable rights against violation by government.

PRINCIPLE THREE

UNALIENABLE RIGHTS—FROM GOD

RIGHTS UNALIENABLE—
BECAUSE GOD-GIVEN

And can the liberties of a nation be thought secure when we have removed their only firm basis, a conviction in the minds of the people that these liberties are the gift of God?

Thomas Jefferson
("Notes on the State of Virginia," 1782)

The Sacred Rights of mankind are not to be rummaged for among old parchments or musty records. They are written, as with a sunbeam, in the whole volume of human nature, by the Hand of the Divinity itself, and can never be erased or obscured by mortal power.

Alexander Hamilton
(An essay, "The Farmer Refuted," 1775)

(Note: entire passage in capital letters in the original.)

UNALIENABLE RIGHTS

Resolved, that the inhabitants of this Province are unalienably entitled to those essential rights ["founded in the law of God and of Nature"] in common with all men: and that no law of society can, consistent with the law of God and nature, divest them of those rights.

Resolutions of House of Representatives, Mass., 1765

In short it is the greatest absurdity to suppose it in the power of one or any number of men at the entering into society, to renounce their essential natural rights, or the means of preserving those rights when the great end of civil government from the very nature of its institution is for the support, protection and defence of those very rights: the principal of which as is before observed, are life liberty and property. If men through fear, fraud or mistake, should *in terms* renounce and give up any essential natural right, the eternal law of reason and the great end of society, would absolutely vacate such renunciation; the right to freedom being *the gift* of God Almighty, it is not in the power of Man to alienate this gift, and voluntarily become a slave—
(Emphasis per original.)

Resolutions of Town of Boston, 1772
("The Rights of The Colonists, . . .")

RIGHT TO KNOWLEDGE—
CAPACITY TO REASON, TO UNDERSTAND

[The people] have a right, from the frame of their nature, to knowledge, as their great Creator, who does nothing in vain, has given them understandings, and a desire to know . . . John Adams
("A Dissertation on the Canon and Feudal Law," 1765)

CONTROL OF SOME RIGHTS QUALIFIED
IN ORDER TO MAKE THE REMAINDER SECURE

Men, when they enter into civil society, relinquish some of their natural rights, in order to their more secure enjoyment of the remainder.
Resolution of Town of Braintree, Mass., 1780
(Concerning the new Constitution of Mass.)

Accordingly it may be Observed, That it appears to Us That in immerging from a State of Nature, into a State of well regulated Society, Mankind gave up some of their natural Rights, in order that others of Greater Importance to their Well-being Safety & Happiness both as Societies and Individuals might be better enjoyed Secured & defended . . .
Resolution of Town of Lexington, Mass., 1778

[All men born with equal rights] Some of those rights are alienable, and may be parted with for an equivalent. Others are unalienable and inherent, and of that importance, that no equivalent can be received in exchange. *Sometimes we shall mention the surrendering of a power to controul our natural rights, which perhaps is speaking with more precision, than when we use the expression of parting with natural rights—but the same thing is intended.* Those rights which are unalienable, and of that importance, are called the rights of conscience. We have duties, for the discharge of which we are accountable to our Creator and benefactor, which no human power can cancel. What those duties are, is determinable by right reason, which may be, and is called, a well informed conscience. What this conscience dictates as our duty, is so; and that power which assumes a controul over it, is an usurper; for no consent can be pleaded to justify the controul, as any consent in this case is void . . . [Men forming government voluntarily delegate some power] . . . No individual, in this case, parts with his unalienable rights, the supreme [governmental] power therefore cannot controul them. (Emphasis added.) "Essex Result"
(Report of Conventions of Towns, Essex County, Mass., rejecting first proposed Constitution for Mass., 1778)

23

LIFE AND LIBERTY INSEPARABLE

The God who gave us life gave us liberty at the same time; the hand of force may destroy, but cannot disjoin them.

Thomas Jefferson
("Rights of British America," 1774)

UNALIENABLE UNLESS SELF-FORFEITED

. . . as all men by nature are free . . . that no man can be deprived of liberty, and subjected to perpetual bondage and servitude, unless he has forfeited his liberty as a malefactor . . .

Pittsfield, Mass., Town-meeting Resolution, 1779

RIGHT OF CONSCIENCE UNALIENABLE

God hath given to every Man an Unalienable Right in Matters of His Worship to Judge for himself as his Conscience reserves ye Rule from God.

Petition from Church Organizations
in 19 Towns in Massachusetts, 1749

BORN RATIONAL AND ENTITLED TO BE FREE

Reason teaches that *all Men* are *naturally equal* in Respect of *Jurisdiction* or *Dominion* one over another. Altho' true it is that *Children* are not born *in* this full State of Equality, yet they are born *to* it . . . [entitled to it . . .] For God having given *Man* an *Understanding* to direct his Actions, has given him therewith a *Freedom* of *Will* and *Liberty* of *Acting*, as properly belonging thereto, within the Bounds of *that Law* he is under . . . [Natural Law, God's Law] . . . So that we are *born Free* as we are *born Rational* . . . *This natural Freedom* is not a Liberty for every one to do what he pleases without any Regard to any *Law;* for a *rational* Creature cannot but be made under a *Law* from its MAKER: But it consists in a *Freedom* from any *superior Power on Earth*, and not being under the Will or legislative Authority of *Man*, and having only the *Law of Nature* (or in other Words, of its MAKER) for his Rule.
(Emphasis per original.) Rev. Elisha Williams
("A Seasonable Plea . . ."—1744)
(Note: a plea primarily for the right to freedom of conscience and private judgment in religious matters.)

24

A Principle of The Traditional American Philosophy

3. UNALIENABLE RIGHTS—FROM GOD

". . . endowed by their Creator with certain <u>unalienable rights</u> . . ."
(Declaration of Independence)

The Principle

1. The traditional American philosophy teaches that Man, The Individual, is endowed at birth with rights which are unalienable because given by his Creator.

The Only Moral Basis

2. This governmental philosophy is uniquely American. The concept of Man's rights being unalienable is based solely upon belief in their Divine origin. Lacking this belief, there is no moral basis for any claim that they are unalienable or for any claim to the great benefits flowing from this concept. God-given rights are sometimes called Natural Rights—those possessed by Man under the Laws of Nature, meaning under the laws of God's creation and therefore by gift of God. Man has no power to alienate—to dispose of, by surrender, barter or gift—his God-given rights, according to the American philosophy. This is the meaning of "unalienable."

One underlying consideration is that for every such right there is a correlative, inseparable duty—for every aspect of freedom there is a corresponding responsibility; so that it is always Right-Duty and Freedom-Responsibility, or Liberty-Responsibility. There is a duty, or responsibility, to God as the giver of these unalienable rights: a moral duty—to keep secure and use soundly these gifts, with due respect for the equal rights of others and for the right of Posterity to their just heritage of liberty. Since this moral duty cannot be surrendered, bartered, given away, abandoned, delegated or otherwise alienated, so is the inseparable right likewise unalienable. This concept of rights being unalienable is thus dependent upon belief in God as the giver. This indicates the basis and the soundness of Jefferson's statement

(1796 letter to John Adams): "If ever the morals of a people could be made the basis of their own government it is our case . . ."

Right, Reason, and Capacity to Be Self-governing

3. For the security and enjoyment by Man of his Divinely created rights, it follows implicitly that Man is endowed by his Creator not only with the right to be self-governing but also with the capacity to reason and, therefore, with the capacity to be self-governing. This is implicit in the philosophy proclaimed in the Declaration of Independence. Otherwise, Man's unalienable rights would be of little or no use or benefit to him. Faith in Man—in his capacity to be self-governing—is thus related to faith in God as his Creator, as the giver of these unalienable rights and this capacity.

Rights—as Prohibitions Against Government

4. Certain specific rights of The Individual are protected in the original Constitution but this is by way of statements "in reverse"— by way of express prohibitions against government. The word "right" does not appear in the original instrument. This is because it was designed to express the grant by the people of specific, limited powers to the central government—created by them through this basic law— as well as certain specific limitations on its powers, and on the pre-existing powers of the State governments, expressed as prohibitions of things forbidden. Every provision in it pertains to power.

The Constitution's first eight (Bill of Rights) amendments list certain rights of The Individual and prohibit the doing of certain things by the central, or Federal, government which, if done, would violate these rights. These amendments were intended by their Framers and Adopters merely to make express a few of the already-existing, implied prohibitions against the Federal government *only*—supplementing the prohibitions previously specified expressly in the original Constitution and supplementing and confirming its general, over-all, implied, prohibition as to all things concerning which it withheld power from this government. Merely confirming expressly some of the already-existing, implied prohibitions, these amendments did not create any new ones. They are, therefore, more properly referred to as a partial list of limitations—or a partial Bill of Prohibitions—as was indicated by Hamilton in *The Federalist* number 84. This hinges upon the uniquely American concepts stated in the Declaration of Independence: that Men, created of God, in turn create their governments and grant to them only "just" (limited) powers—primarily to make and keep secure their God-given, unalienable rights including, in part, the right to Life, Liberty and the pursuit of Happiness. As Hamilton stated, under the American philosophy and system of constitutionally limited government, "the people surrender nothing;" instead, they merely delegate to government—to public servants as public trustees —limited powers and therefore, he added, "they have no need of particular reservations" (in a Bill of Rights). This is the basic reason why the Framing Convention omitted from the Constitution anything in the nature of a separate Bill of Rights, as being unnecessary.

An Endless List of Rights
5. To attempt to name all of these rights—starting with "Life, Liberty and the pursuit of Happiness" mentioned in the Declaration of Independence—would be to start an endless list which would add up to the whole of Man's Freedom (Freedom from Government-over-Man). They would add up to the entirety of Individual Liberty (Liberty against Government-over-Man). Innumerable rights of The Individual are embraced in the Ninth Amendment, which states: "The enumeration in the Constitution of certain rights shall not be construed to deny or disparage others retained by the people." (Here "Constitution" includes the amendments.) Some idea of how vast the list would be is indicated by just one general freedom which leads into almost all of Free Man's activities of daily living throughout life: freedom of choice. This term stands for the right to do—and equally not to do—this or that, as conscience, whim or judgment, taste or desire, of The Individual may prompt from moment to moment, day by day, for as long as life lasts; but always, of course, with due regard for the equal rights of others and for just laws expressive of the above-mentioned "just powers" of government designed to help safeguard the equal rights of all Individuals. Spelled out in detail, this single freedom—freedom of choice—is almost all-embracing.

Right to Be Let Alone
6. In one sense, such freedom to choose involves Man's right to be let alone, which is possessed by The Individual in keeping with the

Declaration and Constitution as against government: in enjoyment of his unalienable rights, while respecting the equal rights of others and just laws (as defined in Paragraph 5 above). This right to be let alone is the most comprehensive of rights and the right most prized by civilized men. This right is, of course, also possessed as against all other Individuals, all obligated to act strictly within the limits of their own equal rights. Consequently any infringement of any Individual's rights is precluded.

Rights Inviolable
by Government or by Others

7. Neither government nor any Individuals—acting singly, or in groups, or in organizations—could possibly possess any "just power" (to use again the significant term of the Declaration) to violate any Individual's God-given, unalienable rights or the supporting rights. No government can abolish or destroy—nor can it rightfully, or constitutionally, violate—Man's God-given rights. Government cannot justly interfere with Man's deserved enjoyment of any of these rights. No public official, nor all such officials combined, could possibly have any such power morally. Government can, to be sure, unjustly and unconstitutionally interfere by force with the deserved enjoyment of Man's unalienable rights. It is, however, completely powerless to abolish or destroy them. It is in defense of these rights of all Individuals, in last analysis, that the self-governing people—acting in accordance with, and in support of, the Constitution—oppose any and all violators, whether public officials as usurpers, or others (par. 9 below).

Each Individual
Consents to Some Limitations

8. In creating governments as their tools, or instruments, and equally in continuing to maintain them—for the purpose primarily of making and keeping secure their unalienable rights—all Individuals composing the self-governing people impliedly and in effect consent to some degree of limitation of their freedom to exercise some of their rights. This does not involve the surrender, or the alienation, of any of these rights but only the partial, conditional and limited relinquishment of freedom to exercise a few of them and solely for the purpose

of insuring the greater security and enjoyment of all of them; and, moreover, such relinquishment is always upon condition that public officials, as public servants and trustees, faithfully use the limited powers delegated to government strictly in keeping with their prescribed limits and with this limited purpose at all times. It was in this sense that George Washington, as President of the Framing Convention in September, 1787, wrote to the Congress of the Confederation—in transmitting to it, for consideration, the draft of the proposed Constitution: ". . . Individuals entering into society, must give up a share of liberty to preserve the rest." Here he meant merely conditional relinquishment of liberty of action in the exercise of certain aspects of unalienable rights—not the surrender of any unalienable rights, which would be impossible because a nullity, a void act.

An Offender's Just Punishment

9. Whenever Man violates either the equal rights of others or the above-mentioned just laws, he thereby forfeits his immunity in this regard; by his misconduct, he destroys the moral and legal basis for his immunity and opens the door to just reprisal against himself, by government. This means that any person, as such offender, may justly be punished by the people's proper instrumentality—the government, including the courts—under a sound system of equal justice under equal laws; that is, under Rule-by-Law (basically the people's fundamental law, the Constitution). Such punishment is justified morally because of the duty of all Individuals—in keeping with Individual Liberty-*Responsibility*—to cooperate, through their instrumentality, government, for the mutual protection of the unalienable rights of all Individuals. The offender is also justly answerable to the aggrieved Individual, acting properly through duly-established machinery of government, including courts, designed for the protection of the equal rights of all Individuals.

It is the offender's breach of the duty aspect of Individual Liberty-Responsibility which makes just, proper and necessary government's punitive action and deprives him of any moral basis for protest. By such breach he forfeits his moral claim to the inviolability of his rights and makes himself vulnerable to reprisal by the people, through government, in defense of their own unalienable rights. By this lack of self-discipline required by that duty, he invites and makes necessary his being disciplined by government.

The Conclusion

10. Man's unalienable rights are sacred for the same reason that they are unalienable—because of their Divine origin, according to the traditional American philosophy.

PRINCIPLE FOUR

MAN ORGANIZES GOVERNMENTS TO BE HIS TOOLS

PUBLIC OFFICIALS ARE PUBLIC SERVANTS

> Rulers are the servants and agents of the people; the people are their masters.
>
> Patrick Henry
> (Va. Ratifying Convention, 1788)

> That all power is vested in, and consequently derived from, the people; that magistrates are their trustees and servants . . .
>
> Virginia Declaration of Rights, 1776

> Here, [in America] the people are masters of the government: there, [in Britain] the government is master of the people.
>
> U.S. Supreme Court Justice James Wilson
> (Lectures, 1790-1791)

> *Governors* have no right to seek what they please; by this, instead of being content with the station assigned them, that of *honourable servants* of the society, they would soon become Absolute masters, Despots, and Tyrants. (Emphasis added.)
>
> Resolutions of Town of Boston, 1772
> ("The Rights of the Colonists . . .")

> The *multitude* I am speaking of, is the *body of the people*—no *contemptible* multitude—for whose sake government is instituted; or rather, who have themselves erected it, solely for *their own* good—to whom even kings and all in subordination to them, are strictly speaking, servants and not masters. (Emphasis Adams'.)
>
> Samuel Adams
> (Essay in Boston Gazette, 1771)

> It seems to have been imagined by some that the returning to the mass of the people was degrading the magistrate. This he thought was contrary to republican principles. In free Governments the rulers are the servants, and the people their superiors & sovereigns. For the former therefore to return among the latter was not to *degrade* but to *promote* them—and it would be imposing an unreasonable burden on them, to keep them always in a State of servitude, and not allow them to become again one of the Masters. (Emphasis per original.)
>
> Benjamin Franklin
> (Remarks in Framing Convention, 1787
> as summarized by Madison in his record)

THE PEOPLE'S POWER TO CONTROL
THEIR CREATURE AND TOOL: GOVERNMENT

All [American] writers on government agree . . . That the origin of all power is in the people, and that they have an incontestible right to check the creatures of their own creation, vested with certain powers to guard the life, liberty, and property of the community . . .

Elbridge Gerry
(An essay, 1788)

THE PEOPLE SUPREME OVER PUBLIC SERVANTS

Rulers surely, even the most dignified and powerful of them, should not be so elevated with the thoughts of their power, as to forget from whom it comes; for what purposes it is delegated to them . . .

Rev. Jonathan Mayhew
(Election Sermon, 1754)

NO POWER IN GOVERNMENT, OR OTHERS,
TO OBSTRUCT A MAN'S EARNING A LIVELIHOOD

I believe . . . that no one has a right to obstruct another, exercising his faculties innocently for the relief of sensibilities made a part of his nature . . .

Thomas Jefferson
(Letter to Dupont de Nemours, 1816)
(Note: refers, for example, to Man's work to earn a livelihood)

UNJUST OF GOVERNMENT TO DENY
FREE USE OF FACULTIES, FREE CHOICE OF OCCUPATIONS

That is not a just government, nor is property secure under it, where arbitrary restrictions, exemptions, and monopolies deny to part of its citizens that free use of their faculties, and free choice of their occupations, which not only constitute their property in the general sense of the word; but are the means of acquiring property strictly so called . . .

James Madison
(Essay, National Gazette, 1792)
(Note: Full text is quoted at pages 232-233 of this study-guide.)

LIKE EVERY OTHER TOOL OF MAN, GOVERNMENT HAS A SPECIAL FUNCTION AND IS RESTRICTED IN USEFULNESS

> . . . government is, or ought to be instituted for the common benefit, protection, and security of the people, nation, or community . . .
>
> **Virginia Declaration of Rights, 1776**

> That government governs best which governs least.
> **(A traditional American maxim)**
> (Erroneously attributed by some to Jefferson's writings, but typical of his views and of the views of most of his fellow Americans.)

> Still one thing more, fellow-citizens—a wise and frugal Government, which shall restrain men from injuring one another, shall *leave them otherwise free to regulate their own pursuits* of industry and improvement, and shall not take from the mouth of labor the bread it has earned. This is the sum of good government, and this is necessary to close the circle of our felicities. (Emphasis added)
>
> **President Thomas Jefferson**
> **(First Inaugural Address)**

> Was the government to prescribe to us our medicine and diet, our bodies would be in such keeping as our souls are now [under a State-established church]. Thus in France the emetic was once forbidden as a medicine, and the potatoe as an article of food. Government is just as infallible, too, when it fixes systems in physics. Galileo was sent to the inquisition for affirming that the earth was a sphere; the government had declared it to be as flat as a trencher, and Galileo was obliged to abjure his error. This error however at length prevailed, the earth became a globe, and Descartes declared it was whirled round its axis by a vortex. The government in which he lived was wise enough to see that this was no question of civil jurisdiction, or we should all have been involved by authority in vortices. In fact the vortices have been exploded, and the Newtonian principle of gravitation is now more firmly established, on the basis of reason, than it would be were the government to step in and to make it an article of necessary faith. Reason and experiment have been indulged, and error has fled before them. It is error alone which needs the support of government. Truth can stand by itself.
>
> **Thomas Jefferson**
> **("Notes on the State of Virginia," 1782)**

34

A Principle of The Traditional American Philosophy

4. MAN ORGANIZES GOVERNMENTS TO BE HIS TOOLS

"That to <u>secure these rights,</u> **Governments are instituted among Men . . ."** (Declaration of Independence)

The Principle

1. The traditional American philosophy teaches that government is merely the creature and a tool, or instrument, of the sovereign people.

Government's Primary Function

2. The people create their governments primarily to serve one supreme purpose: to "secure" the safety and enjoyment of their God-given, unalienable rights. To make and keep them secure is government's primary function and chief reason for existence, according to the philosophy proclaimed in the Declaration of Independence.

Government a Tool

3. This makes clear the correct role of government in relation to the people, as viewed by the American philosophy. It is merely their tool, like any other tool such as a saw, or a plow, or a steam engine, created by them to serve its assigned and limited purpose. As the people's tool, or instrument, any government could never soundly be said to possess sovereign power—that is, unlimited, or total, power over all things and all persons. Under the American philosophy, no legal, meaning governmental, sovereignty exists anywhere; while any political sovereignty is possessed by the people alone and even they are limited by the obligation to keep inviolate the God-given, unalienable rights of every Individual. Government may possess and its officials may exercise, as the people's servants and trustees, only such limited part of the people's power as they see fit from time to time to delegate to it through their fundamental law: the Constitution, as

35

amended by them; and this applies to all governments and Constitutions, Federal and State.

Government Lacks "Just Power" to Violate Rights

4. Therein lies the significance of the limitation by the people of government's role and power, under the American philosophy. The fact that government cannot have any "just" power or authority—as meant by the term "just powers" in the Declaration of Independence—to violate any unalienable right of The Individual follows from the fact that no Individual can have any right, power or authority to violate any other Individual's unalienable rights. Because it is created by the people (a group of Individuals) primarily for the purpose of making secure all rights of all Individuals, this tool of the people, government, could not conceivably derive from them any power or authority, morally or constitutionally, to do the opposite by infringing any such right. Since no Individual possesses, or could grant, any such power or authority, the many Individuals composing the people of a country are similarly lacking; many times zero equals zero. No vote of the people, by however great a majority—even all of the people but one Individual, opposed to that lone Individual—could give to any government any such authority or power. (This is subject, of course, to the point previously discussed in Paragraph 9 of Principle 3, regarding just punishment of offenders against just laws, or against the rights of other Individuals.)

Government Cannot Delegate
Any Power to Violate Man's Rights

5. By the same token, it is impossible for the people's tool, government, to possess any authority from the people—any "just power" (to use the term of the Declaration of Independence)—to delegate to others any power which it does not and could not possess under the traditional American philosophy. As such a tool, government could not possibly possess, could not be given, any power to authorize any person, group or organization to do that which it is itself powerless to do. This precludes, for example, government's authorizing or empowering any person, group, or organization to violate any Individual's unalienable rights—including the right to "Life, Liberty and the pursuit of Happiness"—or any of the supporting rights, such as the right to property and to freedom of association.

Principle Four

No Coercion of Man as to His Labor

6. Under the American philosophy, these supporting rights include, for example, The Individual's right to use all of his faculties, talents, abilities and energies—basically his own labor—as, when and where he sees fit without any restraint by government or by others. This is subject, of course, to his duly respecting the equal rights of other Individuals (in part as discussed regarding Equality in Pars. 8-9 of Principle 7) and just laws expressive of the above-mentioned "just powers" of government designed to help safeguard the equal rights of all Individuals. This means, for example, the enjoyment of this right without any such restraint upon his right to freedom of association, to freedom of choice with regard to joining, or not joining, any organization—for instance, an organization of his fellow employers or an organization of his fellow workers. Violation of this right involves necessarily violation of his unalienable rights to "Life, Liberty and the pursuit of Happiness" as well as of the supporting rights—notably the right to property (money or any other type), including acquiring, possessing and using it. Such violation results in any case of coercion of The Individual to join, or not to join, such an organization. This is true whether perpetrated by government directly, or by it indirectly through others acting with its sanction—for instance, by any group or organization of other Individuals who exert pressures of any kind or degree to induce, or impel, him so to join, or to refrain from joining. As Man's tool, government not only can have no just power so to perpetrate any such violation but is affirmatively obligated, under just laws, not only not to tolerate but actively to prevent such violation by others—always strictly in keeping with its limited powers and related responsibilities as prescribed in the applicable Constitution (as amended), Federal or State, as the case may be. To repeat, any Individual's right to freedom of association (freedom of choice of associates) is always subject to the equal rights of others—including their right to similar freedom of choice of associates. This right's enjoyment always involves the essential factor of mutual consent, free from any element of coercion.

Sovereign Citizen over Public Servant

7. All public officials are subordinate as public servants to all citizens. Under the American philosophy of Man-over-Government, the American heritage assumes that the most modestly circumstanced

37

Individuals among the sovereign people rank higher than any public officials, even those serving as the highest ranking of public servants. It is a case of The Sovereign over servant—each Individual in this regard representing in a sense the sovereign people as the creator of their tool, or instrument: government.

Betrayal of the American Heritage

8. It was the firm conviction of those who founded America—notably the leaders of the period 1776-1787 and their fellow Americans in general—that to forget, neglect, or defy this great American principle is to betray the American heritage of Individual Liberty—Man's Freedom from Government-over-Man—and to contribute in practice to its erosion, or subversion. Sins of omission in this connection are as heinous as sins of commission. Any public servants who ignore this truth are guilty of desecration of the spirit of traditional America and the higher the offender's rank, the worse the offense morally. Any Individual who condones such an offense against this heritage is similarly blameworthy.

The Conclusion

9. Each Individual, among the sovereign and self-governing people, embodies a part of the supreme sovereignty of the people in relation to their creature and tool, or instrument, government, and to its officials as public servants—wholly subservient to the people as their superiors, their masters.

PRINCIPLE FIVE

LIMITED GOVERNMENT

LIBERTIES SAFEGUARDED THROUGH
CHECKS AND BALANCES—TO CREATE DELAYS

The use of checks and balances in the forms of government, is to create delays and multiply diversities of interests, by which the tendency on a sudden to violate them may be counteracted. John Adams
("On Government," 1778)

LIMITS FIXED BY THE CONSTITUTION

Liberty and security in government depend not on the limits, which the rulers may please to assign to the exercise of their own powers, but on the boundaries, within which their powers are circumscribed by the constitution.

With us, the powers of magistrates, call them by whatever name you please, are the grants of the people . . . The supreme power is in them; and in them, even when a constitution is formed, and government is in operation, the supreme power still remains. A portion of their authority they, indeed, delegate; but they delegate that portion in whatever manner, in whatever measure, for whatever time, to whatever persons, and on whatever conditions they choose to fix.
U.S. Supreme Court Justice James Wilson
(Lectures, 1790-1791)

OATH TO SUPPORT THE CONSTITUTION—ONLY

The Senators and Representatives before mentioned, and the Members of the several State Legislatures, and all executive and judicial Officers, both of the United States and of the several States, shall be bound by Oath or Affirmation, to support this Constitution; . . .
Constitution of the U.S., Art. VI
(Note: Art. II, Sec. 1, prescribes a similar oath for the President.)

INSTANT ALARM AND ACTION NEEDED—
"AT THE FIRST EXPERIMENT ON OUR LIBERTIES"

Because, it is proper to take alarm at the first experiment on our liberties. We hold this prudent jealousy to be the first duty of citizens, and one of [the] noblest characteristics of the late Revolution. The freemen of America did not wait till usurped power had strengthened itself by exercise, and entangled the question in precedents. They saw all the consequences in the principle, and they avoided the consequences by denying the principle. James Madison
("Memorial and Remonstrance
Against Religious Assessments"—
Addressed to the General Assembly of Va., 1785)

DANGER OF
USURPATION BY THE SUPREME COURT

... there is no danger I apprehend so much as the consolidation of our government by the noiseless, and therefore unalarming, instrumentality of the supreme court.   Thomas Jefferson
(Letter to Wm. Johnson, 1823)

The executive . . . holds the sword . . . The legislative [Congress] . . . commands the purse . . . The judiciary . . . has no influence over either the sword or the purse . . . can take no active resolution whatever . . . liberty can have nothing to fear from the judiciary alone, [as usurpers] but would have every thing to fear from its union with either of the other departments . . ." [in usurping power]

The Federalist (no. 78, by Alexander Hamilton)

That the Jurisdiction of the Supreme Court of the United States, or of any other Court to be instituted by the Congress, is not in any case to be encreased enlarged or extended by any Fiction Collusion or mere suggestion; . . .

New York Ratifying Convention, 1788
(Part of proposed amendments to the Constitution)

It is not probable that the Supreme Court would long be indulged in a career of usurpation opposed to the decided opinions & policy of the Legislature [Congress]. Nor do I think that Congress, even seconded by the Judicial Power, can, *without some change in the character of the nation,* succeed in *durable* violations of the rights & authorities of the States.

("Durable" emphasized in original; other emphasis added.)
James Madison
(Letter to Judge Spencer Roane, 1821)

A TRUTH ABOUT USURPATION

Another truth respecting the vigilance with which a free people should guard their liberty, that deserves to be carefully observed, is this—that a *real tyranny* may prevail in a state, while the *forms* of a free constitution remain.   John Dickinson
(Emphasis per original.)   ("Notes" in *Political Writings*)

ESPECIALLY PERTINENT EXCERPTS FROM WASHINGTON'S *FAREWELL ADDRESS*
(Full text in Appendix)

ONLY THE PEOPLE CAN CHANGE THEIR CONSTITUTION

The basis of our political systems is the right of the people to make and to alter their Constitutions of Government. But the Constitution which at any time exists, 'till changed by an explicit and authentic act of the whole People, is sacredly obligatory upon all.

"NO CHANGE BY USURPATION" IS THE FUNDAMENTAL MORAL PRINCIPLE UNDERLYING SELF-GOVERNMENT AND RULE-BY-LAW

If in the opinion of the People, the distribution or modification of the Constitutional powers be in any particular wrong, let it be corrected by an amendment in the way which the Constitution designates. *But let there be no change by usurpation;* for though this, in one instance, may be the instrument of good, it is *the customary weapon by which free governments are destroyed.* The precedent must always greatly overbalance in permanent evil any partial or transient benefit which the use can at any time yield. (Emphasis added)

EFFECTIVE CHECKS AND BALANCES NEEDED

It is important, likewise, that the habits of thinking in a free Country should inspire caution in those entrusted with its administration, to confine themselves within their respective Constitutional spheres; avoiding in the exercise of the Powers of one department to encroach upon another. The spirit of encroachment tends to consolidate the powers of all the departments in one, and thus to create whatever the form of government, a real despotism. *A just estimate of that love of power, and proneness to abuse it, which predominates in the human heart* is sufficient to satisfy us of the truth of this position. The necessity of reciprocal checks in the exercise of political power; by dividing and distributing it into different depositories, and constituting each the Guardian of the Public Weal against invasions by the others, has been evinced by experiments ancient and modern; some of them in our country and under our own eyes. To preserve them must be as necessary as to institute them.
(Emphasis added.)

A Principle of The Traditional American Philosophy

5. LIMITED GOVERNMENT

Governments derive "their just powers from the consent of the governed." (Declaration of Independence)

The Principle

1. The traditional American philosophy teaches that government must be limited in power if Individual Liberty is to be safeguarded, if each Individual's God-given, unalienable rights are to be made and kept enduringly secure.

"Just Powers" Defined

2. This philosophy asserts that the self-governing people allow any government they may organize to possess, by grant from them, only the limited and few powers with which the people think the particular government may sensibly be entrusted in order to serve their purposes without endangering their rights—their liberties or freedoms. These powers constitute the "just powers" of government, as the Declaration of Independence phrases it. This is in keeping with the primary purpose for which the people organize governments: to make and keep these unalienable rights secure and most beneficial to themselves and to Posterity—time without end.

"Limited"—a Key Word

3. "Limited government" is a key term in the American philosophy. Its great significance is indicated by describing the purpose of limiting government's power in these words: Limited for Liberty. This summarizes what is meant by the statement in the Declaration of Independence about governments being limited in power "to secure these rights"—to make and keep them ever secure. "Limited" means limited by a written Constitution adopted by the sovereign people as their basic law—never changing in its meaning, as originally intended by

43

The Framers and Adopters, except subject to change by the people only by amendment at any time and to any extent they may see fit. All governments in America are thus limited by written Constitutions —by the United States Constitution as the "supreme Law of the Land" and, as to each State government, by that State's Constitution. (Note again Par. 4 of Principle 3, regarding the first eight, or Bill of Rights, amendments being intended to apply against the Federal government only.)

Limited Powers, Duties, Responsibilities and Limited Threat to Liberty

4. The few and limited powers of the United States government are enumerated and defined in the people's fundamental law—the Constitution, as amended. This is the basis of Rule-by-Law (basically the people's fundamental law, the Constitution) in contrast to Rule-by-Man. The limited quantity of its powers means it is limited in potential threat to the people's liberties. These "just powers," being few and limited, automatically define the limits of the duties which the people assign to this government. It can have no duties, no responsibilities, other than those consistent with the limits of the powers granted to it by the people in the Constitution, as amended. It is equally as violative of the Constitution for government to assume duties—to pretend to have responsibilities—as it is to grasp powers, beyond these prescribed limits.

Division of Powers and Checks and Balances

5. As a further safeguard for the people's rights, The Framers and Ratifiers of the Constitution provided for division of powers not only between the Federal and State governments but also within the Federal government between its three, separate Branches and, further, specified various checks and balances among these Branches, to help prevent either usurpation of power (grasping unauthorized power) or misuse of the limited quantity of power granted to it by the people; as explained, for instance, by Madison in *The Federalist* number 51. Each of the Branches was designed to help restrain the other Branches from any violation of the Constitution. The admonition on this topic expressed in Washington's *Farewell Address* reflected the conviction of all of The Founders. (See third quotation on page 42.)

The Compound Republic

6. The limitation of government's power, by a written Constitution adopted by the people (by the electorate), is the main distinguishing characteristic of a Republic. The correct definition of a Republic is: a constitutionally limited government of the representative type, created by a written Constitution—adopted by the people and changeable (from its original meaning) by them only by its amendment—with its powers divided between three separate Branches: Executive, Legislative and Judicial. Each American government, Federal and State, is a Republic; and such a form of government is expressly guaranteed to each State by the United States Constitution. (Article IV, Section 4.) This makes the American system a combination, or federation, of Republics—a compound Republic as noted in *The Federalist* number 51 by Madison. Although the term "Federal Republic" has sometimes been used to refer both to the central (Federal) government and to the federated system of Republics—including both central government and State governments (all Republics)—it will facilitate clear thinking if this term "Federal Republic" is applied only to the central government while using the phrase "federated system of Republics" or "federation of Republics" to designate the combination, or confederation, of all of these Republics. Clarity of understanding will be best assured by referring to the central government as the central Republic.

The electorate adopt a Constitution as their basic law by utilizing a Constitutional Convention to frame it for their final approval, or ratification, as was done successfully for the first time in history by the people of Massachusetts with regard to its Constitution of 1780; it was so framed by a convention specially chosen by the people for this sole purpose and then submitted to the people for approval. Final adoption, or ratification, may also be effected in behalf of the people by a specially chosen convention for this sole purpose; and later amendments may be so approved for the people or through the regular legislative body—the alternatives specified in the United States Constitution. This Constitution was framed by the Federal (Constitutional) Convention in 1787 and then adopted in 1787-1788 by State Ratifying Conventions especially chosen by the people for this sole purpose;

45

which is the complete and perfect method of Constitution-making. A Constitutional Convention—one chosen by the people for the sole purpose of framing or ratifying a Constitution—is one of America's great contributions, if not her greatest contribution, to the mechanics of self-government through constitutionally limited government.

Federal Delegated-Power, and State Full-Power, Republics

7. The Federal government is a delegated-power Republic which possesses only the comparatively few and limited powers granted to it by the people as enumerated in the United States Constitution, as amended—chiefly the powers concerned with "war, peace, negociation, and foreign commerce" (quoting *The Federalist,* number 45 by Madison). It is in sharpest contrast that each State government is a full-power Republic which possesses the vast and varied powers needed to administer intra-State affairs—"all the objects which, in the ordinary course of affairs, concern the lives, liberties, and properties of the people, and the internal order, improvement, and prosperity of the State" (again quoting number 45). The full-power Republic of each State is subject to the State Constitution, as well as to the United States Constitution as the "supreme Law of the Land." Neither the Federal, nor any State, government therefore possesses legal sovereignty—the unlimited power of sovereignty—while the people's political sovereignty is limited in favor of preserving inviolate the God-given, unalienable rights of each Individual. (See Par. 3, Principle 4.)

The "General Welfare"
in Relation to the Constitution

8. The Preamble of the United States Constitution specifies "the general Welfare" merely as one of the listed goals to be served by the Federal government in the exercise of the limited powers delegated to it, as enumerated in the body of that instrument. This mention of "the general Welfare" in the Preamble was intended, therefore, to serve in effect as a limit on the use of those delegated powers. The Preamble does not constitute a grant of any power whatever to the government. The only other mention of the words "general welfare" in the Constitution is in the Taxing Clause (Article I, Section 8) which authorizes Congress to collect taxes ". . . , to pay the Debts and provide for the common Defence and general Welfare of the United States . . ." Here, too, the words "general Welfare" were designed

to serve as a limitation in effect—as a limit on the power granted under that clause. This excludes any power to tax and spend for all purposes which would not qualify as being for the "general Welfare of the United States" as a whole—for instance, it is excluded if for the benefit merely of a locality or some Individuals in the United States. The clause does not empower Congress to spend tax monies for any and every purpose it might select merely on the pretense, or even in the belief, that it is for the "general welfare." (Discussed also in Pars. 4 and 5 of Principle 11.) Congress possesses no "general legislative authority," as Hamilton stated in *The Federalist* number 83.

Hamilton's Opinion

9. All of those who framed and ratified the Constitution were in agreement on this point of the limited and limiting meaning of the words "general Welfare" in the Taxing Clause. As Secretary of the Treasury, Hamilton contended for the first time in 1791 ("Opinion as to the Constitutionality of the Bank of the United States") in favor of a broader interpretation of this clause than he had formerly espoused and broader than that which Madison—with Hamilton's silent acquiescence—had presented in 1788 in *The Federalist* (especially number 41) as reflecting the controlling intent of the Framing Convention, which Madison and Jefferson consistently supported. Hamilton did not claim, however, that this clause gives to the Federal government any power, through taxing-spending, so as in effect to *control* directly or indirectly anything or anybody, or any activities of the people or of the State governments. Despite his assertion that this clause gives Congress a separate and substantive spending power, Hamilton cautioned expressly (Report on "Manufactures," 1791) that it only authorizes taxing and spending within the limits of what would serve the "general welfare" and does not "imply a power to do whatever else should appear to Congress conducive to the general welfare" —that it does "not carry a power to do any other thing not authorized in the Constitution, either expressly or by fair implication."

The Supreme Court's 1936 Decision Ascertaining and Defining the Original, Controlling Intent

10. As the Supreme Court decided (1936 *Carter* case) in ascer-

taining and defining the original, controlling intent of the Constitution as proved by all pertinent records and confirming its prior decisions over the generations since the adoption of the Constitution, the contentions advanced from time to time that "Congress, entirely apart from those powers delegated by the Constitution, may enact laws to promote the general welfare, have never been accepted but always definitely rejected by this court." It also decided that the Framing Convention "made no grant of authority to Congress to legislate substantively for the general welfare . . . [citing 1936 *Butler* case, page 64] . . . and no such authority exists, save as the general welfare may be promoted by the exercise of the powers which are granted." The American people have never amended the Constitution so as to change the limited and limiting meaning of the words "general Welfare" in the Taxing Clause, as thus originally intended by The Framers and Adopters in 1787-1788.

The Founders' Warnings

11. As Jefferson warned many times in his writings, public and private—for instance in the Kentucky Resolutions (see page 16, *ante*)—in keeping with the traditional American philosophy, strict enforcement of the Constitution's limits on the Federal government's power is essential for the protection of the people's liberties. This point was stressed at great length in *The Federalist* (notably numbers 17, 28, 33 and 78 by Hamilton and 44 and 46 by Madison) in reporting and explaining the intent of the Framing Convention expressed in the Constitution—as was understood and accepted by the State Ratifying Conventions. Hamilton's repeated warnings against permitting public servants to flout the people's mandate as to the limits on government's power, as specified in their basic laws (Constitutions) creating their governments, were in keeping with his words on one occasion in relation to the New York State Constitution. He stated ("Letters of Phocion," 1784) that any such defiance, by public servants, of the Constitution would be "a treasonable usurpation upon the power and majesty of the people . . ." Washington's *Farewell Address* expressed the conviction of The Founders of the Republic and their fellow leaders, in keeping with history's lesson, when he warned that usurpation "is the customary weapon by which free governments are destroyed."

Resistance to Usurpers, as Tyrants,
Is Obedience to God

12. It is a traditional American motto that: "Rebellion to tyrants is obedience to God." That is, resistance against tyranny is a moral duty. This motto was suggested by Benjamin Franklin in mid-1776 in the Congress as being an appropriate one for the seal of the United States; and it was so truly expressive of traditional American thinking that Jefferson adopted it for use on his personal seal.

A major part of the American philosophy underlying the resistance to the tyranny of king and parliament prior to the Declaration of Independence, and in support of that Declaration in 1776, was as follows. Public officials who exceed the limits of the powers delegated to them by the people under their fundamental law and thus violate, or endanger, the people's God-given, unalienable rights thereby and to this extent make of themselves defaulting trustees, usurpers, oppressors and tyrants. They thereby act outside of this supreme law, which defines these limits and the scope of their authority and office, and therefore act without authority from the people. By thus exceeding and violating the restrictions of this law, they act outside of Law: lawlessly, as "out-laws." As Samuel Adams stated: "Let us remember, that 'if we suffer tamely a *lawless* attack upon our liberty, we encourage it, and involve others [Posterity] in our doom.' " (Emphasis added.) They thereby, in practice, replace Rule-by-Law with Rule-by-Man. These defaulting trustees—thus acting lawlessly—thereby free the people from any duty of obedience; because legally and morally, under Rule-by-Law, obedience by the self-governing people is required only to Law and not to law-defying public servants.

The reasoning supporting the above-quoted motto's concept of moral duty is this: Man, being given by his Creator unalienable rights which are accompanied by corresponding duties, has the moral duty —duty to God—to safeguard these rights for the benefit of self and others, including Posterity. Man is therefore obligated to oppose all violators of these rights and to fail to do so is to defy duty to God as the giver of these rights; and such failure betrays Man's duty as the temporary trustee of Posterity's just heritage. This is in keeping with the philosophy of the Declaration of Independence as reiterated in part, for example, in 1788 in the Virginia Ratifying Convention's proposals for amendments to the Constitution including a Bill of Rights stating in part as follows:

". . . that the doctrine of non-resistance against arbitrary power and oppression is absurd slavish, and destructive of the good and happiness of mankind."

Applied to the United States Constitution, which Federal and State officials are sworn to support, this means that—in resisting Federal officials who, as usurpers, defy the limits on their powers imposed by this "supreme Law of the Land"—the people and governments of the States are opposing Rule-by-Man and defending Rule-by-Law (basically the people's fundamental law: the Constitution). They are thus defending the Constitution against its violators: the Federal usurpers; and they are acting in defense of the people's God-given, unalienable rights and the States' reserved powers. The American philosophy and system of constitutionally limited government contemplate that the people of the several States—acting through their State governments—will, *in last resort,* use force to oppose any force employed by the Federal usurpers, that they will use military force (Militia of the States) to oppose any military force used by such usurpers; as Hamilton and Madison explained in detail in *The Federalist,* numbers 28 and 46.

The Conclusion

13. The American philosophy reflects the knowledge that the history of Individual Liberty is the history of the effective limitation of government's power, which is expressed in the traditional principle summarized in the phrase: Limited for Liberty.

PRINCIPLE SIX
DECENTRALIZED GOVERNMENT

NON-RESISTANCE TO USURPERS IS SLAVISH

And he that would palm the doctrine of unlimited passive obedience and non-resistance upon mankind, . . . is not only a fool and a knave, but a rebel against common sense, as well as the laws of God, of Nature, and his Country.   James Otis
("The Rights of the British Colonies," 1764)

And yet I think it may be presumed, a free-born People can never become so servile as to regard them [obey tyrants' edicts], while they have Eyes to see that such Rulers [who violate basic Law] have gone *out of the Line* of their Power.—There is no Reason they should be *Fools* because their Rulers are so . . .   Rev. Elisha Williams
(Emphasis per original.)   ("A Seasonable Plea . . ." 1744)

. . . tyranny and arbitrary power are utterly inconsistent with, and subversive of the very end and design of civil government, and directly contrary to natural law, which is the true foundation of civil government and all politick law: Consequently the authority of a tyrant is of itself null and void . . .   Rev. Samuel West
(Election Sermon, 1776)

The king is as much bound by his oath, not to infringe the legal rights of the people, as the people are bound to yield subjection to him. From whence it follows, that *as soon as the prince sets himself up above law,* he loses the king in the tyrant: *he does to all intents and purposes, unking himself,* by acting out of, and beyond, that sphere which the constitution allows him to move in. And in such cases, he has no more right to be obeyed, than any inferior officer who acts beyond his commission. The subjects obligation to allegiance *then* ceases of course; and to resist him, is no more *rebellion,* than to resist any foreign invader.
(Emphasis added except   Rev. Jonathan Mayhew
in last sentence.)   (Election Sermon, "Unlimited Submission and
Non-Resistance to the Higher Powers," 1750)

Third: That Government ought to be instituted for the common benefit, protection and security of the people; and that the doctrine of non-resistance against arbitrary power and oppression is absurd, slavish, and destructive to the good and happiness of mankind.
North Carolina Ratifying Convention
(Among proposed amendments to the Constitution; and
similarly the Virginia Ratifying Convention)

THE STATES' MILITIA INTENDED, IN PART, FOR DEFENSE AGAINST FEDERAL USURPERS

A well regulated Militia, being necessary to the security of a free State, the right of the people to keep and bear Arms, shall not be infringed.
U.S. Constitution, 2nd Amendment
(in keeping with various States' Bills of Rights, such as Sec. 13 of 1776 Bill of Rights of Virginia)

USE FORCE TO DEFEND LIBERTY BUT ONLY AS THE LAST RESORT

That no man shou'd scruple, or hesitate a moment to use a-ms. [arms] in defence of so valuable a blessing [as liberty], on which all the good and evil of life depends; is clearly my opinion; yet A-ms. [arms] . . . should be the last . . . resort.
George Washington
(Letter to George Mason, 1769)

STATES RIGHTS DEFENDED BY FORCE—IN LAST RESORT

If the representatives of the people betray their constituents [by usurping power], there is then no resource left but in the exertion of that original right of self-defence, which is paramount to all positive forms of government; and which, against the usurpations of the national rulers, may be exerted with infinitely better prospect of success, than against those of the rulers of an individual state. . . . It may safely be received as an axiom in our political system, that the state governments will in all possible contingencies afford complete security against invasions of the public liberty by the national authority.
The Federalist (no. 28, by Alexander Hamilton)
(Note: Means by use of States' Militia in self-defense, in last resort.)

But ambitious encroachments of the federal government, on the authority of the state governments, would not excite the opposition of a single state or of a few states only. They would be signals of general alarm. Every government would espouse the common cause. A correspondence would be opened. Plans of resistance would be concerted. One spirit would animate and conduct the whole. The same combinations in short would result from an apprehension of the federal, as was produced by the dread of a foreign yoke; and unless the projected innovations should be voluntarily renounced, the same appeal to *a trial of force would be made* in the one case, as was made in the other.*
The Federalist (no. 46, by James Madison)
(Note: Emphasis added; means use of States' Militia in self-defense, in last resort.)   * In the American Revolution

THE STATES ESSENTIAL TO LIBERTY—
ACCORDING TO THE THINKING OF THE FOUNDERS

No political dreamer was ever wild enough to think of breaking down the lines which separate the States, and of compounding the American people into one common mass.

John Marshall, Chief Justice of the U.S.
(Speaking for the Court in 1819 *McCulloch v. Md.* case; in 1788 was a member of the Va. Ratifying Convention)

[As to danger of the Supreme Court's misinterpreting the Constitution so as to concentrate power in Washington] To this I am opposed; because, when all government . . . shall be drawn to Washington . . . it will render powerless the checks . . . will become as venal and oppressive . . . [as Great Britain's government] . . . If the States look with apathy on this silent descent of their government into the gulf which is to swallow all, we have only to weep over the human character formed uncontrollable but by a rod of iron, and the blasphemers of man, as incapable of self-government, become his true historians.

Thomas Jefferson
(Letter to Charles Hammond, 1821)

REPEL "LAWLESS ATTACK" ON LIBERTY

The liberties of our Country, the freedom of our civil constitution are worth defending at all hazards: And it is our duty to defend them against all attacks. We have receiv'd them as a fair Inheritance from our worthy Ancestors: They purchas'd them for us with toil and danger and expence of treasure and blood; and transmitted them to us with care and diligence. It will bring an everlasting mark of infamy on the present generation, enlightened as it is, if we should suffer them to be wrested from us by violence without a struggle; or be cheated out of them by the artifices of false and designing men. Of the latter we are in most danger at present: Let us therefore be aware of it. Let us contemplate our forefathers and posterity; and resolve to maintain the rights bequeath'd to us from the former, for the sake of the latter.—Instead of sitting down satisfied with the efforts we have already made, *which is the wish of our enemies,* the necessity of the times, more than ever, calls for our utmost circumspection, deliberation, fortitude and perseverance. Let us remember, that "if we suffer tamely a lawless attack upon our liberty, we encourage it, and involve others in our doom." It is a very serious consideration, which should deeply impress our minds, that *millions yet unborn may be the miserable sharers in the event.*

(Emphasis per original.)

Samuel Adams
(Essay in Boston Gazette, 1771)

A Principle of The Traditional American Philosophy

6. DECENTRALIZED GOVERNMENT

The Principle
1. The traditional American philosophy teaches that decentralization of governmental power, to the maximum practicable extent, is essential to the security of Man's God-given, unalienable rights.

Man's Unalienable Rights
and "States Rights" Doubly Protected
2. It asserts that these rights are most securely protected by a federated system of government—consisting of a central government (a Republic) and State governments (each a Republic). Under this system, the whole quantity of governmental power is not only limited by written Constitutions, Federal and State, but also decentralized so that the vast majority of powers are kept on the State and local levels. The correct definition of a Republic is: a constitutionally limited government of the representative type, created by a written Constitution—adopted by the people and changeable (from its original meaning) by them only by its amendment—with its powers divided between three separate Branches: Executive, Legislative and Judicial. The American system is "a compound Republic"—a federation, or combination, of central and State Republics—under which: "The different governments will control each other . . . ," while within each Republic there are two safeguarding features: (a) a division of powers, as well as (b) a system of checks and balances between separate departments: "Hence a double security arises to the rights of the people." (*The Federalist,* number 51, by Madison.)

Greater Quantity of Power Retained by Each State
3. By far the greater quantity and variety of power was retained by the government of each State when the United States Constitution

was framed and adopted in 1787-1788. Only a comparatively small part of each State's power was delegated by its people to the new central, or Federal, government—chiefly the powers concerning "war, peace, negociation and foreign commerce" (per *The Federalist*, number 45 by Madison). This delegated-power government—the central Republic—was granted few and limited powers; while each State's government is a full-power Republic under the State Constitution, subject to its restrictions, also to that grant, and to the few restrictions specified expressly in the United States Constitution as applying to the governments of the States.

"Home Rule" the Basic, Controlling Principle

4. This federated system of decentralized power is a chief characteristic of the American governmental arrangements. This is in keeping with the controlling intent of those who framed and adopted the Constitution in 1787-1788 and of those who framed and adopted each of its Amendments. The main aim was to preserve maximum "Home Rule" by the States, to keep the greatest feasible quantity of power as close as possible to the source—the people—where they can best watch it alertly so as to check and prevent its abuse or misuse, as well as to prevent its unsound, or unnecessary, expansion, to the peril or perhaps doom of their liberties.

Economic Liberty and Decentralized Government

5. Such decentralized government is favorable, indeed essential, to America's traditional philosophy and system of economic liberty— the inseparable and indispensable economic aspect of the indivisible whole of Individual Liberty-Responsibility. This includes the system of individual, private, competitive enterprise (called Individual Enterprise—the term used by President Jefferson in his 1801 Annual Message to Congress). This system features a free-market economy —free from Government-over-Man *controls,* although subject to just *regulation* (as authorized by the Constitution's pertinent provisions) under just laws expressive of "just powers" (to use the term of the Declaration of Independence) designed to protect the equal rights of all Individuals and thus to safeguard sound competition —which gives full play to individual initiative inspired by the incentive of private profit. The right to Individual Enterprise is of the essence of economic liberty of The Individual and is a main character-

istic of the traditional American philosophy. This right is not a goal or end, in and of itself, but a necessary means, and it is an essential and main support of Man's unalienable rights. It involves freedom of choice by both producer-seller and consumer-buyer, subject always to the potently persuasive influence of community opinion and standards in the sound environment of an ethical society which emphasizes the duty factor of Individual Liberty-Responsibility, including due respect for the equal rights of others. This means that the central government is limited strictly to the consistent role of mere regulation (not control) to these ends—regulation as limited by the Constitution. This excludes any control by the central government directly or indirectly of the whole or any part of the national economy, which includes all of the people's economic activities.

The free-market economy is controlled by the people as a whole through their acting as buyers and sellers—a multitude of Individuals generally acting individually as both buyer and seller of things or services a number of times each day in the ordinary course of life's daily activities, involving transactions great or small—through their exercise of freedom of choice daily, even hourly; for example, the grocer, druggist, barber, taxi-driver, doctor, lawyer and so on. The free-market economy is both result and instrument of the exercise of this freedom of Individuals—not a mechanistic, independently operating "Thing" which oppressively controls human beings.

Sample Warnings by The Founders

6. The American people and their leaders in 1776-1787 were determined that the central government should never be allowed to possess power to act, or be permitted to act, as a "consolidated" government with sovereign, unlimited power over all of the people and things in the country. Vigilant friends of Individual Liberty, including for example leaders such as Thomas Jefferson, Samuel Adams, Alexander Hamilton and James Madison, warned repeatedly and emphatically against the danger of ever permitting such a government to exist in America.

Samuel Adams' Opinion

7. Samuel Adams, firebrand patriot-leader always in the lead for both American Independence and Man's Liberty against Government-over-Man, expressed fear in this regard in 1789 (letter to Richard

Henry Lee) in keeping with his never varying sentiments. He said that he feared misinterpretation of the Constitution would bring about fully centralized (consolidated) power in the Federal government at the expense of the States and "sink both in despotism."

Hamilton's Opinion

8. In the New York Ratifying Convention in 1788, Hamilton warned sharply that the States' powers reserved under the Constitution must be safeguarded for the sake of Individual Liberty and that Congress would never fail to safeguard them: ". . . unless they become madmen."

Hamilton and Madison
in "The Federalist"

9. This sound line of thought was stressed by Hamilton and Madison, in their joint report in *The Federalist* (for example, numbers 17 and 28 by Hamilton, and 45 and 46 by Madison), recording the intent of the 1787 Framing Convention as expressed in the Constitution. The foregoing sentiments of these leaders were shared by their fellow leaders and the American people in general of that day—as reflecting truly American principles—and by Jefferson second to none.

Jefferson's Opinion

10. In his First Inaugural Address as President, Jefferson stated that the State governments are "the surest bulwarks against anti-republican tendencies"—that is, tendencies which conflict with the American form of government: a Republic. He stated in a letter to Destutt de Tracy (1811): "But the true barriers [bulwarks] of our liberty in this country are our State governments . . ." With regard to the people's freedom from Government-over-Man controls by the Federal government, in keeping with the Constitution's limits on that government's powers, Jefferson stated in his Annual Message to Congress, in 1801: "Agriculture, manufactures, commerce, and navigation, the four pillars of our prosperity, are the most thriving when left most free to individual enterprise." In the above-mentioned 1811 letter, Jefferson also discussed the prospective use of the Militia of the States—all acting together—to resist the forces of any Federal

usurpers acting in violation of the Constitution to oppress or dominate the people or government of any State.

Some Peaceable Remedies of the People Against an Offending Federal Government

11. Some of the peaceable remedies of the people of any State against what they consider to be anti-Constitution, or otherwise offensive, conduct by the Federal government—by any of its Branches, or by all of them combined—as contemplated by the Convention which framed the Constitution, were specified in *The Federalist* number 46 by Madison, with the silent acquiescence of his co-author Hamilton, as follows:

"On the other hand, should an unwarrantable measure of the federal government be unpopular in particular states, which would seldom fail to be the case, or even a warrantable measure be so, which may sometimes be the case, the means of opposition to it are powerful and at hand. The disquietude of the people, their repugnance and perhaps refusal to co-operate with the officers of the union, the frowns of the executive magistracy [officials] of the state, the embarrassments created by legislative devices, which would often be added on such occasions, would oppose in any state difficulties not to be despised; would form in a large state very serious impediments, and where the sentiments of several adjoining states happened to be in unison, would present obstructions which the federal government would hardly be willing to encounter."

The most extremely "unwarrantable measure" is an unconstitutional measure. Madison here expressed the understanding also of those who framed the Constitution and of their fellow leaders in the State Ratifying Conventions as well as of the people in general—all extremely jealous of their hard-won liberties and determined to act vigorously against any danger to them from the greatly feared, central government if it should ever threaten to over-step the limits imposed on its powers under the Constitution, as amended. Protests by State legislatures against what they would consider to be abuses of power or usurpations, potential or actual, by the central government were of course included as a main element in what Madison referred to here as "legislative devices . . . impediments . . . obstructions." Actual examples occurring afterward are the Kentucky and Virginia Resolutions of 1798 and the Hartford Convention Resolutions of 1815 (discussed in Principle 2, Pars. 5-6). Some additional remedies of the people, of a peaceable nature, are political action—use of the ballot in elections—and amendment of the Constitution by the people (Art. V); while impeachment by Congress of any officials guilty of acting as defaulting public trustees is provided for (Art. I, Sec. 2, 3).

State's Self-defense by Force, in Last Resort, per "The Federalist"

12. With regard to use by the States of force—use of their Militia forces (all able-bodied males capable of bearing arms)—in self-defense against any Federal usurpers seeking to oppress or dominate one or more States by force in violation of the Constitution's limits on Federal power, Hamilton and Madison discussed at length and in detail in *The Federalist* (numbers 28 by Hamilton and 46 by Madison) the assumption and expectation of The Framers that all States would marshal their forces and act jointly to crush the usurpers' forces. This understanding of The Framers was shared by the members of the State Ratifying Conventions and the leaders and people in general of that day—all fearless foes of any and all enemies of Free Man in America. They believed that all true Americans must be ready to fight and die for Liberty, especially against tyrannical Federal officials who, as usurpers, violate not only the Constitution but also their oath of office: to support the Constitution *only*. It was also contemplated that any non-military force used by the Federal usurpers would be countered by the States' use of their own non-military forces: Sheriff's posses (*posses comitatus*) and any civilian police forces. (See also Par. 12 of Principle 5.)

The Civil over The Military

13. The traditional American philosophy requires, as a fundamental of the system of checks and balances, that The Civil must always be in complete control of The Military. The Founders and their fellow Americans were painfully aware of the lesson of history that large standing armies are, in peacetime, potentially dangerous to the people's liberties. In 1776, the Virginia Declaration of Rights, for example, made this clear in these words: ". . . that standing armies in time of peace should be avoided as dangerous to liberty; and that in all cases the military should be under strict subordination to, and governed by, the civil power." Another, related element in the system

of checks and balances is the requirement of the Constitution (Article VI) that all Federal officials—both civil and military—take an oath to support the Constitution [*only*]; with the result that all military officers, thus controlled fundamentally and supremely by the Constitution, must be obedient to the civil authority—chief of all the President—but only as to orders which are not violative of the Constitution. The Military are, therefore, obligated by the Constitution not only to refuse to obey any orders of Federal usurpers—automatically made by the Constitution itself null and void from the start—but to support the Constitution only, at all times and under all circumstances, as the sovereign people's fundamental law. State officials, civil and military, are likewise so required to take an oath to support the Constitution of the United States—meaning, in part, to resist Federal usurpers by all necessary means: by force in last resort.

The Conclusion

14. The truly American formula, in accordance with the traditional philosophy, for sound and enduring self-government by means of constitutionally limited government with adequate protection assured for Individual Liberty, is this: Limited and Decentralized for Liberty.

PRINCIPLE SEVEN

EQUAL, BY GOD'S GIFT, IN SIGHT OF GOD AND LAW

BY NATURE, EQUALLY FREE AND INDEPENDENT

That all men are by nature equally free and independent . . .

Virginia Declaration of Rights, 1776

DIVERSE FACULTIES CREATE INEQUALITY
OF INTERESTS, PARTIES, POSSESSIONS

As long as the reason of man continues fallible, and he is at liberty to exercise it, different opinions will be formed . . . The diversity in the faculties of men from which the rights of property originate, is not less an insuperable obstacle to an uniformity of interests. The protection of these faculties is the first object of government. From the protection of different and unequal faculties of acquiring property, the possession of different degrees and kinds of property immediately results; And from the influence of these on the sentiments and views of the respective proprietors, ensues a division of the society into different interests and parties.

The Federalist (no. 10, by James Madison)

LIBERTY AND EQUALITY

In the supposed state of nature, all men are equally bound by the laws of nature, or to speak more properly, the laws of the Creator:—They are imprinted by the finger of God on the heart of man. Thou shall do no injury to thy neighbour, is the voice of nature and reason, and it is confirmed by written revelation. In the state of nature, every man hath an equal right by honest means to acquire property, and to enjoy it; in general, to pursue his own happiness, and none can consistently controul or interrupt him in the pursuit . . . [But government is needed to defend the weak and honest against the strong and selfish, so government is organized] for the better security of their natural rights. In this state of society, the unalienable rights of nature are held sacred:— . . . the doctrine of Liberty and Equality is an article in the political creed of the United States . . . without Liberty and Equality, there cannot exist that tranquillity of mind, which results from the assurance of every citizen, that his own personal safety and rights are secure . . . it is the end and design of all free and lawful Governments.

Samuel Adams
(As Lt. Governor of Mass., to the Legislature,
upon the death of Governor John Hancock, 1794)

(Note: "Equality" here—per the Declaration of Independence—means equality in sight of God and Law)

FROM LEATHER APRONS TO LEATHER APRONS
IN THREE GENERATIONS

> Is not one half of the property in the city of Philadelphia owned by men who wear LEATHER APRONS?
> Does not the other half belong to men whose fathers or grandfathers wore LEATHER APRONS?
> An Anonymous Item, Pa. Evening Post, 1776

EQUALITY DESPITE DIFFERING CIRCUMSTANCES

> . . . the important ends of Civil Society, and the personal Securities of Life and Liberty, these remain the same in every Member of the society; and the poorest continues to have an equal Claim to them with the most opulent, whatever Difference Time, Chance, or Industry may occasion in their Circumstances. Benjamin Franklin
> ("Queries etc." regarding Constitution of Pa., 1789)

EQUALITY IN AMERICA GREATER

> [In the U. S.] Every freeman has a right to the same protection & security; and a very moderate share of property entitles them to the possession of all the honors and privileges the public can bestow: hence arises a greater equality, than is to be found among the people of any other country, and an equality which is more likely to continue . . .
> Charles Pinckney
> (In the Framing Convention, 1787)

EQUALITY AND GOVERNMENT

> In the state of nature there was subordination: The weaker was *by force* made to bow down to the more powerful. This is still the unhappy lot of a great part of the world, under government: So among the brutal herd, the strongest horns are the strongest laws. Mankind have entered into political societies, rather for the sake of restoring *equality;* the want of which, in the state of nature, rendered existence uncomfortable and even dangerous. I am not of levelling principles: But I am apt to think, that constitution of civil government which admits equality in the most extensive degree, *consistent with the true design of government*, is the best . . . (Last emphasis added.) Samuel Adams
> (Essay, in Boston Gazette, 1771)

EQUAL LEGAL JUSTICE

Equal and exact justice to all men, of whatever state or persuasion, religious or political . . . [is the goal]
President Thomas Jefferson
(First Inaugural Address)
(Note: "Justice" here means legal justice.)

A DELUSION ABOUT EQUALITY

"Theoretic politicians, who have patronized this species of government [democracy], have erroneously supposed, that by reducing mankind to a perfect equality in their political rights, they would, at the same time, be perfectly equalized and assimilated in their possessions, their opinions, and their passions." *The Federalist* (no. 10 by James Madison)

A NATURAL ARISTOCRACY OF VIRTUE AND TALENTS

For I agree with you that there is a natural aristocracy among men. The grounds of this are virtue and talents . . . The natural aristocracy I consider as the most precious gift of nature, for the instruction, the trusts, and government of society. And indeed, it would have been inconsistent in creation to have formed man for the social state, and not to have provided virtue and wisdom enough to manage the concerns of the society.
Thomas Jefferson
(Letter to John Adams, 1813)

ENDING SLAVERY

I can only say that there is not a man living who wishes more sincerely than I do, to see a plan adopted for the abolition of it [slavery]; but there is only one proper and effectual mode by which it can be accomplished, and that is by Legislative authority; and this, as far as my suffrage will go, shall never be wanting.
George Washington
(Letter to Robert Morris, 1786)

The abolition of domestic slavery is the great object of desire in those colonies, where it was unhappily introduced in their infant state. But previous to the enfranchisement of the slaves we have, it is necessary to exclude all further importations from Africa; yet our repeated attempts to effect this by prohibitions . . . [have been prevented by the King].
Thomas Jefferson
(Rights of British America, 1774)

A Principle of The Traditional American Philosophy

7. EQUAL, BY GOD'S GIFT, IN SIGHT OF GOD AND LAW

". . . all men are created equal . . ."
(Declaration of Independence)

The Principle
1. The traditional American philosophy teaches that all men are created equal, made equal at birth by their Creator, but equal only in the sight of God and of Law.

Basic Definition of Equality
2. This philosophy asserts that equality in the sight of God is in the religious realm and means being equal spiritually, while equality in the sight of Law means being entitled to equal legal justice and having the right to be considered and treated as equal in Freedom from Government-over-Man. Equal legal justice means equal treatment under equal laws—that is, just laws expressive of "just powers" (to quote the term used in the Declaration of Independence) designed to make and keep secure the equal rights of all Individuals and, therefore, compatible with Natural Law (God's Law) on which Man's God-given, unalienable rights are based. It requires respect by government for such equal rights of all Individuals. Also included, of course, is equality as to The Individual's duties underlying Individual Liberty-*Responsibility,* especially the duty to respect the equal rights of others.

The Ideal of Equality in 1776— in the Face of Inherited Slavery System
3. This word equal, according to the American philosophy as defined in the Declaration of Independence, means equal in *freedom* of The Individual. This bars slavery of Man to Man. This truly expressed the American ideal and goal in 1776, despite the laws then making slavery legal in America as the result of an ancient system inherited from the Old World—fostered by the slave trade which was

supported by the king of England despite protests of the Colonies, as noted in Jefferson's "Rights of British America" (1774) and in his first draft of the Declaration of Independence. At the first opportunity to act in this regard, in adopting the Northwest Ordinance of 1787, the Congress prohibited slavery from being practiced in the Northwest Territory. The fact that slavery had to be faced as an existing condition in 1776, and the difficulty and slowness of its ultimate abolition, did not impair the spiritual integrity of the 1776 proclamation of the ideal and goal of the American philosophy in these words of the Declaration of Independence: "all men are created equal"—in the sight of God and of Law. By 1776, a number of slave-owning leaders —notably Washington, Jefferson, and George Mason—were deeply concerned about the need and desirability of abolishing slavery (through appropriate government action). It was generally recognized that the inherited institution of slavery was violative of the principle of Natural Rights and therefore of the American philosophy as proclaimed in the Declaration of Independence. To repeat, the then-existing fact of slavery in America did not lessen the value, or impair the integrity or validity, of the Declaration's definition and proclamation of The American Ideal—the hope and goal of the American philosophy—with which slavery was inconsistent. Indeed, this fact magnified the nobility of this Ideal's proclamation.

Equality in
Freedom of Opportunity
for Self-Development

4. The Declaration's pronouncement assured a sound philosophical basis for equality in *freedom* of opportunity—Freedom from Government-over-Man—to realize to the full The Individual's own highest potential in all aspects of life. This involves maximum freedom of choice. This is always subject to observance of the duties of Individual Liberty-Responsibility under constitutionally limited government, including the duty to respect the equal rights of others.

Equality in
Freedom from Government-over-Man
in the Economic Realm

5. In the economic realm also, this word "equal," as used in the Declaration of Independence, means only equal in *freedom* of oppor-

tunity. That is, freedom from the Government-over-Man type of restrictions upon The Individual's opportunity to strive for material security and advancement through his own self-reliant efforts, as he plans and manages his own life and work and the economic security of himself and his dependents. It means equal in *freedom* from those things which add up to Government-over-Man in general.

Individual Self-reliance and Group Cooperation
Constitute the Sound American Formula

6. The American philosophy makes the question of economic security the responsibility of The Individual and of groups of Individuals. Examples will be clarifying. First and foremost are the family and, further, religious groups as well as fraternal groups—all acting voluntarily. Self-reliance of The Individual is the key here, whether acting singly or cooperatively with other Individuals.

Public "Aid" for the Genuinely Needy
Must Be on Lowest Possible Governmental Level

7. Any locality's necessity to provide public aid for the relatively few persons who are helplessly and genuinely needy, judged by the "means" test (to determine the need of government aid to live), must be met on the lowest possible governmental level, under the traditional American philosophy and system of constitutionally limited government and decentralized power. This is according to the controlling intent of those who framed and adopted the Constitution and each of its amendments, under which the Federal government is prohibited from performing this task either directly, or indirectly through financial aid to State or local governments or to Individuals. (See also Pars. 8-10 of Principle 5 and Pars. 4-5 of Principle 11.) This is partly because Federal aid inescapably results in time in Federal control, either directly or indirectly—sometimes by subtle means. This decentralized power of government to provide public aid to the genuinely needy assures maximum safeguards against fraud, waste, political manipulation, and other adverse results in the administration of such activity. This decentralization saves money for the people as taxpayers whose funds pay the bill, in last analysis, no matter which government does the taxing for this purpose; and, at the same time, best results are obtained for all concerned, including the needy.

Equality as to Non-infringement by Other Individuals

8. The American philosophy also teaches equality in *freedom* of enjoyment of The Individual's unalienable rights, therefore equality in *freedom* from infringement of those rights by other Individuals (who would, by any such infringement, trespass beyond the limits of their own equal rights)—freedom in strict conformity with the Constitution, as amended. This applies whether any would-be infringers act as separate Individuals, or in groups, or in formal organizations such as associations of men in the economic realm—for instance, employers' associations, or employees' organizations. If any such violation of any Individual's unalienable rights, or the supporting rights, be perpetrated with the connivance of government—by its sin of omission or commission, by its sanction through either threat or actual use of force, or by enacted law—the offense is all the more anti-moral, anti-Constitution and anti-American. No allegedly good end can justify use of evil means such as this, according to the American philosophy's code of ethics and the underlying moral code.

Equality of Right to Be Let Alone

9. The ideals and principles, the spirit and lofty vision, of traditional America give highest priority to the concept of the inviolability of each Individual's right to full liberty—including complete freedom of choice—in his own private life and in his choice of associates in all aspects of life. This is limited only by the requirements of the duty aspect of Individual Liberty-Responsibility: due respect for the equal rights of others and for just laws (per Par. 2, above). This refers, for example, to laws such as criminal laws against a conspiracy to commit murder, or a conspiracy to subvert the United States government, or a conspiracy to violate the constitutional rights of any temporarily unpopular group—involving properly punishable guilt by association of persons (not of ideas) for an evil and justly forbidden purpose, the guilt being evidenced basically by the overt act of joining the conspiracy. Also included is the most comprehensive of rights and the right most valued by civilized men—the right of The Individual to be let alone by government. In America, this means to be let alone in the enjoyment of his unalienable rights, under the protection of the safeguards provided by the Constitution. This right to be let alone applies equally against infringement of The Individual's privacy in this regard by other Individuals, whether acting singly, in

groups, or in organizations. This right to be let alone is co-extensive with, and substantially overlaps, the right to freedom of choice: the right to do as one pleases subject only to the above-mentioned duty aspect of Individual Liberty-Responsibility. The anti-morality of the evil precept that the end justifies the means—that an allegedly good end justifies resort to evil means to accomplish it—is most offensive in the eyes of the American philosophy's moral code stemming from the fundamental principle of Man's creation and endowment with rights by God. An example is resort to this evil precept in attempted justification of infringement of The Individual's above-mentioned right to freedom of choice of associates in every realm of private life—the economic, social, religious and community in general; and all the more so when any violation of the Constitution is also involved in any such infringement. This anti-morality is compounded in evil implication if any government coercion is involved; which is true partly because government coercion (always backed by force, or the threat of force), so used, can later be used in reverse to compel disassociation—also violative of The Individual's freedom of choice.

Examples of What "Equality" Does Not Mean

10. To understand the meaning of the word "equal" more clearly and precisely, mention of what it does not mean is needed. For example, it does not mean equal opportunity, much less government-provided equal opportunity—but means equal *freedom* of opportunity as a part of Freedom from Government-over-Man. It does not mean being equal with regard to government-provided security (even if any such phantom goal for all the people were feasible for a long period without their abject slavery to government under a system of prison-type security). Nor does it mean being equal as to anything whatever to be provided by government, except equal legal justice under equally applied laws—the above-mentioned just laws. It certainly does not mean equality in servitude to government in any degree, however disguised—for example as tax-slaves subjected to the tyranny of oppressive, even confiscatory, taxes used for instance by usurpers to buy popular support for activities in furtherance of their usurpations in defiance of the Constitution's limits on their powers.

More Examples

11. The word "equal" in the Declaration of Independence assuredly does not mean being born equal in the sense of being identical

71

—either mentally, or physically, or in intelligence, or in capabilities, or in character, or in virtues, or in potential with regard to accomplishments or attainments, or in any of the various other ways in which men differ by nature's dispensation, from birth to death. It does not mean being equal with regard to any supposed right to material possessions, or to any claimed right to government-provided economic assistance, support, or security.

Equality in Private Life Excluded

12. As a final example, the word "equal" does not mean any kind or degree of government-provided, much less government-forced, equality in private life, such as social equality. Such a meaning would be flagrantly in violation of the spirit of the Declaration of Independence as well as of the spirit and letter of the Constitution, when construed in keeping with the original and always-controlling intent of those who framed and adopted the initial instrument and each of its amendments. Any idea of government-forced equality in Man's private life, social or otherwise—whether the forcing be done by "police state" methods or by any other type or degree of pressure by government or by others (threatened or applied, including "moral" pressure)—is bankrupt spiritually and morally. It is on a par with "forced brotherly love," a monstrous concept which is the product of "confusing the vocabulary." It violates the above-discussed right to be let alone, the right to freedom of choice, of the other Individuals involved, whose right to this aspect of Liberty cannot justly be thus sacrificed in the name of Equality; which would thereby be perverted into inequality as to Liberty, in conflict with the duty aspect of Individual Liberty-Responsibility. The power of government, or of any private group, cannot ever justly and properly be used in connection with any such victimizing of any aspect of any Individual's Liberty.

The Conclusion

13. In sum, the word "equal" in the Declaration of Independence means, first, spiritual equality (equality in the sight of God) and, second, equality in the sight of Law (basically the people's fundamental law, the Constitution)—primarily equality in Freedom from Government-over-man.

PRINCIPLE EIGHT

LIFE AND THE PURSUIT OF HAPPINESS

THE RIGHT TO LIFE

Property must often—reputation must always be purchased:* liberty and life are the gratuitous gifts of heaven.

I shall certainly be excused from adducing any formal arguments to evince, that life, and whatever is necessary for the safety of life, are the natural rights of man. Some things are so difficult; others are so plain, that they cannot be proved.

U.S. Supreme Court Justice James Wilson
(Lectures, 1790-1791)

* (Meaning reputation must be earned.)

The pretence of an absolute, irresistible, despotic power, existing in every government *somewhere*, is incompatible with the first principle of natural right. Take for example the right to life. The moment an infant is born, it has a right to the life which it has received from the Creator . . . no human being, no combination of human beings, has the power, I say not the physical, but the moral power, to take a life not so forfeited [by commission of a crime], unless in self-defense or by the laws of war . . .
(Emphasis per original.) John Quincy Adams
(Address, July 4, 1831)

THE INDIVIDUAL'S HAPPINESS
CONDUCIVE TO THE WELFARE OF OTHERS

The all wise Creator of man imprest certain laws on his nature. A desire of happiness, and of society, are two of those laws. They were not intended to destroy, but to support each other. Man has therefore a right to *promote* the *best* union of both, in order to enjoy both in the *highest* degree. Thus, while this right is properly exercised, desires, that seem *selfish*, by a happy combination, produce the welfare of *others*.
(Emphasis per original.) John Dickinson
(*Political Writings*, 1774)

PROGRESSIVE HAPPINESS—SEEKING PERFECTION

A progressive state is necessary to the happiness and perfection of man. Whatever attainments are already reached, attainments still higher should be pursued. Let us, therefore, strive with noble emulation. Let us suppose we have done nothing, while any thing yet remains to be done. Let us, with fervent zeal, press forward, and make unceasing advances in every thing that can support, improve, refine, or embellish society . . . The commencement of our government has been eminently glorious: let our progress in every excellence be proportionably great. It will—it must be so.
James Wilson
(In an oration, July 4, 1788)

HAPPINESS SELF-CREATED

That Mankind were intended to be happy, at least that God Almighty gave them power of being so, if they would properly exert the means He has bestowed upon them.   James Iredell
(In an Essay, 1775)

SOME TRUTHS ABOUT PUBLIC HAPPINESS

. . . this eternal truth, that *public happiness depends on a virtuous and unshaken attachment to a free constitution.*   Dr. Joseph Warren
(Emphasis per original.)   (Oration, Boston, March 5, 1772)

As the happiness of a people and the good order and preservation of civil government essentially depend upon piety, religion, and morality . . .
Massachusetts Bill of Rights, 1780

RIGHT TO HAPPINESS, FREEDOM, PROPERTY

Kings or parliaments could not *give* the *rights essential to happiness* . . . We claim them from a higher source—from the King of kings, and Lord of all the earth. They are not annexed to us by parchments and seals. They are created in us by the decrees of Providence . . . It would be an insult on the divine Majesty to say, that he has given or allowed any man or body of men *a right to make me miserable.* If no man or body of men has such *a right,* I have a *right to be happy.* If there can be no happiness without freedom, I have a *right to be free.* If I cannot enjoy freedom without security of property, I have a *right to be thus secured.*
(Emphasis per original.)   John Dickinson
(Reply to a Committee in Barbadoes, 1766)

TRUE BASIS OF HAPPINESS—
TO BE ACHIEVED BY EACH INDIVIDUAL

[Through education of the young in public schools] The first elements of morality too may be instilled in their minds; such as, when further developed as their judgments advance in strength, may teach them how to work out their own greatest happiness, by shewing them that it does not depend on the condition of life in which chance has placed them, but is always the result of a good conscience, good health, occupation, and freedom in all just pursuits.   Thomas Jefferson
("Notes on the State of Virginia," 1782)

75

MAN'S HAPPINESS IN RELATION TO.
THE AIM AND FORM OF GOVERNMENT

That government is, or ought to be instituted for the common benefit, protection, and security of the people, nation, or community; of all the various modes and forms of government, that is best which is capable of producing the greatest degree of *happiness* and safety, and is most effectually secured against the danger of maladministration . . .
(Emphasis added.)

Virginia Declaration of Rights, 1776

Our true situation appears to me to be this. —a new extensive Country containing within itself the materials for forming a Government capable of extending to its citizens all the blessings of civil & religious liberty— capable of making them happy at home. This is the great end of Republican Establishments.

Charles Pinckney
(In Framing Convention, 1787)
(Note: "Republican" means those of a Republic.)

We are therefore brought exactly to the same point at last, whether we consider government as it is originally an appointment of Heaven, or, more immediately, the voluntary choice of men. The security and happiness of all the members composing the political body, must be the design and end thereof, considered in both these lights.

Rev. Jonathan Mayhew
(Election Sermon, 1754)

The consequence is, that the happiness of society is the *first* law of every government. This rule is founded on the law of nature: it must control every political maxim: it must regulate the legislature itself. The people have a right to insist that this rule be observed; and are entitled to demand a moral security that the legislature will observe it. If they have not the first [that right], they are slaves; if they have not the second [that moral security], they are, every moment, exposed to slavery.
(Emphasis per original.)

U.S. Supreme Court Justice James Wilson
(Lectures, 1790-1791)

76

A Principle of The Traditional American Philosophy

8. LIFE AND THE PURSUIT OF HAPPINESS

". . . unalienable Rights, that among these are Life . . . and the pursuit of Happiness"   (Declaration of Independence)

The Principle

1. The traditional American philosophy teaches that the words "Life" and "the pursuit of Happiness," as used in the Declaration of Independence, are so inclusive as to defy precise definition.

Ever-Changing Nature of Goals, etc.

2. This is because they mean here the right to Life to be lived, and Happiness to be sought, in keeping with the fundamentals of Man's Liberty against Government-over-Man, according to each Individual's own goals, tastes, aspirations and ideals which are themselves in an ever-changing state of development—from childhood to life's end.

Definition Emphasizes Self-development, Self-discipline

3. "Life" thus means infinitely more than mere continued physical existence. "Happiness" lies in freedom of opportunity of The Individual—chiefly Freedom from Government-over-Man—to strive to realize to the full his own highest potential with regard to all aspects of life. "Happiness" is not a condition but an ideal of ever-changing aspirations, of an ever-expanding vision of self-fulfillment through self-realization and through self-development spiritually, morally, intellectually, in every respect. This ideal and vision are incapable of ever being fully defined, much less completely realized. It is a never-ending process of inner growth, not something external to be pursued and possessed. It is comparable to the horizon—ever-widening as viewed from peak to higher peak of attainment with heightened understanding. As the sages of all ages have taught, true happiness—as distinguished from mere satisfaction of desires—is to be achieved pri-

77

marily through such self-development and growth, with each Individual's progress depending on his own state of being and capacity. This can come mainly through service of lofty goals, whether subjective and personal or objective in character, which are conducive to broadening vision and unceasing effort toward achievement. Each Individual's standard of happiness to be sought for self is fundamentally subjective—not subject to external pressures or controls of any sort from any source, least of all by government, and not subject to being judged by others on any comparative basis, however seemingly eccentric or inadequate in their opinion.

These particular rights to "Life" and to "the pursuit of Happiness," like all of the others among Man's God-given, unalienable rights, are subject to the requirements of the duty factor of Individual Liberty-Responsibility under constitutionally limited government, including especially observance of due respect for the equal rights of others. This involves self-discipline under self-government's system of Rule-by-Law (basically the people's fundamental law, the Constitution). Self-discipline is the alternative to being disciplined.

Innumerable Things of Limitless Scope

4. The things embraced by these words of the Declaration of Independence: "Life" and "the pursuit of Happiness," are innumerable and limitless in scope. They are as incapable of being fully listed and bounded as are the things embraced by that basic freedom: freedom of choice—the freedom to do or not to do—among life's innumerable possibilities hour by hour, day by day, life-long.

The Key:
Voluntary Cooperation Based on Spiritual Unity

5. According to the American philosophy, voluntary cooperation among Individuals and groups of Individuals is the key to expression, in the multitudinous ways of Free Men, of the spirit of harmonious and progressive community life in the ethical environment of a sound society, as a part of the enjoyment of the right to "Life" and to "the pursuit of Happiness." This means, of course, so long as their aims are not violative of the equal rights of others or of just laws expressive of "just powers" (to quote the term of the Declaration of Independence) designed to safeguard the equal rights of all Individuals. Such cooperation is, in truth, an outgrowth of inner unity and

78

Principle Eight

harmony among Men born of Man's spiritual nature—of spiritual brotherhood in the light of the common Fatherhood of God. This is a part of equal freedom for each and every Individual in the separate enjoyment of Life and the pursuit of Happiness, with each one responding voluntarily, from unfettered personal choice only, in any associative or cooperative activity socially, economically, religiously, or politically. Here "voluntary" highlights the key element.

The Practical Application Typical of Americans

6. The American philosophy teaches that in practice this pertains, for example, to charitable, philanthropic, educational, religious, fraternal and other community activities—local, regional, and national. Among such activities by Individuals, illustrations of traditional American practice in neighborhood and community are providing help on the local level for the needy (who are incapable of self-help) as an expression of the benevolent spirit of charity, as well as providing aid to Individuals and institutions in the fields of education, medicine (health), religion and child welfare. The American scene has traditionally been characterized by such a free, generously full, self-fulfilling and unceasing display of this practical idealism of voluntary cooperation for group and community welfare—on such a massive scale within, as well as among, communities generally on a country-wide basis—as to be a highly distinctive feature of American life which elevates its moral tone and, when understood, causes admiration throughout the civilized world. It constitutes, in practice, a vital part of the American concept of Individual Liberty-Responsibility, expressive of The Individual's self-defined duty based on a personal moral code founded on religious-moral considerations and also stemming from the fundamental American idealism of Free Man. The prime motive here is one of Man's loftiest attainments morally and spiritually: compassion for his fellow-man, which ennobles the concept of charity—aid given by The Individual to others.

Coercion Excluded

7. To be spiritual and moral, this cooperation—in the enjoyment of the right to "Life" and to "the pursuit of Happiness"—must never be in any degree involuntary. It must be wholly free from any element of interference or coercion, direct or indirect, by government or by others. If not voluntary, it amounts to seeking a false goal such as

79

"forced brotherly love"—a concept which is self-contradictory. If not voluntary, it can have no relationship to truly moral and spiritual values underlying the principle of Man's concern for the well-being of his fellow-man. The moral and the spiritual, as opposed to coercion, are mutually exclusive. Coerced unity, forced togetherness, can only be external and create increased conflict and separateness because true unity, which is inner or spiritual unity, is possible only among the free in spirit—among genuinely Free Men.

No Sacrifice of Any Right of Any Individual

8. In connection with the meaning of the right to "Life" and to "the pursuit of Happiness," the American philosophy defines the common good, or the general welfare, as being fundamentally and principally the sum of the well-being of all Individuals acting voluntarily—alone as well as cooperatively—in the separate and full enjoyment of their equal, unalienable rights, especially the right to freedom of choice. It cannot be served by any sacrifice of any of these rights of any Individual—for example, by any subordination of any of them to any Government-over-Man philosophy's goals, or coercive system. Any sacrifice of any right of any Individual is morally wrong. It is also dangerous potentially to all rights of all Individuals and, therefore, threatens grave injury to the general welfare, to the common good, which depends basically upon observance of due respect for the equal rights of each and every Individual. Thus to victimize any Individual as to any of his rights—through either government coercion, or by pressures by other Individuals socially, economically, or otherwise—is to victimize potentially every Individual because this sets a precedent which is conducive to later disregard of the rights of others, to Individual Liberty's peril if not grave injury.

The End Does Not Justify the Means

9. No matter how "good" the end may seem to be, there could not possibly be any justification for the use of evil means in pursuing it. The precedent of doing so in one instance could not but be evil and breed evil. No action or pronouncement by government contrary to these guiding precepts could have any validity morally or constitutionally under the American philosophy and system of constitutionally limited government designed primarily to make and keep secure the equal rights of all Individuals.

What Is Not Meant

10. Among the things excluded by the word "Happiness" (of The Individual), under the traditional American philosophy, is any element of Government's providing economic support, or security, for the people—of Government's assuming the role, the authority and responsibility, of satisfying their material desires. Such a role for Government would have been considered by The Founders and their fellow Americans to be the very antithesis of, as utterly hostile to, the American philosophy of Man-over-Government. When they expressed ideas such as that "the happiness of society is the *first* law of every government"—as stated, for example, by James Wilson (per page 76, *ante*)—they contemplated primarily and mainly Government's fulfilling its assigned role, as the creature and instrument of the people, as defined and limited in the Declaration of Independence: to make and keep secure the God-given, unalienable rights of The Individual. This means, above all else, Government's operating strictly and invariably within the confines of its limited, enumerated powers as prescribed by the sovereign people in their fundamental law, the Constitution, through which they create their tool: Government. This is designed to serve the basic goal: of Government's being conducted by all public officials—within the prescribed limits of their respective spheres of constitutional authority and responsibility—so as to ensure to the maximum the people's freedom to enjoy their unalienable rights, notably their right to Liberty: The Individual's Freedom from Government-over-Man. The word "Happiness" and the term "pursuit of Happiness"—as used in the Declaration of Independence and by The Founders and their fellow Americans—exclude everything in conflict with the foregoing considerations.

The Conclusion

11. The American philosophy teaches that the conception of how best to enjoy the benefits of the right to "Life" and to "the pursuit of Happiness" is a strictly personal matter for each Individual as Free Man—free in mind and spirit as well as in body and acting consistently with the duties of Individual Liberty-Responsibility, including chiefly the duty of respecting the equal rights (basically the constitutional rights) of others—to the exclusion of any coercion by government or by others.

PRINCIPLE NINE

LIBERTY—AGAINST GOVERNMENT-OVER-MAN

LIBERTY VERSUS
GOVERNMENT-PROVIDED SECURITY

> However great the tragedy Freedom's experience may be,
> Security in servitude is the dread alternative to
> Individual Liberty.

THE AMERICAN MOTTO

> . . . give me liberty or give me death.
> Patrick Henry
> (Address in second Virginia Convention, 1775)

SECURITY OF LIBERTY PARAMOUNT

> . . . for the efficient management of your common interests, in a country
> so extensive as ours, a Government of as much vigour as is consistent with
> the perfect security of Liberty is indispensable.
> President George Washington, *Farewell Address*

WHO ARE A FREE PEOPLE?

> *For who are a free people?* Not *those,* over whom government is reason-
> ably and equitably exercised, but *those,* who live under a government so
> *constitutionally checked and controuled,* that proper provision is made
> against its being otherwise exercised. John Dickinson
> (Emphasis per original.)
> (*Political Writings,* 1767-1768)

THE CONSTITUTION'S RECONCILIATION
OF MAN'S NEED FOR GOVERNMENT
WITH HIS DESIRE FOR LIBERTY

> Among the difficulties encountered by the [1787 Framing] convention, a
> very important one must have lain, in combining the requisite stability
> and energy in government with the inviolable attention due to liberty, and
> to the republican form [of government].
> *The Federalist* (no. 37, by Madison)

LOSS OF LIBERTY AT HOME
DUE TO FOREIGN DANGERS, REAL OR PRETENDED

> The management of foreign relations appears to be the most susceptible of abuse of all the trusts committed to a Government, because they can be concealed or disclosed, or disclosed in such parts and at such times as will best suit particular views . . . Perhaps it is a universal truth that the loss of liberty at home is to be charged to provisions against danger, real or pretended, from abroad.　　　　　　　　　　James Madison
> (Letter to Jefferson, 1798)

LIBERTY AND FACTION

> Liberty is to faction, what air is to fire, an aliment without which it instantly expires. But it could not be a less folly to abolish liberty, which is essential to political life, because it nourishes faction, than it would be to wish the annihilation of air, which is essential to animal life, because it imparts to fire its destructive agency.
> *The Federalist* (no. 10, by James Madison)

NATURAL RIGHTS

> "Among the Natural Rights of the Colonists are these First a Right to *Life;* Secondly to *Liberty;* thirdly to *Property;* together with the Right to support and defend them in the best manner they can—Those are evident Branches of, rather than deductions from the Duty of Self Preservation, commonly called the first Law of Nature—"
> (Emphasis per original.)　　　　Resolutions of Town of Boston, 1772
> ("The Rights of the Colonists . . .")

SOME SOUND PRINCIPLES

> Secondly, That *every man* . . . is, of common right, and by the laws of God, *a freeman,* and entitled to the free enjoyment of *liberty.* Thirdly, that liberty, or freedom, consists in having *an actual share* in the appointment of those who frame the laws, and who are to be the guardians of every man's life, property, and peace; for the *all* of one man is as dear to him as the *all* of another; and the poor man has an *equal* right, but *more* need, to have representatives in the legislature than the rich one.
> (Emphasis per original.)　　　　　　　　　　Benjamin Franklin
> (Note: "Some Good Whig Principles" approved by Franklin.)

FIRST AMENDMENT CONFIRMS DENIAL
OF POWER TO CONGRESS AS TO RELIGION

Congress shall make no law respecting an establishment of religion, or prohibiting the free exercise thereof . . .
First Amendment, U.S. Constitution
(Note: "establishment" here means an organization, such as the Church of England organization then in some States.)

FREEDOM OF CHOICE—AND RELIGION

From the dissensions among sects themselves arises necessarily a right of chusing & necessity of deliberating to which we will conform, but if we chuse for ourselves, we must allow others to chuse also, & to reciprocally. This establishes religious liberty.
Thomas Jefferson
("Notes on Religion," 1776)

That religion, or the duty which we owe to our Creator, and the manner of discharging it, can be directed only by reason and conviction, not by force or violence; and therefore all men are equally entitled to the free exercise of religion, according to the dictates of conscience . . .
Virginia Declaration of Rights, 1776

Be it enacted by the General Assembly, that no man shall be compelled to frequent or support any religious worship, place or ministry whatsoever, nor shall be enforced, restrained, molested or burthened in his body or goods, nor shall otherwise suffer on account of his religious opinions or belief; but that all men shall be free to profess, and by argument to maintain, their opinion in matters of religion, and that the same shall in no wise diminish, enlarge or affect their civil capacities . . . the rights hereby asserted are of the natural rights of mankind . . .
Virginia Statute of Religious Liberty, 1786

LIBERTY UNDER LAW, BY CONSENT

Political liberty is by some defined, a liberty of doing whatever is not prohibited by law. The definition is erroneous. A tyrant may govern by laws . . . Let it be thus defined; political liberty is the right every man in the state has, to do whatever is not prohibited by laws, TO WHICH HE HAS GIVEN HIS CONSENT. This definition is in unison with the feelings of a free people. (Emphasis per original.)
"Essex Result"
(Report of Convention of Towns, Essex County, Mass., rejecting first proposed Constitution for Mass., 1778)

A Principle of The Traditional American Philosophy

9. LIBERTY—AGAINST GOVERNMENT-OVER-MAN

". . . unalienable Rights, that among these are . . . Liberty"
(Declaration of Independence)

The Principle

1. The traditional American philosophy teaches that the God-given, unalienable right of Man to "Liberty" means primarily Freedom from Government-over-Man—or, otherwise stated, Liberty against Government-over-Man.

The Broader Definition

2. This is the primary meaning of the word "Liberty" as used in the Declaration of Independence and in the Preamble of the United States Constitution. In this fundamental law of the people, The Framers sought to translate into enduring governmental reality, to the maximum practicable extent, the ideals and principles of that 1776 Declaration. They stated in the Preamble the goals to be served by the central (Federal) government in its use of the powers granted to it by the people, as enumerated in the body of that basic law. The word "Liberty" also means, of course, freedom of The Individual from interference or coercion by other Individuals in the enjoyment of his unalienable rights and of the supporting rights. Individual Liberty is an indivisible whole.

Liberty-Responsibility

3. According to this philosophy, Liberty must always be taken to mean Individual Liberty-Responsibility, with emphasis upon the duty of respecting the equal rights of others and just laws expressive of "just powers" (to quote the term of the Declaration of Independence) designed to safeguard the equal rights of all Individuals. Individual Liberty-Responsibility involves the self-governing Individual's being

87

burdened with the duties underlying his share of the responsibility for the safety of the Liberty of all Individuals and of their other unalienable rights. Lacking such a sense of responsibility, Liberty can readily degenerate into license. Individual Liberty-Responsibility denotes that challenging freedom which tests the courage and wisdom of Free Man because of the truth that:

Only the brave dares to be—only the wise can remain—Free Man
By accepting the challenge, performing the duties, of
Individual Liberty-Responsibility under constitutionally limited government.

Freedom of Choice

4. The Liberty of Free Man is basically the Liberty of freedom of choice, with due respect for the equal rights of others. Without this freedom, Man cannot really be free, nor can there be any moral value or merit in his actions because they are not voluntary, not a true self-expression, not based on unfettered election between right and wrong, between good and evil, in the light of conscience and his personal moral code. An example of freedom of choice is freedom of association—for instance, freedom to join, or not to join, any particular organization (such as an organization of employers or of employees) without any compulsion by government or by any others. This means any organization for a lawful purpose—not a conspiracy to commit murder, for example, and not a conspiratorial, subversive organization designed to subvert the United States government, or a conspiracy to violate the constitutional rights of any temporarily unpopular group—involving properly punishable association for evil ends; as to which the overt act of joining the conspiracy is the main factor creating guilt by association of persons, not of ideas. (Discussed also in Par. 6 of Principle 4 and Par. 9 of Principle 7.)

The "Self" Factors of Free Man

5. Liberty means Man's freedom which characterizes a wisely and soundly self-governing people, determined to live up fully to high ideals in the enjoyment of The Individual's rights and in the performance of the accompanying duties defined by these essential elements of the philosophy of truly Free Man:

(1) the spiritual: *self-respect;*
(2) the economic: *self-reliance;*
(3) the political-social: *self-discipline.*

Principle Nine

These are the "self" factors characteristic of the self-governing and genuine Free Man.

Self-respect

6. Fundamentally, self-respect stems from Man's realization of the truth that the Spiritual is supreme and that he is of Divine creation, therefore possessed of a spiritual nature; and that The Individual is therefore of supreme dignity and value. Self-respect is fostered and evidenced by The Individual's striving to maintain the integrity of his unalienable rights. This is manifested partly by insisting that government as well as others respect them—in keeping with the requirements of constitutionally limited government. It is further manifested by his dedication to his own unceasing growth in the fuller realization of his own highest potential—spiritually, morally and intellectually, in every aspect of life.

Self-reliance

7. Self-reliance in the economic field—of the essence of Individual Liberty-Responsibility—is an essential characteristic of Free Man. This is true because dependence upon government for economic support inescapably saps the independence of Man's spirit, robs him of the inspiration and inclination to be individually venturesome and self-reliant, and undermines his willingness and capacity to oppose developments of a Government-over-Man nature including violation by government of the unalienable rights of himself and others. Such violation can be brought about by use of force, or by inducement through subsidy by government which is inescapably accompanied by control. As *The Federalist* (number 79, by Alexander Hamilton) soundly states: "In the general course of human nature, *a power over a man's subsistence amounts to a power over his will.*" (Emphasis Hamilton's.) This truth, in keeping with the adage that "he who pays the piper calls the tune" as well as with the dictates of common sense born of experience, was acknowledged by the United States Supreme Court when it stated (1936 *Butler* case) that: "The power to confer or withhold unlimited benefits is the power to coerce or destroy." Firm belief in the supreme value of Liberty—to the complete subordination always of economic security to Liberty's well-being—and consistent action in support of this belief, are always chief characteristics of every American who is worthy of his heritage of Free Man.

Self-discipline

8. Self-discipline involves, in main part, The Individual's faithful performance of the duties underlying Individual Liberty-Responsibility, in keeping with the truth that there can be no Right apart from Duty, no Liberty or Freedom apart from Responsibility. The self-discipline of the self-governor is the alternative to being disciplined and controlled by government. Self-discipline by The Individual, by respecting the boundary line separating his rights from the equal rights of others, provides the requisite moral basis for prohibiting violation by them of his own rights. Self-discipline, in the political-social realm, is a principal characteristic of Free Man among Free Men in an enduring and ethical environment of freedom. This is the only environment in which Individual Liberty can be secure and flourish.

As to each Individual among a self-governing people under constitutionally limited government, self-discipline involves self-control with regard to making demands upon government. The inherent duties require that nothing be done to help induce government to violate the limits of its powers or corresponding responsibilities as defined in the people's fundamental law: the Constitution, regardless of any seeming benefits temporarily. Such sound conduct is required, in part, in order to help to influence others soundly by proper example in keeping with the moral precept that, in this limited but important sense as to things governmental, each Individual is his "brother's keeper."'

Liberty's Two-fold Meaning

9. Liberty is expressive of that within Free Man which reflects the essence of his mind and spirit—of his very soul, in the religious sense implicit in the uniquely American concept of Man's being endowed by his Creator with unalienable rights. This is what was meant when American leaders of 1776-1787 used the word "Liberty" —for instance, Patrick Henry in his famed cry: "Give me liberty or give me death." This is what was meant by Benjamin Franklin in his profoundly true statement in 1759 that: "They that can give up essential liberty to obtain a little temporary safety deserve neither liberty nor safety." Such convictions typify Americans. These spokesmen for Free Man in America meant primarily Man's Liberty against Government-over-Man. Included also, of course, is Man's right to freedom from violation of his rights by others than government—by any person, group or organization. The "safety" to which Franklin

referred can soundly be said to include also the economic aspect: economic security provided by government—always involving sacrifice of Liberty, in varying degree, however subtle or disguised.

The Lofty Challenge

10. The signers of the Declaration of Independence elevated Patrick Henry's glowing expression of this loftiest of sentiments regarding Liberty to the highest reaches of the human mind and spirit when they closed this 1776 Declaration's uniquely American message, to American Posterity and to all mankind, with these immortal words:

> "And for the support of this Declaration, with a firm reliance on the protection of divine Providence, we mutually pledge to each other our Lives, our Fortunes, and our Sacred Honor."

On a similarly high plane, President Washington's First Inaugural Address defined the great opportunity and responsibility of the American people—as custodians of Individual Liberty-Responsibility in history's first example of a soundly conceived and adequately founded Republic (defined, for example, in Par. 6 of Principle 5) embracing an entire country and its people. His inspiring words were:

> ". . . the preservation of the sacred fire of liberty, and the destiny of the Republican model of Government, are justly considered as *deeply*, perhaps as *finally* staked, on the experiment entrusted to the hands of the American people." (Emphasis Washington's)

(True Republics had been formed in Mass., 1780, and N.H., 1784.) This profound message to all generations of Americans emphasizes their true role and opportunity in relations with other peoples: to seek to influence them chiefly by sound example, as successful self-governors ever faithful to the Constitution's spirit and letter, as never faltering Friends of Individual Liberty—of Man's Freedom from Government-over-Man.

The Conclusion

11. The American philosophy teaches that Individual Liberty is indivisible and for one and all, or for none, in the long run—that the American choice is: Individual Liberty in full, for one and all, always.

91

PRINCIPLE TEN

PRIVATE PROPERTY—LIBERTY'S SUPPORT

"BILL OF RIGHTS" IN FIRST CONSTITUTION

[Right to] . . . lives and liberties . . . acquiring, possessing, and protecting property . . .
Bill of Rights of Mass., 1780

LIBERTY AND PROPERTY—
RIGHTS MUST SHARE THE SAME FATE

There is not a single instance in history in which civil liberty was lost, and religious liberty preserved entire. If therefore we yield up our temporal property, we at the same time deliver the conscience into bondage.
Rev. John Witherspoon
(Sermon, May 17, 1776)

LIFE, LIBERTY, PROPERTY, ETC.

That all men . . . have certain inherent rights . . . namely, the enjoyment of life and liberty, with the means of acquiring and possessing property . . .
Virginia Declaration of Rights, 1776

[Recommending that each Colony form a new government] . . . and it is necessary that . . . all the powers of Government [should be] exerted, under the authority of the people of the colonies, for the preservation of internal peace, virtue, and good order, as well as for the defence of their lives, liberties and properties . . .
Resolutions, Continental Congress, May 15, 1776

RIGHT, PROPERTY AND GOVERNMENT
STAND OR FALL TOGETHER

It is essentially a natural right, that a man shall quietly enjoy, and have the sole disposal of his own property . . . The security of right and property, is the great end of government. Surely, then, such measures as tend to render right and property precarious, tend to destroy both property and government, for these must stand or fall together. Property is admitted to have an existence in the savage state of nature; and if it is necessary for the support of savage life, it by no means becomes less so in civil society.
House of Representatives of Massachusetts
(To the King's representative, 1768)

PROPERTY AND LIBERTY

> Property must be secured, or liberty cannot exist.
>
> John Adams
> ("Discourses on Davila," 1790)

STATE OF PROPERTY, EQUAL OR UNEQUAL

> . . . our wish . . . is, that . . . [there be maintained] . . . that state of property, equal or unequal, which results to every man from his own industry, or that of his fathers. President Thomas Jefferson
> (Second Inaugural Address)

PROPERTY AN ESSENTIAL RIGHT

> That Government is instituted and ought to be exercised for the benefit of the people; which consists in the enjoyment of life and liberty, with the right of acquiring and using property, and generally of pursuing and obtaining happiness and safety. James Madison
> (In 1st Session of Congress of U.S., in proposing "Bill of Rights" amendments to U.S. Constitution)

THE GREAT END OF GOVERNMENT

> . . . the great end of government . . . [after the glory of God, is] . . . the good of man, the common benefit of society . . . instituted for the preservation of mens persons, properties & various rights . . .
> (Per the original.) Rev. Jonathan Mayhew
> (Election Sermon, 1754)

THE BASIS OF THE RIGHT TO PROPERTY

> And as Reason tells us, all are born thus *naturally equal*, i.e., with an *equal Right* to their *Persons;* so also with an equal Right to their *Preservation;* and therefore to *such Things* as Nature affords for their *Subsistence* . . . [Each Man entitled to the fruits of his labor] . . . Thus *every Man* having a *natural Right* to (or being the Proprietor of) his own *Person* and his own *Actions* and *Labour* and to what he can honestly acquire by his Labour, which we call *Property;* it certainly follows, that no Man can have a Right to the *Person* or *Property* of *another* . . . [and a Man has a right to defend his property] . . .
> (Emphasis per original.) Rev. Elisha Williams
> ("A Seasonable Plea . . . ," 1744)
> (Note: "Person" connotes Liberty, "Preservation" connotes Life, and "Subsistence" connotes Property.)

95

PROPERTY IN RIGHTS—
AND RIGHTS OF PROPERTY

> If the United States mean to obtain or deserve the full praise due to wise and just governments, they will equally respect the rights of property, and the property in rights . . .   James Madison
> (Essay, The National Gazette, 1792)
> (Note: full text is quoted at pages 232-233 of this study-guide.)

WICKED PROJECTS, SUCH AS A
FORCED DIVISION OF PROPERTY EQUALLY

> A rage for paper money, for an abolition of debts, for an equal division of property, or for any other improper or wicked project, . . . [will be less likely for the entire Union].
> *The Federalist* (no. 10, by James Madison)

DESPOTIC SCHEMES FOR "LEVELLING"

> . . . The Utopian schemes of levelling, and a community of goods, are as visionary and impracticable, as those which vest all property in the Crown, are arbitrary, despotic, and in our government unconstitutional.
> House of Representatives of Massachusetts
> (1768, to agent in London for the Colonies)
> (Note: the word "unconstitutional" pertains to the British "Constitution.")

SECURITY OF PROPERTY
ONLY ONE OF THE ENDS OF GOVERNMENT

> . . . tho' it is also admitted that the security of property is one end of government, but that of little estimation even in the view of a *miser* when life and liberty of locomotion and further accumulation are placed in competition, it must be a very absurd way of speaking to assert that *one* end of government is the foundation of government . . . [the people delegate power to government only to serve "the good of the whole"] . . . The *end* of government being the *good* of mankind, points out its great duties: It is above all things to provide for the security, the quiet, and happy enjoyment of life, liberty, and property. There is not one act which a government can have a *right* to make, that does not tend to the advancement of the security, tranquility and prosperity of the people.
> (Emphasis per original.)   James Otis
> ("The Rights of the British Colonies," 1764)

A Principle of The Traditional American Philosophy

10. PRIVATE PROPERTY—LIBERTY'S SUPPORT

[Americans] *". . . are entitled to life, liberty and property . . ."*
(Declaration of Rights by First Continental Congress, 1774)

The Principle

1. The traditional American philosophy teaches that Man possesses the right to property as an indispensable support, the principal material support, of his God-given, unalienable rights (notably the right to Liberty) specified in the Declaration of Independence.

Part of Economic Liberty

2. This right to property is a main part of economic liberty, which is the inseparable and indispensable economic aspect of the indivisible whole of Individual Liberty, according to this philosophy. Without economic liberty, the other parts of Individual Liberty are lacking in material support and therefore, for practical purposes, cannot be defended adequately or securely enjoyed enduringly. This right to property in any form—money or any other type—includes all aspects such as acquiring, using, possessing, protecting and disposing of it. Man's unalienable right to Life necessarily involves his derivative right to property, in support of his right to sustain his own life and the lives of his dependents; which requires, in part, acquiring and using food and various other kinds of property necessary to existence or conducive to full enjoyment of God-given, unalienable rights in varied and innumerable ways.

The Underlying Reasoning

3. The American philosophy teaches that the fact that Man is endowed by his Creator with the right to be self-governing, as the Declaration of Independence proclaims, means implicitly that Man is also endowed with the capacity to reason and, therefore, with the

capacity to be self-governing—under a system of Man-over-Government—for the better protection and enjoyment of his unalienable rights. This, in turn, means necessarily that Man is endowed with the capacity of being economically self-reliant and independent, without need of being supported by his creature and tool: government. This is true because to be supported by government would mean to be subject to its control under a system of Government-over-Man; control inevitably accompanies subsidy. As part of his Divine endowment at birth, Man therefore possesses both the right and the capacity to manage his own economic affairs, including his own capability to work in order to support life and his rights in general by acquiring property (money or any other type), free from any degree of Government-over-Man control, directly or indirectly. Any contrary conclusion would inescapably condemn Man to a birthright of servitude to government, which this philosophy rejects as being inconsistent with Divine Creation. This philosophy also teaches that Man is entitled to enjoy this right and to exercise this capability without any interference by others than government as well. The foregoing is subject, of course, to due respect for the equal rights of others and for just laws expressive of "just powers" (to quote the term of the Declaration of Independence) designed to safeguard the equal rights of all Individuals.

The View of The Framers, per "The Federalist"

4. The American philosophy is clear and emphatic on the point that the surest way for Man to become economically dependent upon, and therefore subservient to, government is for it to control or possess his property, or to subsidize him. This is because of the truth stated in *The Federalist* (number 79, by Alexander Hamilton) that: "In the general course of human nature, *a power over a man's subsistence amounts to a power over his will.*" (Emphasis Hamilton's) This truth is also commonly acknowledged in the maxim that "he who pays the piper calls the tune" and it applies especially to a person's income.

The Means of Self-defense

5. This is all the more true to the extent that government controls, or takes from him, his property—not only his current earnings, or income, but also his accumulated savings represented by his property in general. The more government controls or takes from him, and the

less Man possesses and controls, the worse his plight becomes in the face of Government-over-Man practices infringing his unalienable rights. This deprives him of the means of self-defense, of defense of his rights, against violations by government and by others. Lacking such means, his rights are always in danger of being violated or undermined with impunity by transgressors—either oppressive or usurping government officials, or covetously inclined persons who are disregardful of the limits on their own equal rights and are heedless of the duty factor of Individual Liberty-Responsibility, which requires them to respect the equal rights of others.

Property Needed for Defense of Man's Rights

6. According to the American philosophy, Man's purpose in creating governments is primarily "to secure"—to make and keep secure —his unalienable rights, as the Declaration of Independence phrases it. A chief aim of man in this regard is to provide governmental (legal) machinery which can be readily available to each Individual for establishing and maintaining his legal right to his own property and for the equal protection of all Individuals' property under equal laws (basically the people's fundamental laws—their Constitutions, Federal and State). To be able to make effective use of this legal machinery, however, Man needs property (money) to pay the cost.

The 1776 Declaration and the Word "Property"

7. In the years leading up to the American Revolution of 1776, the slogan of the "Sons of Liberty"—most ardent of patriots—was: "Liberty and property." Another popular phrase used throughout America in that period to describe Man's most precious rights, used for example in the "Declaration and Resolves of the First Continental Congress" in 1774, was: "life, liberty and property." This combination of ideas—expressed with regard to protection of Man's ". . . life . . . person . . . goods or estaite . . ."—appeared in America at least by 1641 in Massachusetts in: "The Body of Liberties." This was a law code compiled by Nathaniel Ward, in response to public protests against arbitrary decisions by judges, and adopted by the Massachusetts General Court, the legislative body of the colony. In the phrase of the Declaration of Independence adopted in 1776— "Life, Liberty and the pursuit of Happiness"—the substitution of the phrase "the pursuit of Happiness," in place of the word "property"

customarily used theretofore, assuredly did not mean that the signers of the Declaration disapproved of the idea of the right to property being considered a most important right of Man. Quite the contrary is true, as all pertinent historical records amply prove. A number of these signers were owners of large and valuable property holdings— for example, John Hancock, Thomas Jefferson, Robert Morris, Charles Carroll, Richard Henry Lee and Arthur Middleton, to name only a few. They did, indeed, risk great fortunes, as well as their lives and honor, in signing the 1776 Declaration—as its closing pledge made express, in words made immortal by the exemplary selflessness, the noble self-sacrifice, of these true friends of Independence for America and of Man's Liberty against Government-over-Man. The wealthy of that generation were fully matched by those of little or no means, such as Samuel Adams, in the fervor of belief in, and support of, the right to property as a fundamental part of the Individual's rights. It is noteworthy that among the signers of the Declaration were some who had been members of the above-mentioned First Continental Congress in 1774; and all the signers undoubtedly shared the then popular support of the slogan: "Life, Liberty and Property" as being expressive of the gist of Man's fundamental rights. The emphasis in their thinking regarding the right to property was later reflected in the safeguarding provision included in the "Bill of Rights" amendments to the United States Constitution—in the Fifth Amendment, stating: ". . . nor shall private property be taken for public use, without just compensation." This is expressive of the American philosophy.

The omission of the word "property" from the 1776 Declaration was, presumably, because the right to property was considered by America's leaders in general to be not a primary, God-given, unalienable right—not on a par spiritually with the right to "Life, Liberty and the pursuit of Happiness"—but an essential legal right, a most important supporting right as the material mainstay of Man's unalienable rights including Liberty against Government-over-Man.

An Essential Means, Not an End in and of Itself

8. The right to property is accordingly considered not an end, in and of itself, but an indispensable means needed to sustain Life itself and for the protection and fuller enjoyment of the right to Liberty and to the pursuit of Happiness. The right to property is, therefore, of critical importance to Free Man, whether considered as a support-

ing right or—as some in 1776 occasionally referred to it—as an unalienable right, a Natural Right.

The concept of the property right being derived from every Individual's natural right to Liberty—of its thus being a derivative right rather than a primary, God-given, unalienable right—was expressed for example in an oration in Boston on March 5, 1775 by Dr. Joseph Warren, a leader among the more prominent workers and fighters for Liberty and Independence, as follows:

> "That personal freedom is the natural right of every man, and that *property, or an exclusive right* to dispose of what he has honestly acquired by his own labor, *necessarily arises therefrom,* are truths which common sense has placed beyond the reach of contradiction." (Emphasis added.)

Warren and his fellow leaders in favor of "Liberty and Independence," in Boston especially in that pre-1776 period, were undoubtedly in agreement on this point of derivativeness: "necessarily arises therefrom"—notably Samuel Adams who was very closely associated with Warren in supporting this cause. Adams presumably meant nothing different when he sometimes referred to the right to property as being of the nature of a "Natural Right."

Property Supports Ideals

9. Man's right to property is the principal material support of the idealism of the traditional American philosophy—the idealism of Free Man in America. This idealism would be empty of substance in the absence of the protection provided by such support; it could not be translated into reality and sustained enduringly.

The Conclusion

10. The American philosophy asserts that Man's right to property is a main, indispensable and inseparable part of the indivisible whole of Individual Liberty-Responsibility and the material mainstay of his unalienable right to "Life, Liberty and the pursuit of Happiness."

PRINCIPLE ELEVEN

TAXES—LIMITED TO SAFEGUARD LIBERTY

GOVERNMENT'S POWER TO TAX LIMITED
TO SUPPORT ITS CONSTITUTIONAL DUTIES ONLY—
(NOT ACTIVITIES AS TO USURPED POWER)

A government ought to contain in itself every power [including the power to tax] requisite to the full accomplishment of the objects committed to its care, and to the complete execution of the trusts for which it is responsible . . .   *The Federalist* (no. 31, by Alexander Hamilton)

AVOID, ABOVE ALL ELSE, TAXES
FOR UNCONSTITUTIONAL PURPOSES

[No taxes to provide protection for Stamp-Act collectors] Indeed, we cannot too often inculcate upon you our desires, that all extraordinary grants and expensive measures may, upon all occasions, as much as possible, be avoided. The public money of this country is the toil and labor of the people . . . reasonable frugality ought to be observed. And we would recommend particularly, the strictest care and the utmost firmness to prevent all unconstitutional draughts upon the public treasury.
Instructions of Town of Braintree, Mass.
(To their legislative Representative, 1765)

LIBERTY AND PROPERTY VICTIMIZED
BY ARBITRARY, OPPRESSIVE TAXES

A just security to property is not afforded by that government under which unequal taxes oppress one species of property and reward another species: where arbitrary taxes invade the domestic sanctuaries of the rich, and excessive taxes grind the faces of the poor . . .
James Madison
(Essay, The National Gazette, 1792)
(Note: full text is quoted in Part III, pages 232-233, of this study-guide.)

TO TAX ONE TO GIVE TO ANOTHER
VIOLATES "THE FIRST PRINCIPLE OF ASSOCIATION"

[The tax system must] be equally and fairly applied to all. To take from one, because it is thought that his own industry and that of his fathers has acquired too much, in order to spare [give] to others, who, or whose fathers have not exercised equal industry and skill, is to violate arbitrarily the first principle of association, "the *guarantee* to every one of a free exercise of his industry, and the fruits acquired by it." If the overgrown wealth of an individual be deemed dangerous to the State, the best corrective is the law of equal inheritance to all [of his kin] in equal degree; and the better, as this enforces a law of nature, while extra-taxation violates it. (Emphasis his.)   Thomas Jefferson
(Note in Destutt de Tracy's *Political Economy*, 1816)

CONFISCATORY TAXES ON INCOME AND ESTATES
MAKE THE PEOPLE "A PROPERTY"

> . . . *Great Britain* claims a right to take away nine-tenths of our estates —have we a *right* to the remaining tenth? No.—To say we have, is a "traiterous" position, denying her supreme legislature. So far from *having property*, according to these late found novels, *we are ourselves a property.* (Emphasis and spelling per original.) John Dickinson
> (In Pa. Provincial Convention, 1774)

SLAVERY THROUGH CONFISCATORY TAXES

> Let these *truths* be indelibly impressed on our minds—*that we cannot be* HAPPY, *without being* FREE—that we cannot be free, *without being secure in our property*—that *we* cannot be secure in our property [under a system of taxation without representation, permitting no safeguard against confiscatory taxes]. . . .
>
> ---
>
> [Continuing about government's grasping property by taxes] But if when we plow—sow—reap—gather—and thresh—we find, that we plow—sow —reap—gather—and thresh *for others,* whose PLEASURE is to be the SOLE LIMITATION *how much* they shall *take,* and *how much* they shall *leave,* WHY should we repeat the unprofitable toil?—*Horses* and *oxen* are content with *that portion of the fruits of their work,* which their *owners* assign them, in order to keep them strong enough to raise successive crops; but even *these beasts* will not submit to draw for their *masters,* until they are *subdued* by *whips* and *goads.*
> Let us take care of our *rights,* and we *therein* take care of *our prosperity.* "SLAVERY IS EVER PRECEDED BY SLEEP." [As to officials who usurp power] . . . if *we are not affected* by any reverence for the memory of our ancestors, who transmitted to us that freedom in which they had been blest—if *we are not animated* by any regard for posterity, to whom, by the most sacred obligations, we are bound to deliver down the invaluable inheritance—THEN, indeed, [any official, or his tool, however low] is a *personage* whom it may be dangerous to offend.
> (Emphasis per the original.) John Dickinson
> (See above)

A TAX WITH A BUILT-IN LIMIT

> It is a signal advantage of taxes on articles of consumption, that they contain in their own nature a security against excess . . . If duties are too high they lessen the consumption—the collection is eluded; and the product to the treasury is not so great as when they are confined within proper and moderate bounds. This forms a compleat barrier against any material oppression of the citizens, by taxes of this class, and is itself a natural limitation of the power of imposing them.
> *The Federalist* (No. 21, by Alexander Hamilton)

PUBLIC DEBT A PUBLIC CURSE

> . . . a Public Debt is a Public curse, and in a Rep Govt a greater than in any other.   James Madison
> (Letter to Henry Lee, 1790)
> (Note: "Rep Govt" means that of a Republic.)

POSTERITY—VICTIMS OF DEBTS
CREATED BY PRECEDING GENERATIONS

> As a very important source of strength and security, cherish public credit. . . . use it as sparingly as possible . . . ; avoiding likewise the accumulation of debt . . . in time of Peace . . . discharge the Debts which unavoidable wars may have occasioned, not ungenerously throwing upon posterity the burthen which we ourselves ought to bear.
> President George Washington, *Farewell Address*

NO GENERATION HAS A RIGHT
TO BURDEN THE NEXT WITH VAST PUBLIC DEBT

> What is to hinder them [the government] from creating a perpetual debt? The laws of nature, I answer. The earth belongs to the living, not to the dead. The will and the power of man expire with his life, by nature's law . . . Each generation has the usufruct of the earth during the period of its continuance. When it ceases to exist, the usufruct passes on to the succeeding generation, free and unincumbered . . . [No generation has a right] . . . to bind the succeeding generation . . . [with vast public debts]   Thomas Jefferson
> (Letter to J. W. Eppes, 1813)

A FUNDAMENTAL MAXIM:
CREATION OF PUBLIC DEBT SHOULD ALWAYS
BE ACCOMPANIED BY THE MEANS OF EXTINGUISHMENT

> Persuaded, as the Secretary is, that the proper funding of the present debt will render it a national blessing, yet he is so far from acceding to the position, in the latitude in which it is sometimes laid down, that "public debts are public benefits"—a position inviting to prodigality and liable to dangerous abuse—that he ardently wishes to see it incorporated as *a fundamental maxim in the system of public credit of the United States, that the creation of debt should always be accompanied with the means of extinguishment*. This he regards as *the true secret for rendering public credit immortal*.
> (Emphasis added.)
> Secretary of Treasury Alexander Hamilton
> (First Report on the Public Credit, 1790)

A Principle of The Traditional American Philosophy

11. TAXES—LIMITED TO SAFEGUARD LIBERTY

"He has erected a multitude of New Offices, and sent hither swarms of Officers to harass our people, and eat out their substance."
(Declaration of Independence)

The Principle

1. The traditional American philosophy teaches that tyranny through taxation is one of the most dangerous and oppressive aspects of Government-over-Man and must be guarded against and opposed accordingly, for the protection of Man's God-given, unalienable rights.

The Precedent of 1776

2. Tyrannous abuse of the taxing power was a principal provocation of the American Revolution in 1776 and, according to this philosophy, will always be considered and treated as just cause for prompt, effective, remedial action by every generation of Americans worthy of the American heritage of Individual Liberty—the heritage of Free Man determined to preserve his Freedom from Government-over-Man. This can be done mainly through preserving inviolate the supporting system of constitutionally limited government, designed to restrict government's activities and therefore its cost and taxes.

Limited Taxing Power

3. The traditional American philosophy of constitutionally limited government—limited for Liberty—is hostile to any concept which would permit any unlimited power of taxation to exist to the peril of Man's unalienable rights. Potential danger, not merely present danger, is the crux of the matter and the reason for constitutional safeguards, which are designed to provide protection in the worst imaginable situations. This philosophy prescribes various limitations

107

upon the taxing power of the Federal government, as expressed in the Constitution. For example, Article I, Section 8, of the Constitution authorizes Congress to make only specified levies—within the bounds of certain specific limits as to uses of tax monies: "to pay the Debts and provide for the common Defence and general Welfare of the United States." It also authorizes taxes only to raise revenue to pay for the government's authorized activities, within the bounds of its limited powers and limited duties under the Constitution, as amended—for use directly and openly to accomplish the objects committed to its care and the trusts for which it is made responsible by the people under this basic law. This is according to the controlling intent of those who framed and ratified the Constitution in 1787-1788, and likewise as to each amendment.

Examples of What Is Not Authorized

4. A few examples of what is not authorized by the Constitution in this regard, therefore is impliedly prohibited, will be clarifying. In general, the power of taxation may not be used by the Federal government as a means of bringing about indirectly and subtly any governmental change, or any social or other type of reform, or to achieve indirectly in effect Federal control of anything or anybody, or to accomplish any other result whatever, which the people have not authorized by the Constitution to be accomplished directly and openly. Nor may the power of taxation be used in furtherance of any abuse of the limited powers granted to the Federal government, or in furtherance of activities due to usurpation of any power withheld from it, or denied or prohibited to it, expressly or impliedly, by the people through the Constitution, as amended.

It is especially noteworthy that Hamilton, as Secretary of the Treasury, in urging for the first time in 1791 that the Taxing Clause granted to the Federal government a separate and substantive power for the "application of money," within the limits of what would serve the "general welfare," conceded that such power would "not carry a power to do any other thing not authorized in the Constitution, either expressly or by fair implication." (See Pars. 8-10 of Principle 5.)

Some specific examples are as follows. The power of taxation may not be used so as to prevent criticism of the Federal government by the Press; which would be exercising power over a field of activity withheld from this government by the original Constitution and expressly prohibited by the First Amendment. Nor may taxes be used to obtain funds to subsidize, and in effect to control, any field of activity denied to this government (excluded from its enumerated powers) and reserved to the States by the Constitution—so as in effect to "buy" submission to Federal usurpers: such as agriculture. Hamilton made it expressly clear, in *The Federalist* number 17, that this is a field of activity over which the Federal government had been given no power—a field over which it could never properly be given any power to control. Also, taxes may not be used to stifle, undermine, or destroy any part of the traditional American system's economic aspect of Liberty such as Individual Enterprise (individual, private, competitive, enterprise).

Equally repugnant and prohibited are taxes designed to put into effect the anti-private-property idea, or plan, of "leveling" of ownership of property (money or any other type) by attempting to make all people more "equal" as to property, or as to income, by taking from some to give to others—as a means of achieving social reform or any other purpose not directly and openly authorized by the people in the Constitution. For example, in 1768 a Resolution of the Massachusetts House of Representatives (drafted by James Otis, Samuel Adams *et al*) denounced such leveling as being "despotic and . . . unconstitutional." Two decades later *The Federalist* (number 10, by Madison) condemned it as "improper" and "wicked." Jefferson decried leveling as being unjust and violative of "the first principle of association"—meaning a people's associating for purposes of self-government.

The Examples Continued

5. Congress is not authorized to tax and spend as it pleases, for any and every purpose which it may choose to say, or actually thinks, will serve the "general welfare." Those who framed and ratified the Constitution in 1787-1788 intended the Taxing Clause's words: "general Welfare of the United States," to serve as a limitation on the taxing power. These words were designed to restrict taxing and spending to constitutionally authorized objectives, meaning in part only those which would serve the welfare of the United States as a whole and not merely of a locality, not of individual citizens. Congress does not possess unlimited, sovereign power to tax the people. (See Pars. 8-10 of Principle 5.) It does not even possess "general legislative authority," as Hamilton stated in *The Federalist* number 83.

Congress has, of course, been granted no power to exceed its constitutional authority or responsibilities by being benevolent, by making donations, of money or property at home or abroad at the expense of the American people's income, or other money or property. According to the controlling intent of those who framed and ratified the Constitution, the only words in the Taxing Clause which could possibly be said to sanction any donation to any foreign government, or people, are the words "national defense"—meaning direct and actual military defense of the American homeland. Any and all foreign donations by the Federal government are, therefore, clearly prohibited by inescapable implication unless, and except to the limited extent that, any such donation in actuality helps directly and substantially, on a realistic military basis, to "provide for the common Defence . . . of the United States"—of the States composing the Union.

These few illustrations exemplify prohibited misuse of the limited taxing power as granted by the people to the Federal government under the Constitution, as amended.

Peril to Liberty—Multiplied

6. The traditional American philosophy recognizes that an unlimited power to tax involves the power to destroy—a truth long known. This becomes all the more evilly significant if, when and to the extent that the Federal government becomes guilty of wholesale usurpation of power to expand its activities, at home and abroad, in defiance of the limits on its power imposed by the sovereign people through the Constitution. The evil significance involved is greatly augmented when—in furtherance of such wholesale usurpation—any such official culprits: Federal usurpers, employ oppressive taxation so as in effect to finance their political schemes to keep themselves in power, in control of the government, by using vast sums of public monies to subsidize—in truth to bribe, corrupt and seduce—immense segments of the electorate through distribution of individual money "benefits" to win their votes. This aim and process are furthered by building up a vast governmental bureaucracy which helps to serve this objective but has no sensible relation to sound governmental operations serving constitutionally authorized purposes. Then, indeed, are Individual Liberty and sound self-government in America—also the integrity and safety of the Republic itself—placed in effect on the "auction block." This potentially disastrous condition, of danger com-

110

pounded, becomes almost unlimited in degree of peril for Free Man in America, for American Posterity, when this combination of usurpation and tax tyranny is employed—by such usurpers and their collaborators in all walks of life—to supplant the traditional American system of Man-over-Government with the system of Government-over-Man. The foregoing precepts reflect some aspects of The Founders' thinking in this connection. (Note especially the Jefferson quotation on page xx, *ante,* about taxing—spending—electing.) Any accomplishment of the prohibited objectives by gradual and deceptive steps—rather than directly and openly—highlights the importance of keeping ever in mind a maxim of which the sense was well-known to them and is expressable in verse form as follows:

Great Oaks and Great Tyrannies
Just as surely as "great oaks from little acorns grow,"
So do greatest tyrannies have smallest beginnings;
Yet the mind, uninstructed by knowledge or reason,
Cannot sense either oak or tyranny in the seed.

No Unlimited Income-tax Power
Under the Principle of Limited Government
7. The foregoing holds good even though the traditional American philosophy and system contemplate the Federal government's possessing, by grant of the people under the Constitution, "an unqualified power of taxation in the ordinary modes," as stated in *The Federalist* (number 31, by Alexander Hamilton)—for instance, a consumption tax on sales of goods. Such a tax cannot become dangerous to the people's liberties because it contains an automatic check on abuse by way of such taxation; if the amount of the tax offends them, they can simply refuse to buy the goods and thereby make the tax a failure, leading to its repeal. Even "an unqualified power of taxation" in some mode which was not ordinary in the days of The Founders and was not provided for by them in the Constitution—for instance, a graduated, "escalating" income tax, especially without expressly specifying a maximum rate or "ceiling"—would nevertheless have been considered by them to be impliedly limited in effect because subject to the following factors. First, the principles proclaimed in the Declaration of Independence—notably that governments are granted only "just powers," meaning limited powers, in order to make and keep secure the people's unalienable rights--forbid the existence in Amer-

ica of any system of government or governmental practices which could, in effect and in the unlimited discretion of public servants, impose tax-slavery upon the people through permitting these public servants in peacetime to confiscate most, or all, of the income of the people to be spent as these public servants may please. This assuredly would have been considered by The Founders to be the very definition of tax-tyranny, which was one of the chief causes of the Revolution in 1776. Second, the system intended to be created by The Framers and Adopters of the Constitution—with only the few, limited powers enumerated being granted to the Federal government (for example, per *The Federalist* number 45 by Madison with Hamilton's silent concurrence)—likewise bars tax-tyranny because Congress is authorized to tax and spend only within the scope of its power-limits and its commensurately limited responsibilities; which must always be construed in keeping with that original, controlling intent of The Framers and Adopters, subject only to amendment by the people of the Constitution. Congress may not tax and spend in support of activities in furtherance of abuse of any granted power or in support of usurpation of power not granted.

The Founders would assuredly have stressed these implied limits upon any power to tax incomes of the people—if granted by any constitutional amendment—in the absence of an express, specific and clear mandate from the people to the contrary stated in any such amendment, for instance if it should expressly authorize confiscatory taxes for war needs. Just as they certainly would have condemned any generation of Americans as being unfaithful to the American heritage of Man-over-Government, as being defaulting trustees of Posterity's just heritage, because of any submission to oppressive taxation amounting to tax-tyranny. This applies equally to taxation of accumulated wealth (savings), or property, by way of inheritance, or estate, taxes (death taxes), which are equally subject to the above-mentioned principles and implied limits.

The basic American principles previously discussed: "Limited and Decentralized for Liberty" (per Principles 5 and 6) would therefore have been declared by The Founders to be respected and protected in effect and impliedly by pertinent, controlling limitations despite any income-tax, or any death-tax, provision in any amendment to the Constitution not expressly fixing a maximum rate or "ceiling." They would have agreed that the above-mentioned implied limits would nevertheless be applicable, though not made express, so as to bar unlimited taxing-power opening the door to tax-tyranny, tax-slavery.

Benjamin Franklin's Example

8. When government takes a part of an Individual's earned income, this is the equivalent of government's commandeering, or confiscating, for its own purposes a corresponding portion of his working time; he is deprived of the benefit, of the fruit, of such work and time. A tax-payer's time is employed in the service, or support, of government to the extent that he must devote it to earning the money required to pay the taxes imposed by government. Benjamin Franklin suggested a specific standard or rule by which to judge the character of taxation, presumably in peacetime (not in a national crisis of war), as to whether or not it is oppressive and beyond which the burden of taxation would, in his opinion, presumably have been considered oppressive, if not tyrannous. It was stated by him in a 1758 writing:

"It would be thought a hard Government that should tax its People one-tenth Part of their *Time,* to be employed in its Service." (Emphasis his.)

(Maximum income-tax rate was only seven per cent under 1913 law —the first under the Sixteenth Amendment.)

Under the American philosophy and system of constitutionally limited government, there is and always must be some limit, express or implied, as a standard beyond which the people may properly, indeed should, consider peacetime taxation to amount to impermissible confiscation and therefore oppression and tax-tyranny. Otherwise a mockery is made of the fundamental American principle of limited government. One general test which is unchallengeable, under a system of constitutionally limited government, is this: any and every aspect of taxation which is designed to provide financial support for any governmental activity which involves abuse of granted power, or usurpation of ungranted power, merits condemnation as tax-tyranny.

The Conclusion

9. It is a cardinal principle of the traditional American philosophy that taxes must be limited to safeguard Individual Liberty—to make and keep secure Man's unalienable rights and Posterity's just heritage of Liberty: Freedom from Government-over-Man.

🌿 🌿 🌿

PRINCIPLE TWELVE

THE MAJORITY—LIMITED FOR LIBERTY

THE MAJORITY OMNIPOTENT
FATALLY DANGEROUS TO INDIVIDUAL LIBERTY

[As to Bill of Rights] Repeated violations of these parchment barriers have been committed by overbearing majorities in every State. In Virginia I have seen the bill of rights violated in every instance where it has been opposed to a popular current . . . In our Governments the real power lies in the majority of the Community, and the invasion of private rights is *chiefly* to be apprehended, not from acts of Government contrary to the sense of its constituents, but from acts in which the Government is the mere instrument of the major number of the Constituents. (Emphasis per original.)
James Madison
(Letter to Jefferson, in Paris, 1788)

Since the general civilization of mankind, I believe there are more instances of the abridgement of the freedom of the people, by gradual and silent encroachments of those in power, than by violent and sudden usurpations: but, on a candid examination of history, we shall find that turbulence, violence, and abuse of power, by the majority trampling on the rights of the minority have produced factions and commotions, which, in republics, have more frequently than any other cause, produced despotism. If we go over the whole history of ancient and modern republics, we shall find their destruction to have generally resulted from those causes. If we consider the peculiar situation of the United States, and what are the sources of that diversity of sentiment which pervades its inhabitants, we shall find great danger to fear, that the same causes may terminate here, in the same fatal effects, which they produced in those republics. This danger ought to be wisely guarded against.
James Madison
(Va. Ratifying Convention, 1788)

It is of great importance in a republic, not only to guard the society against the oppression of its rulers; but to guard one part of the society against the injustice of the other part. Different interests necessarily exist in different classes of citizens. If a majority be united by a common interest, the rights of the minority will be insecure. There are but two methods of providing against this evil . . . [The existence of "an hereditary or self-appointed authority" superior to the majority, to the people; or, in the alternative, the existence of so many conflicting interests among the citizens as to constitute a safeguard against any dominant majority likely to become oppressive] . . . The second method will be exemplified in the federal republic of the United States. Whilst all authority in it will be derived from, and dependent on the society, the society itself will be broken into so many parts, interests and classes of citizens, that the rights of individuals or of the minority, will be in little danger from interested combinations of the majority.   *The Federalist* (No. 51, by Madison)

But in every distinct house of these states, the members are equal in their vote; the most ayes make the affirmative vote, and most no's the negative: They don't weigh the intellectual furniture, or other distinguishing qualifications of the several voters in the scales of the golden rule of fellowship; they only add up the ayes, and the no's, and so determine the suffrage of the house.   Rev. John Wise
(Regarding church organizations.)   (*A Vindication etc.*, 1717)

THE CONSTITUTION DESIGNED TO
CHECK ANY OVERBEARING MAJORITY

[The Constitution was designed to remedy existing injustices perpetrated] by the superior force of an interested and overbearing majority.
                                                  The Federalist (No. 10, by Madison)

AN AMERICAN DEVELOPMENT—
A CONSTITUTION TO CONTROL THE LEGISLATURE

The idea of a constitution, *limiting* and superintending the operations of *legislative authority,* seems not to have been accurately understood in Britain. There are, at least, no traces of practice conformable to such a principle. The British Constitution is just what the British Parliament pleases . . . To *control* the power and conduct of *the legislature,* by an overruling constitution, was an improvement in the science and practice of government reserved to the American States.   James Wilson
(Emphasis added.)   (In the Pa. Ratifying Convention, 1788)

THE INDIVIDUAL—THE MINORITY—
VICTIMIZED BY THE MAJORITY UNLIMITED

If a majority are capable of preferring their own private interest, or that of their families, counties, and party, to that of the nation collectively, some provision must be made in the constitution, in favor of justice, to compel all to respect the common right, the public good, the universal law, in preference to all private and partial considerations.

And that the desires of the majority of the people are often for injustice and inhumanity against the minority, is demonstrated by every page of the history of the whole world.

To remedy the dangers attendant upon the arbitrary use of power, checks, however multiplied, will scarcely avail without an explicit admission of some limitation of the right of the majority to exercise sovereign authority over the individual citizen . . . In popular governments, minorities constantly run much greater risk of suffering from arbitrary power than in absolute monarchies . . . [Majority in control of government manipulates public sentiment to suit its aims].   John Adams
                                                        ("On Government," 1778)

117

WISE COUNSEL FROM A CHIEF FRIEND
OF SOUND SELF-GOVERNMENT, BY MAJORITY-RULE,
THROUGH LIMITING THE MAJORITY
BY A WRITTEN CONSTITUTION

I believe . . . that the majority, oppressing an individual, is guilty of a crime, abuses its strength, and by acting on the law of the strongest breaks up the foundations of society . . .

Thomas Jefferson
(Letter to Dupont de Nemours, 1816)

I have seen with deep concern the afflicting oppression under which the republican citizens of Connecticut suffer from an unjust majority. The truths expressed in your letter have been long exposed to the nation through the channel of the public papers, and are the more readily believed because most of the States during the momentary ascendancy of kindred majorities in them, have seen the same spirit of oppression prevail.

President Thomas Jefferson
(Letter to Thomas Seymour, 1807)
(Note: "republican" refers presumably to the Republican Party, which Jefferson founded and headed, in opposition to the Federalist Party.)

[As to the all-powerful legislature in Virginia] All the powers of government, legislative, executive, and judiciary, result to the legislative body. The concentrating these in the same hands is precisely the definition of despotic government. It will be no alleviation that these powers will be exercised by a plurality of hands, and not by a single one. 173 despots would surely be as oppressive as one. Let those who doubt it turn their eyes on the republic of Venice. As little will it avail us that they are chosen by ourselves. An *elective despotism* was not the government we fought for, but one which should not only be founded on free principles, but in which the powers of government should be so divided and balanced among several bodies of magistracy, as that no one could transcend their legal limits, without being effectually checked and restrained by the others . . . [But in forming, in 1776, new State governments (by mere acts of legislatures) the legislatures were made all-powerful and have dominated the Executive and the Judiciary] . . . And this is done with no ill intention. The views of the present members are perfectly upright . . . [But before long it will be different] . . . Mankind soon learn to make interested uses of every right and power which they possess, or may assume. (Emphasis per original.)

Thomas Jefferson
("Notes on the State of Virginia," 1782)

A Principle of The Traditional American Philosophy

12. THE MAJORITY—LIMITED FOR LIBERTY

". . . this sacred principle . . ." [Majority must respect Minority's rights]
(President Jefferson's First Inaugural Address; see below)

The Principle
1. The traditional American philosophy teaches that The Majority must be strictly limited in power, and in the operation of government, for the protection of The Individual's God-given, unalienable rights proclaimed in the Declaration of Independence and, therefore, of the rights of The Minority—of all minorities.

A Restricted Mechanic of Government
2. Self-government's system of rule by majority vote is based on necessity. Rule by majority vote is a necessary mechanic of any government of the popular type, featuring rule by the people through free, periodic elections such as, for example, those held in the United States. Under this philosophy, rule by majority vote is always subject to the "sacred principle" defined in President Jefferson's First Inaugural Address, quoted below.

"This Sacred Principle"
"All, too, will bear in mind this sacred principle, that though the will of the majority is in all cases to prevail, that will to be rightful must be reasonable; that the minority possess their equal rights, which equal law must protect, and to violate would be oppression."

A Minority of One Protected
3. The protection provided by this principle applies fundamentally, of course, in favor of a minority of one: The Individual. No majority, however great—even all of the people but one Individual—may properly infringe, or possess the power to infringe, the rights of any minority, however small—even a minority of a lone Individual.

119

America a Republic—Not a Democracy—
In <u>Form</u> of Government
So As to Limit Effectively The Majority
To Protect The Individual

4. Therein lies the reason why the American leaders who framed and ratified the United States Constitution in 1787-1788 chose, for America's *form* of government, that of a Republic and not a Democracy. (The then existing Confederation was merely a treaty arrangement between completely independent and separate State governments, by agreement of their legislatures only and not by consent of the people, with no real central government—with only a legislative body—and with no power over those governments or over individual citizens; so it provided no protection for the rights of The Individual or The Minority against tyranny by The Majority in any State—later remedied, as to certain rights, by prohibitions in the original Constitution expressly made applicable against the States.) A Republic is a constitutionally limited government of the representative type, created by a written Constitution—adopted by the people and changeable (from its original meaning) by them only by its amendment—with its powers divided between three separate Branches: Executive, Legislative and Judicial. In a Republic, the whole system is designed primarily to protect The Individual's unalienable rights—therefore The Minority, all minorities—against any violation by government or by others. As the Declaration of Independence expresses this American goal of safeguarding these rights, the people form their governments "to secure these rights"—to make and keep them secure.

The Majority Omnipotent in Any Democracy

5. This is not the case under a Democracy, speaking of it as a *form* of government and not merely in the more general sense of its meaning a popular *type* of government. In a Democracy, The Majority is omnipotent, whether it be a Representative Democracy or a Direct Democracy. In the Representative type, the people function governmentally through an elected legislature, which selects and controls the head of the Executive Department, as in Great Britain where "the authority of the parliament is transcendent and uncontrollable" (as stated in *The Federalist* number 53, by Madison)—where in fact the House of Commons alone has by law become supreme. In the Direct type, all of the electorate (those entitled to vote) assemble as a single

group to debate and decide directly and conclusively all governmental questions. This is suitable only for a very small number of people—as in a New England town with a town-meeting system of government, or in a situation like that of the small city-states of ancient Greece. (Decisions of a New England town-meeting are, of course, subject to the State and United States Constitutions which protect the rights of The Individual and The Minority, so such a town-meeting government is not a true Democracy featuring The Majority Omnipotent.)

In a Democracy, The Individual Is Subservient and Must Be Submissive to The Omnipotent Majority

6. Any Democracy, either Representative or Direct, does not even recognize the existence of any unqualified rights of The Individual, much less his possessing God-given, unalienable rights as conceived by the American philosophy. A Democracy in America, as a *form* of government, would therefore provide no protection for these rights. Under a Democracy, Man is considered to have only qualified privileges permitted by The Majority in control of government and revocable by it at any time. This spells Rule by Omnipotent Majority, with The Individual and The Minority as well as all minorities victimized at the pleasure of The Majority, without limit and without any legal basis for objection or practical remedy. The idea of such unlimited rule, as if by "divine right of The Majority," is as abhorrent in the eyes of the traditional American philosophy as is the idea of rule by "divine right of kings."

The Uniquely American Principle Was Thoroughly Understood in 1776

7. The traditional American philosophy requires a Republic's constitutionally limited *form* of government for the security of Man's unalienable rights against violation by The Majority, by government, as well as by others. This philosophy was well understood in America in 1776 but was imperfectly practiced by the States in the post-1776 period, during which rights were violated. This correct understanding was exemplified by the previously noted (Par. 8, Principle 2) town-meeting petition of Pittsfield, Massachusetts, addressed to the legislature of Massachusetts in May, 1776. It urged the adoption by the people—as "the fountain of power"—of a Constitution as their fundamental law, to fill the void created by the end of royal rule, as

"the first step to be taken" by the people in order to guard against despotism—against "the wanton exercise of power"—and it asserted that the only safeguard is "the formation of a fundamental constitution" by the people. Their aim was to safeguard their liberties. This was accomplished by the people of Massachusetts in 1780, by their creating the first true Constitution and Republic in the world. They utilized successfully, for the first time in history, a constitutional convention—which is America's great, if not greatest, contribution to the mechanics of self-government through constitutional government. (Earlier Acts of Legislatures of other States were erroneously classified as "constitutions;" while some countries' governments throughout history had generally been erroneously classified as "republics"—a much-misunderstood and loosely used term. See the correct definition of a Republic in Paragraph 4, above.)

Principle Violated by "Elective Despotism" after 1776

8. The post-1776 period witnessed gross violations by State Legislatures of the unalienable rights of victimized Individuals. In Virginia, for example, Jefferson protested vigorously against the Legislature's acts of tyranny by The Majority, stating: "An *elective despotism* was not the government we fought for . . ." ("Notes on The State of Virginia," 1782; emphasis Jefferson's). Misconduct in this period by The Omnipotent Majority in the legislatures of a number of the States was in reaction against the earlier oppressive rule by the king and his royal governors and judges. At that time, except in Massachusetts und its Constitution of 1780, there were no real State Constitutions to restrain the legislatures, which made sure that the governors and judges were without power to prohibit legislative enactments (by which the violations of unalienable rights were effected). The New Hampshire Constitution, based on this pattern, was not adopted until 1784 after a Constitutional Convention was successful in framing one acceptable to the people—several earlier conventions having been unsuccessful. Other States did not follow suit for a number of years, some not for decades.

"The Excesses of Democracy"

9. This type of tyranny, by Omnipotent Majority, is always possible under any Democracy as a *form* of government. This is what The Framers and Ratifiers of the Constitution and their fellow-

122

Principle Twelve

American leaders meant when, in the 1787-1788 debates with regard to the framing and adoption of the Constitution, they denounced the "excesses of democracy." They were, of course, not criticizing popular government as such—for instance as it exists under the Republic of the United States featuring constitutionally limited government, as limited by the Constitution. They were, therefore, not condemning democracy in the general sense of the term—meaning merely a popular *type* of government. They were speaking in support of America's being a Republic, not a Democracy, as a *form* of government. The more general meaning of Democracy—popular government—also applies to America; but this use of the term is only confusing in any discussion, as here, of the characteristics of different *forms* of popular government: a Republic in contrast to a Democracy.

Federal and State Republics

10. The foregoing explains why the traditional American philosophy requires that the central (Federal) government and the State governments be Republics. (See Pars. 6-7 of Principle 5.) Each State is guaranteed the form of government of a Republic by the United States Constitution (Art. IV, Sec. 4). The foregoing also makes clear why this philosophy requires that The Majority, at any time in temporary charge of government, administer its affairs in keeping with the Constitution's limitations and for the benefit of all Individuals composing the people as a whole, meaning The Minority and all minorities as well as The Majority—not merely for the benefit of those constituting only The Majority of the moment.

The Conclusion

11. The traditional American philosophy demands that the power of The Majority be limited for the protection of The Individual's unalienable rights, for the security of Man's Liberty against Government-over-Man, in keeping with the American formula: The Majority —Limited for Liberty.

PART II
SOME ASPECTS OF
THE TRADITIONAL AMERICAN PHILOSOPHY

BACKGROUND DISCUSSION

PRELIMINARY COMMENT

The following discussion is limited in scope and purpose. It is designed chiefly to provide some background information, as to certain key aspects, which will facilitate the reader's comprehension of the subject of this study-guide.

Any brief presentation such as this, while useful in itself, can also serve the broader purpose of better enabling the reader to pursue the subject further, in part by study of reference sources cited. This is a main aim of this study-guide.

References for all quotations and writings—citing the original sources—are listed in the Appendix.

Like the preceding Principles, separate parts of the following material will be consulted from time to time by various readers when occasion makes some particular topic of special interest for the moment, without having in mind the entire text. For this reason, there is some repetition of especially important points pertinent to different topics discussed, in order to insure adequate understanding of each of them separately—especially by the Young, as well as by others not familiar with the subject. The extremely few (if any) who will scan hastily this entire study-guide as a whole will, it is hoped, bear this in mind and be indulgent toward this aspect of the presentation in the following pages.

127

THE TRADITIONAL AMERICAN PHILOSOPHY

A Definite, Unique, American Philosophy of Government Does Exist—Composed of a Set of Specific, Fundamental, Traditional Principles

When the Declaration of Independence was proclaimed in 1776, and the Constitution of the United States was framed and adopted in 1787-1788, the American people and their leaders firmly believed in, and acted upon the basis of, a definite set of principles—ideas made American principles by being applied governmentally. Some of them were stated in the following words of the Declaration:

> "We hold these truths to be self-evident, that all men are created equal, that they are endowed by their Creator with certain unalienable Rights, that among these are Life, Liberty and the pursuit of Happiness. That to secure these rights, Governments are instituted among Men, deriving their just powers from the consent of the governed, That whenever any Form of Government becomes destructive of these ends, it is the Right of the People to alter or to abolish it, and to institute new Government, laying its foundation on such principles and organizing its powers in such form, as to them shall seem most likely to effect their Safety and Happiness."
> (Text exactly per the original.)

There are those who deny and deplore the idea that there exists a definite group, or set, of fundamental principles—uniquely American as a whole—which constitute the traditional American philosophy of government. Yet there are voluminous historical records which amply prove their existence and definition, the chief source in brief form being this 1776 Declaration—especially the profound sentences quoted above. It was with the gift of foresight—anticipating those in the future who would scoff at the above-mentioned idea and seek to belittle the sincerity and ideals of the generation of Americans of the Revolutionary period—that the town-meeting of Braintree, Massachusetts, adopted on October 14, 1765, a set of "Instructions," drafted by John Adams, to their representatives in the legislature of Massachusetts regarding opposition to the Stamp Act, stating in part as follows:

> "We further recommend the most clear and explicit assertion and vindication of our rights and liberties to be entered on the public records, that the world may know, in the present and all future generations, that we have a clear knowledge and a just sense of them, and, with submission to Divine Providence, that we never can be slaves . . . ."

This indicates what Adams meant when he stated long afterward (letter to Jefferson, 1815) that: "The revolution was in the minds of the people, and this was effected from 1760 to 1775, in the course of fifteen years, before a drop of blood was shed at Lexington."

The above-quoted statement in the Declaration of Independence, of high-minded principles and idealistic goals, is unsurpassed in all the world's writings about Mankind's tortuous struggle throughout history toward the ever-beckoning Light of Individual Liberty. This statement sought to express succinctly the essence of the philosophical basis of the reconciliation of Man's longing for Individual Liberty with the inescapable need for an orderly society, through Government, in order that Man's Liberty may exist. This contemplates the existence of Government adequate for the people's prescribed purposes, for the nation's security and sound functioning, but limited in power so as to make and keep their liberties secure against abuse, or usurpation, of power by public officials as public trustees.

The successful reconciliation of this longing for Individual Liberty with this need for Government makes possible the desired result: Man's Liberty against Government-over-Man. This means Freedom of Man from Government-over-Man. This goal and ideal proclaimed in the Declaration of Independence in 1776 were later translated into governmental reality through adoption of the United States Constitution in 1787-1788, which accomplished this reconciliation in a degree never before attained by any people in all human history. This successful application in the Constitution of the principles of the Declaration was the subject of comment by James Wilson in the Pennsylvania Ratifying Convention. After reading to the members the first few sentences of the Declaration, including those quoted above, he noted their relationship to the constitutional system:

"This is the broad basis on which our independence was placed: on the same certain and solid foundation this system is erected."

This relationship of the Constitution to the Declaration was also commented on in his April 30, 1839 "Jubilee" address by former President John Quincy Adams.

This relationship—this successful application in the Constitution of the Declaration's principles—is a major factor supporting the soundness of the conclusion that a definite, unique, American philosophy of government does exist—composed of a set of specific, fundamental, traditional principles. The governmental realities, created by the constitutional system, gave substance to these principles.

130

The Two Revolutions of 1776—
for Individual Liberty and for Independence

The key goals in America in 1776—for which the colonists had been gradually prepared to fight by their generations-long strivings governmentally and spiritually—were expressed in that period's popular slogan: "Liberty and Independence." This meant Individual Liberty—Freedom from Government-over-Man—and Independence from foreign rule. This slogan was later adopted as the motto on the seal of the State of Delaware.

In the pre-1776 years, the primary goal of most Americans was Individual Liberty—that is, Freedom of Man from Government-over-Man—not by occasional favor of King or Parliament but assured governmentally. They were determined, if *possible,* to attain this goal within the framework of the existing system—within the British Empire—but, if *necessary,* through America's Independence from foreign rule. Being thus determined to attain Liberty in any event, they were equally determined to attain it at all cost—if need be, in last resort, through gaining Independence by revolting against tyrannical rule by King and Parliament. Such exercise by an oppressed people of the right of revolution against tyrants would be, they were convinced, in keeping with the sound philosophy of government—the philosophy long propagated in America and, for some decades prior to 1776, most emphatically by leaders among the New England clergy.

The above-noted priority, of Liberty over Independence, in the minds of the American people and their leaders prior to 1776 was expressed in the closing words of an Address (to the American people) submitted to the Continental Congress on February 13, 1776 by James Wilson as follows: "That the Colonies may continue connected, as they have been, with Britain, is our second Wish: Our first is—THAT AMERICA MAY BE FREE." (Emphasis Wilson's.)

This determination of most Americans, prior to 1776, to gain Individual Liberty at all cost needs to be kept in mind whenever attention is given to the fact that relatively few Americans were in this period openly devoting their activities to seeking revolution against British rule. Yet some leaders, notably those in Boston such as Samuel Adams, had long realized that Liberty could and would be gained in no way other than through revolution and America's Independence. It was not until late 1775 that a great many Americans, and not until early 1776 that a multitude of them, were compelled by events to give up hope of peaceable achievement of the goal of assured Liberty and became convinced of the need of, openly committed to,

Revolution: the remedy of last resort. This is entirely understandable because of the dreadful risks involved not only for each Individual—including risk of Life and all else held dear—but also for the great Cause, due to the then poor prospect of ultimate victory against the massive armaments of the powerful British Empire. Some of the leaders argued up to the last moment for more time in which to work for a peaceable achievement of the desired goal.

The Declaration's principles meant that there was another revolt in 1776, in addition to the one against rule over America by Great Britain; that is, a revolt by Man against being governed and in favor of being self-governing. This was what might be called the Twin Revolution of 1776, though this formal date had been preceded by several years of steadily widening rebellion by the American people against royal tyranny—even by some actual fighting against the tyrant king's troops.

The core-concept of the philosophy of the American revolutionaries in 1776 was the product of the long and bitter experience, of the endless debating and thinking, of the American people in general as well as of their leaders. This core-concept was that there need not be, that in fact there is not, any Controlling Authority on earth to whom the people are justly answerable. That no such Authority exists, and no such pretended Authority should be tolerated, was their firm conviction. This was of the essence of the 1776 Declaration.

This fundamental truth—a basic element of the traditional American philosophy—was phrased by James Wilson during the debates in the Pennsylvania Ratifying Convention as follows (his emphasis):

"The truth is, that, in our governments, the supreme, absolute, and uncontrollable power *remains* in the people. As our constitutions are superior to our legislatures, so the people are superior to our constitutions."

Otherwise stated, from the standpoint of the Natural Law upon which the American philosophy rests, according to the thinking of The Founders: the pretense that an absolute, irresistible, despotic power exists in every government somewhere, is incompatible with the first principle of Natural Right. (Note again J. Q. Adams' quotation page 74, *ante.*) It was merely a sound rephrasing of this traditional, American principle which was included in the Bill of Rights of the 1850 Constitution of Kentucky in words reminiscent of 1776:

"Sec. 2. That absolute, arbitrary power over the lives, liberty, and property of freemen exists nowhere in a republic, not even in the largest majority."

The proclamation of the unprecedented principles in 1776, as the basis of the American people's philosophy and system of self-government, was the greatest act of faith in Man's spirit and mind in all history. It shocked and shook the world and continues to do so to this day. Witness the current upheavals globally among peoples, whose surge toward freedom from colonialism's chains—always so degrading and oppressive, however disguised and however allegedly beneficial or superficially "benevolent"—has convulsed the mid-20th century.

Evolution a Main Part of the Revolution

The Twin Revolution of 1776 was fundamentally in support of conserving well-developed American values governmentally and not for the purpose of their destruction. As the Continental Congress proclaimed on July 6, 1775, in the "Declaration of the Causes and Necessity of Taking Up Arms":

> [We have taken up arms] ". . . for the *preservation* of our liberties . . . in defence of the freedom that is our birth-right, and *which we ever enjoyed* till the late violation of it . . ."

(Emphasis added.) The Twin Revolution was therefore, in general, in defense of established governmental institutions, principles and accustomed rights; but these institutions were then given new functions and significance in the light of the Twin Revolution's goal of complete self-government: Man-over-Government. It was against tyrannous officials acting as usurpers—acting lawlessly, as "out-laws," because outside of the scope of their prescribed authority under Law designed to make and keep secure these things governmental and the people's liberties. It was in pursuit of more complete self-government and Individual Liberty: Freedom from Government-over-Man. An element of evolution governmentally was thus involved: progress through building on the basis of the governmental institutions, customs and civilization in general already established in America. This spelled a vast advance in governmental philosophy and system because— through a century and a half of pioneering governmentally and otherwise—the American people had by 1776 already achieved greater freedom for The Individual from Government-over-Man and a civilization far more advanced politically than any that then existed in the Old World or would exist there for a long time afterward.

The Twin Revolution of 1776 commenced, in truth, a never-ending process of evolution looking towards ever-fuller realization of The

133

American Ideal, of the goals stated in the Declaration of Independence. Therein lies the significance of the call, to endless striving, by James Wilson, one of The Framers, in his oration on July 4, 1788:

> "A progressive state is necessary to the happiness and perfection of man. Whatever attainments are already reached, attainments still higher should be pursued. Let us, therefore, strive with noble emulation. Let us suppose we have done nothing, while any thing yet remains to be done. Let us, with fervent zeal, press forward, and make unceasing advances in every thing that can support, improve, refine, or embellish society . . . The commencement of our government has been eminently glorious: let our progress in every excellence be proportionably great. It will—it must be so."

The fact that the Twin Revolution of 1776 is a continuing process of evolution was highlighted in a 1787 address to the American people by Dr. Benjamin Rush, one of the signers of the Declaration of Independence (quoting the first and the last paragraphs; emphasis his):

> "There is nothing more common, than to confound the terms of *American Revolution* with those of *the late American war*. The American war is over: but this is far from being the case with the American revolution. On the contrary, nothing but the first act of the great drama is closed. It remains yet to establish and perfect our new forms of government; and to prepare the principles, morals, and manners of our citizens, for these forms of government, after they are established and brought to perfection. . . . Patriots of 1774, 1775, 1776—heroes of 1778, 1779, 1780! come forward! your country demands your services!—Philosophers and friends to mankind, come forward! your country demands your studies and speculations! Lovers of peace and order, who declined taking part in the late war, come forward! your country forgives your timidity and demands your influence and advice! Hear her proclaiming, in sighs and groans, in her governments, in her finances, in her trade, in her manufactures, in her morals, and in her manners, 'THE REVOLUTION IS NOT OVER ' "

Uniqueness of the Twin Revolution

There was a great difference between this Twin Revolution of 1776 and the revolution in France which commenced in 1789. The latter had no such sound foundation in the French people's experience but was entirely theoretical—in support of merely abstract ideas of only a few leaders; it was destructive of existing institutions and customs and entirely lacked any element of the constructive based on established principles previously put into practice by the people. This is why the French people, after enduring some years of wanton tyranny and ruthless terror under revolutionary leaders, voted in favor of a return to their own political servitude through restoration of the philosophy and system of Government-over-Man, under Napoleon as emperor. Those destructively revolutionary ideas and theories of the French Revolution's leaders entirely lacked the main characteristic of the principles of the American Revolution—the Twin Revolution of 1776: firm conviction and dedication born of the people's long experience; and, furthermore, those ideas and theories were fundamentally the very antithesis of the American principles—chief of all the godlessness of the French Revolution's philosophy. This element of godlessness made nonsense of the assertion by these French leaders that they considered certain political rights to be unalienable; because rights can properly be termed unalienable only *because* God-given— the element of unalienability depending entirely upon the fact that they are bestowed upon Man by his Creator. (See Par. 2, p. 25, *ante.*)

The uniqueness of the philosophy of the Twin Revolution of 1776 is indicated by the fact that no other people in all history had ever advocated this philosophy's principles, much less proclaimed and acted upon them as a basis for creating such a system of self-government; *although some Old World philosophers had, of course, written about some aspects of a few of these principles but only as abstract ideas unrelated to governmental reality.* Former President John Quincy Adams commented to this effect in his 1839 "Jubilee" address.

This uniqueness is highlighted particularly by the fact that nothing even remotely like it had ever been conceived as a governmental philosophy, much less put into practice, even by the people of Great Britain. There the people had discarded centuries earlier the idea and system of the divine right of kings, of unlimited royal power and rule; but they adopted as a substitute the principle of unlimited power of the national legislature (Parliament) and, therefore, the absolute power of The Majority, so the philosophy and system of Government-over-Man was thus continued, and it continues to the present day. This development reflected a tradition in England of Authority Supreme—over Man, in an environment of a stratified society divided into sharply and rigidly separated classes. Long before the American Revolution, this English tradition was expressed by the famous English judge, Sir William Blackstone, as follows: ". . . there is and must be in all of them [States] a supreme, irresistible, absolute, uncontrolled authority . . ." and he further declared that Parliament is the possessor of this supreme power: ". . . the power of Parliament is absolute and without control." (Quoting his famous *Commentaries.*) The supremacy of Parliament is commented on, for

135

example, in *The Federalist* number 53 by Madison. This supremacy is due to the fact that Britain has no written Constitution—nothing even remotely resembling the United States Constitution. Her so-called "Constitution" is nothing but the aggregate of all laws—which Parliament makes and can change at will—and customs concerning things governmental, all judicial decisions and traditional governmental practices; that is, in a general sense, all basic things of a governmental nature—all subject to Parliament's control.

The supremacy of Parliament is explained in the writings of the English legal authority, Albert V. Dicey, especially his *Introduction to the Study of the Law of the Constitution*. In this authoritative work, Dicey comments expressly about the peculiarly vague meaning of the terms "Constitution" and "constitutional" in England—that their so-called Constitution is not any "more sacred or difficult to change than other laws" and that "the meaning of the word 'constitutional' is in England so vague" that it is seldom used concerning any law. This topic is discussed also in the celebrated volume, *The American Commonwealth,* originally published in Great Britain in 1888 and dedicated to the above-mentioned Dicey, by the famous Englishman, James Bryce—also a legal authority—who was better known as Lord Bryce. He states without qualification that Parliament is omnipotent, can change any "constitutional statutes" such as Magna Carta the same as any other law—for instance a highway act, and can abolish any and all institutions such as the Crown and even Parliament itself; all because it possesses complete power and its will is law—is supreme.

This absolute supremacy of Parliament—in reality today of the House of Commons alone—spells The Majority Omnipotent because the decisions of this House are reached by vote of at least half-plus-one. Any such decision is completely controlling as to everything and everybody in Britain; so The Individual has no inviolable rights there, is completely helpless legally, as against The Majority.

Magna Carta's King-granted Rights

Magna Carta was signed at Runnymede in 1215 by King John under the extreme coercion of the threat of death by the sword, upon demand by the assemblage of armed noblemen that he immediately sign this document. As stated in *The Federalist* number 84 by Hamilton, Magna Carta was "obtained by the Barons, sword in hand, from

136

king John." This document was designed chiefly to clarify and make more formal and definite certain pre-existing, king-granted rights, of the noblemen themselves primarily; and it is a chief example of the application of the principle of king-granted rights—originally based upon the Old World concept of the divine right of kings. Magna Carta is, therefore, in keeping with—was an early expression of—Britain's traditional philosophy and system of Government-over-Man exemplified in modern times, as noted above, by the absolute supremacy of Parliament—now of the House of Commons alone.

Magna Carta's philosophy of king-granted rights stands, therefore, for the antithesis of the traditional American philosophy of Man-over-Government, based upon the uniquely American concept of *God*-given, unalienable rights safeguarded by a system of constitutionally limited government created by the sovereign people, under a written Constitution adopted by them, primarily to make and keep these rights secure.

The conflict between the philosophy underlying Magna Carta and the traditional American philosophy was noted in the address by Secretary of State John Quincy Adams in celebration of the Fourth oι July, 1821, in these words:

"The people of Britain, through long ages of civil war, had extorted from their tyrants not *acknowledgements,* but *grants,* of right. With this concession they had been content to stop in the progress of human improvement. They received their freedom as a donation from their sovereigns; they appealed for their privileges to a sign manual and a seal; they held their title to liberty, like their title to lands, from the bounty of a man; and in their moral and political chronology, the great charter of Runny Mead was the beginning of the world . . . the fabric of their institutions . . . had been founded in conquest; it had been cemented in servitude, . . . instead of solving civil society into its first elements in search of their rights, they looked back only to conquest as the origin of their liberties, and claimed their rights but as donations from their kings. This faltering assertion of freedom is not chargeable indeed upon the whole nation. There were spirits capable of tracing civil government to its foundation in the moral and physical nature of man; but conquest and servitude were so mingled up in every particle of the social existence of the nation, that they had become vitally necessary to them . . ."

(Runny Mead is also spelled Runnymede; emphasis per original.) To repeat, the traditional American philosophy of Man-over-Government based upon the concept of *God*-given, unalienable rights is utterly antithetical to the philosophy of Magna Carta's Government-over-Man, with its *king*-granted rights.

Understanding the American Heritage

If they fail to comprehend the profound significance of the fore-going points—of the fundamental difference between the philosophy and system of Great Britain, featuring Government-over-Man and The Majority Omnipotent, on the one hand, and, on the other hand, the American philosophy and system of Man-over-Government fea-turing constitutionally limited government designed primarily for the protection of Man's God-given, unalienable rights—the American people can have no adequate conception of the Twin Revolution of 1776 or of their heritage. Without such comprehension and steadfast loyalty to the traditional American principles and values involved, they cannot fulfill their duty as temporary trustees—of the American heritage—for America's youth today and Posterity.

The spirit of Free Men such as Patrick Henry and Samuel Adams, the pioneering Daniel Boone and other frontiersmen, for example, is expressive of the true spirit of traditional America. To those benighted souls who cry for "security"—either that of the subjects of a benev-olent king, or of a paternalistic system of Government-over-Man with its government-provided economic "security" accompanied inesca-pably by only a limited degree of Liberty, namely a system of Man subservient to Authority—The American Spirit replies:

> Better Liberty with the challenge
> And dangers of the untried, unknown,
> Than Servitude's deadly certainty
> Of economic security.

The principles stated in the Declaration of Independence were truly expressive of the deep-rooted convictions in 1776 not only of its signers and other American leaders but of the people in general. As its chief draftsman, Jefferson wrote later that in it he sought to express no new ideas but only those commonly prevailing throughout the country. As he put it in 1825 (letter to Henry Lee), the Declaration was designed not to present new principles, or arguments, but "to place before mankind the common sense of the subject, . . . in-tended to be an expression of the American mind . . ." In the same year (letter to Dr. James Mease) he stated that the Declaration was ". . . the genuine effusion of the soul of our country at that time." The same sentiments, in substance, were expressed in 1822 by John Adams—one of the drafting committee's members and chiefly re-sponsible for insisting that Jefferson do the actual, initial drafting— (letter to Timothy Pickering) stating:

138

"As you justly observe, there is not an idea in it but what had been hackneyed in Congress for two years before. The substance of it is contained in the declaration of rights and the violation of those rights, in the Journals of Congress, in 1774. Indeed, the essence of it is contained in a pamphlet, voted and printed by the town of Boston, before the first Congress met . . ."

As noted in the Introduction to this study-guide, a somewhat similar observation had been made by John Adams in a letter to Samuel Chase in July, 1776. The records fully bear out these concurring statements by Jefferson and John Adams. The sentiments expressed in the Declaration of Independence were, indeed, those of the American people in general—loyal to the aims of the two Revolutions of 1776: the Revolution for Independence and the Twin Revolution in support of Individual Liberty: Freedom of Man from Government-over-Man.

The deep-seated and long-developing nature of "the common sense of the subject"—of the thinking of the American people expressed in the Declaration—is illustrated by the striking fact that a book published over half a century earlier by one of the New England clergy, Reverend John Wise, expounded and espoused with remarkable clarity and great assurance, born of firm conviction, most of the principal ideas, or principles, presented in this 1776 document. The idea of Equality was discussed—for instance, there is a "natural equality of men amongst men," which must be "favored" (respected). The fundamental rights: "life, liberty, estate" (property) were commented on. The fact that the primary role and aim of Government is the protection of these rights and to serve the common good, as well as the topic of Man's relationship to Government, were also discussed. For instance, he noted that Man delegates power to government— (part of) his "original liberty" is "resigned"—not unconditionally but "under due restrictions" (namely, permitting government to possess only limited powers) and that Man's reserved rights "ought to be cherished in all wise Governments; or otherwise a man in making himself a subject, he alters himself from a freeman, into a slave, which to do is repugnant to the law of nature." Here he noted, in effect, not only the limited-power nature of Government, by grant of power under "restrictions" by the people, but also the fact that its granted powers should be such as to be consistent with a Freeman's Liberty. He also emphasized the "Compact" theory: that Men enter into Society, form their governments, by contract freely entered into and "not of divine institution" (not in keeping with the rejected theory of the Divine Right of Kings), and that government "is the

produce of mans reason, of human and rational combinations . . ."
Furthermore, this book stressed the fundamental, political tenet of
the 1776 Declaration: that the source of Government's power "is
the People."

All of this advanced and forward-looking political thought, and
much more, is found in this Ipswich, Massachusetts, clergyman's 1717
book, *A Vindication of the Government of New-England Churches.*
It is unexcelled among all such writings of the Colonial period. Although he did not discuss that other great political idea of the 1776
Declaration: the people's right to revolt against tyrannical government,
yet he observed that "the prince who strives to subvert the fundamental laws of the society, is the traytor and the rebel"—that is, public
officials who act outside of their granted authority and violate its
limits as prescribed by the people under the fundamental law are the
traitors and rebels and not the people who resist their tyranny. It is
also noteworthy that this clergyman was in the lead of the revolt of
the Town of Ipswich in 1687 against Royal Governor Andros and his
tax levied without consent of the popular legislative body—a revolt
based upon the principle of popular sovereignty as to taxation; the
Town-meeting refused to authorize collection of the tax and, for his
refusal to pay the tax, Clergyman Wise was tried, fined and suspended
from the Ministry—also jailed during the proceedings. This is com-
memorated by the inscription on the town's official seal: "The Birth-
place of American Independence, 1687."

This 1717 book of Reverend Wise emphasized the relationship of
Man to the Law of Nature and his capacity to understand it through
use of his faculty of reason; the Law of Nature is "the dictate of right
reason." Note also the statement in an oration on July 4, 1787 by
Joel Barlow at Hartford, Connecticut, in celebration of the anniversary of the proclamation of the Declaration of Independence, that:

"The present is an age of philosophy, and America the empire of reason.
Here, neither the pageantry of courts, nor the glooms of superstition, have
dazzled or beclouded the mind. Our duty calls us to act worthy of the age
and the country that gave us birth. Though inexperience may have betrayed
us into errors—yet they have not been fatal: and our own discernment will
point us to their proper remedy."

This "discernment"—the capacity to reason—was considered by The
Founders and their fellow leaders of that period, as well as those like
Reverend Wise of earlier generations, to be self-governing Man's
salvation, if soundly exercised. His 1717 book makes it clear that this

"age of philosophy" and this "empire of reason" in America did not originate in the 1776 period but was in bud, if not in flower in remarkable degree, in Wise's day—based of course upon much older roots in American thinking and experience in government, with the benefit of wide reading of Old World writings.

The steadily developing American character of this early thinking, of these precepts, stemmed from the fact that the American people were applying them in practice, living by them, in increasing degree; *though some abstract ideas, or ways of expressing them, were selectively adapted from theoretical writings of foreign authors. Ideas applied governmentally became uniquely American principles.*

Comments About
A Few of the Sources Consulted
Regarding Definition of the American Principles

The definitions of the "Twelve Basic American Principles," in the preceding Part I, are based upon the results of many years of research by the present writer in the writings of American leaders of the period 1750-1800, including particularly those eminent among the Signers of the Declaration of Independence and the Constitution. Special attention was given to what might be called the Jefferson-Madison list of sound sources in this connection.

In collaboration with Madison, who is often and justly called "the father of the Constitution" because of his exceptionally valuable and diligent service in 1787 in the Federal (framing) Convention, Jefferson provided an especially interesting and most persuasive piece of evidence that they, and assuredly their fellow leaders in general, accepted a certain set of principles as being fundamental American principles of government—together constituting the uniquely American philosophy of government; made genuinely American by being put into practice by the people. This was the resolution which these two members of the Board of Visitors of the University of Virginia offered and caused to be adopted by the Board at its meeting in March 1825 (Jefferson then being the Rector). It stated that all students shall be "inculcated" with the basic American governmental principles and that "none should be inculcated which are incompatible with those on which the Constitutions of this State, and of the U. S. were genuinely based, in the common opinion." The faculty was thus required to teach positively and affirmatively ("inculcate" and "indoctrinate" being synonymous under the word "teach") these principles *only*. Such sound teaching does not preclude, indeed it requires, students being taught *about* conflicting principles in order to enable them to understand the unsoundness of the latter—judged by the sound standard of the American principles, with which the students must, of course, first be made familiar so as to have a "yardstick" by which to judge soundly.

Jefferson, Madison and their fellow leaders were undoubtedly in agreement on this point: that in order to inculcate the sound American principles—partly by teaching uninformed and impressionable Youth *about* the conflicting principles which are unsound, judged by this "yardstick," so as to enable them to understand fully the soundness and value of the American principles, considered comparatively— it is of course necessary that the reasons for the comparative unsoundness of the conflicting principles be stressed comprehensively, clearly and positively through adequate teaching, with scholarly competence and intellectual honesty, in keeping with the duty aspect of Academic Freedom-Responsibility, which is in a very real sense closely related to Individual Liberty-Responsibility in general. Otherwise the students are deprived of the substance of their right to freedom of choice; they cannot choose soundly between alternatives which they do not know, or do not understand adequately in all their implications for the long term. The exact wording of the Preamble to the Board's above-mentioned resolution is as follows:

> "Whereas it is the duty of this board to the government [of the United States] under which it lives, and especially to that [of Virginia] of which this University is the immediate creation, to pay especial attention to the principles of government which shall be inculcated therein, and to provide that none shall be inculcated which are incompatible with those on which the Constitutions of this State, and of the U. S. were genuinely based in the common opinion: and for this purpose it may be necessary to point out specifically where these principles are to be found legitimately developed . . ."

For this purpose, the resolution specified six writings (named below) as being, in the Board's opinion, such authoritative sources.

This resolution did not express merely the Board members' personal views. It was in effect certifying to the truth of an important point, accepted and firmly supported with unanimity by the American people in 1776 and through all succeeding generations for about a century and a half: that America does have a distinctive, indeed a unique and definable, governmental philosophy which is firmly rooted in her well-defined traditions; and that youth should be indoctrinated accordingly.

142

Four of the six writings, reflecting long experience in government in America, were referred to as embodying these American principles. They are: (1) the Declaration of Independence; (2) Washington's *Farewell Address;* (3) the Virginia Resolutions of 1799 (adopted by the Virginia Legislature); and (4) *The Federalist.* These are the American sources cited. The remaining two of the six writings are much earlier volumes by Old World authors, concerning abstract theories of government: John Locke's *Essay Concerning The True Original Extent and End of Civil Government* (originally published in 1690), and Algernon Sidney's *Discourses Concerning Government* (1698). These two writings were listed in that resolution as being sound sources of "the general principles of liberty and the rights of man in nature and society;" that is, as theoretical discussions. These six writings were prescribed as textbooks for law students.

In the Appendix of this study-guide, there are presented, for ready reference, the text of some of these sources: the Declaration of Independence; the *Farewell Address;* and the above-mentioned Virginia Resolutions. The Appendix also presents selected parts of several essays of *The Federalist.* These sources constitute a part of the reliable proof—on the authority of Jefferson, Madison and their fellow members of the University's Board of Visitors—that there does exist a distinctive and definable American philosophy consisting of a set of specific, traditional principles as applied governmentally.

The American sources cited, in the University resolution, alone contain adequate evidence of the soundness of the definitions of the Twelve Basic American Principles presented in the preceding Part I of this study-guide. Among the many other writings consulted in this regard, those especially of Washington, Jefferson, Madison, Hamilton, and John and Samuel Adams—to name a few of the most prominent leaders—offer a wealth of supporting evidence. Brief comment concerning five of the above-listed sources, and extended discussion of *The Federalist,* are in order at this point.

Madison wrote Jefferson on February 8, 1825, that the writings of Sidney and Locke ". . . are admirably calculated to impress on young minds the right of Nations to establish their own Governments, and to inspire a love of free ones . . ." and, further, that the Declaration of Independence is ". . . rich in fundamental principles . . ." Madison also stated that he had considered Jefferson's suggestion of a textbook for the University's Law School and added: "It is certainly very material that the true doctrines of liberty, as exemplified in our Political System, should be inculcated on those who are to sustain and may administer it."

It is noteworthy, in passing, that Locke's and Sidney's writings are soundly considered not to have originated the basic ideas, or principles, entertained by American leaders but principally to have helped to clarify the expression of some which were already a part of the thinking of these leaders—clarification by way of logical exposition and lucid expression. Note also that the frequency of quotation by American leaders in this period of a few of Locke's statements as to some main ideas should not be permitted to lead to the erroneous conclusion that writings of other foreign philosophers also in this field were not similarly utilized; because many of these leaders were familiar with them. It should never be lost sight of, moreover, that the fundamental American principles of government were the outgrowth mainly of generations of painful experience in self-government in America and were not merely theoretical ideas drawn from books —this being true as to the principles of the Declaration of Independence as well as of the Constitution and the constitutional system. *These principles, derived mainly from experience in America, were thus given support—in application in practical affairs—by selective, not imitative, use of the foreign writings, which were themselves chosen on a similar, selective basis.* The Americans made use of the parts of any writing which served their purpose but did not embrace in their entirety any foreign writer's set of ideas. Then, as now, American thinking was more practical than theoretical—as John Adams stated (1778, "Thoughts On Government"): "It must be conceded that, as yet, philosophical generalization upon abstract questions of the highest class is not the characteristic of the American mind."

The Virginia Resolutions of 1799, drafted by Madison and adopted January 4, 1799—and his lengthy 1799 Report to the General Assembly (adopted January 7, 1800) in explanation and support of its Resolutions of December 21, 1798—were intimately related to the famous Kentucky Resolutions drafted by Jefferson and adopted by the Kentucky Legislature on November 10, 1798. All of these Resolutions were in defense of the rights of the people and of the States, as reserved by the Constitution and expressly by the Ninth and Tenth Amendments to the Constitution, against what were considered to be the recent usurpations and abuses of power by the Federal government in various respects, chiefly through the Alien and Sedition Laws of 1798. These resolutions were not the first such protest by a legislature;

in 1790, for instance, the Virginia Legislature had protested against the Federal government's assumption of the war debts of the States as being unconstitutional. Other States did not support the Virginia Resolutions of 1798, but this legislative protest helped to start the creation of public opinion in opposition to these 1798 laws with the result that their end was assured by the next election. Use of legislative protests, exemplified by Kentucky and Virginia in 1798, was moreover resorted to in the succeeding decades by the governments of various States—in New England, the North in general, the Midwest as well as in the South—in support of their own respective complaints from time to time against what they deemed to be abuses, or usurpations, of power by the Federal government, including especially the Supreme Court, in violation of the reserved rights of the States under the Constitution. These developments are recorded in detail and at length in the book, *State Documents on Federal Relations: the States and the United States,* by Dr. Herman V. Ames of the faculty of the History Department of the University of Pennsylvania, which published it in 1906.

An impressive example of such later, legislative protests is the set of resolutions adopted in 1815 (during the war with England) by the Hartford Convention—representing the governments of Massachusetts, Connecticut, Rhode Island, Vermont and New Hampshire—protesting against what were considered to be Federal usurpations, potential or actual, regarding use of the States' Militia by the Federal government in war operations and concerning other matters involved in national defense. (See quotation from these Hartford Resolutions page 14, *ante.*) The Fugitive Slave Law and the Supreme Court's decision in the 1857 *Dred Scott* case, *Scott versus Sandford,* concerning slavery, as well as later decisions of the Court involving this subject, aroused violent protests by the governments and especially the legislatures of various States. A notable example is the resolution adopted by the Massachusetts' Legislature in 1858, against the *Dred Scott* decision, asserting that the people of Massachusetts would never consent to any invasion of their liberties by reason of the Supreme Court's "usurpations of political power" and, further, "That no part of the decision of the supreme court of the United States, in the case of Scott *versus* Sandford, is binding, which was not necessary to the determination of that case . . ." This referred to what were considered to be political parts of the decision. A more extreme protest, against a decision of the Supreme Court involving the subject of slavery, was that of the Wisconsin Legislature in 1859 asserting that the Court's decision was "an arbitrary act of power, unauthorized by the constitution . . . and therefore without authority, void, and of no force . . . and that a *positive defiance* . . . is the rightful remedy." (Emphasis per original.) This meant the proper remedy of the States in self-defense and defense of the Constitution against usurpation of power by the Federal government, including the Supreme Court. Other States in the North and the Mid-west were vigorous in their legislative protests in this pre-Civil War period regarding the *Dred Scott* case and matters involving the Fugitive Slave Law.

It is noteworthy that the Virginia Resolutions of 1798, pertaining to Federal laws, did not use any language such as that used by the above-quoted Wisconsin Resolutions: "void, and of no force." In the 1830's Madison wrote a lengthy manuscript: "Notes on Nullification" in which he emphasized that the Virginia Resolutions were not intended to attempt nullification of any Federal law and therefore were not a precedent for the 1832 "Ordinance of Nullification" of South Carolina, which he considered unsound. He had also discussed this topic at length in an 1830 letter to Edward Everett and an 1832 letter to N. P. Trist. Madison well knew, of course, what Hamilton had made entirely clear in 1787-1788 in *The Federalist* (especially number 78, also number 33) to have been the understanding of the Framing Convention: that it is the Constitution only, as the "supreme Law of the Land," which can—and does automatically—make null and void any conflicting Act of Congress. This applies equally to other things governmental, such as Supreme Court decisions. The State Ratifying Conventions also understood this. The controlling principle is this: no legislature, or government, of a State has any power, under the constitutional system, to nullify any Federal law, or Federal court decision, and the converse is equally true. This basic principle was noted in *The Federalist* number 34 by Hamilton (referring to a law as an act): ". . . there is no power on either side to annul the acts of the other." Any annulling is by the Constitution.

An important consideration needs stressing at this point. It is that a protest by a State legislature against claimed Federal usurpation, or abuse, of power is entirely sound constitutionally and traditionally as one of the peaceable remedies (within the constitutional system) available to the States, in any such situation, as indicated expressly in *The Federalist* number 46 by Madison. Any such protest by a State legislature, thus acting within the constitutional system, amounts of course to *nothing more than a declaration of opinion* of that body without in the least affecting the *fact* of constitutionality, or unconstitutionality, as the case may be, of the Act of Congress in question. Madison made this point expressly in his clarifying discussion in his above-mentioned "Notes on Nullification" with regard to the Virginia Resolutions of 1798 and 1799. The basic importance of this topic makes it deserving always of most thoughtful consideration.

The foregoing brief discussion of these resolutions and their historical significance must suffice for present purposes due to lack of space for more extended consideration.

The inclusion of the Declaration of Independence in this list of writings needs no explanation; but it is fitting to note the unusually interesting statement about it in the July 4th oration by Secretary of State John Quincy Adams in 1821 (destined soon thereafter to become President):

"It was the first solemn declaration by a nation of the only *legitimate* foundation of civil government. It was the corner stone of a new fabric, destined to cover the surface of the globe. It demolished at a stroke the lawfulness of all governments founded upon conquest. It swept away all the rubbish of accumulated centuries of servitude. It announced in practical form to the world the transcendent truth of the unalienable sovereignty of the people. It proved that the social compact was no figment of the imagination; but a real, solid, and sacred bond of the social union."

(Emphasis per original.) He continued his eulogy by adding this poetic but just estimate of the Declaration:

"It stands, and must for ever stand, alone, a beacon on the summit of the mountain, to which all the inhabitants of the earth may turn their eyes for a genial and saving light till time shall be lost in eternity, and this globe itself dissolve, nor leave a wreck behind. It stands for ever, a light of admonition to the rulers of men, a light of salvation and redemption to the oppressed . . . [as the delineation of] the boundaries of their respective rights and duties, founded in the laws of nature, and of nature's God."

The profound and invaluable *Farewell Address* was prepared by President Washington over a period of several years with the elaborate attention merited by his last official utterance to the people of his day and to Posterity. He was assisted in this task by some of his associates, notably Alexander Hamilton and James Madison. The fact that it contains "political lessons of peculiar value"—to use the words of the 1825 University resolution—is obvious to even the casual reader possessing any familiarity with history's lessons in this field.

147

The *Farewell Address* reflected the accumulated wisdom of the ages regarding the topics discussed, as understood not only by Washington, Madison and Hamilton but also by their fellow leaders as well as by that period's multitude of well-informed and thoughtful Americans so alert intellectually and profoundly concerned with regard to things governmental, chief of all the philosophy of government in relation to Man's Liberty. This address reflected the teachings of history and of governmental experience not only in America but in the Old World, with which The Founders were thoroughly familiar. An especially interesting book concerning the development of this address is entitled *Washington's Farewell Address,* edited by Victor Hugo Paltsits, published in 1935 by the New York (City) Public Library.

"The Federalist"—
A Rich Source of Sound Knowledge

In the above-noted resolution of the University of Virginia Board, *The Federalist* was lauded as "being an authority to which appeal is habitually made by all, and rarely declined or denied by any as evidence of the general opinion of those who framed, and of those who accepted the Constitution of the U.S. on questions as to its genuine meaning." This referred to the Federal (framing) Convention of 1787 and to the State Ratifying Conventions of 1787-1788 which ratified, or adopted, the Constitution and thereby made it the fundamental law of the people. As Madison wrote Jefferson on February 8, 1825:

> "The 'Federalist' may fairly enough be regarded as the most authentic exposition of the text of the federal Constitution, as understood by the Body which prepared & the Authority which accepted it."

He here referred to the Federal (framing) Convention "which prepared"—and the State Ratifying Conventions "which accepted"— the Constitution.

The Federalist has long been famous as an authoritative volume of greatest pertinence to important governmental problems, especially those involving constitutional principles. Jefferson praised it highly in late 1788 in a letter to Madison written from Paris (where he was then the American Minister), saying that it is: ". . . in my opinion, the best commentary on the principles of government which ever was written." Washington's high opinion of *The Federalist,* expressed from the standpoint of having presided over the Framing Convention and having read probably all current writings of any consequence

148

about the proposed new Constitution, were expressed repeatedly in his correspondence and most interestingly in a letter to Hamilton (August 28, 1788):

> "As the perusal of the political papers under the signature of Publius has afforded me great satisfaction, I shall certainly consider them as claiming a most distinguished place in my Library. I have read every performance which has been printed on one side and the other of the great question lately agitated (so far as I have been able to obtain them) and, without an un-meaning compliment, I will say, that I have seen no other so well calculated (in my judgment) to produce conviction on an unbiased Mind, as the *Production* of your *triumvirate*. When the transient circumstances and fugitive performances which attended this Crisis shall have disappeared, That Work will merit the Notice of Posterity; because in it are candidly and ably discussed the principles of freedom and the topics of government, which will be always interesting to mankind so long as they shall be connected in Civil Society."

(Emphasis per original.) By "triumvirate," Washington referred to the three authors of *The Federalist:* Hamilton, Madison and Jay. All of the essays were published over the signature "Publius," in keeping with the custom of that time of using pen names in publishing political views; but the identity of the authors was a poorly kept secret.

Praised abroad over the generations, where it has been reprinted in various languages in different countries from time to time—for example, in France in 1792, in Brazil (in Portuguese) in 1840, in Argentina (in Spanish) in 1868, in Germany in 1864, and in 1911 in Britain in an edition designed for British readers—*The Federalist* has been so admired and prized in America that the domestic editions published are now counted in the dozens, several having appeared in recent years.

This book's 85 essays were written by Hamilton and Madison, two of the most distinguished leaders who had been members of the Framing Convention, and by John Jay—equally distinguished as a lawyer and political leader of New York, also in charge of foreign affairs under the Confederation in 1787, and in 1789 chosen by President Washington to be the first Chief Justice of the United States. Of these essays, Jay wrote five chiefly on foreign affairs, Hamilton wrote fifty one, and Madison wrote the remainder—a few with some data from Hamilton. Most of the essays were first published in a long series of articles in newspapers in New York City in 1787-1788 —commencing on October 27, 1787, and continuing at irregular intervals until mid-1788. (See page xxix, *ante,* as to authorship.)

149

They were presented as an authoritative and *joint report* of the thus well-publicized intent of the Framing Convention expressed in the Constitution and, therefore, of its original and true meaning; which is always controlling, subject to change by the people only by its amendment. *Each one's contribution was acquiesced in silently by his co-authors,* in keeping with the joint-report nature of the essays. The authors' immediate purpose was to help to win support for its ratification, based upon sound understanding of its real meaning in keeping with this intent, and to dispel the confused thinking in this regard which was then widely prevalent due largely to uninformed assumptions about it. These essays were also published in book form (two volumes) in March and May, 1788 under the title, *The Federalist: A Collection of Essays, written in favour of the New Constitution. As agreed upon by the Federal Convention, September 17, 1787.* Their publication in book form was Hamilton's self-appointed responsibility. (This volume's essays, written when there were no political parties such as came into being later, had no connection of course and should not be confused with the party created later and led by John Adams and Hamilton—called the Federalist Party—which strongly opposed, and was vigorously fought by, Jefferson and Madison as leaders of the Republican Party founded by Jefferson.)

In these articles Hamilton, Madison and Jay discussed comprehensively and authoritatively, in the light of both American and Old World history, the nature and significance of the fundamental principles underlying the American philosophy of Man-over-Government, as well as the actual intent with which the Constitution was framed —the intent expressed in its provisions. This philosophy and the Constitution's meaning cannot be understood adequately without understanding what is presented in *The Federalist.* Hence its vital importance today to all Americans desirous of being adequate defenders of the Constitution, of the Republic, of their own and the people's liberties, of the cause of safeguarding constitutionally limited government as the bulwark of Individual Liberty, and of the just heritage of the helpless children of today and of Posterity in America.

The true meaning of the Constitution, as intended by the Framing Convention, was well known to the members of the State Ratifying Conventions when they adopted it. This knowledge came partly through members of the latter Conventions who had been members of the Framing Convention or who were in touch with some of its members when the State Conventions were held between October 1787 and mid-1788. It also came through some dissemination of *The Federalist* articles after their initial publication in newspapers of New York City as well as in book form in the Spring of 1788. It is reasonable to assume, for instance, that copies of many if not most of these newspaper articles were promptly mailed by interested leaders in New York to similarly interested leaders in all of the States—especially those seeking ratification and able to inform the State Ratifying Conventions and others of the substance of these articles; also reasonable to assume that some of the articles were reprinted and circulated among leaders in the States. Note, for example, that in November and December 1787, Washington received from Hamilton and Madison copies of the newspaper essays published in that period and passed them on to a Richmond newspaper, through an intermediary, for republication; he also asked that he be sent copies of future essays, in this newspaper series, when published; and he wrote to Madison in February 1788 asking for several copies of the volume of those about to be republished in book form. (Letters: to Hamilton November 10, 1787; to David Stuart, in Richmond, November 30, 1787; also to Madison December 7, 1787, and February 5, 1788.) Another example is Hamilton's sending in May-June 1788 to Governor Randolph in Richmond, Virginia, 52 sets of the two volumes of these essays, in book form, for use during the Virginia Ratifying Convention—over which Randolph presided as chairman. Madison took a leading part in that Convention and he, too, of course had them available; and presumably some other members of the Convention also had copies (in either newspaper, or book, form). Evidence of *The Federalist's* contemporary use elsewhere has also been found.

The proceedings of the Framing Convention had been kept secret, in order to prevent unsound and distracting pressures from being applied to its members during their deliberations. As soon as they adjourned, however, in September 1787 and *The Federalist* articles began to appear in the following month, the public—and especially those who were soon to serve as members of the State Ratifying Conventions—commenced to gain fuller information about the background and meaning of the provisions of the proposed Constitution; that is, the meaning as intended by the Framing Convention as reported in these essays. Some Framers were also Ratifiers.

The meaning of the Constitution's provisions, as reported in *The Federalist,* is the same as was understood by the State Ratifying Conventions. This fact is fundamentally important because the true sanction and authority of the Constitution, as the people's basic law, stems from the actions of these Ratifying Conventions in adopting it as the sovereign people's specially chosen representatives, authorized to act for them in this regard—each State acting independently.

It is especially noteworthy, in connection with the Constitution as framed, that Madison stated in Congress in 1796 that "life and validity were breathed into it by the voice of the people, speaking through the several State [Ratifying] Conventions . . ."—that is, the understanding by these Ratifying Conventions of its meaning is controlling. He reiterated this in 1831 (letter to N. P. Trist), stating that it was the proceedings "of the State Conventions which gave it all the validity & authority it possesses." To the same effect, Chief Justice John Marshall stated for the Supreme Court in the 1819 *McCulloch* case (page 403 of opinion) that it is from these State Conventions that "the constitution derives its whole authority" as the basic law of the people. (The Framing Convention produced nothing but a draft of a proposed Constitution.) This was well understood by The Founders.

Note again the statement (page 148, *ante*) by Madison, in his 1825 letter to Jefferson, that *The Federalist* is "the most authentic" report of the meaning of the Constitution as understood and intended by both the Framing Convention and the State Ratifying Conventions.

Any adequate examination of the pertinent historical records will, it is believed, satisfy all competent and reliable scholars as to the soundness of the conclusion that, in the period of ratification as well as in the subsequent years, *The Federalist* was familiar to, and accepted by, those best able to judge—notably the leading and most active members of the Framing and Ratifying Conventions—as being a dependable and authoritative report, jointly by the authors (each acquiescing silently in the essays written by the others), of the intent of the Framing Convention expressed in the words of the Constitution and of its true meaning as understood and accepted by the State Ratifying Conventions. Here "the authors" refers primarily to Hamilton and Madison because Jay, due to illness, wrote only five essays (on foreign affairs in the main) and was not involved in intimate collaboration in this connection as were the other two authors.

The greatness of this volume is conceded by all who are qualified to judge, especially on the basis of competence of scholarship and intellectual integrity—with no axe to grind by way of misconstruction so as to serve some ulterior purpose. Its greatness is due in part to the fact that it was the first work in all history to define and discuss adequately the, theory and realities of self-government through constitutionally limited government and of the principles of federated government: a federation of republics. This was done moreover in a thorough, comprehensive, realistic and authoritative manner, with adequate consideration of history's teachings in the field of government—duly respecting Man's experience as a guide, in keeping with the motto: "foresight through hindsight." It constitutes a unique and magnificent contribution to the science of government.

The Federalist has always been accepted by all who are qualified to judge (as specified above)—including the United States Supreme Court in scores of cases during the century and a half after 1787—not only as reporting correctly the original intent with which the Constitution had been framed and ratified and, therefore, its true meaning, but also as an authoritative exposition of the American philosophy (of constitutionally limited government, in a Republic) reflecting the essence of the principles, ideals and goals of the Declaration of Independence as best summarized in the Constitution's Preamble:

"WE THE PEOPLE of the United States, in Order to form a more perfect Union, establish Justice, insure domestic Tranquility, provide for the common defence, promote the general Welfare, and secure the Blessings of Liberty to ourselves and our Posterity, do ordain and establish this Constitution for the United States of America."

(Per original.) Here the word "Liberty" serves as a principal connecting link between the two documents. The words: "We, the people of the United States," were intended to refer to the people of each of the States acting separately—through a State Ratifying Convention—and not to the people of the nation as a consolidated whole, as all competent and reliable authorities have always agreed; for example Madison in *The Federalist* number 39.

The United States Supreme Court's early opinion of *The Federalist*, as such a sound guide to the meaning of the Constitution, was expressed for example in the statements of Chief Justice Marshall, for the Court, in the 1819 case of *McCulloch v. Maryland* (page 433) and the 1821 case of *Cohens v. Virginia* (page 418); and see the 1895 *Pollock* case (pages 625, 627)—references being to pages of the opinions in the official reports. It is of special interest to note that, in this last-named case in 1895, the Supreme Court decided that the argument which had been presented by Hamilton as counsel in a 1796 case—arguing that a provision of the Constitution had a meaning which conflicted with its meaning as reported in 1787-1788 by him and his co-authors in *The Federalist* in keeping with the intent of the Framing Convention—had to be rejected because, said the Court (page 627 of opinion), the report in *The Federalist* was so authoritative that it "should not and cannot be disregarded." This was the consistent attitude of the Court toward *The Federalist,* as being authoritative and reliable in this regard, through the first century and a half of the life of the Republic.

The authors of *The Federalist* explained with great particularity the Constitution's plan for an enduring system of Man-over-Government (limited, decentralized government) which, as a dependable safeguard of the people's liberties, would serve well these American ideals and goals. However, these authors warned expressly and repeatedly that this would be true only if, and so long as, the people would require their public servants, the officials of the Federal government, to respect in practice the Constitution's limits on its powers; only if, and so long as, the people would prevent these public servants, these public trustees, from committing the gravest of civic crimes: usurpation of power—that is, misusing granted power, or grasping power in violation of, and beyond, the limits prescribed by the sovereign people in the Constitution, as amended by them.

Another important principle, which the authors of *The Federalist* made clear (notably in No. 43), deserves mention here. It is that the people's power to amend the Constitution as and when they see fit, to meet changing conditions, was expressed in the amending clause (Article V) and was intended to give it the needed flexibility, while preserving the necessary stability of the people's basic law and the federated system of government (featuring decentralized power through its division between a central government and State governments). This indicates the nonsensical, indeed preposterous, nature of any claim that usurpation of power is justified by the "rigidity" of the Constitution, especially in the light of the fact that when the people are ready for a particular amendment they will have it approved quickly—as in 1933 in about eleven months (the 21st Amendment repealing the 18th, or "Prohibition," Amendment); also in 1960-1961 in less than ten months (the 23rd Amendment). Any such claim— in effect that public servants, especially judges by "interpreting" the Constitution to suit themselves, may properly grasp power by usurpation—mocks the entire American philosophy and system of constitutionally limited government and amounts to assumption by these public servants of the role of the masters with the people treated as subject to the Will of these usurpers, in effect as their servants. Usurpation is, of course, never justifiable but always unconscionable—the end does not justify the means; and to tolerate it is, in reality, to sanction and foster the ultimate doom of constitutionally limited government and consequently the people's liberties—as well as Posterity's just heritage and the Republic—given enough time. This topic will be discussed later more fully concerning the role of the Supreme Court.

The Federalist also made clear a profound truth which refutes the fallacy that the Constitution is out-of-date, that it was suited only to the comparatively "simple" civilization of the period of The Founders: "the horse and buggy days." This truth is that these constitutional safeguards will always be necessary because they are designed to protect the people's liberties against the never-changing weaknesses of human nature in government; that, just as *these weaknesses will never change, so the need for these safeguards can never change.* This is all the more true because of the corresponding weaknesses of human nature among the electorate; these mutual and inter-related frailties of the people and of their public servants play upon and support each other to the ceaseless peril of Individual Liberty, as history proves. (Note again the very significant Jefferson quotation on page xx, *ante.*) Therein lies the key to sound understanding of the enduring value of the Constitution. It can, of course, fill its safeguarding role only if respected in practice—only if the people exercise not only vigilance but self-discipline by themselves respecting the Constitution and compelling their public servants to abide faithfully by the limits on their power as provided in this fundamental law (per their oath of office).

It is important to note that in *The Federalist,* especially numbers 33 and 78, Hamilton made perfectly clear The Framers' understanding and intent with regard to the controlling effect of the Constitution as the sovereign people's basic law, as the "supreme Law of the Land," in its original, true and always-controlling meaning: that is, in keeping with the intent with which the original instrument, and later each of its amendments, was framed and adopted. This point will be discussed more fully later. (The Appendix to this study-guide presents some excerpts from *The Federalist* pertinent to this topic.)

To understand the message of *The Federalist* is to understand, in its essential aspects, the traditional American philosophy and system of constitutionally limited government, of Man-over-Government through Rule-by-Law on the basis of the Constitution. This is why

155

this unique volume is of enduring and inestimable value, of supreme importance, to all Americans of all generations—critically so with regard to the present generation's need of the knowledge required for the adequate and sound discharge of the daily duties of self-governing in keeping with the duty aspect of Individual Liberty-Responsibility.

(The text of *The Federalist* is available in bookshops in various editions including some in paperback form; but only those are dependable which reproduce the exact and complete text of the original essays as published initially in newspapers, or in book form in 1788 under Hamilton's supervision, and without any change by the editor unless clearly and expressly brought to the reader's attention in each and every instance. Any editor's comments merit cautious scrutiny.)

The foregoing indicates some of the main sources studied by the present author during his extensive research over many years in the numerous, authoritative writings of the period 1776-1787 pertinent to full understanding of the background and meaning of the Declaration of Independence and of the Constitution, including especially the voluminous writings of a number of the leading signers of these documents; also writings of many leaders of American political thought in the more extended period from 1750 to 1800. The records of the Framing Convention and of the State Ratifying Conventions in 1787-1788 are authoritative and invaluable sources in this connection.

Because of the importance of economic liberty—the economic aspect of the indivisible whole of Individual Liberty—it is noteworthy that two writings in the field of economics, of political economy, were looked upon with great respect and special favor by the generation of those who signed the Declaration of Independence and the Constitution. One was Adam Smith's famous *Wealth of Nations,* first published on March 9, 1776. He was professor of Moral Philosophy at the University of Glasgow. The other was Jean-Baptiste Say's less well-known volume, *A Treatise on Political Economy,* first published in Paris in 1803. It was so popular in America that seven American editions, English translation, had been published by 1867. (Smith's book is readily available to the American people in bookshops, for example in the Modern Library edition.) Jefferson wrote of Smith's book that: "In political economy I think Smith's *Wealth of Nations* the best book extant . . ." (Letter to T. M. Randolph, 1790; title not italicized in the original.) On another occasion, after mentioning various writings, he wrote (letter to John Norvell, 1807) that:

"If your views of political inquiry go further, to the subjects of money & commerce, Smith's *Wealth of Nations* is the best book to be read, unless Say's *Political Economy* can be had, which treats the same subject on the same principles, but in a shorter compass & more lucid manner."

(Titles not italicized in the original. Several editions of Say's book are available in the Library of Congress. Full title of Smith's book is, *An Inquiry Into the Nature and Causes of the Wealth of Nations*.)

The Federalist is especially enlightening with regard to a topic about which there is widespread confusion, now to be discussed. The volume needs, however, to be considered carefully in this regard in all of its pertinent parts—not merely this or that part separately—for full comprehension. This is true partly because each of the various essays (of newspaper-article length) which refers to the topic could often note only some particular aspect due to the need of brevity; also they were addressed to a public far better informed in this regard than is today's generation, therefore much knowledge could be assumed.

An Important Distinction:
Democracy versus Republic

It is important to keep in mind the difference between a Democracy and a Republic, as dissimilar *forms* of government. Understanding the difference is essential to comprehension of the fundamentals involved. It should be noted, in passing, that use of the word Democracy as meaning merely the popular *type* of government—that is, featuring genuinely free elections by the people periodically—is not helpful in discussing, as here, the difference between alternative and dissimilar *forms* of popular government: a Democracy versus a Republic. This double meaning of Democracy—a popular-*type* government in general, as well as a specific *form* of popular government—needs to be made clear in any discussion, or writing, regarding this subject, for the sake of sound understanding.

These two *forms* of government: Democracy and Republic, are not only dissimilar but antithetical, reflecting the sharp contrast between (a) The Majority Unlimited, in a Democracy, lacking any legal safeguard of the rights of The Individual and The Minority, and (b) The Majority Limited, in a Republic under a written Constitution safeguarding the rights of The Individual and The Minority; as we shall now see.

157

A Democracy

The chief characteristic and distinguishing feature of a Democracy is: Rule by Omnipotent Majority. In a Democracy, The Individual, and any group of Individuals composing any Minority, have no protection against the unlimited power of The Majority. It is a case of Majority-over-Man.

This is true whether it be a Direct Democracy, or a Representative Democracy. In the direct type, applicable only to a small number of people as in the little city-states of ancient Greece, or in a New England town-meeting, all of the electorate assemble to debate and decide all governmental questions, and all decisions are reached by a majority vote (of at least half-plus-one). Decisions of The Majority in a New England town-meeting are, of course, subject to the Constitutions of the State and of the United States which protect The Individual's rights; so, in this case, The Majority is not omnipotent and such a town-meeting is, therefore, not an example of a true Direct Democracy. Under a Representative Democracy like Britain's parliamentary form of government, the people elect representatives to the national legislature—the elective body there being the House of Commons—and it functions by a similar vote of at least half-plus-one in making all legislative decisions.

In both the Direct type and the Representative type of Democracy, The Majority's power is absolute and unlimited; its decisions are unappealable under the legal system established to give effect to this form of government. This opens the door to unlimited Tyranny-by-Majority. This was what The Framers of the United States Constitution meant in 1787, in debates in the Federal (framing) Convention, when they condemned the "excesses of democracy" and abuses under any Democracy of the unalienable rights of The Individual by The Majority. Examples were provided in the immediate post-1776 years by the legislatures of some of the States. In reaction against earlier royal tyranny, which had been exercised through oppressions by royal governors and judges, little real authority was allowed the governors and judges of the new State governments, while the legislatures acted as if they were virtually omnipotent. There were no effective State Constitutions to limit the legislatures because most State governments were operating under mere Acts of their respective legislatures which were mislabelled "Constitutions." Neither the governors nor the courts of the offending States were able to exercise any substantial and effective restraining influence upon the legislatures in defense of The Individual's unalienable rights, when violated by legislative infringements. (Connecticut and Rhode Island continued under their old Charters for many years.) It was not until 1780 that the first genuine Constitution, creating the world's first genuine Republic through constitutionally limited government, was adopted by Massachusetts—next New Hampshire in 1784, other States later.

It was in this connection that Jefferson, in his "Notes On The State of Virginia" written in 1781-1782, protested against such excesses by the Virginia Legislature in the years following the Declaration of Independence, saying: "An *elective despotism* was not the government we fought for . . ." (Emphasis Jefferson's.) He also denounced the despotic concentration of power in the Virginia Legislature, under the so-called "Constitution"—in reality a mere Act of that body:

> "All the powers of government, legislative, executive, and judiciary, result to the legislative body. The concentrating these in the same hands is precisely the definition of despotic government. It will be no alleviation that these powers will be exercised by a plurality of hands, and not by a single one. 173 despots would surely be as oppressive as one. Let those who doubt it turn their eyes on the republic of Venice."

This topic—the danger to the people's liberties due to the turbulence of democracies and an omnipotent, legislative majority—is discussed in *The Federalist,* for example in numbers 10 and 48 by Madison (in the latter noting Jefferson's above-quoted comments).

The Framing Convention's records prove that by decrying the "excesses of democracy" The Framers were, of course, not opposing a popular *type* of government for the United States; their whole aim and effort was to create a sound system of this type. To contend to the contrary is to falsify history. Such a falsification not only maligns the high purpose and good character of The Framers but belittles the spirit of the truly Free Man in America—the people at large of that period—who happily accepted and lived with gratification under the Constitution as their own fundamental law and under the Republic which it created, especially because they felt confident for the first time of the security of their liberties thereby protected against abuse by all possible violators, including The Majority momentarily in control of government. The truth is that The Framers, by their protests against the "excesses of democracy," were merely making clear their sound reasons for preferring a Republic as the proper *form* of government. They well knew, in the light of history, that nothing but a Republic can provide the best safeguards—in truth in the long run the only effective safeguards (if enforced in practice)—for the people's liberties which are inescapably victimized by Democracy's *form* and system of unlimited Government-over-Man featuring The Majority Omnipotent. They also knew that the American people would not consent to any form of government but that of a Republic. It is of special interest to note that Jefferson, who had been in Paris as the American Minister for several years, wrote Madison from there in March 1789 that:

> "The tyranny of the legislatures is the most formidable dread at present, and will be for long years. That of the executive will come in it's turn, but it will be at a remote period."

(Text per original.) Somewhat earlier, Madison had written Jefferson about violation of the Bill of Rights by State legislatures, stating:

> "Repeated violations of those parchment barriers have been committed by overbearing majorities in every State. In Virginia I have seen the bill of rights violated in every instance where it has been opposed to a popular current."

It is correct to say that in any Democracy—either a Direct or a Representative type—as a *form* of government, there can be no legal system which protects The Individual or The Minority (any or all minorities) against unlimited tyranny by The Majority. The undependable sense of self-restraint of the persons making up The Majority at any particular time offers, of course, no protection whatever. Such a *form* of government is characterized by The Majority Omnipotent and Unlimited. This is true, for example, of the Representative Democracy of Great Britain; because unlimited governmental power is possessed by the House of Commons, as noted earlier; it even has the power to abolish the House of Lords, under an Act of Parliament of 1949—indeed, it has power to abolish anything and everything governmental in Great Britain.

For a period some centuries ago, some English judges did argue that their decisions could restrain Parliament; but this theory had to be abandoned because it was found to be untenable in the light of sound political theory and governmental realities in a Representative Democracy. Under this *form* of government, neither the courts nor any other part of the government can effectively challenge, much less block, any action by The Majority in the legislative body, no matter how arbitrary, tyrannous, or totalitarian they might become in practice. The parliamentary system of Great Britain is a perfect example of Representative Democracy and of the potential tyranny inherent in its system of Unlimited Rule by Omnipotent Majority. This pertains only to the potential, to the theory, involved; governmental practices there are irrelevant to this discussion.

Madison's observations in *The Federalist* number 10 are noteworthy at this point because they highlight a grave error made through the centuries regarding Democracy as a *form* of government. He commented as follows:

"Theoretic politicians, who have patronized this species of government, have erroneously supposed, that by reducing mankind to a perfect equality in their political rights, they would, at the same time, be perfectly equalized and assimilated in their possessions, their opinions, and their passions."

Democracy, as a *form* of government, is utterly repugnant to—is the very antithesis of—the traditional American system: that of a Republic, and its underlying philosophy, as expressed in essence in the Declaration of Independence with primary emphasis upon the people's forming their government so as to permit them to possess only "just powers" (limited powers) in order to make and keep secure the God-given, unalienable rights of each and every Individual and therefore of all groups of Individuals.

A Republic

A Republic, on the other hand, has a very different purpose and an entirely different *form*, or system, of government. Its purpose is to control The Majority strictly, as well as all others among the people, primarily to protect The Individual's God-given, unalienable rights and therefore for the protection of the rights of The Minority, of all minorities, and the liberties of the people in general. The definition of a Republic is: a constitutionally limited government of the representative type, created by a written Constitution—adopted by the people and changeable (from its original meaning) by them only by its amendment—with its powers divided between three separate Branches: Executive, Legislative and Judicial. Here the term "the people" means, of course, the electorate.

The people adopt a Constitution as their fundamental law by utilizing a Constitutional Convention—especially chosen by them for this express and sole purpose—to frame it for consideration and approval by them either directly or by their representatives in a Ratifying Convention, similarly chosen. Such a Constitutional Convention, for either framing or ratification, is one of America's great contributions, if not her greatest contribution, to the mechanics of government—of self-government through constitutionally limited government, comparable in importance to America's greatest contribution to the science of government: the formation and adoption by the sovereign people of a written Constitution as the basis for self-government. One of the earliest, if not the first, specific discussions of this new American development (a Constitutional Convention) in the historical records is an entry in June 1775 in John Adams' "Autobiography" commenting on the framing by a convention and ratification by the people as follows:

"By conventions of representatives, freely, fairly, and proportionably chosen . . . the convention may send out their project of a constitution, to the people in their several towns, counties, or districts, and the people may make the acceptance of it their own act."

Yet the first proposal in 1778 of a Constitution for Massachusetts was rejected for the reason, in part, as stated in the "Essex Result" (the result, or report, of the Convention of towns of Essex County), that it had been framed and proposed not by a specially chosen convention but by members of the legislature who were involved in general legislative duties, including those pertaining to the conduct of the war.

The first genuine and soundly founded Republic in all history was the one created by the first genuine Constitution, which was adopted by the people of Massachusetts in 1780 after being framed for their consideration by a specially chosen Constitutional Convention. (As previously noted, the so-called "Constitutions" adopted by some States in 1776 were mere Acts of Legislatures, not genuine Constitutions.) That Constitutional Convention of Massachusetts was the first successful one ever held in the world; although New Hampshire had earlier held one unsuccessfully—it took several years and several successive conventions to produce the New Hampshire Constitution of 1784. Next, in 1787-1788, the United States Constitution was framed by the Federal Convention for the people's consideration and then ratified by the people of the several States through a Ratifying Convention in each State specially chosen by them for this sole purpose. Thereafter the other States gradually followed in general the Massachusetts pattern of Constitution-making in adopting genuine Constitutions; but there was a delay of a number of years in this regard as to some of them, several decades as to a few.

This system of Constitution-making, for the purpose of establishing constitutionally limited government, is designed to put into practice the principle of the Declaration of Independence: that the people form their governments and grant to them only "just powers," limited powers, in order primarily to secure (to make and keep secure) their God-given, unalienable rights. The American philosophy and system of government thus bar equally the "snob-rule" of a governing Elite and the "mob-rule" of an Omnipotent Majority. This is designed, above all else, to preclude the existence in America of any governmental power capable of being misused so as to violate The Individual's rights—to endanger the people's liberties.

With regard to the republican form of government (that of a republic), Madison made an observation in *The Federalist* (no. 55) which merits quoting here—as follows·

> "As there is a degree of depravity in mankind which requires a certain degree of circumspection and distrust: So there are other qualities in human nature, which justify a certain portion of esteem and confidence. *Republican government* [that of a Republic] *presupposes the existence of these qualities in a higher degree than any other form.* Were the pictures which have been drawn by the political jealousy of some among us, faithful likenesses of the human character, the inference would be that there is not sufficient virtue among men for self government; and that nothing less than the chains of despotism can restrain them from destroying and devouring one another." (Emphasis added.)

It is noteworthy here that the above discussion, though brief, is sufficient to indicate the reasons why the label "Republic" has been misapplied in other countries to other and different forms of government throughout history. It has been greatly misunderstood and widely misused—for example as long ago as the time of Plato, when he wrote his celebrated volume, *The Republic;* in which he did not discuss anything governmental even remotely resembling—having the essential characteristics of—a genuine Republic. Frequent reference is to be found, in writings of the period of the framing of the Constitution for instance, to "the ancient republics," but in any such connection the term was used loosely—by way of contrast to a monarchy or to a Direct Democracy—often using the term in the sense merely of a system of Rule-by-Law featuring Representative government; as indicated, for example, by John Adams in his "Thoughts on Government" and by Madison in *The Federalist* numbers 10 and 39. But this is an incomplete definition because it can include a Representative Democracy, lacking a written Constitution limiting The Majority.

The Planning in 1776-1788
That the New Government Be a Republic

The creation of the new, central government by the Constitution in 1787-1788 as a genuine Republic was in fulfillment of public demand for precisely such a government, then designated as such. One of the most interesting pronouncements regarding this topic before the Declaration of Independence was in the "Instructions of the Inhabitants of Malden, Massachusetts to their Representatives in Congress" on May 27, 1776, as follows:

> "For these reasons, as well as many others which might be produced, we are confirmed in the opinion, that the present age will be deficient in their duty to God, their posterity and themselves, if they do not establish an American republic. This is the only form of government which we wish to see established; for we can never be willingly subject to any other King than he who, being possessed of infinite wisdom, goodness and rectitude, is alone fit to possess unlimited power . . . if they [the Continental Congress] should declare America to be a free and independent republic, your constituents would support and defend the measure, to the last drop of their blood, and the last farthing of their treasure."

The King referred to here is, of course, Man's Creator: God. The Malden resolution's prescription of a Republic for America was matched by other substantially similar declarations in that period—for instance that reported in the previously-mentioned "Essex Result" (report of the 1778 Convention of the towns of Essex County, Massachusetts) stating that: "A republican form [of government] is the only one consonant to the feelings of the generous and brave Americans." This was in rejecting this State's first proposed Constitution.

On July 1, 1776, John Adams—on the eve of the Declaration—in a letter to Archibald Bullock, hailed the new prospect in these words: "May Heaven prosper the new-born republic . . ." Realizing that the Articles of Confederation did not and could not satisfy the need, or provide, for a Republic, Hamilton wrote on July 4, 1782 ("The Continentalist," number 6), that: "There is something noble and magnificent in the perspective of a great Federal Republic, closely linked in the pursuit of a common interest, tranquil and prosperous at home, respectable abroad . . ." In the Framing Convention on June 1, 1787, James Wilson asserted that America's manners were "so republican, that nothing but a great confederated Republic would do for it." He commented further on this topic in the Convention: "A confederated republic joins the happiest kind of Government with the most certain security to liberty." He also used the same term, or one

164

comparable such as "Federal Republic," to describe the form of the new government in several instances during his remarks in the debates in the Pennsylvania Ratifying Convention. Using the term "republican government" to refer to the form of a Republic, Hamilton stated in the New York Ratifying Convention: "We all, with equal sincerity, profess to be anxious for the establishment of a republican government, on a safe and solid basis. It is the object of the wishes of every honest man in the United States . . ." In *The Federalist* number 39, Madison—referring to the proposed central government as "strictly republican" (meaning a Republic)—stated:

"It is evident that no other form would be reconcileable with the genius of the people of America; with the fundamental principles of the revolution; or with that honorable determination, which animates every votary of freedom, to rest all our political experiments on the capacity of mankind for self-government."

He also used the terms "republican form" (no. 37) and "a compound republic," "federal republic" and "extended republic" (no. 51).

These examples sufficiently illustrate the point that The Founders and other leaders, as well as many other thoughtful people in that day —such as the inhabitants of Malden and of Essex County mentioned above—well understood the nature of a Republic and were determined that the United States government be a Republic, such as the central government created later by the United States Constitution. (Note also the 1776 Pittsfield Resolution, page 18, *ante*.)

The Federated System of Republics in America

The Federal government is a Republic and this form of government is guaranteed to each of the States, under the Constitution (Article IV, Section 4). This Republic (the central Republic) is, however, different in a most important respect from the State Republics. To lose sight of this fact, of this difference between them, is to overlook the deep significance of America's federated system—a federation of Republics featuring decentralized power. (See also pages 45, 55, *ante*).

The principal difference, for present purposes, is as to quantity of power. The central Republic is a delegated-power government which possesses only the comparatively few and limited powers granted to it by the people as enumerated in the United States Constitution, as amended. These include chiefly the powers concerned with "war, peace, negociation, and foreign commerce" (quoting *The Federalist*,

165

number 45 by Madison). Each State Republic is a full-power government which possesses the vastly varied powers needed to administer intra-State affairs—"all the objects, which, in the ordinary course of affairs, concern the lives, liberties, and properties of the people; and the internal order, improvement and prosperity of the State" (again quoting *The Federalist* number 45). The full-power government of each State is, nevertheless, subject to the State Constitution as well as to the United States Constitution's grant of power to the Federal government and its limitations which are expressly specified as applying to the State governments. A State government, therefore, does not possess the unlimited power of legal sovereignty—that is, total power over all persons and things within its jurisdiction. The central and the State Republics are constitutionally limited governments, in keeping with the American formula: Limited for Liberty.

Governments of such limited-power character as these Republics are to be distinguished from the type possessing sovereign power, unlimited or total power as mentioned above, such as Great Britain's Representative Democracy, previously discussed. This clear and precise definition of the term "sovereign power" is different from, and preferable to, the more general and loose use of the word "sovereign" as meaning merely a government exercising the usual powers of self-government, and of declaring war and peace, without outside control. Under the American philosophy and system, the people alone possess *political* sovereignty and as the creators of their tools—the Federal and State governments—they do not permit any of these governments to possess the total powers of *legal* sovereignty. This political sovereignty of the people, moreover, is limited by the traditional American philosophy in favor of protection of The Individual's God-given, unalienable rights. As Supreme Court Justice James Wilson, one of The Framers, stated in his separate opinion in the 1793 *Chisholm* case, in discussing at length the concept of sovereignty in relation to the American philosophy and system of constitutionally limited government, they bar from the American governmental scene every pretense of sovereign power governmentally (emphasis per original):

"To the Constitution of the *United States* the term SOVEREIGN, is totally unknown. There is but one place where it could have been used with propriety. But, even in that place it would not, perhaps, have comported with the delicacy of those, who *ordained* and *established* the Constitution. They *might* have announced themselves "SOVEREIGN" people of the *United States:* But serenely conscious of the *fact,* they avoided the *ostentatious declaration.*"

Here he referred to two entirely different things: *legal* sovereignty of government—entirely lacking in the limited-power government of the United States—and *political* sovereignty of the people. The legislative body (the General Court) of Massachusetts, in its Proclamation of January 23, 1776, also meant *legal* power (legal sovereignty) of government in contrast to *political* power (political sovereignty) of the people, in stating (and in effect defining "sovereign power"):

"It is a maxim that in every government, there must exist, somewhere, a supreme, sovereign, absolute, and uncontrolable power; but this power resides always in the body of the people; and it never was, or can be delegated to one man, or a few; the great Creator has never given to men a right to vest others with authority over them, unlimited either in duration or degree."

To repeat, no government in the United States—least of all the limited-power, delegated-power, central government—possesses *legal* power of sovereignty: sovereign power. (See also page 132, *ante.*)

The difference between the Federal government's power and that of the government of each of the States is more easily understood in the light of the situation existing in 1787-1788 when the Constitution was being framed and ratified, in order to bring into existence the Federal government. At that time, the original thirteen States were already in existence. They ante-dated the creation of the Federal government by the Constitution, which supplanted the Articles of Confederation by consent of the people expressed through the State Ratifying Conventions. Under those Articles, there had been no central government with any power over the individual citizen or over the State governments. The Confederation was a mere treaty arrangement between the independent governments of the several States—by approval of their legislatures only and not by any direct authorization by the people of each State. The Confederation had no Executive Department and no Judicial Department—nothing but a legislative body, the Congress, which was completely powerless and could only request the States to provide money for it, or to do other things. The Confederation was, in truth, not a real government; and the State governments freely flouted with impunity the Articles of Confederation whenever this suited the pleasure of any of them. By 1787, the collapse of any pretense that the Confederation Congress possessed any governmental power, or authority, or any effectiveness governmentally, was complete—a topic to be discussed in detail in Part III.

Each of the State governments was, therefore, actually exercising

167

without any check virtually full governmental power whenever, and to the extent that, it chose so to do by the time the proposed, new Constitution, as framed in 1787, was submitted to the States for ratification. By action of the State Ratifying Conventions in 1787-1788, the sovereign people of each ratifying State exercised their indubitably reserved right and power by completely ignoring the Confederation and consenting to the creation of the new government—granting to it only that comparatively small part of the State government's powers which was specified in the Constitution as being so delegated. This is how the Federal government came into being as a delegated-power Republic possessed of only a few, limited powers as enumerated in the Constitution. All of the remaining powers of each State government and its people were reserved by them—as later expressly stated in the Ninth and Tenth Amendments, which merely confirmed the already-existing fact of this reservation, or retention, of power by them; subject only to the few limitations expressly specified in the Constitution as applying against the States. This is made clear beyond possibility of doubt by the writings of the leaders of that period, including especially various signers of the Constitution. The clearest and most comprehensive exposition is contained in *The Federalist,* particularly numbers 17, 32, 33 and 83 by Hamilton and numbers 39, 40, 41 and 45 by Madison. Before 1789, Americans were unified in spirit and philosophy but not as to governmental system.

The foregoing exposes the unsoundness of any claim that the central government possesses inherent powers amounting to sovereign power—or any power whatever other than, or in excess of the limits of, those enumerated in the Constitution, as amended, as being delegated to it expressly or related to such express powers by necessary implication. If such a claim were true, the Federal government would be a government not of definitely limited powers but of powers without definable limits. Nothing could be more antithetical to the truth, as proved by all pertinent historical records, notably *The Federalist.* Nothing could be more violative of the controlling intent of those who framed and adopted the Constitution in 1787-1788, in keeping with the principle of the Declaration of Independence—that government is permitted to possess only "just powers" (limited powers). Any use of the term "sovereign," or "sovereignty," in seeking to define the limited, delegated, power of the central government is unsound.

As the Supreme Court stated in 1936—for perhaps the thousandth time since 1789—(*Butler* case, at its page 63), each State possesses full governmental powers except such as the people, by the Constitution, either conferred on the Federal government, denied to the States, or reserved to themselves. This is true according to the original intent of those who framed and ratified the Constitution and, therefore, of the people for whom they acted; and this intent is forever controlling, subject only to the people's changing the Constitution, by amendment.

The Federal government thus started out with nothing like the full powers of one of the State governments, much less the unlimited power of a sovereign government. Under the Constitution, as amended, the Federal government still retains its original, strictly limited-power character—limited to the relatively few enumerated powers which have been delegated to it as discussed above. All of the amendments to the Constitution combined have not altered this fundamental of its character. On the contrary, each amendment which granted to this government any additional, specific and limited power only served to confirm its limited power character and the underlying principle of constitutionally limited government.

A main aspect of the federated system of republics, as contemplated by those who framed and adopted the Constitution, was the system of political checks by the States upon the central government—as explained, in part, by Madison in a 1787 letter to Jefferson (then in Paris), soon after the Framing Convention adjourned:

"In the American Constitution The general authority [of the central government] will be derived entirely from the subordinate authorities. The Senate will represent the States in their political capacity; the other House will represent the people of the States in their individual capac'y [capacity]. The former will be accountable to their constituents at moderate, the latter at short periods. The President also derives his appointment from the States, and is periodically accountable to them. This dependence of the General [central] on the local authorities, seems effectually to guard the latter against any dangerous encroachments of the former; whilst the latter, within their respective limits, will be continually sensible of the abridgement of their power, and be stimulated by ambition to resume the surrendered portion of it."

By the words "the subordinate authorities" Madison meant the States —through the people and the government of each of the separate States. The original system provided that the Senators from each State would be chosen by its Legislature (changed by the 17th Amendment); while the system of Electors of each of the States choosing the President is provided for in Section 1 of Article II, as modified by the 12th Amendment.

169

Representative Government—
a Chief Characteristic of a Republic

One of the chief characteristics of a government which constitutes a Republic is the representative feature, as noted earlier. America made an important contribution to the science of government with regard to development of this feature. Several of The Founders commented upon this great, forward step brought about in their day. Madison, for instance, observed in *The Federalist* number 14 that:

". . . even in modern Europe, to which we owe the great principle of representation, no example is seen of a government wholly popular, and founded at the same time wholly on that principle. If Europe has the merit of discovering this great mechanical power in government, by the simple agency of which, the will of the largest political body may be concentred, and its force directed to any object, which the public good requires: America can claim the merit of making the discovery the basis of unmixed and extensive republics."

Another member of the Framing Convention, James Wilson, commented on this topic while he was a member of the United States Supreme Court—in one of a series of lectures in 1790-1791, as follows:

"The extension of the theory and practice of representation through all the different departments of the state is another very important acquisition made, by the Americans, in the science of jurisprudence and government. To the ancients, this theory and practice seem to have been altogether unknown. To this moment, the representation of the people is not the sole principle of any government in Europe. . . . The American States enjoy the glory and the happiness of diffusing this vital principle [of representation] throughout all the different divisions and departments of the government."

In *The Federalist* number 56, Madison commented on the inadequacy of Great Britain's application of the principle of representation; and he discussed the general topic of representation in numbers 57 and 58 with particular reference to the prospective operation of the principle under the Constitution.

The role of the people's representatives—all sworn to support the Constitution faithfully—in relation to public opinion concerning particular issues to be voted upon, or decided, was the subject of comment by Madison and Hamilton which merits mention here. Speaking in the First Congress on August 15, 1789, Madison stated in part (as summarized in the report of his remarks):

"The right of freedom of speech is secured; the liberty of the press is expressly declared to be beyond the reach of this Government; the people may therefore publicly address their representatives, may privately advise them, or declare their sentiments by petition to the whole body; in all these ways they may communicate their will. If gentlemen mean to go further, and to say that the people have a right to instruct their representatives in such a sense as that the delegates are obliged to conform to those instructions, the declaration is not true. Suppose they instruct a representative, by his vote, to violate the Constitution; is he at liberty to obey such instructions? Suppose he is instructed to patronise certain measures, and from circumstances known to him, but not to his constituents, he is convinced that they will endanger the public good; is he obliged to sacrifice his own judgment to them?"

Madison's answer was unequivocally in the negative, as he had made clear in *The Federalist* (No. 63). Hamilton also made some observations to like effect in *The Federalist* (No. 71), stating in part with regard to the principles of a Republic, or republican principles:

"The republican principle demands, that the deliberate sense of the community should govern the conduct of those to whom they intrust the management of their affairs; but it does not require an unqualified complaisance to every sudden breeze of passion, or to every transient impulse which the people may receive from the arts of men, who flatter their prejudices to betray their interests. It is a just observation, that the people commonly *intend* the PUBLIC GOOD. This often applies to their very errors. But their good sense would despise the adulator, who should pretend that they always *reason right* about the *means* of promoting it. They know from experience, that they sometimes err; and the wonder is, that they so seldom err as they do; beset as they continually are by the wiles of parasites and sycophants by the snares of the ambitious, the avaricious, the desperate; by the artifices of men, who possess their confidence more than they deserve it, and of those who seek to possess, rather than to deserve it. When occasions present themselves in which the interests of the people are at variance with their inclinations, it is the duty of the persons whom they have appointed to be the guardians of those interests, to withstand the temporary delusion, in order to give them time and opportunity for more cool and sedate reflection. Instances might be cited, in which a conduct of this kind has saved the people from very fatal consequences of their own mistakes, and has procured lasting monuments of their gratitude to the men, who had had courage and magnanimity enough to serve them at the peril of their displeasure."

(Emphasis per original.) Hamilton made a further, pertinent comment in number 78, in connection with the duty of public servants to avoid any violation of the Constitution and not to yield to any popular opinion of the moment which would involve such violation —instead, adhering to the Constitution as it exists at the time until the people properly amend it to suit their purposes: ". . . and no presumption, or even knowledge of their sentiments, can warrant their representatives in a departure from it, prior to such an act." An exceptionally enlightening statement of the governing principle involved—especially as to the limited authority of the courts under the constitutional system, chief of all the Supreme Court as the highest judicial authority—was made by the Supreme Court in the 1905 *South Carolina* case, quoting the 1857 *Dred Scott* case. Its statement is presented in a special section of the Appendix and it is believed that the reader will find it most interesting and instructive, meriting careful study. (See pages 291-293, *post.*)

Such unvarying fidelity by all public servants, as public trustees, to the Constitution—construed according to the original intent with which it was framed and adopted (as to the initial instrument and each amendment)—is required by the oath of office and is the prime requisite for the successful and enduring functioning of constitutionally limited government and, therefore, for the security of the people's liberties and the Republic.

Limited Government
in Relation to
the "Bill of Rights" (or Prohibitions)

The "Bill of Rights" amendments (the first eight, specifying particular rights, supplemented by the Ninth and Tenth Amendments expressly reserving to the people and to the States their non-delegated rights and powers) are, in reality, express prohibitions against the Federal government additional to those previously stated in the body of the Constitution. They are therefore properly considered to be a partial and supplementary Bill of Prohibitions which particularize some of the previously created boundaries, or limits, of this government's powers. They may be likened to additional posts put in a fence to strengthen it—the fence built around the field of powers of the Federal government, to "fence in" this potential monster of power. As made clear in *The Federalist* (number 84, by Hamilton), this concept, of these "Bill of Rights" amendments being in truth a Bill of Prohibitions, is in keeping with the American philosophy of the people's deriving their rights from God and, in turn, creating governments with limited powers to keep these rights secure; which is diametrically opposed to the philosophy of king-granted rights and the related statement of such rights in a Bill of Rights. (See also no.

172

26.) A Bill of Rights is not only not necessary in connection with American Constitutions (Federal and State) but, in theory, is inconsistent with the American philosophy of limited government created by the people, because there can be no need of listing merely a few of the powers not granted. However, as those who advocated the addition of the "Bill of Rights" amendments had in mind, such an express statement of certain prohibitions against the Federal government—for instance, against violation of freedom of religion, of the Press, of speech, and so on—could serve as a focus of the people's attention and affection and a readily available rallying point for opposition by the people to any Federal infringements; and experience has proved this to be true. In other words, the addition of the "Bill of Rights" (Prohibitions), as amendments to the Constitution, can be useful even though not essential; as Madison, for example, explained in his letter to Jefferson (then in Paris) of October 17, 1788 and in his speech on this subject in the First Congress on June 8, 1789.

It is of particular interest to note that the main point made in the explanation, as presented by Hamilton in *The Federalist* number 84 as mentioned above, of the omission by The Framers from the Constitution of any Bill of Rights, was publicized soon after the Framing Convention adjourned by one of its members, James Wilson. This was in an address on October 6, 1787 in which he stated, in part, with regard to the people's creation of the central government, that:

". . . it would have been superfluous and absurd to have stipulated with a foederal body of our own creation, that we should enjoy those privileges, of which we are not divested either by the intention or the act, that has brought that body into existence."

(By "foederal body," Wilson meant the Federal government; and by "privileges" he meant the rights reserved to the people.) The fact that Wilson's explanation, which he soon thereafter stated more fully in the Pennsylvania Ratifying Convention, reflected the thinking of The Framers as a group, is further indicated by the fact that Washington referred to it with approval in a letter to Lafayette of April 28, 1788; just as Hamilton's similar explanation in *The Federalist* (number 84)—in which Madison silently acquiesced—reflected the thinking of the Framing Convention.

The "Bill of Rights" (first eight) amendments are thus seen to have created no new limits, or prohibitions, as to Federal power. Instead, they merely confirmed expressly and specifically a few of the multitude of prohibitions which had already been implied as a part

173

of the original Constitution's over-all prohibition through its denial of all powers other than the few it enumerated as being delegated to the Federal government. The Constitution's limits on the power of this government would have been the same if these amendments had never been adopted, as Hamilton and Wilson made clear.

It is most important to keep in mind, moreover, that these "Bill of Rights" amendments were intended by the framing Congress, and by the legislatures of the States which ratified them, to apply against the Federal government *only*. They were not intended to be applicable, or to operate, against the governments of the States; as all competent and reliable authorities have always agreed. This has continued to be true ever since, to the present writing, because the Constitution has never been amended so as to make any change in this regard— so as to make these amendments apply against the States. It is especially noteworthy that the Fourteenth Amendment was not intended by the Congress which framed it, or by the State legislatures which ratified it, to make any such change—to make the first eight amendments apply against the States. No such change was expressed in this Amendment's words or was intended by implication, as all competent and reliable authorities have always agreed. During the approximate century which has elapsed since the adoption of this Amendment, the Supreme Court has repeatedly and consistently so decided, as in the 1959 *Bartkus* case stating (page 124 of opinion):

> "We have held from the beginning and uniformly that the Due Process Clause of the Fourteenth Amendment does not apply to the States any of the provisions of the first eight amendments as such. *The relevant historical materials have been canvassed by this Court and by legal scholars. **These materials demonstrate conclusively that the Congress and the members of the legislatures of the ratifying States did not contemplate that the Fourteenth Amendment was a short-hand incorporation of the first eight amendments making them applicable as explicit restrictions upon the States."

(*Citing earlier cases. **Citing Fairman article mentioned below.) Two scholars here referred to are Stanford University's former Law Professors, Charles Fairman and Stanley Morrison, whose superb articles in the Stanford Law Review of December, 1949 are conclusive in their presentation and discussion of the exhaustively researched, historical evidence proving their proposition: that neither the framing Congress nor the ratifying legislatures of the States intended, or understood, that the words of the Fourteenth Amendment would make the first eight amendments applicable against the States.

The massive historical evidence resulting from the sound and thorough research by these two scholars, as presented especially in the Fairman article, abundantly supports the above-stated proposition and leaves no room for doubt that to pretend to the contrary is to falsify history, wittingly or unwittingly. Furthermore, it proves that the word "liberty" in the Fourteenth was intended merely to give all persons (notably colored) *in any State* the same Liberty then enjoyed by *that State's* white Majority (except as to voting, covered later by the Fifteenth); but not to give Federal judges any blank-check power, typical of Rule-by-Man, to make "Liberty" mean whatever their changing whims might dictate from time to time so as, for example, to permit them to make applicable against the States this or that part of the Bill of Rights. (This would be prohibited law-*making* by judges, as discussed later—pages 195-197, 199.) The intent was the same as to the Fourteenth's words "equal protection of the laws."

An additional and especially persuasive item of evidence, indeed conclusive in and of itself, as to the intent of the Congress which framed the first eight amendments—that it did not intend them to apply against the States—is this. When considering the first group of amendments, the House of Representatives debated a considerable number of proposed amendments, of which only twelve received final approval by both Senate and House and were referred to the States for ratification (of which only ten were ratified). One which did not receive such final approval was a proposed amendment—adopted by the House on August 17, 1789—designed expressly to prohibit the States from infringing freedom of speech and the press. This was already prohibited to the Federal government under a separate, proposed amendment (which finally became the First Amendment). The fact that the House at first considered it necessary to have the above-noted amendment expressly specifying the States, in order to be applicable against the States, is additional evidence that the ratified amendments were not intended to apply against the States.

The American philosophy and system of limited government was made express by the Constitution—as supplemented by the "Bill of Rights" Amendments, applying against the Federal government *only*.

Limited Government
In Relation to Some Fields of Power
Prohibited to the Federal Government

The Constitution's enumeration of powers granted to the Federal government is summed up by Madison in *The Federalist* number 45, as we have seen, as being: ". . . few and defined . . . will be exercised principally on external objects, as war, peace, negociation, and foreign commerce . . ." It is of interest to note briefly some principal examples of fields of power which are prohibited to the Federal government by the Constitution, as amended to the present writing.

In *The Federalist* number 17, Hamilton decried the idea that the new Federal government—to be created under the Constitution, then in process of ratification—would not respect the strict limits on its powers as prescribed in this fundamental law but would usurp the reserved powers of the States; as was being asserted by those who were extremely fearful of any central government with substantial powers and were arguing in favor of stricter and clearer limits on Federal power. Chief among these were Patrick Henry, Richard Henry Lee and Samuel Adams. Hamilton here mentioned commerce, finance, negotiation, and war as being the principal fields of power properly delegated to the Federal government but he expressly made it clear that agriculture is excluded. He classified agriculture as a field belonging to the reserved powers of the States—as one which could never properly be under the control of the central government:

> "The administration of private justice between the citizens of the same state, the supervision of agriculture and of other concerns of a similar nature, all those things in short which are proper to be provided for by local legislation, can never be desireable cares of a general jurisdiction."

By "general jurisdiction" he meant the Federal government. The field of agriculture was no doubt chosen by Hamilton for specific mention here because it was common knowledge—not only among those who had framed the Constitution but among all other leaders as well as the people at large—that nothing would have been considered more unarguably and absurdly false than any claim that the activities of people engaged in agriculture would be subject to Federal regulation or control, directly or indirectly, under the Constitution's wording as understood by The Framers and Adopters and everyone else.

Several other illustrations of prohibited power were provided by President Jefferson in his Second Inaugural Address. He discussed the constructive uses of any possible surplus revenues of the Federal government and mentioned some which he stated are outside of the scope of power of this government under the Constitution, expressly noting that an amendment of the fundamental law would be necessary before such use could be made of any surplus of tax monies:

". . . by a just repartition among the states, and a *corresponding amendment of the constitution*, be applied, *in time of peace*, to rivers, canals, roads, arts, manufactures, education, and other great objects within each state."

(Emphasis added, except "in time of peace" emphasized in the original.) In other words, Federal spending for these specified purposes was not authorized by the Constitution—these fields of activity being excluded from the scope of the Federal government's power under the Constitution; so an amendment would be necessary in order to give any such spending the necessary sanction through the properly expressed consent of the people. In his sixth annual Message to the Congress in 1806, Jefferson again discussed possible surplus revenues and their use in such fields requiring a constitutional amendment:

". . . application to the great purposes of the public education, roads, rivers, canals, and such other objects of public improvement as it may be thought proper to *add to the constitutional enumeration* of federal powers . . . I suppose *an amendment to the constitution, by consent of the States, necessary*, because the objects now recommended are *not among those enumerated in the constitution*, and to which it permits the public moneys to be applied."

(Emphasis added.) It is particularly interesting to note that Jefferson here soundly distinguished between using Federal *monies* to aid education (mentioning particularly a national institution of scientific learning)—which he stated is unauthorized, unless and until an amendment to the Constitution would be adopted authorizing it; and, on the other hand, aiding education by making *land-grants* from the colossal holdings of virgin and unsettled land already owned by the Federal government (by occupation, purchase or conquest from the Indians and foreign governments), which he stated the Congress "now have it in their power" so to use. Such aid to education by Federal land-grants was already customary; it had been commenced under the Confederation and was generally considered to be within the powers of the Federal government under the Constitution—but not so as to tax-monies in the Federal treasury.

Special emphasis is needed with regard to the basis of this distinction between such Federal *land*-grants and *money*-grants, as to constitutionality: the Federal government has the power to dispose of land and other property it owns (Art. IV, Sec. 3) and, furthermore, single-transaction land-grants could not possibly accomplish the unconstitutional objective of permitting it to obtain, in effect, any control over the recipients. On the other hand, the Constitution did not specify aid to education as one of the purposes for which the Federal

177

government (specifically the Congress) might tax and spend; and furthermore periodic, or regular, grants of money could not but have the practical effect of giving this government—perhaps indirectly, gradually and subtly but nevertheless inescapably—substantially controlling influence over the recipient institutions, or persons. This is due partly to the reason cited by Hamilton in *The Federalist* number 79: "In the general course of human nature, *a power over a man's subsistence amounts to a power over his will.*" (Emphasis Hamilton's.) In other words, "he who pays the piper calls the tune." Such control can even be effectively manifested negatively, by creating inhibitions on the part of the recipient of the subsidy or grant of funds, rather than through control affirmatively and outrightly. For example, those who would hope for a Federal grant in the future—such as a scholar, or a college—would be strongly inclined to refrain from criticism of this government regarding things which would otherwise be freely and vigorously condemned as unsound.

This is why Hamilton, as Secretary of the Treasury, carefully restricted his contention in 1791 so as to *exclude Federal control,* when he first argued in favor of the idea that the Taxing Clause gives the Federal government a separate and substantive power for the "application of money," within the limits of what would serve the general welfare. He also stated, in another document, that it would not ". . . imply a power to do whatever else should appear to Congress conducive to the general welfare" and continued:

"A power to appropriate money with this latitude, which is granted, too, in express terms, would not carry a power to do any other thing not authorized in the Constitution, either expressly or by fair implication."

(1791 "Opinion as to the Constitutionality of the Bank of the United States"; and 1791 Report on "Manufactures.") The Taxing Clause, using the words "general Welfare," (Art. I, Sec. 8) states: "The Congress shall have Power To lay and collect Taxes, Duties, Imposts and Excises, to pay the Debts and provide for the common Defence and general Welfare of the United States . . ."

Hamilton always denied that this clause gives Congress a general legislative authority—to legislate regarding, and so as to achieve, whatever Congress might consider to be for the common good. He never varied from his assertion in *The Federalist* number 83, regarding the plan of the Framing Convention expressed in the Constitution, with regard to such authority, as follows:

178

"The plan of the convention declares that the power of congress or in other words of the *national legislature,* shall extend to certain enumerated cases. This specification of particulars evidently excludes all pretension to a general legislative authority; because an affirmative grant of special powers would be absurd as well as useless, if a general authority was intended."

(Emphasis per original.) Hamilton never contended for—indeed, he evidently would have opposed strenuously—use of the Federal power to tax and spend so as in effect to give the Federal government indirectly any *control* over anything, or anybody, which is not directly and openly authorized by the Constitution and its amendments through enumeration of the powers granted to it by the people. He would undoubtedly have agreed with the distinction which Jefferson drew—in the above-mentioned addresses made after Hamilton's death—with regard to Federal aid to Education: that land-grants in aid of education are constitutional, partly because they could not possibly produce any degree of control over the recipient institutions due to such grants being a single-transaction measure as to each of the recipient institutions.

The opposite would be true as to Federal grants of monies periodically, because they could not possibly avoid producing the effect of substantial control over the recipient—however gradual, or subtle, or indirect, or negative (by creating inhibitions) and regardless of how arranged so as to conceal the element of control. In the 1936 *Butler* case, the Supreme Court truly stated (pages 70-71 of opinion): "The power to confer or withhold unlimited benefits is the power to coerce or destroy;" and it restated (pages 73-74) and applied the cardinal, constitutional principle that what the Constitution does not specifically empower the Federal government to do directly, so as to be able to exercise control, ". . . it may not indirectly accomplish those ends by taxing and spending to purchase compliance." In other words, a power granted by the Constitution may not be misused by this government so as in effect to enable it indirectly to exercise a power which has not been so granted and therefore has been prohibited to it. While in the related *Wickard* case (1942) the Court asserted [correctly, but *only* if it be true that the particular subsidy is authorized by the Constitution] that: "It is hardly lack of due process for the Government to regulate that which it subsidizes." (Page 131 of opinion; here "regulate" means control.) Judged by his writings, including his 1791 assertions noted above, Hamilton would have agreed and would have disapproved, as unconstitutional,

179

any and all subsidy-and-control schemes of the Federal government except such as might be directly and clearly authorized by the people, by a constitutional amendment, empowering this government so to control openly and directly the persons, or institutions, subsidized. Madison and all of the other Framers and Adopters of the Constitution also would have agreed—Jefferson, too.

The fields of power denied to the Federal government by the Constitution, according to both Hamilton and Jefferson—agriculture, education and so on, as noted above—could be multiplied by citing other writings by them and other Founders; but this is unnecessary for present purposes and would not take into account any additions to Federal power authorized by subsequent amendments. It is desirable, therefore, to quote here a modern writing which correctly reflects the views of The Framers and Adopters as to the initial instrument's exclusion of fields of power from Federal control and, in addition, takes into account all amendments to the present period.

A 1930 writing which fills this need is available; and, in addition, it is an excellent and concise discussion of the traditional American philosophy and system of government regarding especially the nature and importance of decentralization of power ("States Rights") as a mainstay of the security of the people's liberties. The Constitution has not been amended since 1930 to increase Federal power, so this writing in effect speaks as of today with regard to the extent of Federal powers; indeed, they have since been decreased by repeal of the 18th ("Prohibition") Amendment by adoption in 1933 of the 21st Amendment. This 1930 writing is cited for the further reason that it is couched in simple terms and presents only ideas which were then common knowledge and accepted truths among the American people—even among Youth with a normal high-school education for that period—as well as among the people through all generations from 1787 to 1930. The writing is cited not because it expressed anything new, or any original thinking of its author but, on the contrary, because it did *not* do so. Its special usefulness and value stem from the fact that it merely *re*-stated the traditional view as always understood and supported up to 1930 by all competent scholars and authorities—including the three Branches of the Federal government, especially the Supreme Court—as well as by leaders and the American people in general. This widespread understanding was such in 1930 that, if the valedictorian of a graduating class of a college, or even of a high school, had then made this address as the one usual on such an occasion, the audience would justly have applauded on the ground that there was nothing in it but long-accepted truths so well known that it merely evidenced the young orator's being soundly and reasonably well-informed regarding the elementary simplicities of the traditional American philosophy and system of constitutionally limited and decentralized power and its fundamental importance to the safety of the American people's God-given, unalienable rights.

This writing referred to is the March 2, 1930 "States Rights" address of Governor Franklin D. Roosevelt of New York—the full text of which, for the foregoing reasons, is set forth in the Appendix to this study-guide. This Address—made as an appeal to the American people for support of his plan to be elected President and present-ing some of the basic principles which, he impliedly assured them, he would if elected faithfully support—was in criticism of any con-centration of power in Washington in violation of the Constitution's limits on Federal power.

The entire address merits careful study for the reasons previously noted; but, at this point in the present discussion of fields of power prohibited to the Federal government by the Constitution as amended, the following short quotation will suffice:

> "As a matter of fact and law, the governing rights of the States are all of those which have not been surrendered to the National Government by the Constitution or its amendments. Wisely or unwisely, people know that under the Eighteenth Amendment Congress has been given the right to legislate on this particular subject, but this is not the case in the matter of a great number of other vital problems of government, such as the conduct of *public utilities,* of *banks,* of *insurance,* of *business,* of *agriculture,* of *educa-tion,* of *social welfare* and of a dozen other important features. In these, Washington must not be encouraged to interfere."

(Emphasis added.) To repeat, the Constitution has never been amended since 1930 so as to increase the Federal government's power. Since then, no amendment has granted it any power to control any of the prohibited fields of power specified by Hamilton, Jefferson and Roosevelt as mentioned above. It is of unusual interest to note that agriculture—expressly listed by Hamilton in 1787 and by Roosevelt as of 1930 as being among the fields of power prohibited to the Federal government by the Constitution—was the subject of the above-mentioned *Butler* case (1936). There the Supreme Court confirmed the fact of such prohibition, in deciding that the Federal law under consideration—seeking to subsidize and control agriculture

181

—violated the Constitution's limits on Federal power and therefore was null and void, judged by this instrument's original meaning which the Court correctly ruled is controlling unless and until the people change these limits by due amendment of this basic law.

It is a fundamental principle of the American philosophy that the people themselves, as well as their public servants who are sworn to support the Constitution faithfully, must respect the existing limits on the Federal government's power under the Constitution, as amended; which can be changed by the people only by its amendment. Referring to the amending process as a "solemn and authoritative act," Hamilton stated the principle (previously noted) in *The Federalist* number 78 as follows: "Until the people have by some solemn and authoritative act annulled or changed the established form, it is binding upon themselves collectively, as well as individually; and no presumption, or even knowledge of their sentiments, can warrant their representatives in a departure from it, prior to such an act." (Here "sentiments" refers to public opinion in favor of some measure not authorized by the Constitution.) The reason why this principle is so basically important was stressed in Washington's *Farewell Address* as follows:

"If in the opinion of the People, the distribution or modification of the Constitutional powers be in any particular wrong, let it be corrected by an amendment in the way which the Constitution designates. But let there be no change by usurpation; for though this, in one instance, may be the instrument of good, it is the customary weapon by which free governments are destroyed. The precedent must always greatly overbalance in permanent evil any partial or transient benefit which the use can at any time yield."

This highlights the tremendous importance of the American people's being always soundly informed with respect to the limits on the Federal government's power under the Constitution, as amended, in order to be able to perform adequately the duties inherent in Individual Liberty-Responsibility and thus make possible the enduring safety of their God-given, unalienable rights and Posterity's just heritage of Individual Liberty and its supporting system.

Limited Government
in Relation to
The Constitution's Treaty Clause
(a) Treaties

The Constitution is the "supreme Law of the Land." It is controlling as to all officials of the three Branches of the Federal government

—Executive, Legislative and Judicial—with regard to all of their pronouncements, actions, decisions, agreements and legislative Acts. Each of them is sworn, by oath of office, to support the Constitution *only*. To be valid, any treaty must be strictly in conformity to—free from any conflict with—the Constitution. A treaty is like a Federal law in this respect.

The Constitution is supreme over laws and treaties; it expressly states (Article VI, Section 2) that: "This Constitution, and the Laws of the United States which shall be made in Pursuance thereof; and all Treaties made, or which shall be made, under the Authority of the United States, shall be the supreme Law of the Land . . ." This means that any such Law (Act of Congress) which violates the Constitution is automatically made null and void to start with—*nullified by the Constitution itself*—and therefore cannot be a part of the "supreme Law of the Land." This is also true as to treaties.

The only reason for the special language used in Article VI regarding Treaties was to make it cover those made previously, under the Confederation (notably the Peace Treaty with Great Britain terminating the Revolutionary War), as well as future Treaties. Madison's official record of the Framing Convention's proceedings states that, upon his motion, there was inserted in the Treaty Clause the words "or which shall be made" following the words "all treaties made." Then his record states:

"This insertion was meant to obviate all doubt concerning the force of treaties pre-existing, by making the words 'all treaties made' to refer to them, as the words inserted would refer to future treaties."

(In the original, the word pre-existing appears as prëexisting.) The words of Article VI: "under the Authority of the United States" were used regarding Treaties—instead of the words: "in Pursuance thereof" (referring to the Constitution) with regard to laws to be enacted thereafter by Congress—because the prior Treaties could not, of course, be said to have been entered into pursuant to the Constitution because they had been made before the Constitution was framed. The term "the United States" was intended to embrace both the new government and the one existing under the Articles of Confederation which had made the prior Treaties. The intent was that any and every agreement entered into by the new government, including new Treaties, should be pursuant—in conformity—to the Constitution because this government would possess no authority except that granted to it under this instrument. The fact that the above-mentioned, special language was used merely so as to embrace both past and future Treaties was noted, for example, in the 1825 book, *A View of the Constitution of the United States of America* (pages 59-60), written by William Rawle, a lawyer of Philadelphia who was prominent during President Washington's Administration and was one of his appointees to Federal office.

In the "Camillus" essays—in defense of the Jay Treaty with Great Britain—published by Hamilton and written mostly by him (some by Rufus King, one of The Framers), Hamilton stated in number 37 that the Constitution itself gives ". . . the force of law to treaties, making them equal with the acts of Congress, the supreme law of the land, . . ." This necessarily means they are valid only if not in conflict with the Constitution, as Article VI expressly provides concerning Federal laws. This limitation on these laws (Acts of Congress) is discussed by Hamilton in *The Federalist*, number 33, as follows:

> "Hence we perceive that the clause which declares the supremacy of the laws of the union, . . . only declares a truth, which flows immediately and necessarily from the institution of a federal government. It will not, I presume, have escaped observation, that it *expressly* confines this supremacy to laws made *pursuant to the constitution;* which I mention merely as an instance of caution in the convention; since that limitation would have been to be understood, though it had not been expressed."

(Emphasis per original.) This is equally applicable to treaties.

In the Virginia Ratifying Convention, Patrick Henry voiced the fears of many when he took the position that the language of the Treaty Clause was not sufficiently clear in limiting Federal power with regard to treaties. Speaking in the light of his intimate knowledge of the intent of the Framing Convention, Madison refuted this contention, stating:

> "Does it follow, because this power is given to Congress, that it is absolute and unlimited? I do not conceive that power is given to the President and Senate to dismember the empire [Union], or to alienate any great, essential right. I do not think the whole legislative authority have this power. The exercise of the power must be consistent with the object of the delegation . . . The object of treaties is the regulation of intercourse with foreign nations, and is external."

The understanding of the Virginia Convention in this connection, in keeping with Madison's statement, was even more specifically expressed by member George Nicholas as follows: "They can, by this,

184

make no treaty which shall be repugnant to the spirit of the Constitution, or inconsistent with the delegated powers. The treaties they make must be under the authority of the United States, to be within their province." The question of the Treaty Clause being limited by the Constitution as a whole was discussed in the United States House of Representatives on April 6, 1796 concerning the Jay Treaty (with Great Britain), when the point was made by Madison and other members that the record of debates with regard to ratification in the Pennsylvania, Virginia and North Carolina Conventions in 1787-1788 had made it clear that the understanding was "that the Treaty-making power was a limited power" (limited by the Constitution as a whole).

An especially interesting piece of evidence supporting the conclusion that the Treaty Clause was intended and understood by the Framing and Ratifying Conventions not to authorize the President and Senate, by a treaty, either (a) to override the Constitution, in whole or in part, or (b) to make domestic law (as distinguished from governance of relations with foreign governments), was provided by a statement by Jefferson—presumably reflecting at the time the prevailing opinion among governmental leaders also and especially leaders in Congress—in his 1801 *A Manual of Parliamentary Practice.* It was written by him as Vice President, while serving as the presiding officer of the Senate. It was reprinted in many editions in the following generations, being incorporated in full in the "Manual" of the Senate and in the "Manual" of the House of Representatives (as to the part applicable to the particular body in each case). Use of his Manual to some extent continues at the present writing. In this guide, Jefferson stated with regard to the Treaty Clause and power:

> [Section 52.] "Treaties are legislative acts. A treaty is a law of the land. It differs from other laws only as it must have the consent of a foreign nation, being but a contract with respect to that nation . . . 2. By the general power to make treaties, the Constitution must have intended to comprehend only those objects which are usually regulated by treaty, and cannot be otherwise regulated. 3. *It must have meant to except out of these the rights reserved to the States;* for surely the President and Senate cannot do by treaty what the whole Government is interdicted from doing in any way."

(Emphasis added.) This brief review of even a small part of the pertinent, historical evidence is sufficient to make inescapable the conclusion that the Framing and Ratifying Conventions intended the Treaty Clause to be limited by the Constitution; that in order to be valid a treaty, like any Federal law (Act of Congress), must be in

185

strict conformity to the Constitution, as amended. The pertinent evidence supporting this proposition is so conclusive that not to accept it would mean (to use Jefferson's striking phraseology in another connection) that human reason must be surrendered as a vain and useless faculty, given to bewilder and not to guide us. The United States Supreme Court has repeatedly decided that the foregoing conclusion is correct, that the treaty-power under the Treaty Clause is limited by the Constitution as a whole; and the Court most recently confirmed this, upon full consideration, in the 1957 *Reid* case.

It merits repetition here, for emphasis, that—as observed earlier in this Part II—the Federal government was not intended by the Framing and Ratifying Conventions to be given under the Constitution any implied power of sovereignty, nor any power whatever other than as enumerated in this instrument. This applies, of course, to the Treaty Clause. Any pretense to the contrary violates historical truth. If such a pretense were sound, it would mean that the Federal government was meant to be a government not of definitely limited powers but, instead, of unlimited and indefinable powers; than which nothing could be more violative of the intent of the Framing and Ratifying Conventions.

(b) Executive Agreements

Executive Agreements with foreign governments made by the President alone are, at the minimum, as limited as treaties insofar as concerns the President's power to enter into them being limited by the Constitution; that is, any such agreement must be in strict conformity to the Constitution in order to be valid. The previously quoted statement by Hamilton, in *The Federalist* number 33, about the supremacy of the Constitution over any Federal law being implied, even if it had not been made express in the Constitution, is as applicable to Executive Agreements as it is to treaties. If they had had occasion to express themselves on the topic, The Framers and Adopters would unquestionably have stressed the strict limits under the Constitution upon any such power of the President alone, even more than with regard to treaties—as to which they required approval by the Senate. The grave danger inherent in allowing any single official, specifically the President, to have the sole power to make international agreements was discussed by Hamilton in *The Federalist* number 75. He stated, with regard to the power to make treaties: ". . . it would be utterly unsafe and improper to entrust that power to an elective magistrate of four years duration." After discussing in detail the weaknesses of human nature in government and the danger of excessive power to deal with foreign governments being given to one man occupying the Presidency, he continued:

> "The history of human conduct does not warrant that exalted opinion of human virtue which would make it wise in a nation to commit interests of so delicate and momentous a kind as those which concern its intercourse with the rest of the world to the sole disposal of a magistrate, created and circumstanced, as would be a president of the United States."

Hamilton further commented that, though it would be "imprudent to confide in him solely so important a trust," his being joined with the Senate in this regard provides reasonably adequate protection of the public interest. The danger involved was highlighted in a statement by Madison (in a letter to Jefferson, 1798) as follows:

> "The management of foreign relations appears to be the most susceptible of abuse of all the trusts committed to a Government, because they can be concealed or disclosed, or disclosed in such parts and at such times as will best suit particular views . . . Perhaps it is a universal truth that the loss of liberty at home is to be charged to provisions against danger, real or pretended, from abroad."

This makes clear the reason why Executive Agreements, entered into with foreign governments by the President alone, are not only potentially dangerous in highest degree but undoubtedly violate the limits imposed by the Constitution upon the power of the Federal government whenever this device (an Executive Agreement) is used to bring into being any international agreement of a type which traditionally would have been considered to require a treaty to be entered into by the President with the advice and consent of the Senate. Under this principle, only Executive Agreements as to very minor matters would be exempted and permitted to the President alone. The danger involved in any one-man power to make agreements with foreign governments is all the more apparent in the light of this truth stated in Washington's *Farewell Address* (emphasis per original):

> "Against the insidious wiles of foreign influence, (I conjure you to believe me fellow citizens) the jealousy of a free people ought to be *constantly* awake; since history and experience prove that foreign influence is one of the most baneful foes of Republican Government."

(Here "Republican" means that of a Republic.) For the President to resort to an Executive Agreement in order to evade the Constitution's limits on his power in international dealings constitutes usurpation of power and is as offensive from the standpoint of the American philosophy and system of constitutionally limited government as it is according to the principles of sound morality.

The foregoing discussion also makes clear the reasons why certain fallacious statements, which have sometimes been made by supposedly responsible sources, are utterly unsound. An example is the false pretense that a treaty completely and permanently binds the hands of Congress. The truth is that Congress has the power to revoke a treaty at any time, just as Congress has the power to annul one of its own enactments; because Federal laws and treaties are on a par in this respect. As the above-quoted statement by Jefferson notes, treaties are legislative acts; they are on a par with laws. Another fallacious statement is that a treaty "can override the Constitution;" which defies historical truth, as we have seen. A related and most preposterous allegation is that a treaty "can cut across the rights given the people by the constitutional Bill of Rights"—than which nothing could be further from the truth, partly for two reasons: the Constitution does not authorize any such treaty and, secondly, the people are, of course, given their rights by God and not by themselves through their own creation: the Constitution (including its Bill of Rights, or Bill of Prohibitions, Amendments). The quoted statement is farcical.

There is no limit to the madness which could be perpetrated by Federal officials in violation of the rights of their masters, the sovereign people, if there were any soundness in this monstrous doctrine—that the Treaty Clause gives these officials unlimited authority so to impose their Will, and even a system of tyrannous Government-over-Man, upon the people regardless of, indeed in defiance of, the Constitution as a whole. So to contend is to deal in nonsense.

(c) Foreign Aid

The Constitution (including its Treaty Clause) was designed to accomplish—as to limiting the powers of the Federal government—what is contemplated with regard to all governments created by the people as their instruments: primarily to make and keep secure their God-given, unalienable rights (and the supporting rights, notably the right to property) according to the Declaration of Independence. It is a violation of this fundamental law of the people for the Federal government to deprive the people of their property by taxation in order to donate to foreign governments, or peoples, the funds thus obtained, or things purchased with these funds—whether or not sanctioned ostensibly by a treaty; that is, except to the extent that this is authorized by the words "common Defence" in the Constitution's Taxing Clause: "provide for the common Defence and general Welfare of the United States." This means that any donation abroad of funds or things, military or any other kind, by the Federal government —in order to be authorized by the Constitution—must contribute substantially and directly to the "common Defence . . . of the United States," meaning the national defense: the actual, military, physical defense of the American homeland. Under the Constitution as amended, Congress and the President completely lack any power to act the benevolent role abroad with the American people's property —money or any other type. This is true as to all so-called "foreign aid"—whether military, economic or financial—however accomplished: by gift, or loan, or by any other device or method, and whether done openly, or by subterfuge. *Individuals may, of course, give such aid out of their own property (money) as they please.*

The words "general Welfare" in the Taxing Clause refer expressly to the welfare of the people "of the United States." This excludes the people of any foreign country. The fact that this provision does not give Congress a general legislative power, to provide even for the American people's general welfare in any way Congress sees fit, has been established earlier, citing as one reference *The Federalist* number 83 by Hamilton. The further fact that this clause grants no power, or authority, to Congress to provide for the welfare of the people of any foreign country—a self-evident truth: that is, one too obvious to need any supporting evidence—was discussed by Madison in the debates in the House of Representatives on January 10, 1794, concerning a proposal to grant funds for the relief of a group of citizens of France—refugees from the French possession, San Domingo—then being given asylum in Baltimore, Maryland, where they had recently arrived and were already being given relief locally. According to the report in a Philadelphia newspaper, Dunlap & Claypoole's American Daily Advertiser of January 14, 1794 (reporting the debate of January 10th), Madison expressed sympathy for the refugees and stated his hope that some way could be devised for their relief other than a grant of financial aid by Congress because, he stated, this would be beyond the authority of Congress under the Constitution. The newspaper's summary of his remarks is, in part:

". . . the government of the United States is a definite government, confined to specified objects—it is not like the state governments whose powers are more general. Charity is no part of the legislative duty of the [Federal] gov-

189

ernment; it would puzzle him to lay his finger on any part of the constitution which would authorise the government to interpose in this business . . . He concluded his remarks by saying, that tho' he was of opinion that the relief contemplated could not be granted in the way proposed . . ." [because in violation of the Constitution, yet a constitutional way might be found.]

His remarks as reported in another newspaper, The Philadelphia Gazette and Universal Daily Advertiser, of January 14, 1794, were used later as the basis for the official report in the *Annals* of Congress—due to lack of an official reporter in that period—and were to the same general effect, in part as follows:

"Mr. Madison . . . was afraid of establishing a dangerous precedent, which might hereafter be perverted to the countenance of purposes, very different from those of charity. He acknowledged, for his own part, that he could not undertake to lay his finger on that article in the Federal Constitution, which granted a right to Congress of expending, on objects of benevolence, the money of their constituents. And if once they broke the line laid down before them [in the Constitution], for the direction of their conduct, it was impossible to say, to what lengths they might go, or to what extremities this practice might be carried."

He further commented that the Congress was not like the British Parliament possessing unlimited power to tax and spend for any purpose it might please; then, according to the report, he continued: ". . . this house certainly did not possess an undefined authority correspondent with that of a British Parliament." The plight of the numerous refugees—including many women and children—was so severe, however, that intense sympathy was felt for them. One member, Nicholas, was so affected that he asserted he was willing to vote for the grant of relief, though unconstitutional, and then ask for forgiveness by his constituents for thus violating the Constitution; but the Constitution, and the oath of office to support it (faithfully and unvaryingly), permit no such usurpation of power and allow for no such transgression and forgiveness. Nor does morality, because the end does not justify the means. Note again the previously-quoted warning in Washington's *Farewell Address* regarding the evil of such a precedent and the fact that usurpation is the "customary weapon by which free governments are destroyed." (See page 182, *ante*.)

The question of constitutionality of expenditures under the Taxing Clause, for the common defense and general welfare, was discussed by the famous Justice Joseph Story—a long-time member of the United States Supreme Court (1811-1845)—in his celebrated *Com-*

mentaries on the Constitution of the United States (1833), where he stated in this connection (Section 919):

"A power to lay taxes for any purposes whatsoever is a general power; a power to lay taxes for certain specified purposes is a limited power. A power to lay taxes for the common defence and general welfare of the United States is not in common sense a general power. It is limited to those objects. It cannot constitutionally transcend them. If the defence proposed by a tax be not the common defence of the United States, if the welfare be not general, but special, or local, as contradistinguished from national, it is not within the scope of the constitution. If the tax be not proposed for the common defence, or general welfare, but for other objects, wholly extraneous, (as for instance, *for propagating Mahometanism among the Turks, or giving aids and subsidies to a foreign nation, to build palaces for its kings, or erect monuments to its heroes,) it would be wholly indefensible upon constitutional principles.* The power, then, is, under such circumstances, necessarily a qualified power." (Emphasis added.)

The purpose of constitutionally limiting government in America is defeated to the extent that Federal officials fail to respect invariably the limits imposed upon their power by the entire Constitution—including its subordinate (not independent) Treaty Clause—construed in keeping with the original and controlling intent of those who framed and adopted the initial instrument and later each amendment. Sometime support of the Constitution is the equivalent of no support, from the standpoint of this "supreme Law of the Land" as well as of the oath of office and of sound morality.

It merits emphasis that any violation of the Constitution so as to accomplish an unauthorized purpose—for example, granting relief to such foreign refugees being sheltered within the United States, or perhaps within their own country, or by way of aid to any foreign country in any form whatever which is not directly related to the actual military defense of the American homeland, as explained previously—can never alter in the least the constitutional situation with regard to the power granted to Congress. Such an act of usurpation, or even a great number of successive acts of usurpation, can never increase the power of Congress—can never change, or impair, or destroy, the limits on its power as prescribed by the sovereign people in the Constitution. The power of Congress, as so limited, remains unchanged unless and until increased by the people only by amendment of the Constitution. Any act of usurpation produces zero increase in power; and many acts of usurpation still produce zero increase. Many times zero equals zero.

191

No precedent, no quantity of precedents, by way of actions of government, can alter the Constitution. As Madison remarked in 1831 (letter to N. P. Trist), there was a fallacy prevalent "in confounding a question whether precedents could expound a Constitution, with a question whether they could alter a Const." (Madison's abbreviation.) He correctly concluded, of course, that such precedents could help to expound (clarify), but not to alter, this fundamental law.

Limited Government
in Relation to
the Role of the Supreme Court

The Judicial Branch of the Federal government—authorized by Article III of the Constitution—is a creation and an instrument of the sovereign, self-governing people. By their permission and grant of limited power to the Judiciary, this Branch is assigned the role, in principal part, of helping to enforce the Constitution's system of limited-power government through acting as a check—as intended under the constitutional system—upon the other two Branches to the end of keeping them within the prescribed limits of their power, respectively; while the judges themselves are, of course, obligated to keep strictly within the limits of their own power as fixed by the same system. The limited-power and limited-function character of the Federal courts, including the Supreme Court as the highest judicial authority, is in keeping with the basic purpose of all governments in America as defined in the Declaration of Independence: to exercise the "just powers" (limited powers) granted to them by their creator, the people, in order primarily to make and keep secure the people's God-given, unalienable rights.

The Constitution's limits on the power of government, including the limits on the power of the courts, are of real significance only to the extent that they are respected in practice. The limits on the power of the Federal courts, chief of all the Supreme Court, under the constitutional system, merit careful consideration in this discussion of limited government.

The Federalist is a rich source of knowledge in this regard. In the following comments, reference is made to some of its pertinent essays —notably numbers 78-83 devoted mainly to the subject of the Judiciary. It is believed that readers of this study-guide will find certain portions of that material of such great interest and practical value to the clarity of their thinking, which is of the gravest importance to enlightened and sound self-government in America, that it will be helpful if ready reference can be made to these selected portions of the original text; so they are presented in a special section in the Appendix (pages 271-286, *post*). Main additional references are the volumes reporting the debates in the Framing Convention of 1787 and in the State Ratifying Conventions in 1787-1788: *The Records of the Federal Convention of 1787,* four volumes edited by Max Farrand, and *The Debates in the Several State Conventions on the Adoption of the Federal Constitution,* etc., edited by Jonathan Elliot, in five volumes (fifth presenting debates in Framing Convention).

It merits stressing at this point that there is no mystery about the fundamentals of self-government under a written Constitution. Common sense is all that is needed to understand the subject in its essentials. As John Adams stated, with regard to the virtues of the forefathers in America before his day:

"They knew that government was a plain, simple, intelligible thing, founded in nature and reason, and quite comprehensible by common sense."

This applies to all aspects of constitutionally limited government, including the meaning of the Constitution which is readily understandable if considered with common sense and studied adequately. As Chief Justice John Marshall stated for the Supreme Court in the 1824 *Gibbons* case (page 188 of opinion):

"As men, whose intentions require no concealment, generally employ the words which most directly and aptly express the ideas they intend to convey the enlightened patriots who framed our constitution, and the people who adopted it, must be understood to have employed words in their natural sense, and to have intended what they have said."

During the ratification debates in 1787-1788, one of The Framers, Oliver Ellsworth, who later became Chief Justice of the United States, highlighted the common-sense wording of the Constitution, stating:

"It is an excellency of this Constitution that it is expressed with brevity, and in the plain, common language of mankind."

The common-sense approach applies to all aspects of constitutionally limited government including the limited role assigned, and the limited power granted, by the people to the Supreme Court as a part of the constitutional system.

Some essentials regarding this limited role and power of the Supreme Court will now be considered—*as understood and intended by those who framed and adopted the Constitution and created the con-*

193

stitutional system, according to their writings, notably *The Federalist,* as is clear when they are studied with requisite competence and intellectual integrity: free from warping bias stemming from any hostility to The Founders and their handiwork.

1. The Constitution is controlling, as the "supreme Law of the Land." Article VI makes it supreme over all laws (legislative Acts) —as well as over treaties, as we have seen—and requires all judges and other officials, Federal and State, to be "bound by Oath or Affirmation, to support this Constitution." It automatically makes null and void all governmental Acts (laws), decisions, orders, pronouncements, and actions in conflict with it—null and void from the time each one may occur. (See, for example, *The Federalist,* nos. 33 and 78 by Hamilton.) "Affirmation" is permitted for those whose religion forbids "swearing."

2. The original meaning is controlling, as determined by the intent of those who framed and adopted the Constitution in 1787-1788 and by those who framed and adopted each amendment on behalf of the sovereign people, who alone can change it as their fundamental law and only by amending it. This was commonly understood in the 1776-1787 period, as noted in *The Federalist* number 53 by Madison:

> "The important distinction so well understood in America between a constitution established by the people, and unalterable by the government; and a law established by the government, and alterable by the government, seems to have been little understood and less observed in any other country."

The government is powerless to change the Constitution; and this applies to the Judiciary, acting alone or in collaboration with the other Branches. A particularly impressive restatement by the Supreme Court—of the basic rule that "the original meaning is controlling"—in the 1905 *South Carolina* case, is presented in a special section of the Appendix (page 291, *post*).

3. The original meaning is ascertainable from the Constitution's own words—construed in the light of the intent of the framing and ratifying bodies with respect to the particular provision (of the original instrument, or any amendment) under consideration—as supplemented by all pertinent historical records which cannot change or be changed, just as that intent is unchangeable.

4. The strictly limited role of judges in "interpreting" the Constitution—the role as clearly defined under the constitutional system and well understood by all competent and reliable authorities ever since

194

1788—is to *ascertain, define and apply* this intent and meaning solely on the basis of its words and the above-mentioned historical records. That is, merely to clarify—not to *make*—the fundamental law (which the Constitution itself determines) as intended by those who framed and adopted it (per pars. 2 and 3 above). As explained particularly in *The Federalist* number 78 by Hamilton, in so doing judges are obligated to apply their honest Judgment to such ascertainment, definition and application; and not to indulge their Will, or whim, in disregard of the original intent and meaning mentioned above. As Hamilton there also emphasizes, in deciding cases thus involving principles of the Constitution, judges—chief of all those on the Supreme Court as the highest judicial authority—are obligated to respect precedent (to abide by prior decisions which have so ascertained, defined, and applied that unchangeable intent and meaning on the basis of those historical records). Therefore, they may not change their minds as and when they please concerning the meaning of this fundamental law, concerning the definition of these principles. Any such power so to change their minds could not but result in its belittlement, if not doom, as the intended source and basis of stability of limited government in America—as the reliable guide for the conduct of the people and the dependable bulwark of their liberties. In this connection, decisions by the Supreme Court must be made impartially, "according to the rules of the Constitution," as Madison asserted in *The Federalist* number 39. (See also number 81, by Hamilton.)

5. Interpreting, or construing, the provisions of the Constitution properly, in keeping with the foregoing traditional precepts—which is all that judges are empowered and authorized to do under the constitutional system—is entirely different, and must always be distinguished, from the role of judges in the entirely separate field of ordinary, day-to-day, law (called Common Law) which involves not the Constitution but *judge*-made rules pertaining to matters such as contracts, Wills, real estate transactions, and so on. Judges may, of course, change the legal rules which they themselves have power to make (separate and apart from the Constitution and legislative Acts); but they have no power to change either legislative Acts—which the enacting, legislative body alone may make and change—or the Constitution, which the people alone may make and change. This is elementary, and a controlling principle, in constitutional law—under the constitutional system—as intended by The Framers and Adopters.

The principle of *stare decisis* (meaning "adhere to prior decisions and do not disturb settled points") is the general rule even in the field of judge-made law (Common Law), because Law is designed primarily to provide a stable guide for the people's conduct of their affairs and not to be changed from day to day according to the whims of judges; which indicates the difference between the antithetical systems of Rule-by-Law and Rule-by-Man. If Justice requires, however, in a particular case in this field of judge-made law, the judge of course has power to disregard prior *judge*-made rules and to make a new rule to fit the facts of that case. This *stare decisis* principle permits such changing *only* in the field of *judge*-made law (the Common Law) because it has nothing to do with the field of *people*-made law: that is, the people's fundamental law, the Constitution, which the people alone have the power to make and change; as various Supreme Court cases have made entirely clear, notably the 1935 *Dimick* case. Nothing but common sense is needed to understand this vitally important difference between the two entirely separate fields of *judge*-made law and *people*-made law.

6. Judges possess the power of "judicial review" (reviewing legislative Acts, or any governmental pronouncements or actions—so as to decide their validity under the Constitution) under the American constitutional system due to the basic principles of limited government, although there is no express mention of this judicial power in the Constitution, as Hamilton pointed out in *The Federalist* number 81—also noting there the point that the Constitution must always be considered the controlling standard and supreme over laws. (This point is discussed in other numbers also, for example 33, 39, 78 and 80.) The fact that the courts have the power, and are under an obligation, so to enforce the Constitution—by deciding in appropriate cases that all laws found to be in conflict with the Constitution are null and void from the start—was well understood and repeatedly stated in the Framing Convention and in the State Ratifying Conventions: notably by Madison, Gerry, King and Mason in the Framing Convention and, in State Ratifying Conventions, by a number of members including two who later became Chief Justice of the United States: Oliver Ellsworth (Conn.) and John Marshall (Va.), also by James Wilson (Pa.) who became a member of the Supreme Court. It is important to keep in mind that it is only the Constitution itself which makes a conflicting law void, from the start, and not the decision of the Court—which has power merely to *ascertain and declare* this to be the fact; therefore the court has the power thus to *clarify*

196

and explain the existing legal situation (under the Constitution), meaning the existing law, but not *create* it—not *make* law in the constitutional field. The principle that a constitution is supreme and makes void all laws in conflict with it was well understood in America long before the United States Constitution was framed—for instance, in arguing in 1761 in a Boston court against the infamous "Writs of Assistance" law enacted by Parliament, James Otis declared: "An act against the constitution is void." (Likewise in 1764 in his "The Rights of the British Colonies.") Debatable as to that (British) "constitution," it is unchallengeable as to a written Constitution of the American type. This is unquestionably correct as to a law in conflict with a written Constitution such as the United States Constitution.

7. Judges are limited by Article III, Section 2, to deciding genuine controversies in cases properly brought before any court, including the Supreme Court—controversies which are capable of final settlement by a court in accordance with legal principles. They have no power to offer "advisory opinions," or to consider political issues (which are properly determinable only by the Executive or the Legislative Branches). This is in accordance with the Constitution's definition of the judicial authority and jurisdiction of the Federal courts. Judges are, of course, powerless to enlarge their own authority, or jurisdiction; as Hamilton emphasized in *The Federalist* number 83.

8. Supreme Court decisions do not constitute the "supreme Law of the Land." Its decision in a case is limited by the facts involved and constitutes only "the law of the case," binding merely the parties to the case. This is true as to all cases and all courts, including the Supreme Court. Even in a case involving consideration of the Constitution, therefore, the Supreme Court's decision—involving a mixture of legal rules and principles as applied to the facts involved—cannot and does not constitute a part of the "supreme Law of the Land;" which the Constitution (Article VI) defines as including only this fundamental law itself, as well as Federal Laws, meaning Acts of Congress, and treaties (which conform to the Constitution).

9. Once the meaning of any part of the Constitution has been properly *ascertained,* in keeping with the original intent (Paragraphs 2 and 3 above), and *defined* accordingly as a principle of the Constitution by the Supreme Court as the highest judicial authority on the basis of all pertinent, historical records (which can never change or be changed), so as to *clarify* the original intent and meaning, this definition—as *first* determined by the Supreme Court—becomes in effect a

part of the Constitution's words thus construed (as concerns the Court's power to interpret) and cannot thereafter be changed by the Court; because the records and intent are unchangeable. This meaning and principle—as so ascertained and defined for the *first* time—may thereafter be nullified and supplanted only by the people and only by amendment. Once the Supreme Court thus *first* determines the definition in any particular, it thereby exhausts its power and authority as to this particular topic and thereafter has no power to make any new and conflicting definition of the Constitution's words involved—according to the constitutional system as understood and intended by the Framers and Adopters in 1787-1788. This is necessarily true because any power of the Court to "change its mind" at its pleasure—to re-define at will the words of the people's fundamental law—would be a power without limit; and the effect would be endless "changing of mind" and endless changing of definitions so as to have *judge*-made law in placé of the Constitution's *people*-made law to the doom of the intended stability as a guide for the people's conduct and as a bulwark of their liberties. This would be a monstrous absurdity, according to the American philosophy of Man-over-Government proclaimed in the Declaration of Independence—necessarily put into practice through constitutionally *limited* government. Such changeability by judges would spell unlimited Rule-by-Man.

10. Any judge's decision is null and void if in conflict with the Constitution in its original meaning (per paragraph 2 above)—so nullified automatically from the start by the Constitution itself due to the fact of such conflict. This applies to all judges and all courts. Any judge, acting alone or as one of a group of judges on a court, who makes such a conflicting decision thereby acts outside of the scope of his judicial authority under the Constitution—therefore outside of the Law, in violation of Rule-by-Law (basically the people's fundamental law: the Constitution). It amounts to Rule-by-Man.

11. Any judge who violates the Constitution acts as a usurper, in conflict with his oath of office. Every Federal judge is sworn to support the Constitution *only* (necessarily in its original and controlling meaning) so his responsibility and culpability—legally and morally—as a usurper is individual and personal in each case. Usurpation by a higher court cannot excuse violation of his oath of office and the Constitution by a lower-court judge, through his adhering to the anti-Constitution policy and decisions of the higher court and claiming their leadership as an excuse for his default as a public trustee.

198

12. The real chaos of Rule-by-Man, supplanting Rule-by-Law (basically the people's fundamental law, the Constitution), would inescapably result from any violation of the Constitution—in its original and controlling meaning—by judges who would misinterpret it so as to make it *seem* to mean something different, to suit their own wishes, changing from time to time according to their changing aims. This would apply especially to the highest judicial authority: the Supreme Court. Considered from the standpoint of the stability and security of the Republic and of the God-given rights of every Individual—entirely dependent for their security upon a stable Constitution—any such Rule-by-Man practices could not but produce judge-made chaos. For any lower-court judge to violate his oath of office (to support the Constitution *only*) by collaborating with higher-court judges in any such usurpation of power would amount to his helping to produce this chaos of Rule-by-Man, this judge-made chaos. (It is pertinent at this point to refer to the comment on page 175, *ante,* about judges not being given the Rule-by-Man type of power to construe the words of the Fourteenth Amendment, in relation to the Bill of Rights, according to their changing whims.)

13. What is sometimes referred to as "judicial chaos"—meaning the situation created by a lower-court judge's refusal to give unlimited and unquestioning submission to judges on a higher court—could apply only to a Rule-by-Man system under which highest judges would be omnipotent and fill the role of The Authority Supreme (not bound by any Constitution as the supreme law); than which nothing could be more hostile to the American philosophy and system of constitutionally limited government. The term "judicial chaos" obviously has no place, therefore, under the American philosophy and system of Rule-by-Law based upon the Constitution as the "supreme Law of the Land" with every judge sworn, as a public servant and trustee of the people, to support the Constitution *only* (necessarily in its original and controlling meaning). Every judge is not only not obligated to obey any usurper-judges on a higher court but is clearly obligated to defy and denounce such violators of the Constitution as defaulting trustees.

14. Any violation of oath of office by way of usurpation of power is the gravest of civic offenses. It is "treasonable usurpation upon the power and majesty of the people," as Alexander Hamilton correctly characterized any flouting of the people's fundamental law. ("Letters of Phocion," 1784: regarding violation of the New York Constitution.) Any such usurpation "is criminal and odious," as declared by

President John Quincy Adams in his first annual Message to Congress (1825). Such condemnation of usurpation—either by misusing granted power, or by grasping power which has not been granted—is in keeping with *The Federalist's* denunciation of this most heinous offense by any public official as a defaulting public trustee, including especially any and every judge because especially charged with the particular duty of enforcing respect in practice for this basic law.

15. Just as the Constitution and its prescribed oath of office allow for no exceptions in requiring faithful support of this fundamental law by every official including every judge, so does the moral law permit no exception to its pertinent precept that the end does not justify the means—that an alleged good end can never justify resort to evil means. Usurpation by an oath-breaking judge (or by any other public official) is therefore, in effect, despite any "good intentions," anti-Constitution, anti-moral, anti-Rule-by-Law, anti-Republic, and anti-Liberty (Freedom of Man from Government-over-Man); it is utterly hostile to the security of the God-given rights of every Individual and to the principles of the Declaration of Independence. It is hostile to everything governmental for which America has stood traditionally

To repeat, the foregoing considerations (in the numbered paragraphs)—presenting some essentials of the American constitutional system—reflect in substance the thinking of those who framed and adopted the Constitution, according to their pertinent writings (notably *The Federalist*) when judged on the basis of the requisite competence and intellectual integrity: free from any warping bias stemming from hostility to The Founders and their handiwork.

The foregoing points, considered together with the related portions of the text of *The Federalist* presented in a special section of the Appendix (pages 271-286, *post*), are sufficient to clarify the strictly limited authority and role of all judges—notably all the members of the Supreme Court—under the American philosophy and system of constitutionally limited government. (This is a principal subject of the present author's writings—separate and apart from this book—based upon many years of exhaustive research in this field.)

The critical importance—from the standpoint of the security of the people's liberties and of Posterity's just heritage—of the constitutional system's prohibition against the Judiciary's intruding into the field of political policy was emphasized in his Lectures in 1790-1791 by Justice James Wilson of the United States Supreme Court (who was one of The Framers) in these words:

"Nothing is more to be dreaded than maxims of law and reasons of state blended together by judicial authority. Among all the terrible instruments of arbitrary power, decisions of courts, whetted and guided and impelled by considerations of policy, cut with the keenest edge, and inflict the deepest and most deadly wounds."

The subject of limited government, under the Constitution, involves various important aspects other than those discussed up to this point; but, for present purposes, the foregoing will suffice to make clear some most important considerations, conducive to research by readers.

Before concluding this presentation of background material, there are two other topics which merit special mention because of their profound significance in relation to the traditional American philosophy—one in the religious realm and the other in the economic realm. They will be discussed briefly.

Limited Government
under the Constitution
in Relation to Religious Considerations
Which the Declaration of Independence Makes Express

The Constitution was designed to translate into enduring, governmental reality the ideals, goals and principles of the Declaration of Independence. This is made clear by the inspiring words of the Constitution's Preamble. It provides the connection between these two documents—the chief link being the word "Liberty" in both—with regard especially to the expressly stated religious considerations underlying the traditional American philosophy as defined in the Declaration, notably the concept of God-given, unalienable rights.

Belief in God as the Creator of Man and the giver of his unalienable rights—unalienable *because* God-given—is the basis of this philosophy; which is an indivisible whole and must be accepted, or rejected, as such. The Constitution's primary role, or function, was intended to be the safeguarding of these rights of every Individual— partly through so limiting the power of the Federal government that it could never interfere with the religious life and practices of the people of the separate States (the people in each State being in complete control of pertinent policy for themselves), always involving implicitly recognition of belief in God as the only basis of the unalienable character of these rights.

The traditional American philosophy's first and fundamental principle is that "The Spiritual Is Supreme," that Man is of Divine origin

201

and his spiritual, or religious, nature is of supreme value and importance compared with things material. This principle was the basis of the assertion in the Declaration of Independence that ". . . all men are created . . . endowed by their Creator . . ." This philosophy teaches that belief in God is the fundamental link which unites the adherents of all religions in a spiritual brotherhood under the common fatherhood of God; and it allows for no differentiation between them as to this unifying conviction.

This applies not only to those who adhere to some one of the organized religions but also to The Individual holding a strictly personal, but genuinely religious, belief—however unorthodox or strange it may seem to others. Belief in God is the common denominator here; but no element of required, religious conformity is involved.

America was colonized originally by adherents of the Christian religion, in the main, and the vast majority of them were Protestants of various denominations. The Founding Fathers nevertheless adhered faithfully to the all-embracing character of the approach of the American philosophy to religion, as indicated by the affirmative and express statement in the Declaration, quoted above. This approach was also indicated, negatively, in the Constitution by way of its denying to the Federal government any power pertaining to religion—no such power was included among the few powers which were delegated to this government by the people. This denial of such power was confirmed by the later addition of the First Amendment, which expressly prohibits the Federal government from making any law "respecting an establishment of religion, or prohibiting the free exercise thereof . . ." (Here "an establishment of religion" was intended to mean only an official church organization—one controlled, supported and preferred by the government—such as the Church of England organization which then existed in some of the States.) America is, in fact, a haven for all religions and their adherents; her traditional philosophy in this regard is actually practiced.

This aspect of the American philosophy was emphasized strikingly when discussion was in progress in the legislature of Virginia regarding the Bill to establish religious freedom—finally adopted in 1786. As Jefferson observed in his "Autobiography," it was proposed during the long-continued discussion of the Bill that the reference to "the holy author of our religion" (meaning God) be changed so as to refer to Jesus Christ; but the proposal was rejected by vote of "a great majority," as Jefferson (the author of the first draft) stated:

202

"... in proof that they meant to comprehend, within the mantle of its protection, the Jew and the Gentile, the Christian and Mahometan, the Hindoo, and Infidel of every denomination."

("Mahometans" means Moslems, also called "Musselmen." Here "Infidel" means any religious believer although a non-Christian.) The foregoing comment about America's being a haven for all religions is sound even though in some early colonial communities of a strongly religious character, such as the initial ones in Massachusetts, there was extreme intolerance on the part of the governing group which impelled some dissenters, such as Roger Williams, to leave and found settlements elsewhere. By the time of the Declaration of Independence, however, insofar as government was concerned, religious toleration was widespread in America; although it was some decades before every "establishment of religion" (to use the term of the First Amendment), as defined above, had been abolished by all of the States which had one in 1791 when the First Amendment was adopted.

It is true that the traditional American philosophy is basically religious and that America and Americans in general are a religious country and people. It is equally true that the American people are predominantly Christian in their beliefs. It is, however, unsound to characterize the Constitution of the United States government as being either religious, or Christian. The Constitution is a charter adopted by the people for defining the framework of the federated system of government composed of the central Republic and the State Republics. No such charter, in and of itself, can properly be classified as being religious; just as a government, in and of itself, cannot be so classified. This truth was the basis of the statement in the Treaty of Peace and Friendship entered into by President John Adams, a devoutly religious man and a steadfast Christian, in 1797, between the United States and Tripoli of Barbary, that:

"As the government of the United States of America is not in any sense founded on the Christian Religion,—as it has in itself no character of enmity against the laws, religion, or tranquillity of Musselmen . . ." [Moslems]

The non-religious character of government becomes more obvious when it is considered that, under the American philosophy, the sovereign people create their governments as their tools; and no tool can be called religious. To continue with this metaphor, the government, as a tool, is created by the people according to the "blueprint" (the Constitution) which they design in order to help define the

203

characteristics and operating limits of this tool; and no "blueprint" can be classified as religious. As a further illustration, consider the architect's "blueprints" (drawings) for a church building; the edifice will be for religious purposes but the "blueprints" cannot properly be labelled religious in nature, in and of themselves.

This would be true even if it were possible for certain purposes to classify as "religious" a government which is completely dominated by, and an official reflection of, the hierarchy of some church or denomination. Nothing could be more antithetical to the American philosophy than to consider the United States government in any such category. As President Jefferson observed in his Second Inaugural Address (1805):

> "In matters of religion, I have considered that its free exercise is placed by the constitution independent of the powers of the general government. I have therefore undertaken, on no occasion, to prescribe the religious exercises suited to it; but have left them, as the constitution found them, under the direction and discipline of state or church authorities acknowledged by the several religious societies."

By "state" authorities acknowledged by the several religious societies, Jefferson referred to those States in which the previously-mentioned, official, church organizations, or establishments—"establishments of religion"—still existed; some of which continued to exist thereafter for a number of years, in Massachusetts until 1834.

No Constitution or government, Federal or State, in America can soundly be called "religious"; and it is equally unsound, of course, to classify any of them as being Christian. This applies also to the Declaration of Independence because it is a political statement; which is true despite the fact that it expresses, in part, the fundamentally religious nature of the American philosophy. To confuse the religious with the political in this connection impedes clear thinking and sound comprehension of the real values in both of these fields.

The infinite greatness of the Declaration of Independence and the Constitution as political documents, and their supreme and timeless value to all Americans—and as guidelights to all peoples—do not depend on mistaken adulation due to confused thinking on the basis of the erroneous assumption that they are religious in nature.

The foregoing conclusions do not, of course, conflict with the idea held by many people that the men who framed the Constitution were religiously inspired in performing this great task. This view is the basis, for example, of one of the tenets of two religious sects—the

Church of Christ, Scientist (Christian Scientists) and the Church of Jesus Christ of Latter Day Saints (Mormons)—whose members are admonished, if not obligated, by the teachings of their respective founders, as a matter of religious duty, to be loyal to the Constitution. There is striking and express support for the belief in such religious inspiration on the part of The Framers in a statement by Benjamin Franklin—not ardently affiliated with any organized religion, with any "establishment of religion," but ever a firm believer in God; though he is erroneously assumed by some to have been a skeptic, a non-believer in God, because of his fame as a scientific-minded person. This statement was published by him during the period of ratification of the Constitution, in The Federal Gazette & the Philadelphia Evening Post of April 8, 1788, in part as follows:

"To conclude, I beg I may not be understood to infer, that our general convention was divinely inspired when it formed the new federal constitution, merely because that constitution has been unreasonably and vehemently opposed; yet I must own, I have so much faith in the general government of the world by PROVIDENCE, that I can hardly conceive a transaction of such momentous importance to the welfare of millions now existing, and to exist in the posterity of a great nation, should be suffered to pass without being in some degree influenced, guided and governed by that omnipotent, omnipresent and beneficent Ruler, in whom all inferior spirits live and move and have their being."

(Text per newspaper original.) In the preceding year, during the debates in the Framing Convention, Franklin had recommended the invocation of Divine guidance of the deliberations of that body, partly in these words:

"The small progress we have made after 4 or five weeks . . . is methinks a melancholy proof of the imperfection of the Human Understanding . . . how has it happened, Sir, that we have not hitherto once thought of humbly applying to the Father of lights to illuminate our understandings?"

(The Franklin quotations on page 5, *ante*, are of particular interest here.) That Divine Providence—Man's Creator, as proclaimed in the Declaration of Independence—was influential in guiding The Framers in their work in the 1787 Convention is a belief shared by others, too. Note, for example, the assertion by Charles Pinckney, one of this group, in 1788 that he was skeptical at the outset as to the prospect of success of the undertaking due to the conflicting interests involved, and was amazed at the final result, believing that:

205

"Nothing less than that superintending hand of Providence, that so miraculously carried us through the war (in my humble opinion), could have brought it [the Constitution] about so complete, upon the whole."

Hamilton expressed a similar view soon after the Framing Convention adjourned, in a published essay commenting on the proposed Constitution's system of government:

"For my own part, I sincerely esteem it a system, which, without the finger of *God*, never could have been suggested and agreed upon by such a diversity of interests." (Emphasis Hamilton's.)

Madison agreed, as he made expressly clear in *The Federalist* (no. 37). One more illustration is the resolution adopted by the U.S. House of Representatives on September 25, 1789 recommending that the President proclaim a day of Thanksgiving to God and prayer by the people of the entire nation:

"acknowledging, with grateful hearts, the many signal favors of Almighty God, especially by affording them an opportunity peaceably to establish a Constitution of government for their safety and happiness."

It is sometimes mistakenly asserted that the words of the original Constitution contain no recognition of the existence of God. Besides a formal reference in the closing (execution) clause: "the year of our Lord 1787," Article VI requires an oath, or affirmation, of office by all officials, Federal and State, to support the Constitution. This is in the same sentence prohibiting any religious test for Federal office; which makes it clear that such an oath of office was not considered by The Framers and Adopters of the Constitution to be such a prohibited test. As understood by them, as well as their fellow leaders and the people in general, such an oath (or affirmation, in the alternative, by those whose religious convictions bar their "swearing") is fundamentally religious—in effect and impliedly acknowledging belief in, and invoking punishment by, a Supreme Being (as the oath-taker conceives such a Being, without any degree of enforced, religious conformity) for any failure to tell the truth or other falsification, as the case may be. The reference by The Framers in this document in this indirect way to religion, evidencing recognition of God, was emphasized by John Quincy Adams in his previously quoted "Jubilee" address on April 30, 1839:

"The constitution had provided that all the public functionaries of the Union, not only of the general but of all the state governments, should be under oath or affirmation for its support. The homage of religious faith was thus

206

superadded to all the obligations of temporal law, to give it strength; and this confirmation of an appeal to the responsibilities of a future omnipotent judge, was in exact conformity with the whole tenor of the Declaration of Independence—guarded against abusive extension by a further provision . . ." [against a religious test for Federal office].

To repeat, the Constitution cannot soundly be classified as a religious document; but in the foregoing respects, for example, it is intimately bound up with recognition of the existence of God and with an assumption of the profound connection of this recognition with sound self-government. Furthermore, as the pertinent quotations presented in the first portion of this study-guide indicate, it was the firm conviction of The Founders that religion is the basis of morality and that firm religious conviction and faith are, therefore, essential to sound morality among a people; just as sound morality was considered by them to be essential to sound character of Individuals and of the people of a country, as the only firm basis upon which successful self-government could be created and endure.

It is also of special interest to note in this connection that the philosophy of the American people, through the generations preceding the period of the Declaration of Independence and the framing of the Constitution as well as during this period, was characterized in the main by a dominant element of the religious. This philosophy, underlying these two instruments as discussed previously, was as we have seen actively and substantially influenced by religious leaders— chief of all clergymen of New England—in the long course of their own gradually developing struggle toward "Liberty and Independence" within the realm of religion as well as with regard to their role as citizens in the field of government: that is, independence of country from foreign control accompanied by Individual Liberty, especially in the realm of conscience and all things religious—freedom of conscience and freedom of The Individual to reason and to decide religious questions himself without interference by any superintending, earthly Authority. These developments within the realm of religious thinking strongly influenced and fostered the kindred developments, in the governmental realm, which culminated in the Declaration of Independence and the Constitution. Various sound volumes devoted to this subject—especially the role of the New England clergy in the development of the philosophy leading up to 1776, make inspiring and enlightening reading for any student of the fundamentals of the traditional American philosophy. They participated in governmental activities, moreover—notably in Town-meetings—during consideration of fundamental matters; and, for instance, thirteen clergymen were members of the Constitutional Convention of 1779-1780 in Massachusetts which framed this State's first Constitution.

There is an important consideration which needs to be kept in mind by every generation, including especially the Clergy and all others particularly interested in preserving religious liberty—freedom of conscience—in America, with fullest protection under the Constitution. This is that freedom of conscience and religion is only one aspect of the indivisible whole of Individual Liberty and must stand or fall with the other parts; it cannot be treated separately and preserved, as observed in 1776 by the Reverend John Witherspoon—president of Princeton College and a signer of the Declaration of Independence:

> "There is not a single instance in history in which civil liberty was lost, and religious liberty preserved entire. If therefore we yield up our temporal property, we at the same time deliver the conscience into bondage."

Samuel Adams asserted the same conclusion as to civil and religious liberty in 1774: "they rise and fall together." Hamilton also observed in the same year in this regard that: "if the foundation of the one be sapped, the other will fall of course." In the 1785 document drafted by Madison: "A Memorial and Remonstrance Against Religious Assessments"—opposing a tax in Virginia to support "teachers of the Christian religion," it was stated in conclusion:

> "Because, finally, 'the equal right of every citizen to the free exercise of his Religion according to the dictates of conscience' is held by the same tenure with all our other rights."

An impressive expression of a similar view was contained in a letter written by the General Association of Congregational Ministers of Connecticut, in their Annual Meeting on June 22, 1774, to the clergy of beseiged Boston, stating:

> "We consider you as suffering in the common cause of *America*—in the cause of civil liberty; which, if taken away, we fear would involve the ruin of religious liberty also . . ."

In other words, religious liberty and all other liberties stand, or fall, together; they can be secure only to the extent that their governmental foundation is preserved in its full integrity, only to the extent that the Constitution is respected in its original, true and only meaning—as intended by those who framed and adopted the initial instrument and each amendment—subject only to the people's exclusive power to change it, which can be done solely by amendment.

The final topic, in this presentation of background material, concerns the economic aspect of Individual Liberty and will now be considered in some detail.

Limited Government
and
Individual Enterprise and the Profit Motive—
Soundness Ethically, Morally, Socially and Otherwise

The traditional American philosophy and system of limited government require strict limitation of the power of the Federal government, in the economic field, to *regulation* in the particulars specified in the Constitution—excluding any *control* by government of the people's economic activities, according to the controlling intent of those who framed and adopted the Constitution in 1787-1788 and thereafter each of its amendments. This economic aspect of the philosophy and system is entirely in harmony with the other aspects—notably the related ethical, moral and social aspects in their broadest and most inclusive connotations. Brief consideration of this view is of particular significance and value at this point.

Individual Enterprise, as contemplated and featured by the traditional American philosophy and system, means private, competitive, individual enterprise or activity concerning things economic. The soundness of this philosophy and system as a whole—ethically, morally, socially and otherwise—necessarily characterizes each and every one of their constituent parts, including Individual Enterprise.

The right to enjoy the freedom of Individual Enterprise, for private profit, together with the intimately related right to private property, constitute the main elements of Man's economic liberty. This right to economic liberty is the inseparable and indispensable economic aspect of the indivisible whole of Individual Liberty. As Jefferson stated in his first annual Message to Congress in 1801:

"Agriculture, manufactures, commerce, and navigation, the four pillars of our prosperity, are the most thriving when left most free to individual enterprise."

Jefferson's statement holds true equally as to all other parts of the economic realm, according to the American philosophy. Benjamin

209

Franklin expressed a similar view (perhaps about 1766) in his "Remarks on the Plan for Regulating the Indian Affairs" as follows:

> "It seems contrary to the Nature of Commerce, for Government to interfere in the Prices of Commodities . . . It therefore seems to me, that Trade will best find and make its own Rates; and that Government cannot well interfere, unless it would take the whole Trade into its own hands (as in some Colonies it does), and manage it by its own Servants, at its own Risque."

During the colonial period, the British government exercised full control over major aspects of the empire's economy and manipulated trade to Britain's benefit at the expense of the economy of the colonies. Some of the ethical, moral and social aspects of this part of economic Liberty—the Individual Enterprise part of Man's Freedom in the economic realm—as viewed by the traditional American philosophy, will now be considered.

First, Individuals must deal with each other by free choice, by mutual and voluntary arrangement, so that the result can be mutual trade for mutual benefit in the light of rational self-interest, with due respect by each for the other's equal rights.

Second, the gain permitted by the private-profit feature of the Individual Enterprise system is The Individual's reward for giving superior service, or superior benefits (of the product purchased), to those with whom he deals—offering them what they prefer to buy in the face of competition with all other offerings. The more the sales and resulting profit he makes, due to the greater value he offers, and the more firmly his superior service becomes established through "repeat" sales to well-satisfied customers, the greater the proof of the value of his services to them as well as to society, to the general welfare, in various ways. This special service, in some instances, takes the form of making various standard items offered more conveniently available to the customer, as in the case of the neighborhood drug-store; the special convenience is the special service. The seller's successful demonstration of sound practices and superior standards helps to influence others to emulate his example and thereby to raise the level of performance by other sellers. This gradually improves the material environment of the people generally, directly and indirectly in a number of ways, while giving evidence of the soundness of the system and making its foundations more secure economically and in the minds of the people, which helps to form beneficent customs and traditions.

Third, Man's freedom in the economic realm—that is, freedom

from Government-over-Man—including the freedom of the "free market" economy operating on the basis of the private-profit motive, presupposes the existence of an ethical environment. Such an environment is created by the multiple, beneficent influences within any group, neighborhood, community and society stemming from all of the sound and constructive aspects of life. These influences include, for example, the religious, ethical, moral, social, educational, civic, fraternal, political, as well as the material. An additional and most compelling factor is self-interest based on the desire of The Individual to be known and accepted as an honorable, dependable and entirely worthy participant in the activities of the society—including mutual-trade transactions. In the background always is fear of society's potential disciplinary measure—fear by an offender of being driven out of business by group and community ostracism due to any dishonest or unfair treatment of others, including grossly avaricious conduct.

The potency of the foregoing elements combined, contributing to self-discipline among traders in the "free market," can be readily understood by any one familiar with neighborhood and community life in any locality in America, viewed traditionally. It needs to be kept in mind that any large community, even a city, is merely an aggregation of a number of such neighborhoods. For instance, even in a huge section of a big city such as the "Wall Street" financial community in New York City, nothing is more valuable than a man's reputation for probity ("his word is as good as his bond") and nothing is more disastrous for him in business than publicity of his violating an agreement; and all the more true the smaller the community.

A man's reputation for honest dealing is not only a big asset in economic life but so vitally important to profit-making over the years that the number of these who offend seriously against community or trade-group standards are relatively few indeed. The percentage of such offenders is probably quite similar to the percentage of those who prove themselves unworthy and unacceptable in other ways and in other walks of life. Any instance of an exception, for some special reason peculiar to a particular period or trade or locality, only serves to prove the general rule.

In America the traditional philosophy and system of government —designed primarily to make secure each Individual's unalienable rights against infringement by other Individuals, as well as by government—safeguards against evils in the economic realm such as monopolies through which a person or group might try to disrupt, or

211

eliminate, the freedom of action of others and the free play of the "free market" economy with regard to some commodity or type of business. The worst type of monopoly, government monopoly, through either government control or government ownership, is of course barred above all else under the traditional American philosophy and system. The correctness of the foregoing statements is not affected by the fact that it took time to evolve effective measures to combat the proneness of some men to seek monopolistic control in this or that part of the national economy; nor by the fact that violators are occasionally discovered and punished—their relative fewness being proof of the main point here.

Under the traditional American philosophy and system, the resulting ethical environment in the economic realm helps greatly to give reasonable assurance of ethical conduct by Individuals. This applies to Individuals acting singly, in groups and in organizations such as associations and corporations. This makes the surrounding atmosphere of the "free market" economy in general anything but sordid, evil or degrading to Man. On the contrary, this helps to make it sound, constructive and enduringly fruitful, judged by longtime records of the traditional American system. It has proved to be the most beneficent system of economic operation by a people—from the standpoint of the people in general through the generations—ever devised in human history to serve the supreme end and goal, which are to make fruitful and secure Man's Liberty against Government-over-Man. This means to make secure Man's unalienable rights in general, through the effective operation of his economic liberty as an inseparable part and the material mainstay of the indivisible whole of Individual Liberty. Any exceptions from time to time have only served to prove the rule.

Fourth, as proved by life in any American community, the property (including money) accumulated by Individuals, through operation of the Individual Enterprise system stimulated by the private-profit motive, is generally used soundly. This means constructively and even beneficently in the main. It is used by most Individuals not only for the support of self and of all of his dependents, so they can enjoy continued physical existence (the minimum meaning of life), but also for that supremely important purpose: the support of their unalienable rights in general. By this course, The Individual sets a good example for all others. This encourages all Individuals in the community and in the larger society to stand up for their equal rights, especially the

212

right to Freedom from Government-over-Man, while demonstrating how this can be done successfully. This creates a salutary "climate" conducive to the well-being of Free Man in the neighborhood and in the entire country.

This indicates the impregnable foundation, the firm basis, for the sound ethics of rational self-interest for each Individual. Multiplied by the number of people involved—for the whole country—this contributes to a strong, constructive, enduring community of Free Men operating normally on a reasonably high plane, morally and governmentally, in a manner always consistent with the duty factor of Individual Liberty-Responsibility and with the primary meaning of Individual Liberty—Freedom of Man from Government-over-Man. Again, any relatively few violators of this standard constitute merely the exceptions which help to prove the general rule.

Fifth, as Man operates successfully on the basis of the private-profit motive, he accumulates property beyond the requirements of his and his dependents' necessities and normal life in general, judged by neighborhood and community standards. This generally results in most Individuals making financial and other contributions to betterment of group, neighborhood, community and society at large—to the higher things of life, to be shared by self and others, embraced by the all-inclusive words: "Life, Liberty and the pursuit of Happiness." Such contributions, varying in form and frequency, are made moreover on the voluntary basis of the freedom of choice of Man, free in mind and spirit—much of the time on his own initiative, without request by others. Contributions by way of personal service in infinitely varied ways are commonly made by a multitude of persons daily in the communities of America. This helps greatly to create and maintain the previously-mentioned ethical environment. The average American community has over the generations proved this to be true in such remarkable degree as to cause this aspect of life, in the traditionally "free economy" civilization in America, to constitute a high goal to which other peoples have long looked with amazement and most with admiration and longing. The fact that an Individual's service to community often leads to material benefits to him—for instance, the additional rewards through increased employment by the public in his work or profession due to prominence gained in serving the community—as well as to inner fulfillment, does not alter the soundness of such service or the integrity of The Individual's motivation in this connection.

The mixture of direct self-interest with indirect self-interest through community service, traditionally so typical of the American scene, is potent proof of the efficacy of the private-profit motive (within an ethical environment) in serving the higher things of life for The Individual and for society—for the "general welfare." This reflects the truth that society's ethical level is but the sum of that of all Individuals, on the average, whether considered from the standpoint of neighborhood, community, region, or country as a whole. (Note especially the Dickinson quotation on page 74, *ante.*)

Sixth, Man's indulging the demands of rational self-interest, through operating on the basis of the private-profit motive, is in harmony with the "self" factors of self-governing, genuine Free Man. These factors are major elements of Individual Liberty-Responsibility. They are as follows—the spiritual: *self-respect;* the economic: *self-reliance;* and the political-social: *self-discipline.* (See pages 88-90, *ante.*)

Effective self-discipline by Individuals, in making the "free market" economy function soundly, contributes to the reality of the surrounding ethical environment which is essential to its enduring success. This forestalls and precludes any real, or pretended, excuse for discipline being imposed by the government. In last analysis, this is the best safeguard against Government-over-Man. Self-discipline is a main element of Individual Liberty-Responsibility. It is the alternative to being disciplined, just as self-government is the alternative to being governed.

The foregoing six considerations are, of course, only a part of those embraced by the subject as a whole. They help to clarify the fundamental value of economic liberty—including Individual Enterprise and the related private-profit motive—as an inseparable part of the indivisible whole of Individual Liberty-Responsibility.

A point needs noting here to clarify thinking. It is that the frequently heard term "free enterprise" is not accurately descriptive and involves some misleading connotations. It is an inadequate translation of the French phrase: *laissez faire et laissez passer;* which, roughly translated, means leave me alone and let me work. This phrase became popular in France generations ago as a protest against the strict and infinitely-detailed government controls of the people's economic activities, such as manufacturing. The term "free enterprise" is often misinterpreted as meaning free in the sense of license—not in the true sense of Free Man operating in an ethical environment and with due respect for the equal rights of others and, of great importance, with freedom from Government-over-Man, as discussed above. The term should, therefore, be avoided in favor of the more soundly and accurately descriptive phrase: "Individual Enterprise"—meaning individual, private, competitive enterprise within an ethical environment, as exemplified by the American scene traditionally, operating always with due respect for the equal rights of others. The foregoing assumes, of course, showing in practice due regard for just laws which are expressive of "just powers" (to use the term of the Declaration of Independence) and designed to protect the equal rights of all Individuals through proper government regulation—as authorized by the Constitution—but not government control, or ownership.

The conclusion, as to this aspect of Man's Freedom, is that on the basis of the foregoing considerations alone—though merely a brief and partial commentary—it must be conceded that the morality and sound ethics of rational self-interest of The Individual are readily apparent and soundly founded. Even this brief discussion proves the point here: that the private-profit motive is sound, constructive and an essential element of the economic system required for the preservation and support of The Individual's God-given, unalienable rights—chief of all Liberty against Government-over-Man.

Any human activities, like human nature, have their weaknesses and imperfections. Though true with regard to the American people's activities in the economic aspect of life, this has to be judged comparatively—in contrast to the infinitely greater imperfections of any alternative, economic system ever devised by Man, especially any other system which could ever be conceived but would lack the prime requisite: Freedom of Man from Government-over-Man, which is of the essence of the traditional American system. The American philosophy condemns this lack and rests secure in its comparative virtue —its infinitely greater value to Free Man. The unsoundness of any unfavorable comparison of this American system with some theoretically perfect system, which has never existed anywhere in the world in all history—a tactic resorted to only by critics who are either themselves confused or seek to confuse others—is so self-evident as to need mere mention in passing and not any discussion.

Concluding Comment
as to Background Material

The foregoing sample, of available material, presented in this Part II is not only indicative of the profoundly sound basis of the Twelve

Basic American Principles discussed in Part I but is itself sufficient to make clear the magnificent role in history, and especially in American history, which was played by The Founders—notably the signers of the Declaration of Independence and of the Constitution. It is fitting, however, to continue this discussion by considering in some detail, in the following pages, some additional aspects of the obligation of the present generation and American Posterity to The Founders—why respect should be shown in practice for the Twelve Basic American Principles as an important way in which the people can render due honor to The Founders.

PART III
ALL HONOR TO THE FOUNDERS

Respect Due The Founders

The indebtedness to The Founders on the part of American Posterity knows no bounds. The more prominent leaders of the pre-Revolutionary years, as well as of the period 1774-1788—embracing the life of the Continental Congress, the Declaration of Independence, and the framing and adoption of the Constitution, also of the formative years of the Republic in the first decade of its life to 1800—constituted a group unparalleled in all history with regard to knowledge of government gained from sound scholarship and experience in self-governing; high character, exemplified in practice with such consistency as to be reflected in life-long reputation; such devotion in practice to professed principles as to prove themselves to be men of genuine convictions; and dedication to the highest ideals known to Man in the governmental field as exemplified by those recited in the Declaration of Independence and in the Preamble to the Constitution.

This is unquestionably true of them as a group, judged by the entire record, despite the inescapable frailties of human nature to which every human being is subject and at time exhibits in some degree, as history proves. Such high praise of the group has been accorded them uniformly and consistently in the light of sound understanding by various leaders abroad as well as by all in America who have been competent to judge adequately on the basis of sound scholarship and intellectual integrity—with freedom from bias due, for example, to a desire (revealed or concealed, conscious or unconscious) to belittle the philosophy and handiwork of the group so as to undermine and change, if not destroy, the governmental system and the traditional values involved, in considerable part if not as a whole.

It should, of course, never be lost sight of that this group of eminent leaders—such as the signers of the Declaration of Independence and the Constitution and the other famous governmental figures of that period—were truly representative of a multitude of less prominent leaders, in the localities throughout the country, who in substantial degree possessed comparable virtues within more circumscribed limits, especially as to experience governmentally. It is also well to keep in mind that the American people in general of that period were unique in their active experiences in the developing art of self-governing in the light of their heritage, of which they were so keenly aware and alert in expounding as well as fearless and vigorous in defending.

Notable among these less famous leaders, for instance, were New England clergymen who, as we have seen, were so potently influential in helping to develop and nurture what ripened into the traditional American philosophy and system of government: meaning basically constitutionally limited government. A striking example is the Reverend Andrew Eliot of Boston who on May 29, 1765—the very day that Patrick Henry introduced his famous Resolutions against the Stamp Act in the Virginia House of Burgesses, in connection with which he made his celebrated oration against royal tyranny—preached the Election Sermon, before the royal Governor and the legislature of Massachusetts, in which he stressed the right of resistance against usurped power, asserting that submission to tyranny is an offense against God, mankind and the State. These factors need to be remembered in any commendatory discussion of The Founders—chief of all the above-mentioned Signers.

Many books and other writings have been produced in praise of The Founders and their handiwork. The only purpose of the present discussion of this topic, so limited necessarily by lack of space, is to call attention to certain facts and points as a stimulus to thought and, it is hoped, as an influential inducement to further reading regarding this subject—preferably of the original writings.

One of the most striking and persuasive testimonials, regarding the virtues and talents of the members of the Continental Congress, is a statement by William Pitt, the Earl of Chatham, former Prime Minister of Great Britain, in the House of Lords on December 20, 1775, during the discussion of, and strongly supporting, the proposal that British troops be removed from Boston. It is to be found in the useful collection of writings and speeches of the general Revolutionary period: *Principles and Acts of the Revolution in America,* edited by Hezekiah Niles (1876). Regarding communications from the Continental Congress to the Parliament presenting the American viewpoint, Pitt stated in part:

"When your lordships look at the papers transmitted us from America, when you consider their decency, firmness and wisdom, you cannot but respect their cause, and wish to make it your own—for myself I must declare and avow that, in all my reading and observation, and it has been my favorite study—I have read Thucydides, and have studied and admired the master statesmen of the world—that for solidity and reasoning, force of sagacity, and wisdom of conclusion, under such a complication of different circumstances, no nation or body of men can stand in preference to the general congress at Philadelphia.—I trust it is obvious to your lordships, that all attempts to impose servitude on such men, to establish despotism over such a mighty continental nation—must be vain—must be futile."

The last quoted statement was induced by his sound estimate of the staunchness of spirit of Free Man in America—including not only these leaders in the Continental Congress but the American people as a whole—as stated by him earlier in this speech:

"Of this general spirit existing in the American *nation* . . . of this spirit of independence, animating the *nation* of America, I have the most authentic information. It is not new among them; it is, and ever has been their established principle, their confirmed persuasion; it is their nature and their doctrine. [Referring to an eminent and reliable informant] he assured me with a certainty which his judgment and opportunity gave him, that these were the prevalent and steady principles of America: That you might destroy their towns, and cut them off from the superfluities, perhaps the conveniences of life, but that they were prepared to despise your power, and would not lament their loss, whilst they had, what, my lords?—Their woods and liberty. . . . [They] prefer poverty with liberty, to golden chains and sordid affluence; . . . will die in defence of their rights, as men—as freemen. . . . 'Tis liberty to liberty engaged, that they will defend themselves, their families and their country. In this great cause they are immovably allied. It is the alliance of God and nature—immutable, eternal, fixed as the firmament of Heaven!" (Emphasis per original.)

This American spirit was manifested in one of the papers to which Pitt referred: "Declaration of the Causes and Necessity of Taking Up Arms," adopted by the Continental Congress, July 6, 1775, in which it was emphatically asserted:

"Our cause is just. Our union is perfect . . . [our arms] we will, in defiance of every hazard, with unabating firmness and perseverance, employ for the preservation of our liberties; being with one mind resolved to dye Free-men rather than to live Slaves." ["one" is "our" in original.]

Pitt's just estimate of the American leaders in the Continental Congress in 1775 was, of course, equally true of the members of the same body which issued the Declaration of Independence a few months after his tribute quoted above. Its President, John Hancock, truly reflected the American spirit in this entire period in an oration he delivered in Boston on March 5, 1774, on the anniversary of the "Boston Massacre" of Americans by British troops, in which he extolled the restraint showed by the Americans in not executing reprisals:

"May that magnificence of spirit which scorns the low pursuits of malice, may that generous compassion which often preserves from ruin, even a guilty villain, forever actuate the noble bosoms of Americans! But let not

221

the miscreant host vainly imagine that we feared their arms. No; them we despised; we dread nothing but slavery. Death is the creature of a poltroon's brains; 'tis immortality to sacrifice ourselves for the salvation of our country. We fear not death."

It was in this address that Hancock reiterated the typical American sentiment so scornful of unqualified submissiveness to government:

". . . it is to the last degree vicious and infamous to attempt to support a government, which manifestly tends to render the persons and properties of the governed insecure. Some boast of being friends to government; I am a friend to righteous government founded upon the principles of reason and justice; but I glory in publicly avowing my eternal enmity to tyranny."

Those principles were a main part of the basis of the Declaration of Independence—of the Twin Revolution of 1776: for Freedom from Government-over-Man, as previously discussed. As a leading spokesman of the philosophy of 1776, Jefferson summed it up—and, at the same time, noted the effect of the Declaration on the minds and spirits of the peoples of the world—only a few days before he died (letter to R. C. Weightman, June 24, 1826):

"All eyes are opened, or opening, to the rights of man. The general spread of the light of science has already laid open to every view the palpable truth, that the mass of mankind has not been born with saddles on their backs, nor a favored few booted and spurred, ready to ride them legitimately, by the grace of God."

The fact that the glorious significance and value to Free Man in America of the proclamation of the principles of the Declaration could be fully realized and preserved enduringly only through endless and great efforts was noted at the time by John Adams (letter to Mrs. Adams, July 3, 1776), who urged that annual celebrations take place —"from this time forward forever"—to help keep alive the Spirit of '76, stating:

"You will think me transported with enthusiasm, but I am not. I am well aware of the toil, and blood, and treasure, that it will cost us to maintain this declaration, and support and defend these States. Yet, through all the gloom, I can see the rays of ravishing light and glory. I can see that the end is more than worth all the means, and that posterity will triumph in that day's transaction, even although we should rue it, which I trust in God we shall not."

With regard to The Framers of the Constitution, it is of interest to quote another Prime Minister of Great Britain, William E. Gladstone, who expressed himself in 1887 in a letter to an official committee in

America in charge of the celebration of the centennial of the framing of the Constitution, in part as follows:

"I have always regarded that Constitution as the most remarkable work known to me in modern times to have been produced by the human intellect, at a single stroke (so to speak), in its application to political affairs."

Earlier he had expressed a like sentiment more briefly (North American Review, September 1878): ". . . the American Constitution is the most wonderful work ever struck off at a given time by the brain and purpose of man."

The Framers were paid a high tribute during their deliberations by Jefferson—then resident in Paris as the American Minister—in a letter to John Adams of August 30, 1787: "It is really an assembly of demigods." One of the most striking aspects of the Framing Convention's accomplishment, noted by Madison and others, was the entire lack of any model (for a federated system of Republics) to go by in this Constitution-making in 1787. One of the Framers, James Wilson, commented on this and other aspects of great significance in the following statement in the Pennsylvania Ratifying Convention:

"Permit me to add, in this place, that the science even of government itself seems yet to be almost in its state of infancy. Governments, in general, have been the result of force, of fraud, and of accident. After a period of six thousand years has elapsed since the creation, the United States exhibit to the world the first instance, as far as we can learn, of a nation, unattacked by external force, unconvulsed by domestick insurrections, assembling voluntarily, deliberating fully, and deciding calmly, concerning that system of government, under which they would wish that they and their posterity should live."

He called attention to the peaceful change from the Articles of Confederation to the Constitution, in sharp contrast to other nations' changes by war and revolution, in these words:

". . . the scene, hitherto unparalleled, which America now exhibits to the world—a gentle, a peaceful, a voluntary, and a deliberate transition from one constitution of government to another."

The foregoing brief presentation is sufficient, by way of illustration, to indicate the more than deserved reputation of The Founders for highest qualities and superb performance. Any attempt to belittle them in either regard can only serve to prove either incompetence or evil intent—either a state of being confused or an intent to confuse others—on the part of the one culpable, when judged with intellectual honesty by any one adequately informed. One striking illustration of such an attempt in the present generation will be stressed as the discussion proceeds because of its great, evil and continuing influence.

Refutation of the Charge
That The Framers Perpetrated a Coup d'état

For a multitude of reasons, political and otherwise, partly inspired by deep-seated fear of any central government with real powers, however limited on parchment—in a written Constitution—the framing of the Constitution was harshly criticized by a number of people throughout the period of the ratification debates. One of the principal arguments was that the Framing Convention acted beyond the scope of its authority, because it did not limit itself to proposing amendments to the Articles of Confederation, in keeping with the original "call" for the Convention. (Instead it proposed, in draft form, an entirely new instrument for submission to the people for consideration through their specially chosen Ratifying Convention in each State.) Madison devoted the entire essay number 40 of *The Federalist* to refutation of this argument. Among the numerous and convincing reasons which he presented in support of the soundness of the Convention's course, a main one was "the crisis" then confronting the country but only incidentally, in passing, in the process of his analysis. Yet the crisis, caused by the complete breakdown of all pretense of effective government by the Confederation, was alone sufficient to justify the Convention's new approach to the problem. The record shows overwhelming evidence of the completeness of this breakdown and of the impossibility of amending the Articles of Confederation so as to produce any effective remedy within its framework. Besides, earlier attempts to amend the Articles had failed. Lacking a real central government, there was for example no possibility of national security through sound national defense, or sound interstate relations economically, financially or politically, much less sound relations with foreign governments. (The previous comments about the Confederation, at pages 120 and 167, are pertinent here.)

The collapse of the Confederation was so complete that in a statement in Congress on April 8, 1789, Madison referred to it as having suffered from "imbecility" and this word, and comparable terms, are found in the records repeatedly as the expression of opinion by various leaders in describing the utter collapse of the Confederation. During the Framing Convention, George Mason wrote that:

224

"At a time when our Government is approaching to Dissolution, when some of its Principals have been found utterly inadequate to the Purposes for which it was establish'd, & and it is evident that without some material Alterations it can not much longer subsist . . ."

(Mason's use here of the word "Principals," as it appears in the original of Madison's notes of the proceedings, seemingly referred to principles.) In 1787 in *The Federalist* number 30, Hamilton observed that "the government of the union has gradually dwindled into a state of decay, approaching nearly to annihilation." In 1788 in the Virginia Ratifying Convention, Madison commented in this connection:

"What is the situation of this country at this moment? Is it not rapidly approaching to anarchy? Are not the bands of the Union so absolutely re-laxed as almost to amount to a dissolution?"

Madison's reference to "anarchy" was echoed by Washington in February 1788 in a letter to Lafayette in which he stated:

"I will only add, as a further opinion founded on the maturest deliberation, that there is no alternative, no hope of alteration, no intermediate resting place, between the adoption of this [Constitution], and a recurrence to an unqualified state of Anarchy, with all its deplorable consequences."

Washington had declared earlier, at the close of the Framing Convention in September 1787—in his letter to the Congress conveying to them a copy of the draft Constitution—that there was at stake "perhaps our national existence." At the outset of the Convention, he wrote to Jefferson (in Paris) this grim estimate of its prospects:

"Much is expected from it by some; but little by others; and nothing by a few. That something is necessary, all will agree; for the situation of *the General Governmt.* (*if it can be called a governmt.*) is shaken to its foundation, and liable to be overset by every blast. In a word, it is at an end, and unless a remedy is soon applied, anarchy and confusion will inevitably ensue."

(Emphasis added.) In his previously-quoted "Jubilee" address of April 30, 1839, John Quincy Adams summed up the situation, which had existed prior to the adoption of the Constitution, in these words:

"The nation fell into an atrophy. The Union languished to the point of death. . . . The system was about to dissolve in its own imbecility—impotence in negotiation abroad—domestic insurrection at home, were on the point of bearing to a dishonourable grave the proclamation [in 1776] of a government founded on the rights of man . . . [when the Framing Convention met and brought forth the Constitution]: the complement to the Declaration of Independence . . ."

225

Another point of special interest in this regard is the fact that the Articles of Confederation were inconsistent with the Declaration of Independence because the people themselves should form their governments according to the Declaration (by means of Constitutional Conventions and Constitutions), whereas the Articles of Confederation had been approved only by the legislatures of the States and not directly by the people of each State. In *The Federalist* number 22, Hamilton noted this as one reason for the Confederation's infirmities or defects (which were discussed also in numbers 15-21.)

The Articles of Confederation were in reality of the nature of a treaty entered into between separate and independent States, as observed earlier (pages 120 and 167, *ante*). One of the chief points made by James Wilson during the debate in the Pennsylvania Ratifying Convention pertained to this aspect, mentioned also by Madison in his April 1787 writing: "Vices of the Political System of the United States," in which he presented various reasons why the failure of the Confederation was so complete that it permitted no remedy within its framework. Madison there stated that: ". . . it is in fact nothing more than a treaty of amity of commerce and of alliance, between independent and Sovereign States." He also made the point that there was no sanction to support its laws. It had, in fact, no power whatever, as we have seen previously, in relation to persons individually and no power whatever to compel the State governments to do anything —it could only request, even as to money for its support; and the States frequently flouted its requests for money. In that 1787 writing, Madison made the above-noted point that the sovereign people of each of the States had not themselves created the Confederation but only their agent, the legislature, from which he soundly concluded that the people could properly overrule their agent at any time they should see fit and replace the Confederation with some other system. This was all the more true of this unsoundly formed, futile, and hopelessly impotent pretense of a government because of the principle stated in the Declaration of Independence that, when a people's government "becomes destructive of these ends" (to make and keep secure the people's God-given, unalienable rights), they may alter, or abolish, it and create a satisfactory substitute. The Confederation provided no security whatever for these rights. Madison's list of topics among the "vices" of the existing political system, in that April 1787 writing, are enlightening (using the word "want" as meaning "lack") —as presented in his own wording:

1. Failure of the States to comply with the Constitutional requisitions.
2. Encroachments by the States on the federal authority.
3. Violations [by the States] of the law of nations and of treaties.
4. Trespasses of the States on the rights of each other.
5. Want of concert in matters where common interest requires it.
6. Want of Guaranty to the States of their Constitutions & laws against internal violence.
7. Want of sanction to the laws, and of coercion in the Government of the Confederacy.
8. Want of ratification by the people of the Articles of Confederation.
9. Multiplicity of laws in the several States.
10. Mutability of the laws of the States.
11. Injustice of the laws of the States.

Some of the contemporary criticism of The Framers has been translated unsoundly by some modern writers into the ridiculous accusation that, by framing the Constitution instead of proposing amendments to the Articles of Confederation, The Framers perpetrated a *coup d'état*. Nothing could be more absurd—indeed, violative of historical truth—than this charge, made with the evident purpose of belittling these leaders and undermining respect for them and their handiwork in the minds of the American people and especially the Young. Brief discussion will make obvious the absurdity of any such contention which all pertinent historical records prove to be false.

A dictionary, and the popular, definition of a *coup d'état* is: "A sudden decisive political move overthrowing an existing government." Such "overthrowing" necessarily involves either the use of force, or the threat of its use. As every competent scholar well knows, there was not even the slightest threat of this—much less the actuality —involved in the situation in 1787-1788. Instead, the Framing Convention consisted of delegates appointed, and it met, in response to a resolution of the Continental Congress of February 21, 1787—inspired by State governments, which in turn appointed these delegates. This was the result of years of public discussion of the grave need of effective action to the end of remedying the disastrous governmental situation. Furthermore, as Hamilton stressed in *The Federalist* number 2, this Convention produced nothing but a paper proposal: the draft of a proposed Constitution for final approval by the sovereign

227

people of each State, if found acceptable to them. This was in keeping with the fundamental American principle, restated in *The Federalist* number 22 by Hamilton that:

> "The fabric of American empire [the Union] ought to rest on the solid basis of THE CONSENT OF THE PEOPLE. The streams of national power ought to flow immediately from that pure original fountain of all legitimate authority."

(Emphasis per original.) In number 43, Madison also discussed the point that the proposed, new Constitution would supersede the Articles of Confederation (only by consent of the people, if ratified).

The foregoing considerations were among those, in support of ratification, which were brought to the attention of the American people in various ways during the ratification debates in 1787-1788. One of the principal ways was the publication of *The Federalist* essays as newspaper articles, originally in New York City; also in book form in two volumes published in March and May, 1788. (The distribution of this material has been discussed earlier, pages 150-151.)

As planned all the while, The Framers took elaborate and formal steps to have their draft of a proposed Constitution properly submitted to the people of each State, through action by the Confederation Congress, in keeping with the spirit of a resolution of the Framing Convention of June 13, 1787, which expressly specified that in each State the matter should be considered by an assembly of representatives especially chosen by the people for this purpose upon recommendation by the legislature. At the close of the Convention on September 17, it adopted a resolution transmitting the draft of the proposed Constitution to Congress and reciting that the Convention considered that the draft document should be submitted by the Congress "to a Convention of delegates, chosen in each State by the People thereof, under the Recommendation of its Legislature, for their Assent and Ratification;" and that each Ratifying Convention which would approve it should notify Congress of such approval. This resolution also specified recommendations as to steps by which the Constitution, after ratification by nine States, should be put into effect. The resolution, accompanied by a copy of the proposed Constitution, was forwarded to Congress with a letter dated September 17 from George Washington, as President of the Convention. This letter reflects so accurately the high purposes and ideals and the background thinking of the members of the Convention as a group that it should be considered here in its entirety, so the full text is presented:

228

"WE HAVE now the honor to submit to the consideration of the United States in Congress assembled, that Constitution which has appeared to us the most adviseable.

"The friends of our country have long seen and desired, that the power of making war, peace and treaties, that of levying money and regulating commerce, and the corresponding executive and judicial authorities should be fully and effectually vested in the general government of the Union: but the impropriety of delegating such extensive trust to one body of men is evident— Hence results the necessity of a different organization.

"It is obviously impracticable in the foederal government of these States, to secure all rights of independent sovereignty to each, and yet provide for the interest and safety of all—Individuals entering into society, must give up a share of liberty to preserve the rest. The magnitude of the sacrifice must depend as well on situation and circumstance, as on the object to be obtained. It is at all times difficult to draw with precision the line between those rights which must be surrendered, and those which may be reserved; and on the present occasion this difficulty was encreased by a difference among the several States as to their situation, extent, habits, and particular interests.

"In all our deliberations on this subject we kept steadily in our view, that which appears to us the greatest interest of every true American, the consolidation of our Union, in which is involved our prosperity, felicity, safety, perhaps our national existence. This important consideration, seriously and deeply impressed on our minds, led each State in the Convention to be less rigid on points of inferior magnitude, than might have been otherwise expected; and thus the Constitution, which we now present, is the result of a spirit of amity, and of that mutual deference and concession which the peculiarity of our political situation rendered indispensable.

"That it will meet the full and entire approbation of every State is not perhaps to be expected; but each will doubtless consider, that had her interest alone been consulted, the consequences might have been particularly disagreeable or injurious to others; that it is liable to as few exceptions as could reasonably have been expected, we hope and believe; that it may promote the lasting welfare of that country so dear to us all, and secure her freedom and happiness, is our most ardent wish."

By "one body," Washington referred to the Congress of the Confederation. By the word "consolidation," he meant effective, though partial, unification politically of the States through the federation of Republics (central and State) as provided in the Constitution. With regard to his reference to giving up "a share of liberty to preserve the rest," attention is called to Paragraph 8 of Principle 3 in Part I.

The lofty tone and high-principled approach which is reflected by the above communication on behalf of the Convention to the Congress —both being representative bodies—was in keeping with the characteristic and profoundly moving plea made by Washington to the Framing Convention to counter the prevailing gloom at one point

229

during their sessions, as reported by Gouverneur Morris in an oration on the occasion of Washington's death:

> " 'It is (said he) too probable that no plan we propose will be adopted. Perhaps another dreadful conflict is to be sustained. If to please the people, we offer what we ourselves disapprove, how can we afterwards defend our work? *Let us raise a standard to which the wise and the honest can repair. The event is in the hand of God.'*—this was the patriotic voice of WASHINGTON; and this the constant tenor of his conduct." (Emphasis added.)

The Congress considered the above-mentioned letter, resolution and draft of the proposed Constitution for several days and then adopted a resolution on September 28 providing that they "be transmitted to the several legislatures in Order to be submitted to a convention of Delegates chosen in each state by the people thereof in conformity to the resolves of the Convention made and provided in that case." The legislature of each State acted in accordance with these resolutions and the draft of the proposed Constitution was submitted to a Constitutional Convention in each State chosen by the people for the sole and express purpose of considering and then, on behalf of the people of the State, ratifying or rejecting it. The Constitution ceased to be a mere paper proposal and became binding governmentally only when approved by nine States and only as to those which so approved it. (North Carolina acted in 1789, Rhode Island in 1790.)

Never before in all history in any other country had any such steps —in part, or as a whole—been taken to insure the people's consent to the establishment of their form of government. The foregoing summary of events presents irrefutable evidence of an unprecedented performance by all public servants involved—including the members of the Framing and Ratifying Conventions—acting strictly in accordance with their limited duty as the agents of the people, to the end of enabling the sovereign people of each of the States to exercise to the full freedom of choice in forming a central government for the greater security of their unalienable rights, in keeping with the ideals, goals and principles of the Declaration of Independence as summarized in the Preamble to the Constitution. Nothing in history even matches, much less surpasses, this record when judged by the severest standards of integrity and all other pertinent tests of the highest type.

In the light of the foregoing discussion, it is self-evident that any one who asserts that The Framers perpetrated a *coup d'état* thereby flouts historical truth and exhibits lack of either scholarly competence, or intellectual integrity. If one thus culpable be a professional educator, such misconduct also involves betrayal of the duty aspect of Academic Freedom-Responsibility, which includes above all else the above-mentioned elements: scholarly competence and intellectual integrity; and, furthermore, it robs the affected students of their right to freedom of choice based upon correct information and instruction which is sound in every respect. Any such unjust attempt to defame The Framers, or others among The Founders, amounts moreover to character assassination—a grossly anti-moral offense—which is as cowardly as it is indefensible when perpetrated against our fore-fathers, unable to refute with the truth.

The Founders are also sometimes attacked as having been crass money-seekers at the expense of the people's liberties, which historical records prove to be false. This topic merits extended discussion but lack of space requires brevity in the following comments about it.

The Founders' Concept of "Property"— Embracing All Rights—Not Merely Things Material

The Founders considered the right to property to be subordinate, and a supporting right in relation, to The Individual's God-given, un-alienable rights; as discussed in Part I, under Principle 10. (Note the especially pertinent quotation of John Adams on page xviii.) As the main, material support of all of Man's rights, the right to property was rated by them as being of great importance—essential to the enjoy-ment and security of all rights. This was true of all of The Founders and their fellow leaders as well as of their fellow countrymen in gen-eral—notably those who were in the forefront of the fight for "Liberty and Independence," especially for Freedom from Government-over-Man, but not possessed of great wealth, such as Samuel Adams. His writings, for example, contain numerous, pertinent essays published in newspapers prior to 1776.

Furthermore, the thinking of The Founders and of their fellow Americans did not limit the meaning of the word "property" so as to apply merely to things material: physical things. They considered that Man's rights in general—separate and apart from material posses-sions—were also an extremely important, if not the most valuable, part of his property; that Man has not only a right to property but a property in his rights. This general line of thought—reflecting truly American thinking of that day, of The Founders second to none—was never expressed more soundly and clearly than in the essay on

"Property" by Madison published in The National Gazette (one of a series of essays by him on various topics so published) on March 29, 1792. Brief but comprehensive in presenting this characteristically American viewpoint, the full text of the essay deserves consideration here (emphasis Madison's). Note that the expression "excess of liberty" refers to license.

Property

"This term in its particular application means 'that dominion which one man claims and exercises over the external things of the world, in exclusion of every other individual.'

"In its larger and juster meaning, it embraces every thing to which a man may attach a value and have a right; and *which leaves to every one else the like advantage.*

"In the former sense, a man's land, or merchandize, or money is called his property.

"In the latter sense, a man has property in his opinions and the free communication of them.

"He has a property of peculiar value in his religious opinions, and in the profession and practice dictated by them.

"He has property very dear to him in the safety and liberty of his person.

"He has an equal property in the free use of his faculties and free choice of the objects on which to employ them.

"In a word, as a man is said to have a right to his property, he may be equally said to have a property in his rights.

"Where an excess of power prevails, property of no sort is duly respected. No man is safe in his opinions, his person, his faculties or his possessions.

"Where there is an excess of liberty, the effect is the same, tho' from an opposite cause.

"Government is instituted to protect property of every sort; as well that which lies in the various rights of individuals, as that which the term particularly expresses. This being the end of government, that alone is a *just* government, which *impartially* secures to every man, whatever is his *own.*

"According to this standard of merit, the praise of affording a just security to property, should be sparingly bestowed on a government which, however scrupulously guarding the possessions of individuals, does not protect them in the enjoyment and communication of their opinions, in which they have an equal, and in the estimation of some, a more valuable property.

"More sparingly should this praise be allowed to a government, where a man's religious rights are violated by penalties, or fettered by tests, or taxed by a hierarchy. Conscience is the most sacred of all property; other property depending in part on positive law, the exercise of that, being a natural and inalienable right. To guard a man's house as his castle, to pay public and enforce private debts with the most exact faith, can give no title to invade a man's conscience which is more sacred than his castle, or to withold from it that debt of protection, for which the public faith is pledged, by the very nature and original conditions of the social pact.

"That is not a just government, nor is property secure under it, where the property which a man has in his personal safety and personal liberty, is violated by arbitrary seizures of one class of citizens for the service of the rest. A magistrate issuing warrants to a press gang, would be in his proper functions in Turkey or Indostan, under appellations proverbial of the most compleat despotism.

"That is not a just government, nor is property secure under it, where arbitrary restrictions, exemptions, and monopolies deny to part of its citizens that free use of their faculties, and free choice of their occupations, which not only constitute their property in the general sense of the word; but are the means of acquiring property strictly so called. What must be the spirit of legislation where a manufacturer of linen cloth is forbidden to bury his own child in a linen shroud, in order to favour his neighbour who manufactures woolen cloth; where the manufacturer and wearer of woolen cloth are again forbidden the economical use of buttons of that material, in favor of the manufacturer of buttons of other materials!

"A just security to property is not afforded by that government under which unequal taxes oppress one species of property and reward another species: where arbitrary taxes invade the domestic sanctuaries of the rich, and excessive taxes grind the faces of the poor; where the keenness and competitions of want are deemed an insufficient spur to labor, and taxes are again applied by an unfeeling policy, as another spur; in violation of that sacred property, which Heaven, in decreeing man to earn his bread by the sweat of his brow, kindly reserved to him, in the small repose that could be spared from the supply of his necessities.

"If there be a government then which prides itself on maintaining the inviolability of property; which provides that none shall be taken *directly* even for public use without indemnification to the owner, and yet *directly* violates the property which individuals have in their opinions, their religion, their persons, and their faculties; nay more, which *indirectly* violates their property, in their actual possessions, in the labor that acquires their daily subsistence, and in the hallowed remnant of time which ought to relieve their fatigues and soothe their cares, the inference will have been anticipated, that such a government is not a pattern for the United States.

"If the United States mean to obtain or deserve the full praise due to wise and just governments, they will equally respect the rights of property, and the property in rights: they will rival the government that most sacredly guards the former; and by repelling its example in violating the latter, will make themselves a pattern to that and all other governments."

As the foregoing indicates—and as proved by the discussion of the Twelve Basic American Principles in Part I, especially Principle 10 —the traditional American philosophy considers that the right to material property is only a small but important part of The Individual's over-all rights; and that the higher things of life—those intangible reflections of Man's spiritual, moral and intellectual being—are infinitely superior in value if they could be considered separately. This

233

philosophy is, however, an indivisible whole. It recognizes, further, that the desire for material property is merely one of Man's driving urges, or chief motivations; also that it is, in truth, most valuable and helpful to Man when harnessed in the service of his ideals and higher aspirations, as discussed for instance in Part II (page 209) in connection with Individual Enterprise in its ethical, moral and social aspects.

A part of the particular value today of the above-quoted essay by Madison on "Property" is that it highlights the core-concept of the traditional American philosophy in such a way as to expose the fallacy in modern attempts to make it appear that there is something inherently antithetical in the right to material property in relation to what are referred to as "human rights." There can be no such thing as "human rights" which are different from the traditional American philosophy's God-given, unalienable rights and their supporting rights, including the right to material property—always accompanied by correlative duties, as discussed earlier. The definition and discussion of the Twelve Basic American Principles, in Part I of this study-guide, are believed to demonstrate adequately the inescapably inter-related nature of this entire group of rights, including the right to material property, as understood and accepted by The Founders and their fellow Americans. If, indeed, the so-called "human rights" were in any respect different from, and in conflict with, The Individual's God-given, unalienable rights and the supporting rights, then there would be no room in the American philosophy for such "human rights." This is all the more true to the extent that so-called "human rights" are an integral part of any Government-over-Man philosophy and system— the antithesis of the traditional American philosophy and system.

No conclusion appears more clearly and impressively, it is believed, even from consideration merely of the limited material presented in this study-guide, than the idea that—from the viewpoint of this philosophy—the economic is subordinate to higher values not only in such comparative rating but also among Man's motivating influences. Assuredly any adequate examination of pertinent historical materials proves this to be unquestionably true of the thinking of the entire generation in America of the period 1776-1787 and, second to none, of The Founders as a group. They rated their economic interests and security as secondary to their ideals in seeking "Liberty and Independence"—a truth which is highlighted, for example, by the Declaration of Independence, especially its closing words: "And for the support of this Declaration, with a firm reliance on the protection of divine Providence, we mutually pledge to each other our Lives, our Fortunes and our sacred Honor." The record proves they meant it, and equally the almost-naked, ever-hungry and shoeless men at Valley Forge who stained the snow with bleeding feet, yet fought on.

Among the writings which make this truth apparent is *The Federalist,* partly through its making clear the fundamental goals—chief of all the security of Man's God-given, unalienable rights—which were intended to be served by the constitutional system as discussed in detail in this volume's essays. This assumes that these essays are read with adequate understanding: with scholarly competence and intellectual honesty—free from warping bias stemming from a desire to undermine respect for this philosophy, The Founders and their handiwork.

An Example

Some have nevertheless so grossly misread *The Federalist,* for example, as to contend that Madison's discussion in number 10 of the relationship of property to political factions shows that he considered the economic to be the most influential—even determinative—factor among Man's motivations. Nothing could be further from the truth as to Madison's own thinking, or as to his representation of the nature of the American philosophy, in his writings in general (for instance, the above-quoted essay) as well as in his report—jointly with Hamilton and Jay—in *The Federalist* of the thinking of the Framing Convention. This applies equally to Hamilton and all The Founders.

In one widely-known, still widely-disseminated, writing by a prominent educator in the present generation, for example, it is asserted that Hamilton, like Madison, clearly believed in the economic interpretation of history. This 1937 writing praised, as being brilliant, the 1913 book, *An Economic Interpretation of the Constitution of the United States,* by the historian Dr. Charles A. Beard, who was on the faculty of Columbia University in 1913. In Beard's book, as generally understood and widely condemned by many leaders in various walks of life in the period following its publication, he made it appear, first: that The Framers designed the Constitution primarily so as to benefit themselves and their "class" financially—especially as to their Confederation-government securities—at the expense of the people's liberties; and second: that the economic motive is the dominant one, indeed the decisive factor, in the affairs of mankind in keeping with the theory of the economic interpretation of history. These were in substance his two main propositions; which he helped greatly to popularize for decades, most strikingly in the 1930's. His attack on The Framers and the Constitution started a trend which has had gravely harmful effects, continuing today, within education and government.

The phrase "economic interpretation of history" refers to the thesis that the economic is the determining, the decisive, factor in shaping history—that it is controlling in influencing and motivating Man and in shaping history's development. In one aspect, this thesis asserts that social evolution is due basically to economic causes. This is also referred to as "economic determinism"—in the more blunt and un-compromising language of Marxist Socialism-Communism.

Later in life, Beard tried to make it appear that he did not intend to espouse "economic determinism" in that 1913 book but he was unsuccessful in this attempt; the book was unmistakably clear in this regard. Note, for example, the contemporaneous criticism of the book in a book-review by Dr. Edwin S. Corwin—then (and for many years afterward) a full professor of Politics at Princeton University—in History Teachers Magazine for February 1914. Corwin stated that had Beard "been less bent on demonstrating the truth of the Socialistic theory of economic determinism and class struggle as an interpretation of history, his own performance would be less open to criticism."

The complete unsoundness of the Beard book, judged from the standpoint of sound scholarship, has been proved conclusively in the volume: *Charles Beard and the Constitution, A Critical Analysis of "An Economic Interpretation of the Constitution"* by Dr. Robert E. Brown of the faculty of Michigan State University, published in 1956 by the Princeton University Press. Brown's devastating and unanswer-able analysis exposes what he calls "the many ways" in which Beard violated "the concepts of historical method"—meaning violation of sound scholarship and of sound writing requiring the use of sound methods in dealing with historical materials. At one point, Brown notes some of these "ways" in connection especially with Beard's pre-tense of offering historical "evidence" that The Framers designed the Constitution largely to benefit their holdings of government securities, primarily "as an economic document" for their own financial benefit:

"These ran the gamut from omission to outright misrepresentation of evi-dence, and included the drawing of conclusions from evidence that not only did not warrant the conclusions but actually refuted them. To say that the Constitution was designed in part to protect property is true; to say that it was designed only to protect property is false; and to say that it was designed only to protect *personalty* is preposterous."

(Emphasis per original. Personalty means personal property, such as government securities like bonds, as distinguished from real property: land and buildings.)

Many years later, Beard disclaimed any intent of attacking the integrity, the good character, of The Framers; but this obviously amounted to a dissembling tactic, because the burden and effect of his presentation—in substance making it appear that they framed the Constitution primarily so as to "feather their own nest"—was precisely such an attack and was generally accepted as such (accepted by some, who approved, with praise but many leaders criticized it harshly with great hostility). The net effect of his attack was to charge them with being so lacking in moral and intellectual integrity, in framing the Constitution, as to sacrifice the people's liberties in favor of their own financial benefit; than which nothing could have been further from the truth, as all pertinent historical records amply prove when judged competently and without such bias. Supreme Court Justice Oliver Wendell Holmes, for example, stated in a 1916 letter about this book that Beard's disclaimer (of any intent to impute to The Framers self-seeking motives) was discredited by the book's presentation of "all the facts" about their holdings of government securities. In other letters in later years, Holmes asserted that he rejected this disparaging thesis of Beard and still believed that Washington and the other Founders ". . . had for their dominant motive a patriotic desire . . ."—that they had not ". . . talked patriotism because they had invested . . . ;" and Holmes charged Beard with dealing in "drivelling cant" by implying in this connection that The Framers represented the rich indulging in "exploitation" of the poor.* Holmes also stated that Beard's approach to the subject was "ignoble" and dealt in "innuendo" and avowed his own belief (as opposed to Beard's, as evidenced by the 1913 book's thesis) "that high-mindedness is not impossible to man"—for instance, that it characterized The Framers.**   *(1928 to J. C. H. Wu) **(1928 to Pollock)

Lack of space precludes adequate discussion here of the motive which prompted Beard in making this attack in 1913 upon The Framers and, therefore, upon their handiwork: the Constitution. The topic is, however, a most important one because of the vast, harmful influence of that Beard book and thesis, especially within the educational world (upon many teachers, textbook writers, and a multitude of students), setting a trend for decades. Some supplementary comments

237

are made at the end of the "References" section of the Appendix (pages 345-347), in part quoting a book of special interest about him published after his death—an appraisal of him and his record in a series of essays mainly by prominent educators who had known him well: *Charles A. Beard—An Appraisal* (1954), edited by Howard K. Beale. As these essays make clear, his great influence, especially upon students in his classes during his teaching at Columbia University, was due in considerable part to his lovable and admirable character as a person—always so gracious, gentle and warm-hearted in his personal relationships—to which the present writer can testify most sincerely; which makes all the more distressing the need of criticism such as is presented here. (Dr. Beard died in 1948.)

In connection with any false and defamatory claim, in effect, that The Framers sought to "feather their own nest" by framing the Constitution chiefly to benefit their Confederation-government securities, several facts merit emphasis. One is that such securities owned by these patriotic leaders and other leaders as well, considered as a group, were in the main purchased to help the government win the Revolutionary War (like buying "war bonds" in modern times), or to support the struggling government of the Confederation after the war ended, during the years when the governmental situation was nothing less than desperate financially. Also, there was even a very good prospect all the while that the "securities" would turn out to be virtually worthless, like the wartime paper currency after some years of extreme inflation (the ill-fated "Continentals"). Indeed, through the entire period 1776-1788, there was only a slim chance that the government would ever repay the sums borrowed by its selling these "securities" to patriotic Americans such as The Framers and the multitude of others willing to risk their money to aid their country. Furthermore, wealthy men like Washington helped to "make a market" for such securities (there was no such thing then as an established "stock market" where anyone could readily buy and sell such securities) when neighbors and friends were in need of selling their own securities of any such type—thereby performing an important and patriotic task by thus helping to maintain confidence in the government and make it possible for it to sell other securities from time to time, when necessary to support government activities. Without such aid by men like Washington, these necessitous sellers would not have been able to get needed funds by selling such securities—bought for patriotic reasons mainly—and would thus have been penalized for

238

indulging their patriotism; while the government would have been virtually paralyzed financially because people generally would have refused to buy its unsalable securities. Here Washington is cited merely as a shining example because he was one of the wealthiest men in the country and his exalted patriotism was and is impregnable. The other Framers—also unjustly maligned, in effect, in Beard's book—were undoubtedly also uncontaminated by any such compelling lust for money, at the expense of the people's liberties, as that book's pretended "evidence" purported to prove had motivated them. This is a case where any exception, if one could actually be *proved* to have existed, would only serve to prove the general rule just stated.

The Beard book's utter unsoundness is thus seen to make equally unsound the contention that it was brilliant in its thesis that The Framers were part of a "class" with a conscious solidarity of interests (economic interests which they preferred over all else). This unsound contention is found in that 1937 writing, by a prominent educator, which falsely alleges that Madison and Hamilton believed in economic interpretation (page 235, *ante*). A third false pretense in this 1937 writing is that The Framers perpetrated a *coup d'état,* which we have seen to be a gross falsification of history. This writing thus provides an excellent example of modern ones which, in effect, foster public opinion conducive to *dis*honor of The Founders, on the basis of false information in defiance of historical truth—in some cases accompanied by lip-service to them, or even genuine praise, in other respects. This writing, which is also seriously defective in other major respects from the standpoint of sound scholarship and American history, nevertheless continues to receive wide distribution—being a 1937 "Introduction," to an edition of *The Federalist,* by the late Edward M. Earle, then and afterward associated with the Institute for Advanced Study, Princeton, New Jersey. (He died in 1955.) The evil influence of the Beard book is continuing.

The Just Heritage of Posterity
Always Uppermost in The Founders' Minds

The historical records are replete with expressions of The Founders' profound concern for the enduring safety of the God-given, unalienable rights of future generations in America—time without end, for the preservation of Posterity's just heritage of Individual Liberty: Freedom of Man from Government-over-Man, under a securely functioning system of constitutionally limited government to be in practice inviolate in its full integrity. This concern of all of The Founders, indeed of all their fellow leaders and of their fellow Americans in general, was soundly reflected in 1774 in "Resolutions of Committee for the Province of Pennsylvania" which constituted "Instructions from the Committee to the Representatives in Assembly" of Pennsylvania as drafted by John Dickinson, a signer of the Constitution and distinguished in other respects as a leader in the period 1774-1787. These resolutions contained the following stirring appeal, to be always solicitous of moral obligation stemming from the fact that, in any period, the living generation is only temporary trustee of the just heritage of Posterity (emphasis per original):

> "*Honour, justice* and *humanity* call upon us to hold, and to transmit to our posterity, that liberty, which we received from our ancestors. It is not our duty to leave wealth to our children: but it is our duty, to leave liberty to them. No infamy, iniquity, or cruelty, can exceed our own, if we, born and educated in a country of freedom, intitled to its blessings, and knowing their value, pusillanimously deserting the post assigned to us by Divine Providence, surrender succeeding generations to a condition of wretchedness, from which no human efforts, in all probability, will be sufficient to extricate them; the experience of all states mournfully demonstrating to us, that when arbitrary power has been established over them, even the wisest and bravest nations, that ever flourished, have, in a few years, degenerated into abject and wretched vassals."

It was in this sense, in part, that Washington referred to the American people—meaning those of each and every generation—in his previously-noted statement in his First Inaugural Address (referring to the form of a Republic as "the Republican model of Government"):

> ". . . the preservation of the sacred fire of liberty, and the destiny of the Republican model of Government, are justly considered as *deeply*, perhaps as *finally* staked, on the experiment entrusted to the hands of the American people."

(Emphasis Washington's.) This indicates the double burden of responsibility of each generation of Americans, according to the thinking of The Founders, as the trustee of "the republican model of government" not only for American Posterity but for all other peoples of future generations—for whom The Founders intended the American "experiment" to be a model: to serve as the Light of Liberty which could inspire other peoples as an ideal and goal and to which they

240

could turn for sound guidance whenever any people, of any country, might feel so inclined in the course of their own self-development governmentally; without any attempt by America, of course, to impel—to "pressure"—any people in this connection.

Samuel Adams' Warning

To any who seek to condemn, if not to defame, The Founders for alleged mistakes, an appropriate answer would be the one hurled by Samuel Adams at detractors of "our ancestors" who proffered "excuses" for their errors (essay, Boston Gazette, 1771):

> "But we want no excuse for any *supposed* mistakes of our ancestors. Let us first see it prov'd that they were mistakes. 'Till then we must hold ourselves obliged to them for sentiments transmitted to us so worthy of their character, and so important to our security: . . ."

(Emphasis added.) It is of interest to note here a remark of President John Quincy Adams in his First Inaugural Address, after reciting the felicitous situation of the American people under the Constitution's governmental system:

> "To admit that this picture has its shades is but to say that it is still the condition of men upon earth. From evil—physical, moral, and political—it is not our claim to be exempt."

A particularly misleading and effective but most unfair and entirely unsound technique used in criticizing The Founders merits stressing here: comparison of their ideas and handiwork with a false standard of theoretical perfection—never existing in the world then, or before, or since; also unsoundly comparing their ideas and handiwork with developments of a later period instead of using the only sound comparison: what had been known in the Old World throughout history. The error and unsoundness involved in such false comparisons is too obvious to need more than mere mention in order to make clear the fallacy involved.

It is a tremendously important and never-ending problem for the self-governing American people to be not only adequately informed but ever alert and vigorously active in forestalling whenever possible, and combating whenever necessary, any and all threats to Individual Liberty and to its supporting system of constitutionally limited government. In this connection, it is essential to keep in mind that the greatest danger lies in the subtle and gradual, or piecemeal, approach of danger—by which the foundations are gradually eroded rather than by open and outright assault; accompanied by harsh attacks

241

upon all who seek to alert the people to such danger whenever it threatens. This was stressed by Samuel Adams—always in the forefront, as a firebrand patriot, in the fight for Liberty and Independence, for the rights of Free Man through Freedom from Government-over-Man—in an essay published in 1771 in the Boston Gazette, signed "Candidus" (quoted exactly as in original text, including emphasis):

> "If the liberties of America are ever compleatly ruined, of which in my opinion there is now the utmost danger, it will in all probability be the consequence of a mistaken notion of *prudence*, which leads men to acquiesce in measures of the most destructive tendency for the sake of present ease. When designs are form'd to rase the very foundation of a free government, those few who are to erect their grandeur and fortunes upon the general ruin, will employ every art to sooth the devoted people into a state of indolence, inattention and security, which is forever the fore-runner of slavery— They are alarmed at nothing so much, as attempts to awaken the people to *jealousy* and *watchfulness;* and it has been an old game played over and over again, to hold up the men who would rouse their fellow citizens and countrymen to a sense of their *real* danger, and spirit them to the most zealous activity in the use of all proper means for the preservation of the public liberty, as *'pretended patriots,' 'intemperate politicians,' rash, hot-headed* men, *Incendiaries*, wretched *desperadoes*, who, as was said of the best of men, would turn the world upside down, or have done it already."

These remarks pertained to internal dangers to Individual Liberty equally as much as to external dangers in that day, then involving potentially the values inherent in the approaching Twin Revolution of 1776 (discussed at pages 132-136, *ante*). These internal dangers to Individual Liberty are ever present, potentially or actually in greater or lesser degree, in every generation—from year to year and day to day. This 1771 warning by Samuel Adams constitutes also one of his most salutary admonitions to Posterity.

A 1765 Call to Action—
"Educate Young and Old: For Liberty"—
As Timely Today as When Originally Made

If only a single idea could be said to have been held in common by all of The Founders, none would have a better claim to this distinction than the idea that sound information and education constitute the essential and best foundation upon which to build securely and enduringly—for The Individual and for the people as a whole, for the nation. The writings of The Founders are filled with appeals and admonitions to make sure of a fair future for Liberty in America through widest possible use of sound information and education; and

John Adams was second to none in this regard. An especially impressive appeal of this character was made by him as part of a 1765 writing: "A Dissertation on the Canon and the Feudal Law" which was first published as a series of essays in the Boston Gazette. Its value lies, in part, in its enduring quality—valuable in every year and generation and as pertinent today as when first published. This is so true, and its message is so important to the well-being of Man's Freedom from Government-over-Man in America today and in the future, that an extended quotation is believed to be justified. First he assumed to be true then a favorable situation which, it must be admitted, does not exist in America today:

> "Let us presume, what is in fact true, that the spirit of liberty is as ardent as ever among the body of the nation, though a few individuals may be corrupted. . . ."

True today as to independence from foreign rule, it is not true today regarding Individual Liberty: Freedom from Government-over-Man. This melancholy fact of deterioration of the situation of Free Man in America only serves to make more important the main part of his message:

> "Let us tenderly and kindly cherish, therefore, the means of knowledge. Let us dare to read, think, speak, and write. Let every order and degree among the people rouse their attention and animate their resolution. Let them all become attentive to the grounds and principles of government . . ."

After thus expressing the key idea, he continued by directing attention to one of the main areas of knowledge which should be fostered and inculcated:

> "Let us read and recollect and impress upon our souls the views and ends of our own more immediate forefathers, in exchanging their native country for a dreary, inhospitable wilderness. Let us examine into the nature of that power, and the cruelty of that oppression, which drove them from their homes. Recollect their amazing fortitude, their bitter sufferings,—the hunger, the nakedness, the cold, which they patiently endured—the severe labors of clearing their grounds, building their houses, raising their provisions, amidst dangers from wild beasts and savage men, before they had time or money or materials for commerce. Recollect the civil and religious principles and hopes and expectations which constantly supported and carried them through all hardships with patience and resignation."

After this invitation to relive the harsh realities of those days in our imaginations, with emphasis however upon the sustaining things of the mind and heart and soul, he reached the key word, "liberty":

"Let us recollect it was liberty, the hope of liberty for themselves and us and ours, which conquered all discouragements, dangers, and trials. In such researches as these, let us all in our several departments cheerfully engage,—but especially the proper patrons and supporters of law, learning, and religion!"

By "learning" he referred not only to formal education but to all knowledge-gaining, in all its facets by all possible means. Then he focused attention upon the group which, in New England especially, was in that time—as before and later—so potently influential in helping to develop, nurture and propagate the ideas of "Liberty and Independence": Independence from foreign rule and Liberty of Man against Government-over-Man. This was the clergy. He appealed to them as follows:

"Let the pulpit resound with the doctrines and sentiments of religious liberty. Let us hear the danger of thraldom to our consciences from ignorance, extreme poverty, and dependence, in short, from civil and political slavery. Let us see delineated before us the true map of man. Let us hear the dignity of his nature, and the noble rank he holds among the works of God,—that consenting to slavery is a sacrilegious breach of trust, as offensive in the sight of God as it is derogatory from our own honor or interest or happiness, —and that God Almighty has promulgated from heaven, liberty, peace, and good-will to man!"

By "slavery" he of course meant, in part, subjection to tyrannous rule by a British king and Parliament. Here Adams was not urging the clergy to do something new for their group—some of them had been doing this for generations in America. Instead, he was emphasizing the need of more of the clergy to participate in this educational program in support of "Liberty and Independence" and all of them to give more attention to this cause, so crucially important to freedom of religion. He then called upon the Bar—the profession which was expected to take the lead actively in the fight and which, in every generation, is obligated to do so morally as well as otherwise; partly today because every member of the Bar—like every judge and other public official—is sworn to support the Constitution—necessarily in its true and original meaning (per page 194, *ante*) as intended by those who framed and adopted the initial instrument and later each of its amendments. He continued:

"Let the bar proclaim, 'the laws, the rights, the generous plan of power' delivered down from remote antiquity,—inform the world of the mighty struggles and numberless sacrifices made by our ancestors in defence of freedom . . ."

Next he came to the leading group in the realm of formal education, the colleges:

"Let the colleges join their harmony in the same delightful concert. Let every declamation turn upon the beauty of liberty and virtue, and the deformity, turpitude, and malignity, of slavery and vice [meaning mainly governmental evils from the standpoint of Free Man]. Let the public disputations become researches into the grounds and nature and ends of government, and the means of preserving the good and demolishing the evil. Let the dialogues, and all the exercises, become the instruments of impressing on the tender mind, and of spreading and distributing far and wide, the ideas of right and the sensations of freedom. In a word, let every sluice of knowledge be opened and set a-flowing."

He continued by warning of Britain's plan to enslave American colonists through the Stamp Act and other such measures; then continued:

"These are not the vapors of a melancholy mind, nor the effusions of envy, disappointed ambition, nor of a spirit of opposition to government, but the emanations of a heart that burns for its country's welfare. No one of any feeling, born and educated in this once happy country, can consider the numerous distresses, the gross indignities, the barbarous ignorance, the haughty usurpations, that we have reason to fear are meditating for ourselves, our children, our neighbors, in short, for all our countrymen and all their posterity, without the utmost agonies of heart and many tears."

The distinguished clergyman, Jonathan Mayhew, was mentioned expressly by Adams with praise for his valuable writings in support of the cause of Man's freedom in America.

This message has great significance today for all parts of American society because of the pressing need at present for sound information and education, to the end that Individual Liberty may be made and kept secure under constitutionally limited government—respected in practice and preserved in full integrity for the sake of the present generation as well as for the benefit of Posterity, for whom the present generation is merely temporary trustee.

It is only through living the principles which The Founders lived, and serving the ideals which they served, that in each generation any and every American can, in truth, render all honor to The Founders.

Could they return to the American scene now and speak a word of warning in behalf of the cause of Individual Liberty, they would perhaps be satisfied to repeat the remark of Dr. Joseph Warren— President of the Massachusetts Congress and a Major General, killed in action at Bunker Hill on June 17, 1775—in his oration in Boston on March 5, 1775 (the anniversary of the "Boston Massacre" by British troops). His words were in effect addressed to every American of every generation, faced with the never-ending need for Friends of Liberty to be faithful, vigilant and active in support of the institutions and principles which are essential to Liberty's well-being:

"Our country is in danger, but not to be despaired of . . . On you depend the fortunes of America. You are to decide the important·question, on which rest the happiness and liberty of millions yet unborn. Act worthy of yourselves."

PART IV
APPENDIX

EXPLANATORY NOTE
REGARDING THE ROOSEVELT ADDRESS
(see facing page)

(Quoting from main text, page 180, *ante*)

It is desirable, therefore, to quote here a modern writing which correctly reflects the views of the Framers and Adopters as to the initial instrument's exclusion of fields of power from Federal control and, in addition, takes into account all amendments to the present period.

A 1930 writing which fills this need is available; and, in addition, it is an excellent and concise discussion of the traditional American philosophy and system of government regarding especially the nature and importance of decentralization of power ("States Rights") as a mainstay of the security of the people's liberties. The Constitution has not been amended since 1930 to increase Federal power, so this writing in effect speaks as of today with regard to the extent of Federal powers; indeed, they have since decreased by repeal of the 18th ("Prohibition") Amendment by adoption in 1933 of the 21st Amendment. This 1930 writing is cited for the further reason that it is couched in simple terms and presents only ideas which were then common knowledge and accepted truths among the American people—even among Youth with a normal high-school education for that period—as well as among the people through all generations from 1787 to 1930. The writing is cited not because it expressed anything new, or any original thinking of its author but, on the contrary, because it does *not* do so. Its special usefulness and value stems from the fact that it merely *re*-stated the traditional view as always understood and supported up to 1930 by all competent scholars and authorities—including the three Branches of the Federal government, especially the Supreme Court—as well as by leaders and the American people in general. This widespread understanding was such in 1930 that, if the valedictorian of a graduating class of a college, or even of a high school, had then made this address as the one usual on such an occasion, the audience would justly have applauded on the ground that there was nothing in it but long-accepted truths so well known that it merely evidenced the young orator's being soundly and reasonably well informed regarding the elementary simplicities of the traditional American philosophy and system of constitutionally limited and decentralized power and its fundamental importance to the safety of the American people's God-given, unalienable rights.

ADDRESS OF FRANKLIN D. ROOSEVELT

as Governor of New York, March 2, 1930

(per text in his *Public Papers and Addresses*, 1938, I, 569—
also *New York Times* March 3, 1930)

I have been asked to talk about the respective powers of the National and the State Governments to rule and regulate, where one begins and the other ends. By some curious twist of the public mind, under the terms "Home Rule" or "States' Rights," this problem has been considered by many to apply, primarily, to the prohibition issue.

As a matter of fact and law, the governing rights of the States are all of those which have not been surrendered to the National Government by the Constitution or its amendments. Wisely or unwisely, people know that under the Eighteenth Amendment Congress has been given the right to legislate on this particular subject, but this is not the case in the matter of a great number of other vital problems of government, such as *the conduct of public utilities, of banks, of insurance, of business, of agriculture, of education, of social welfare and of a dozen other important features. In these, Washington must not be encouraged to interfere.*

The proper relations between the government of the United States and the governments of the separate States thereof depend entirely, in their legal aspects, on what powers have been voluntarily ceded to the central government by the States themselves. What these powers of government are is contained in our Federal Constitution, either by direct language, by judicial interpretation thereof during many years, or by implication so plain as to have been recognized by the people generally.

The United States Constitution has proved itself the most marvelously elastic compilation of rules of government ever written. Drawn up at a time when the population of this country was practically confined to a fringe along our Atlantic coast, combining into one nation for the first time scattered and feeble States, newly released from the autocratic control of the English Government, its preparation involved innumerable compromises between the different Commonwealths. Fortunately for the stability of our Nation, it was already apparent that the vastness of our territory presented geographical and climatic differences which gave to the States wide differences in the nature of their industry, their agriculture and their commerce. Already the New England States had turned toward shipping and manufacturing, while the South was devoting itself almost exclusively to the easier agriculture which a milder climate permitted. *Thus, it was clear to the framers of our Constitution that the greatest possible liberty of self-government must be given to each State, and that any national administration attempting to make all laws for the whole Nation, such as was wholly practical in Great Britain, would inevitably result at some future time in a dissolution of the Union itself.*

The preservation of this "Home Rule" by the States is not a cry of jealous Commonwealths seeking their own aggrandizement at the expense of sister States. It is *a fundamental necessity if we are to remain a truly united country.* The whole success of our democracy has not been that it is a democracy wherein the will of a bare majority of the total inhabitants is imposed upon the minority, but that it has been a democracy where through a division of government into units called States the rights and interests of the minority have been respected and have always been given a voice in the control of our affairs. This is the principle on which the little State of Rhode Island is given just as large a voice in our national Senate as the great State of New York.

The moment a mere numerical superiority by either States or voters in this country proceeds to ignore the needs and desires of the minority, and, for their own selfish purposes or advancement, hamper or oppress that minority, or debar them in any way from equal privileges and equal rights—that moment will mark the failure of our constitutional system.

For this reason a proper understanding of the fundamental powers of the States is very necessary and important. There are, I am sorry to say, danger signals flying. A lack of study and knowledge of the matter of the sovereign power of the people through State government has led us to drift insensibly toward that dangerous disregard of minority needs which marks the beginning of autocracy. Let us not forget that there can be an autocracy of special classes or commercial interests which is utterly incompatible with a real democracy whose boasted motto is, "of the people, by the people and for the people." Already the more thinly populated agricultural districts of the West are bitterly complaining that rich and powerful industrial interests of the East have shaped the course of government to selfish advantage.

The doctrine of regulation and legislation by "master minds," in whose judgment and will all the people may gladly and quietly acquiesce, has been too glaringly apparent at Washington during these last ten years. Were it possible to find "master minds" so unselfish, so willing to decide unhesitatingly against their own personal interests or private prejudices, men almost god-like in their ability to hold the scales of Justice with an even hand, such a government might be to the interest of the country, but *there are none such on our political horizon, and we cannot expect a complete reversal of all the teachings of history.*

Now, to bring about government by oligarchy masquerading as democracy, it is fundamentally essential that practically all authority and control be centralized in our National Government. The individual sovereignty of our States must first be destroyed, except in mere minor matters of legislation. *We are safe from the danger of any such departure from the principles on which this country was founded just so long as the individual home rule of the States is scrupulously preserved and fought for whenever it seems in danger.*

Thus it will be seen that this "Home Rule" is a most important thing, a most vital thing, if we are to continue along the course on which we have so far progressed with such unprecedented success.

Let us see, then, what are the rights of the different States, as distinguished from the rights of the National Government. The Constitution says that "the powers not delegated to the United States by the Constitution, nor prohibited by it to the States, are reserved to the States, respectively, or to the people," and Article IX, which precedes this, reads: "The enumeration in the Constitution of certain rights shall not be construed to deny or disparage others retained by the people."

Now, what are the powers delegated to the United States by the Constitution? First of all, the National Government is entrusted with the duty of protecting any or all States from the danger of invasion or conquest by foreign powers by sea or land, and in return the States surrender the right to engage in any private wars of their own. This involves, of course, the creation of the army and navy and the right to enroll citizens of any State in time of need. Next is given the treaty-making power and the sole right of all intercourse with foreign States, the issuing of money and its protection from counterfeiting. The regulation of weights and measures so as to be uniform, the entire control and regulation of commerce with foreign nations and among the several States, the protection of patents and copyrights, the erection of minor Federal tribunals throughout the country, and the establishment of postoffices are specifically enumerated. The power to collect taxes, duties and imposts, *to pay the debts for the common defense and general welfare* of the country is also given to the United States Congress, as the law-making body of the Nation.

It is interesting to note that under the power to create postoffices the Constitution specifically provides for the building of post roads as a Federal enterprise, thus early recognizing that good roads were of benefit to intercommunication between the several States, and that districts too poor to afford to construct them at their own expense were entitled to some measure of Federal assistance. It is on this same principle that New York and other States are aiding rural counties, or constructing entirely at State expense improved through-thoroughfares suited to modern traffic. The Constitution also contains guarantees of religious freedom, of equality before the law of all citizens, of protection from confiscation of property and from other possible acts of injustice to the individual citizens; and Congress is empowered to pass laws enforcing these guarantees of the Constitution, which is declared to be the supreme law of the land.

On such a small foundation have we erected the whole enormous fabric of Federal Government which costs us now $3,500,000,000 every year, and if we do not halt this steady process of building commissions and regulatory bodies and special legislation like huge inverted pyramids over every one of the simple Constitutional provisions, we shall soon be spending many billions of dollars more.

A few additional powers have been granted to the Federal Government by subsequent amendments. Slavery has been prohibited. All citizens, including women, have been given the franchise; the right to levy taxes on income, as well as the famous Eighteenth Amendment regarding intoxicating liquors, practically complete these later changes.

So much for what may be called the "legal side of national versus State sovereignty." *But what are the underlying principles on which this Government is founded? There is, first and foremost, the new thought that every citizen is entitled to live his own life in his own way so long as his conduct does not injure any of his fellowmen.* This was to be a new "Land of Promise" where a man could worship God in the way he saw fit, where he could rise by industry, thrift and intelligence to the highest places in the Commonwealth, where he could be secure from tyranny and injustice—*a free agent, the maker or the destroyer of his own destiny.*

But the minute a man or any collection of men sought to achieve power or wealth by crowding others off the path of progress, by using their strength, individually or collectively, to force the weak to the wall—that moment the whole power of Government, backed, as is every edict of the Government, by the entire army and navy of the United States, was pledged to make progress through tyranny or oppression impossible.

On this sure foundation of the protection of the weak against the strong, stone by stone, our entire edifice of Government has been erected. As the individual is protected from possible oppression by his neighbors, so the smallest political unit, the town, is, in theory at least, allowed to manage its own affairs, secure from undue interference by the larger unit of the county which, in turn, is protected from mischievous meddling by the State.

This is what we call the doctrine of "Home Rule," and the whole spirit and intent of the Constitution is to carry this great principle into the relations between the National Government and the Governments of the States.

Let us remember that from the very beginning differences in climate, soil, conditions, habits and modes of living in States separated by thousands of miles rendered it necessary to give the fullest individual latitude to the individual States. Let us further remember that the mining States of the Rockies, the fertile savannas of the South, the prairies of the West, and the rocky soil of the New England States created many problems and introduced many factors in each locality, which have no existence in others. *It must be obvious that almost every new or old problem of government must be solved, if it is to be solved to the satisfaction of the people of the whole country, by each State in its own way.*

There are many glaring examples where exclusive Federal control is manifestly against the scheme and intent of our Constitution.

It is, to me, unfortunate that under a clause in our Constitution, itself primarily intended for an entirely different purpose, our Federal Courts have been made a refuge by those who seek to evade the mandates of the State Judiciary.

I think if we understand what I have tried to make clear tonight as to the fundamental principles on which our Government is built, and what the underlying idea of the relations between individuals and States and States and the National Government should be, we can all of us reason for ourselves what should be the proper course in regard to Federal legislation on any of the questions of the day.

(Italics added)

WASHINGTON'S
FAREWELL ADDRESS
United States, September 19, 1796

Friends, and Fellow-Citizens: The period for a new election of a Citizen, to Administer the Executive government of the United States, being not far distant, and the time actually arrived, when your thoughts must be employed in designating the person, who is to be clothed with that important trust, it appears to me proper, especially as it may conduce to a more distinct expression of the public voice, that I should now apprise you of the resolution I have formed, to decline being considered among the number of those, out of whom a choice is to be made.

I beg you, at the same time, to do me the justice to be assured, that this resolution has not been taken, without a strict regard to all the considerations appertaining to the relation, which binds a dutiful citizen to his country, and that, in with drawing the tender of service which silence in my situation might imply, I am influenced by no diminution of zeal for your future interest, no deficiency of grateful respect for your past kindness; but am supported by a full conviction that the step is compatible with both.

The acceptance of, and continuance hitherto in, the office to which your Suffrages have twice called me, have been a uniform sacrifice of inclination to the opinion of duty, and to a deference for what appeared to be your desire. I constantly hoped, that it would have been much earlier in my power, consistently with motives, which I was not at liberty to disregard, to return to that retirement, from which I had been reluctantly drawn. The strength of my inclination to do this, previous to the last Election, had even led to the preparation of an address to declare it to you; but mature reflection on the then perplexed and critical posture of our Affairs with foreign Nations, and the unanimous advice of persons entitled to my confidence, impelled me to abandon the idea.

I rejoice, that the state of your concerns, external as well as internal, no longer renders the pursuit of inclination incompatible with the sentiment of duty, or propriety; and am persuaded whatever partiality may be retained for my services, that in the present circumstances of our country, you will not disapprove my determination to retire.

The impressions, with which I first undertook the arduous trust, were explained on the proper occasion. In the discharge of this trust, I will only say, that I have, with good intentions, contributed towards the Organization and Administration of the government, the best exertions of which a very fallible judgment was capable. Not unconscious, in the outset, of the inferiority of my qualifications, experience in my own eyes, perhaps still more in the eyes of others, has strengthned the motives to diffidence of myself; and every day the encreasing weight of years admonishes me more and more, that the shade of retirement is as necessary to me as it will be welcome. Satisfied that if any circumstances have given peculiar value to my services, they were temporary, I have the consolation to believe, that while choice and prudence invite me to quit the political scene, patriotism does not forbid it. [Word "strengthned" above per original.]

In looking forward to the moment, which is to terminate the career of my public life, my feelings do not permit me to suspend the deep acknowledgment of that debt of gratitude wch. [which] I owe to my beloved country, for the many honors it has conferred upon me; still more for the stedfast confidence with which it has supported me; and for the opportunities I have thence enjoyed of manifesting my inviolable attachment, by services faithful and persevering, though in usefulness unequal to my zeal. If benefits have resulted to our country from these services, let it always be remembered to your praise, and as an instructive example in our annals, that, under circumstances in which the Passions agitated in every direction were liable to mislead, amidst appearances sometimes dubious, vicissitudes of fortune often discouraging, in situations in which not unfrequently want of Success has countenanced the spirit of criticism, the constancy of your support was the essential prop of the efforts, and a guarantee of the plans by which they were effected. Profoundly penetrated with this idea, I shall carry it with me to my grave, as a strong incitement to unceasing vows that Heaven may continue to you the choicest tokens of its beneficence; that your Union and brotherly affection may be perpetual; that the free constitution, which is the work of your hands, may be sacredly maintained; that its Administration in every department may be stamped with wisdom and Virtue; that, in fine, the happiness of the people of these States, under the auspices of liberty, may be made complete, by so careful a preservation and so prudent a use of this blessing as will acquire to them the glory of recommending it to the applause, the affection, and adoption of every nation which is yet a stranger to it.

Here, perhaps, I ought to stop. But a solicitude for your welfare, which cannot end but with my life, and the apprehension of danger, natural to that solicitude, urge me on an occasion like the present, to offer to your solemn contemplation, and to recommend to your frequent review, some sentiments; which are the result of much reflection, of no inconsiderable observation, and which appear to me all important to the permanency of your felicity as a People. These will be offered to you with the more freedom, as you can only see in them the disinterested warnings of a parting friend, who can possibly have no personal motive to bias his counsel. Nor can I forget, as an encouragement to it, your endulgent reception of my sentiments on a former and not dissimilar occasion.

Interwoven as is the love of liberty with every ligament of your hearts, no recommendation of mine is necessary to fortify or confirm the attachment.

The Unity of Government which constitutes you one people is also now dear to you. It is justly so; for it is a main Pillar in the Edifice of your real independence, the support of your tranquility at home; your peace abroad; of your safety; of your prosperity; of that very Liberty which you so highly prize. But as it is easy to foresee, that from different causes and from different quarters, much pains will be taken, many artifices employed, to weaken in your minds the conviction of this truth; as this is the point in your political fortress against which the batteries of internal and external enemies will be most constantly and actively (though often covertly and insidiously) directed, it is of infinite moment, that you should properly estimate the immense value of your national Union to your collective and individual happiness; that you should cherish a cordial, habitual and immoveable attachment to it; accustoming yourselves to think and speak of it as of the Palladium of your political safety and prosperity; watching for its preservation with jealous anxiety; discountenancing whatever may suggest even a suspicion that it can in any event be abandoned, and indignantly frowning upon the first dawning of every attempt to alienate any portion of our Country from the rest, or to enfeeble the sacred ties which now link together the various parts.

For this you have every inducement of sympathy and interest. Citizens by birth or choice, of a common country, that country has a right to concentrate your affections. The name of AMERICAN, which belongs to you, in your national capacity, must always exalt the just pride of Patriotism, more than any appellation derived from local discriminations. With slight shades of difference, you have the same Religion, Manners, Habits and political Principles. You have in a Common cause fought and triumphed together. The independence and liberty you possess are the work of joint counsels, and joint efforts; of common dangers, sufferings and successes.

But these considerations, however powerfully they address themselves to your sensibility are greatly outweighed by those which apply more immediately to your Interest. Here every portion of our country finds the most commanding motives for carefully guarding and preserving the Union of the whole.

The *North*, in an unrestrained intercourse with the *South,* protected by the equal Laws of a common government, finds in the productions of the latter, great additional resources of Maratime and commercial enterprise and precious materials of manufacturing industry. The *South* in the same Intercourse, benefitting by the Agency of the *North,* sees its agriculture grow and its commerce expand. Turning partly into its own channels the seamen of the *North,* it finds its particular navigation envigorated; and while it contributes, in different ways, to nourish and increase the general mass of the National navigation, it looks forward to the protection of a Maratime strength, to which itself is unequally adapted. The *East,* in a like intercourse with the *West,* already finds, and in the progressive improvement of interior communications, by land and water, will more and more find a valuable vent for the commodities which it brings from abroad, or manufactures at home. The *West* derives from the *East* supplies requisite to its growth and comfort, and what is perhaps of still greater consequence, it must of necessity owe the *secure* enjoyment of indispensable *outlets* for its own productions to the weight, influence, and the future Maritime strength of the Atlantic side of the Union, directed by an indissoluble community of Interest as *one Nation.* Any other tenure by which the *West* can hold this essential advantage, whether derived from its own separate strength, or from an apostate and unnatural connection with any foreign Power, must be intrinsically precarious.

While then every part of our country thus feels an immediate and particular Interest in Union, all the parts combined cannot fail to find in the united mass of means and efforts greater strength, greater resource, proportionably greater security from external danger, a less frequent interruption of their Peace by foreign Nations; and, what is of inestimable value! they must derive from Union an exemption from those broils and Wars between themselves, which so frequently afflict neighboring countries, not tied together by the same government; which their own rivalships alone would be sufficient to produce, but which opposite foreign alliances, attachments and intriegues would stimulate and imbitter. Hence likewise they will avoid the necessity of those overgrown Military establishments, which under any form of Government are inauspicious to liberty, and which are to be regarded as particularly hostile to Republican Liberty: In this sense it is, that your Union ought to be considered as a main prop of your liberty, and that the love of the one ought to endear to you the preservation of the other.

These considerations speak a persuasive language to every reflecting and virtuous mind, and exhibit the continuance of the Union as a primary object of Patriotic desire. Is there a doubt, whether a common government can embrace so large a sphere? Let experience solve it. To listen to mere speculation in such a case were criminal. We are authorized to hope that a proper organization of the whole, with the auxiliary agency of governments for the respective Sub divisions, will afford a happy issue to the experiment. 'Tis well worth a fair and full experiment With such powerful and obvious motives to Union, affecting all parts of our country, while experience shall not have demonstrated its impracticability, there will always be reason, to distrust the patriotism of those, who in any quarter may endeavor to weaken its bands.

In contemplating the causes wch. [which] may disturb our Union, it occurs as matter of serious concern, that any ground should have been furnished for characterizing parties by *Geographical* discriminations: *Northern* and *Southern; Atlantic* and *Western;* whence designing men may endeavour to excite a belief that there is a real difference of local interests and views. One of the expedients of Party to acquire influence, within particular districts, is to misrepresent the opinions and aims of other Districts. You cannot shield yourselves too much against the jealousies and heart burnings which spring from these misrepresentations. They tend to render Alien to each other those who ought to be bound together by fraternal affection. The inhabitants of our Western country have lately had a useful lesson on this head. They have seen, in the Negociation by the Executive, and in the unanimous ratification by the Senate, of the Treaty with Spain, and in the universal satisfaction at that event, throughout the United States, a decisive proof how unfounded were the suspicions propagated among them of a policy in the General Government and in the Atlantic States unfriendly to their Interests in regard to the Mississippi. They have been witnesses to the formation of two Treaties, that with G: [Great] Britain and that with Spain, which secure to them every thing they could desire, in respect to our Foreign relations, towards confirming their prosperity. Will it not be their wisdom to rely for the preservation of these advantages on the Union by wch. [which] they were procured? Will they not henceforth be deaf to those advisers, if such they are, who would sever them from their Brethren and connect them with Aliens?

To the efficacy and permanency of Your Union, a Government for the whole is indispensable. No Alliances however strict between the parts can be an adequate substitute. They must inevitably experience the infractions and interruptions which all Alliances in all times have experienced. Sensible of this momentous truth, you have improved upon your first essay, by the adoption of a Constitution of Government, better calculated than your former for an intimate Union, and for the efficacious management of your common concerns. This government, the offspring of our own choice uninfluenced and unawed, adopted upon full investigation and mature deliberation, completely free in its principles, in the distribution of its powers, uniting security with energy, and containing within itself a provision for its own amendment, has a just claim to your confidence and your support. Respect for its authority, compliance with its Laws, acquiescence in its measures, are duties enjoined by the fundamental maxims of true Liberty. The basis of our political systems is the right of the people to make and to alter their Constitutions of Government. But the Constitution which at any time exists, 'till changed by an explicit and authentic act of the whole People, is sacredly obligatory upon all. The very idea of the power and the right of the People to establish Government presupposes the duty of every Individual to obey the established Government.

All obstructions to the execution of the Laws, all combinations and Associations, under whatever plausible character, with the real design to direct, controul counteract, or awe the regular deliberation and action of the Constituted authorities are distructive of this fundamental principle and of fatal tendency. They serve to organize faction, to give it an artificial and extraordinary force; to put in the place of the delegated will of the Nation, the will of a party; often a small but artful and enterprising minority of the Community; and, according to the alternate triumphs of different parties, to make the public administration the Mirror of the ill concerted and incongruous projects of faction, rather than the organ of consistent and wholesome plans digested by common councils and modefied by mutual interests. However combinations or Associations of the above description may now and then answer popular ends, they are likely, in the course of time and things, to become potent engines, by which cunning, ambitious and unprincipled men will be enabled to subvert the Power of the People, and to usurp for themselves the reins of Government; destroying afterwards the very engines which have lifted them to unjust dominion.

Towards the preservation of your Government and the permanency of your present happy state, it is requisite, not only that you steadily discountenance irregular oppositions to its acknowledged authority, but also that you resist with care the spirit of innovation upon its principles however specious the pretexts. one [*sic*] method of assault may be to effect, in the forms of the Constitution, alterations which will impair the energy of the system, and thus to undermine what cannot be directly overthrown. In all the changes to which you may be invited, remember that time and habit are at least as necessary to fix the true character of Governments, as of other human institutions; that experience is the surest standard, by which to test the real tendency of the existing Constitution of a country; that facility in changes upon the credit of mere hypotheses and opinion exposes to perpetual change, from the endless variety of hypotheses and opinion: and remember, especially, that for the efficient management of your common interests, in a country so extensive as ours, a Government of as much vigour as is consistent with the perfect security of Liberty is indispensable. Liberty itself will find in such a Government, with powers properly distributed and adjusted, its surest Guardian. It is indeed little else than a name, where the Government is too feeble to withstand the enterprises of faction, to confine each member of the Society within the limits prescribed by the laws and to maintain all in the secure and tranquil enjoyment of the rights of person and property.

I have already intimated to you the danger of Parties in the State, with particular reference to the founding of them on Geographical discriminations. Let me now take a more comprehensive view, and warn you in the most solemn manner against the baneful effects of the Spirit of Party, generally[.]

This spirit, unfortunately, is inseperable from our nature, having its root in the strongest passions of the human Mind. It exists under different shapes in all Governments, more or less stifled, controuled, or repressed; but, in those of the popular form it is seen in its greatest rankness and is truly their worst enemy.

The alternate domination of one faction over another, sharpened by the spirit of revenge natural to party dissention, which in different ages and countries has perpetrated the most horrid enormities, is itself a frightful despotism. But this leads at length to a more formal and permanent despotism. The disorders and miseries, which result, gradually incline the minds of men to seek security and repose in the absolute power of an Individual: and sooner or later the chief of some prevailing faction more able or more fortunate than his competitors, turns this disposition to the purposes of his own elevation, on the ruins of Public Liberty.

Without looking forward to an extremity of this kind (which nevertheless ought not to be entirely out of sight) the common and continual mischiefs of the spirit of Party are sufficient to make it the interest and the duty of a wise People to discourage and restrain it.

It serves always to distract the Public Councils and enfeeble the Public administration. It agitates the Community with ill founded jealousies and false alarms, kindles the animosity of one part against another, foments occasional riot and insurrection. It opens the door to foreign influence and corruption, which find a facilitated access to the government itself through the channels of party passions. Thus the policy and and [*sic*] the will of one country, are subjected to the policy and will of another.

There is an opinion that parties in free countries are useful checks upon the Administration of the Government and serve to keep alive the spirit of Liberty. This within certain limits is probably true, and in Governments of a Monarchial cast Patriotism may look with endulgence, if not with favour, upon the spirit of party. But in those of the popular character, in Governments purely elective, it is a spirit not to be encouraged. From their natural tendency, it is certain there will always be enough of that spirit for every salutary purpose. And there being constant danger of excess, the effort ought to be, by force of public opinion, to mitigate and assuage it. A fire not to be quenched; it demands a uniform vigilance to prevent its bursting into a flame, lest instead of warming it should consume.

It is important, likewise, that the habits of thinking in a free Country should inspire caution in those entrusted with its administration, to confine themselves within their respective Constitutional spheres; avoiding in the exercise of the Powers of one department to encroach upon another. The spirit of encroachment tends to consolidate the powers of all the departments in one, and thus to create whatever the form of government, a real despotism. A just estimate of that love of power, and proneness to abuse it, which predominates in the human heart is sufficient to satisfy us of the truth of this position. The necessity of reciprocal checks in the exercise of political power; by dividing and distributing it into different depositories, and constituting each the Guardian of the Public Weal against invasions by the others, has been evinced by experiments ancient and modern; some of them in our country and under our own eyes. To preserve them must be as necessary as to institute them. If in the opinion of the People, the distribution or modification of the Constitutional powers be in any particular wrong, let it be corrected by an amendment in the way which the Constitution designates. But let there be no change by usurpation; for though this, in one instance, may be the instrument of good, it is the customary weapon by which free governments are destroyed. The precedent must always greatly overbalance in permanent evil any partial or transient benefit which the use can at any time yield.

Of all the dispositions and habits which lead to political prosperity, Religion and morality are indispensable supports. In vain would that man claim the tribute of Patriotism, who should labour to subvert these great Pillars of human happiness, these firmest props of the duties of Men and citizens. The mere Politician, equally with the pious man ought to respect and to cherish them. A volume could not trace all their connections with private and public felicity. Let it simply be asked where is the security for property, for reputation, for life, if the sense of religious obligation *desert* the oaths, which are the instruments of investigation in Courts of Justice? And let us with caution indulge the supposition, that morality can be maintained without religion. Whatever may be conceded to the influence of refined education on minds of peculiar structure, reason and experience both forbid us to expect that National morality can prevail in exclusion of religious principle.

'Tis substantially true, that virtue or morality is a necessary spring of popular government. The rule indeed extends with more or less force to every species of free Government. Who that is a sincere friend to it, can look with indifference upon attempts to shake the foundation of the fabric[?]

Promote then as an object of primary importance, Institutions for the general diffusion of knowledge. In proportion as the structure of a government gives force to public opinion, it is essential that public opinion should be enlightened[.]

As a very important source of strength and security, cherish public credit. One method of preserving it is to use it as sparingly as possible: avoiding occasions of expence by cultivating peace, but remembering also that timely disbursements to prepare for danger frequently prevent much greater disbursements to repel it; avoiding likewise the accumulation of debt, not only by shunning occasions of expence, but by vigorous exertions in time of Peace to discharge the Debts which unavoidable wars may have occasioned, not ungenerously throwing upon posterity the burthen which we ourselves ought to bear. The execution of these maxims belongs to your Representatives, but it is necessary that public opinion should cooperate. To facilitate to them the performance of their duty, it is essential that you should practically bear in mind, that towards the payment of debts there must be Revenue; that to have Revenue there must be taxes; that no taxes can be devised which are not more or less inconvenient and unpleasant; that the intrinsic embarrassment inseperable from the selection of the proper objects (which is always a choice of difficulties) ought to be a decisive motive for a candid construction of the Conduct of the Government in making it, and for a spirit of acquiescence in the measures for obtaining Revenue which the public exigencies may at any time dictate.

Observe good faith and justice towds. [towards] all Nations. Cultivate peace and harmony with all. Religion and morality enjoin this conduct; and can it be that good policy does not equally enjoin it? It will be worthy of a free, enlightened, and, at no distant period, a great Nation, to give to mankind the magnanimous and too novel example of a People always guided by an exalted justice and benevolence. Who can doubt that in the course of time and things the fruits of such a plan would richly repay any temporary advantages wch. [which] might be lost by a steady adherence to it? Can it be, that

Providence has not connected the permanent felicity of a Nation with its virtue? The experiment, at least, is recommended by every sentiment which ennobles human Nature. Alas! is it rendered impossible by its vices?

In the execution of such a plan nothing is more essential than that permanent, inveterate antipathies against particular Nations and passionate attachments for others should be excluded; and that in place of them just and amicable feelings towards all should be cultivated. The Nation, which indulges towards another an habitual hatred, or an habitual fondness, is in some degree a slave. It is a slave to its animosity or to its affection, either of which is sufficient to lead it astray from its duty and its interest. Antipathy in one Nation against another, disposes each more readily to offer insult and injury, to lay hold of slight causes of umbrage, and to be haughty and intractable, when accidental or trifling occasions of dispute occur. Hence frequent collisions, obstinate envenomed and bloody contests. The Nation, prompted by ill will and resentment sometimes impels to War the Government, contrary to the best calculations of policy. The Government sometimes participates in the national propensity, and adopts through passion what reason would reject; at other times, it makes the animosity of the Nation subservient to projects of hostility instigated by pride, ambition and other sinister and pernicious motives. The peace often, sometimes perhaps the Liberty, of Nations has been the victim.

So likewise, a passionate attachment of one Nation for another produces a variety of evils. Sympathy for the favourite nation, facilitating the illusion of an imaginary common interest, in cases where no real common interest exists, and infusing into one the enmities of the other, betrays the former into a participation in the quarrels and Wars of the latter, without adequate inducement or justification: It leads also to concessions to the favourite Nation of priviledges denied to others, which is apt doubly to injure the Nation making the concessions; by unnecessarily parting with what ought to have been retained; and by exciting jealousy, ill will, and a disposition to retaliate, in the parties from whom eql. [equal] priviledges are withheld: And it gives to ambitious, corrupted, or deluded citizens (who devote themselves to the favourite Nation) facility to betray, or sacrifice the interests of their own country, without odium, sometimes even with popularity; gilding with the appearances of a virtuous sense of obligation a commendable deference for public opinion, or a laudable zeal for public good, the base or foolish compliances of ambition corruption or infatuation.

As avenues to foreign influence in innumerable ways, such attachments are particularly alarming to the truly enlightened and independent Patriot. How many opportunities do they afford to tamper with domestic factions, to practice the arts of seduction, to mislead public opinion, to influence or awe the public Councils! Such an attachment of a small or weak, towards a great and powerful Nation, dooms the former to be the satellite of the latter.

Against the insidious wiles of foreign influence, (I conjure you to believe me fellow citizens) the jealousy of a free people ought to be *constantly* awake; since history and experience prove that foreign influence is one of the most baneful foes of Republican Government. But that jealousy to be useful must be impartial; else it becomes the instrument of the very influence to be avoided, instead of a defence against it. Excessive partiality for one foreign nation and excessive dislike of another, cause those whom they actuate to see danger only on one side, and serve to veil and even second the arts of influence on the other. Real Patriots, who may resist the intriegues of the favourite, are liable to become suspected and odious; while its tools and dupes usurp the applause and confidence of the people, to surrender their interests.

The Great rule of conduct for us, in regard to foreign Nations is in extending our commercial relations to have with them as little *political* connection as possible. So far as we have already formed engagements let them be fulfilled, with perfect good faith. Here let us stop.

Europe has a set of primary interests, which to us have none, or a very remote relation. Hence she must be engaged in frequent controversies, the causes of which are essentially foreign to our concerns. Hence therefore it must be unwise in us to implicate ourselves, by artificial ties, in the ordinary vicissitudes of her politics, or the ordinary combinations and collisions of her friendships, or enmities:

Our detached and distant situation invites and enables us to pursue a difference course. If we remain one People, under an efficient government, the period is not far off, when we may defy material injury from external annoyance; when we may take such an attitude as will cause the neutrality we may at any time resolve upon to be scrupulously respected; when belligerent nations, under the impossibility of making acquisitions upon us, will not lightly hazard the giving us provocation; when we may choose peace or war, as our interest guided by our justice shall Counsel.

Why forego the advantages of so peculiar a situation? Why quit our own to stand upon foreign ground? Why, by interweaving our destiny with that of any part of Europe, entangle our peace and prosperity in the toils of European Ambition, Rivalship, Interest, Humour or Caprice?

'Tis our true policy to steer clear of permanent Alliances, with any portion of the foreign world. So far, I mean, as we are now at liberty to do it, for let me not be understood as capable of patronising infidility to existing engagements (I hold the maxim no less applicable to public than to private affairs, that honesty is always the best policy). I repeat it therefore, let those engagements be observed in their genuine sense. But in my opinion, it is unnecessary and would be unwise to extend them.

Taking care always to keep ourselves, by suitable establishments, on a respectably defensive posture, we may safely trust to temporary alliances for extraordinary emergencies.

Harmony, liberal intercourse with all Nations, are recommended by policy, humanity and interest. But even our Commercial policy should hold an equal and impartial hand: neither seeking nor granting exclusive favours or preferences; consulting the natural course of things; diffusing and deversifying by gentle means the streams of Commerce, but forcing nothing; establishing with Powers so disposed; in order to give to trade a stable course, to define the rights of our Merchants, and to enable the Government to support them; conventional rules of intercourse, the best that present circumstances and mutual opinion will permit, but temporary, and liable to be from time to time abandoned or varied, as experience and circumstances shall dictate; constantly keeping in view, that 'tis folly in one Nation to look for disinterested favors from another; that it must pay with a portion of its Independence for whatever it may accept under that character; that by such acceptance, it may place itself in the condition of having given equivalents for nominal favours and yet of being reproached with ingratitude for not giving more. There can be no greater error than to expect, or calculate upon real favours from Nation to Nation. 'Tis an illusion which experience must cure, which a just pride ought to discard.

In offering to you, my Countrymen these counsels of an old and affectionate friend, I dare not hope they will make the strong and lasting impression, I could wish; that they will controul the usual current of the passions, or prevent our Nation from running the course which has hitherto marked the Destiny of Nations: But if I may even flatter myself, that they may be productive of some partial benefit, some occasional good; that they may now and then recur to moderate the fury of party spirit, to warn against the mischiefs of foreign Intriegue, to guard against the Impostures of pretended patriotism; this hope will be a full recompence for the solicitude for your welfare, by which they have been dictated.

How far in the discharge of my Official duties, I have been guided by the principles which have been delineated, the public Records and other evidences of my conduct must Witness to You and to the world. To myself, the assurance of my own conscience is, that I have at least believed myself to be guided by them.

In relation to the still subsisting War in Europe, my Proclamation of the 22d. of April 1793 is the index to my Plan. Sanctioned by your approving voice and by that of Your Representatives in both Houses of Congress, the spirit of that measure has continually governed me; uninfluenced by any attempts to deter or divert me from it.

After deliberate examination with the aid of the best lights I could obtain I was well satisfied that our Country, under all the circumstances of the case, had a right to take, and was bound in duty and interest, to take a Neutral position. Having taken it, I determined, as far as should depend upon me, to maintain it, with moderation, perseverence and firmness.

The considerations, which respect the right to hold this conduct, it is not necessary on this occasion to detail. I will only observe, that according to my understanding of the matter, that right, so far from being denied by any of the Belligerent Powers has been virtually admitted by all.

The duty of holding a Neutral conduct may be inferred, without any thing more, from the obligation which justice and humanity impose on every Nation, in cases in which it is free to act, to maintain inviolate the relations of Peace and amity towards other Nations.

The inducements of interest for observing that conduct will best be referred to your own reflections and experience. With me, a predominant motive has been to endeavour to gain time to our country to settle and mature its yet recent institutions, and to progress without interruption, to that degree of strength and consistency, which is necessary to give it, humanly speaking, the command of its own fortunes.

Though in reviewing the incidents of my Administration, I am unconscious of intentional error, I am nevertheless too sensible of my defects not to think it probable that I may have committed many errors. Whatever they may be I fervently beseech the Almighty to avert or mitigate the evils to which they may tend. I shall also carry with me the hope that my country will never cease to view them with indulgence; and that after forty five years of my life dedicated to its Service, with an upright zeal, the faults of incompetent abilities will be consigned to oblivion, as myself must soon be to the Mansions of rest.

Relying on its kindness in this as in other things, and actuated by that fervent love towards it, which is so natural to a Man, who views in it the native soil of himself and his progenitors for several Generations; I anticipate with pleasing expectation that retreat, in which I promise myself to realize, without alloy, the sweet enjoyment of partaking, in the midst of my fellow Citizens, the benign influence of good Laws under a free Government, the ever favourite object of my heart, and the happy reward, as I trust, of our mutual cares, labours and dangers.

GEO. WASHINGTON.

UNITED STATES,
17th September, 1796.

Note

Text as presented in *The Writings of George Washington* from the Original Manuscript Sources 1745-1799; prepared under the direction of the United States Bicentennial Commission and published by authority of Congress; John C. Fitzpatrick, Editor; 1931-1944; 39 Volumes; Volume 35 at pages 214-238. Spelling, punctuation and capitalization per the original.

THE FEDERALIST

Excerpts
Regarding the Judiciary

(Text per 1788 M'Lean edition in book form, published under the personal supervision of Hamilton; taken from numbers 78-83 discussing the Judiciary. Emphasis Hamilton's.)

Number 78 by Hamilton
(in its entirety)

WE proceed now to an examination of the judiciary department of the proposed government.

In unfolding the defects of the existing confederation, the utility and necessity of a federal judicature have been clearly pointed out. It is the less necessary to recapitulate the considerations there urged; as the propriety of the institution in the abstract is not disputed: The only questions which have been raised being relative to the manner of constituting it, and to its extent. To these points therefore our observations shall be confined.

The manner of constituting it seems to embrace these several objects—1st. The mode of appointing the judges—2d. The tenure by which they are to hold their places—3d. The partition of the judiciary authority between different courts, and their relations to each other.

First. As to the mode of appointing the judges: This is the same with that of appointing the officers of the union in general, and has been so fully discussed in the two last numbers, that nothing can be said here which would not be useless repetition.

Second. As to the tenure by which the judges are to hold their places: This chiefly concerns their duration in office; the provisions for their support; and the precautions for their responsibility.

According to the plan of the convention, all the judges who may be appointed by the United States are to hold their offices *during good behaviour,* which is conformable to the most approved of the state constitutions; and among the rest, to that of this state. Its propriety having been drawn into question by the adversaries of that plan, is no light symptom of the rage for objection which disorders their imaginations and judgments. The standard of good behaviour for

271

the continuance in office of the judicial magistracy is certainly one of the most valuable of the modern improvements in the practice of government. In a monarchy it is an excellent barrier to the despotism of the prince: In a republic it is a no less excellent barrier to the encroachments and oppressions of the representative body. And it is the best expedient which can be devised in any government, to secure a steady, upright and impartial administration of the laws.

Whoever attentively considers the different departments of power must perceive, that in a government in which they are separated from each other, the judiciary, from the nature of its functions, will always be the least dangerous to the political rights of the constitution; because it will be least in a capacity to annoy or injure them. The executive not only dispenses the honors, but holds the sword of the community. The legislative not only commands the purse, but prescribes the rules by which the duties and rights of every citizen are to be regulated. The judiciary on the contrary has no influence over either the sword or the purse, no direction either of the strength or of the wealth of the society, and can take no active resolution whatever. It may truly be said to have neither FORCE nor WILL, but merely judgment; and must ultimately depend upon the aid of the executive arm even for the efficacy of its judgments.

This simple view of the matter suggests several important consequences. It proves incontestibly that the judiciary is beyond comparison the weakest of the three departments of power*; that it can never attack with success either of the other two; and that all possible care is requisite to enable it to defend itself against their attacks. It equally proves, that though individual oppression may now and then proceed from the courts of justice, the general liberty of the people can never be endangered from that quarter: I mean, so long as the judiciary remains truly distinct from both the legislative and executive. For I agree that "there is no liberty, if the power of judging be not separated from the legislative and executive powers†." And it proves, in the last place, that as liberty can have nothing to fear from the judiciary alone, but would have everything to fear from its union with either of the other departments; that as all the effects of such an union must ensue from a dependence of the former on the latter, not-

* The celebrated Montesquieu speaking of them says: "of the three powers above mentioned, the JUDICIARY is next to nothing."—*Spirit of Laws,* Vol. I, page 186.
† Idem, page 181.

withstanding a nominal and apparent separation; that as from the natural feebleness of the judiciary, it is in continual jeopardy of being overpowered, awed or influenced by its co-ordinate branches; and that as nothing can contribute so much to its firmness and independence, as permanency in office, this quality may therefore be justly regarded as an indispensable ingredient in its constitution; and in a great measure as the citadel of the public justice and the public security.

The complete independence of the courts of justice is peculiarly essential in a limited constitution. By a limited constitution I understand one which contains certain specified exceptions to the legislative authority; such for instance as that it shall pass no bills of attainder, no *ex post facto* laws, and the like. Limitations of this kind can be preserved in practice no other way than through the medium of the courts of justice; whose duty it must be to declare all acts contrary to the manifest tenor of the constitution void. Without this, all the reservations of particular rights or privileges would amount to nothing.

Some perplexity respecting the right of the courts to pronounce legislative acts void, because contrary to the constitution, has arisen from an imagination that the doctrine would imply a superiority of the judiciary to the legislative power. It is urged that the authority which can declare the acts of another void, must necessarily be superior to the one whose acts may be declared void. As this doctrine is of great importance in all the American constitutions, a brief discussion of the grounds on which it rests cannot be unacceptable.

There is no position which depends on clearer principles, than that every act of a delegated authority, contrary to the tenor of the commission under which it is exercised, is void. No legislative act therefore contrary to the constitution can be valid. To deny this would be to affirm that the deputy is greater than his principal; that the servant is above his master; that the representatives of the people are superior to the people themselves; that men acting by virtue of powers may do not only what their powers do not authorize, but what they forbid.

If it be said that the legislative body are themselves the constitutional judges of their own powers, and that the construction they put upon them is conclusive upon the other departments, it may be answered, that this cannot be the natural presumption, where it is not to be collected from any particular provisions in the constitution. It is not otherwise to be supposed that the constitution could intend to enable the representatives of the people to substitute their *will* to that of their constituents. It is far more rational to suppose that the courts were designed to be an intermediate body between the people and the legislature, in order, among other things, to keep the latter within the limits assigned to their authority. The interpretation of the laws is the proper and peculiar province of the courts. A constitution is in fact, and must be, regarded by the judges as a fundamental law. It therefore belongs to them to ascertain its meaning as well as the meaning of any particular act proceeding from the legislative body. If there should happen to be an irreconcileable variance between the two, that which has the superior obligation and validity ought of course to be preferred; or in other words, the constitution ought to be preferred to the statute, the intention of the people to the intention of their agents.

Nor does this conclusion by any means suppose a superiority of the judicial to the legislative power. It only supposes that the power of the people is superior to both; and that where the will of the legislature declared in its statutes, stands in opposition to that of the people declared in the constitution, the judges ought to be governed by the latter, rather than the former. They ought to regulate their decisions by the fundamental laws, rather than by those which are not fundamental.

This exercise of judicial discretion in determining between two contradictory laws, is exemplified in a familiar instance. It not uncommonly happens, that there are two statutes existing at one time, clashing in whole or in part with each other, and neither of them containing any repealing clause or expression. In such a case, it is the province of the courts to liquidate and fix their meaning and operation: So far as they can by any fair construction be reconciled to each other; reason and law conspire to dictate that this should be done: Where this is impracticable, it becomes a matter of necessity to give effect to one, in exclusion of the other. The rule which has obtained in the courts for determining their relative validity is that the last in order of time shall be preferred to the first. But this is mere rule of construction, not derived from any positive law, but from the nature and reason of the thing. It is a rule not enjoined upon the courts by legislative provision, but adopted by themselves, as consonant to truth and propriety, for the direction of their conduct as interpreters of the law. They thought it reasonable, that between the interfering acts of an *equal* authority, that which was the last indication of its will, should have the preference.

But in regard to the interfering acts of a superior and subordinate authority, of an original and derivative power, the nature and reason of the thing indicate the converse of that rule as proper to be followed. They teach us that the prior act of a superior ought to be preferred to the subsequent act of an inferior and subordinate authority; and that, accordingly, whenever a particular statute contravenes the constitution, it will be the duty of the judicial tribunals to adhere to the latter, and disregard the former.

It can be of no weight to say, that the courts on the pretence of a repugnancy, may substitute their own pleasure to the constitutional intentions of the legislature. This might as well happen in the case of two contradictory statutes; or it might as well happen in every adjudication upon any single statute. The courts must declare the sense of the law; and if they should be disposed to exercise WILL instead of JUDGMENT, the consequence would equally be the substitution of their pleasure to that of the legislative body. The observation, if it proved any thing, would prove that there ought to be no judges distinct from that body.

If then the courts of justice are to be considered as the bulwarks of a limited constitution against legislative encroachments, this consideration will afford a strong argument for the permanent tenure of judicial offices, since nothing will contribute so much as this to that independent spirit in the judges, which must be essential to the faithful performance of so arduous a duty.

This independence of the judges is equally requisite to guard the constitution and the rights of individuals from the effects of those ill humours which the arts of designing men, or the influence of particular conjunctures sometimes disseminate among the people themselves, and which, though they speedily give place to better information and more deliberate reflection, have a tendency in the mean time to occasion dangerous innovations in the government, and serious oppressions of the minor party in the community. Though I trust the friends of the proposed constitution will never concur with its enemies* in questioning that fundamental principle of republican government, which admits the right of the people to alter or abolish the established constitution whenever they find it inconsistent with their happiness; yet it is not to be inferred from this principle, that the representatives of the people, whenever a momentary inclination happens to lay hold of a majority of their constituents incompatible with the provisions

* Vide Protest of the minority of the convention of Pennsylvania, Martin's speech, etc.

in the existing constitution, would on that account be justifiable in a violation of those provisions; or that the courts would be under a greater obligation to connive at infractions in this shape, than when they had proceeded wholly from the cabals of the representative body. Until the people have by some solemn and authoritative act annulled or changed the established form, it is binding upon themselves collectively, as well as individually; and no presumption, or even knowledge of their sentiments, can warrant their representatives in a departure from it, prior to such an act. But it is easy to see that it would require an uncommon portion of fortitude in the judges to do their duty as faithful guardians of the constitution, where legislative invasions of it had been instigated by the major voice of the community.

But it is not with a view to infractions of the constitution only that the independence of the judges may be an essential safeguard against the effects of occasional ill humours in the society. These sometimes extend no farther than to the injury of the private rights of particular classes of citizens, by unjust and partial laws. Here also the firmness of the judicial magistracy is of vast importance in mitigating the severity, and confining the operation of such laws. It not only serves to moderate the immediate mischiefs of those which may have been passed, but it operates as a check upon the legislative body in passing them; who, perceiving that obstacles to the success of an iniquitous intention are to be expected from the scruples of the courts, are in a manner compelled by the very motives of the injustice they meditate, to qualify their attempts. This is a circumstance calculated to have more influence upon the character of our governments, than but few may be aware of. The benefits of the integrity and moderation of the judiciary have already been felt in more states than one; and though they may have displeased those whose sinister expectations they may have disappointed, they must have commanded the esteem and applause of all the virtuous and disinterested. Considerate men of every description ought to prize whatever will tend to beget or fortify that temper in the courts; as no man can be sure that he may not be tomorrow the victim of a spirit of injustice, by which he may be a gainer to-day. And every man must now feel that the inevitable tendency of such a spirit is to sap the foundations of public and private confidence, and to introduce in its stead, universal distrust and distress.

That inflexible and uniform adherence to the rights of the constitution, and of individuals, which we perceive to be indispensable in the courts of justice, can certainly not be expected from judges who hold their offices by a temporary commission. Periodical appointments, however regulated, or by whomsoever made, would in some way or other be fatal to their necessary independence. If the power of making them was committed either to the executive or legislative, there would be danger of an improper complaisance to the branch which possessed it; if to both, there would be an unwillingness to hazard the displeasure of either; if to the people, or to persons chosen by them for the special purpose, there would be too great a disposition to consult popularity, to justify a reliance that nothing would be consulted but the constitution and the laws.

There is yet a further and a weighty reason for the permanency of the judicial offices; which is deducible from the nature of the qualifications they require. It has been frequently remarked with great propriety, that a voluminous code of laws is one of the inconveniences necessarily connected with the advantages of a free government. To avoid an arbitrary discretion in the courts, it is indispensable that they should be bound down by strict rules and precedents, which serve to define and point out their duty in every particular case that comes before them; and it will readily be conceived from the variety of controversies which grow out of the folly and wickedness of mankind, that the records of those precedents must unavoidably swell to a very considerable bulk, and must demand long and laborious study to acquire a competent knowledge of them. Hence it is that there can be but few men in the society, who will have sufficient skill in the laws to qualify them for the stations of judges. And making the proper deductions for the ordinary depravity of human nature, the number must be still smaller of those who unite the requisite integrity with the requisite knowledge. These considerations apprise us, that the government can have no great option between fit characters; and that a temporary duration in office, which would naturally discourage such characters from quitting a lucrative line of practice to accept a seat on the bench, would have a tendency to throw the administration of justice into hands less able, and less well qualified to conduct it with utility and dignity. In the present circumstances of this country, and in those in which it is likely to be for a long time to come, the disadvantages on this score would be greater than they may at first sight appear; but it must be confessed that they are far inferior to those which present themselves under the other aspects of the subject.

Upon the whole there can be no room to doubt that the convention acted wisely in copying from the models of those constitutions which have established *good behaviour* as the tenure of their judicial offices in point of duration; and that so far from being blameable on this account, their plan would have been inexcusably defective if it had wanted this important feature of good government. The experience of Great Britain affords an illustrious comment on the excellence of the institution.

Number 79 by Hamilton
(excerpt)

NEXT to permanency in office, nothing can contribute more to the independence of the judges than a fixed provision for their support. The remark made in relation to the president, is equally applicable here. In the general course of human nature, *a power over a man's subsistence amounts to a power over his will.* And we can never hope to see realized in practice the complete separation of the judicial from the legislative power, in any system, which leaves the former dependent for pecuniary resources on the occasional grants of the latter. . . .

The precautions for their responsibility are comprised in the article respecting impeachments. They are liable to be impeached for malconduct by the house of representatives, and tried by the senate, and if convicted, may be dismissed from office and disqualified for holding any other. This is the only provision on the point, which is consistent with the necessary independence of the judicial character, and is the only one which we find in our own constitution in respect to our own judges.

[Editorial note: "our" refers to New York State.]

Number 80 by Hamilton
(excerpt)

To judge with accuracy of the proper extent of the federal judicature it will be necessary to consider, in the first place, what are its proper objects. . . .

[Editorial note: omitted part lists fields of jurisdiction of Federal courts.]

The first point depends upon this obvious consideration that there ought always to be a constitutional method of giving efficacy to constitutional provisions. What for instance would avail restrictions on the authority of the state legislatures, without some constitutional mode of enforcing the observance of them? The states, by the plan of the convention are prohibited from doing a variety of things; some of which are incompatible with the interests of the union, and others with the principles of good government. The imposition of duties on imported articles, and the emission of paper money, are specimens of each kind. No man of sense will believe that such prohibitions would be scrupulously regarded, without some effectual power in the government to restrain or correct the infractions of them. This power must either be a direct negative on the state laws, or an authority in the federal courts, to over-rule such as might be in manifest contravention of the articles of union. There is no third course that I can imagine. The latter appears to have been thought by the convention preferable to the former, and I presume will be most agreeable to the states.

As to the second point, it is impossible by any argument or comment to make it clearer than it is in itself. If there are such things as political axioms, the propriety of the judicial power of a government being co-extensive with its legislative, may be ranked among the number. The mere necessity of uniformity in the interpretation of the national laws, decides the question. Thirteen independent courts of final jurisdiction over the same causes, arising upon the same laws, is a hydra in government, from which nothing but contradiction and confusion can proceed. . . .

[*Editorial note: Omitted portion discusses Federal courts' jurisdiction over matters involving U.S. government and foreigners.*]

The power of determining causes between two states, between one state and the citizens of another, and between the citizens of different states, is perhaps not less essential to the peace of the union than that which has been just examined. History gives us a horrid picture of the dissensions and private wars which distracted and desolated Germany prior to the institution of the IMPERIAL CHAMBER by Maximilian, towards the close of the fifteenth century; and informs us at the same time of the vast influence of that institution in appeasing the disorders and establishing the tranquillity of the empire. This was a court invested with authority to decide finally all differences between the members of the Germanic body. . . .

It may be esteemed the basis of the union, that "the citizens of each state shall be entitled to all the privileges and immunities of citizens of the several states." And if it be a just principle that every government *ought to possess the means of executing its own provisions by its own authority,* it will follow, that in order to the inviolable maintenance of that equality of privileges and immunities to which the citizens of the union will be entitled, the national judiciary ought to preside in all cases in which one state or its citizens are opposed to another state or its citizens. To secure the full effect of so fundamental a provision against all evasion and subterfuge, it is necessary that its construction should be committed to that tribunal, which, having no local attachments, will be likely to be impartial between the different states and their citizens, and which, owing its official existence to the union, will never be likely to feel any bias inauspicious to the principles on which it is founded. . . .

From this review of the particular powers of the federal judiciary, as marked out in the constitution, it appears, that they are all conformable to the principles which ought to have governed the structure of that department, and which were necessary to the perfection of the system. If some partial inconveniences should appear to be connected with the incorporation of any of them into the plan, it ought to be recollected that the national legislature will have ample authority to make such *exceptions* and to prescribe such regulations as will be calculated to obviate or remove these inconveniences. The possibility of particular mischiefs can never be viewed by a well-informed mind as a solid objection to a general principle, which is calculated to avoid general mischiefs, and to obtain general advantages.

Number 81 by Hamilton
(excerpt)

LET us now return to the partition of the judiciary authority between different courts, and their relations to each other.

"The judicial power of the United States is (by the plan of the convention) to be vested in one supreme court, and in such inferior courts as the congress may from time to time ordain and establish." *

That there ought to be one court of supreme and final jurisdiction is a proposition which has not been, and is not likely to be contested. The reasons for it have been assigned in another place, and are too obvious to need repetition. The only question that seems to have been

* Article 3, Section 1.

raised concerning it, is whether it ought to be a distinct body, or a branch of the legislature. . . .

The arguments or rather suggestions, upon which this charge is founded, are to this effect: "The authority of the proposed supreme court of the United States, which is to be a separate and independent body, will be superior to that of the legislature. The power of construing the laws, according to the *spirit* of the constitution, will enable that court to mould them into whatever shape it may think proper; especially as its decisions will not be in any manner subject to the revision or correction of the legislative body. This is as unprecedented as it is dangerous. In Britain, the judicial power in the last resort, resides in the house of lords, which is a branch of the legislature; and this part of the British government has been imitated in the state constitutions in general. The parliament of Great-Britain, and the legislatures of the several states, can at any time rectify by law, the exceptionable decisions of their respective courts. But the errors and usurpations of the supreme court of the United States will be uncontrolable and remediless." This, upon examination, will be found to be altogether made up of false reasoning upon misconceived fact.

In the first place, there is not a syllable in the plan under consideration, which *directly* empowers the national courts to construe the laws according to the spirit of the constitution, or which gives them any greater latitude in this respect, than may be claimed by the courts of every state. I admit however, that the constitution ought to be the standard of construction for the laws, and that wherever there is an evident opposition, the laws ought to give place to the constitution. But this doctrine is not deducible from any circumstance peculiar to the plan of the convention; but from the general theory of a limited constitution; and as far as it is true, is equally applicable to most, if not to all the state governments. There can be no objection therefore, on this account, to the federal judicature, which will not lie against the local judicatures in general, and which will not serve to condemn every constitution that attempts to set bounds to the legislative discretion. . . .

These considerations teach us to applaud the wisdom of those states, who have committed the judicial power in the last resort, not to a part of the legislature, but to distinct and independent bodies of men. Contrary to the supposition of those, who have represented the plan of the convention in this respect as novel and unprecedented, it is but a copy of the constitutions of New-Hampshire, Massachusetts,

Pennsylvania, Delaware, Maryland, Virginia, North-Carolina, South-Carolina, and Georgia; and the preference which has been given to these models is highly to be commended. . . .

It may in the last place be observed that the supposed danger of judiciary encroachments on the legislative authority, which has been upon many occasions reiterated, is in reality a phantom. Particular misconstructions and contraventions of the will of the legislature may now and then happen; but they can never be so extensive as to amount to an inconvenience, or in any sensible degree to affect the order of the political system. This may be inferred with certainty from the general nature of the judicial power; from the objects to which it relates; from the manner in which it is exercised; from its comparative weakness, and from its total incapacity to support its usurpations by force. And the inference is greatly fortified by the consideration of the important constitutional check, which the power of instituting impeachments, in one part of the legislative body, and of determining upon them in the other, would give to that body upon the members of the judicial department. This is alone a complete security. There never can be danger that the judges, by a series of deliberate usurpations on the authority of the legislature, would hazard the united resentment of the body entrusted with it, while this body was possessed of the means of punishing their presumption by degrading them from their stations. While this ought to remove all apprehensions on the subject, it affords at the same time a cogent argument for constituting the senate a court for the trial of impeachments.

Number 82 by Hamilton
(excerpt)

The principles established in a former paper* teach us, that the states will retain all *pre-existing* authorities, which may not be exclusively delegated to the federal head; and that this exclusive delegation can only exist in one of three cases; where an exclusive authority is in express terms granted to the union; or where a particular authority is granted to the union, and the exercise of a like authority is prohibited to the states, or where an authority is granted to the union with which a similar authority in the states would be utterly incompatible. Though these principles may not apply with the same force to the judiciary as to the legislative power; yet I am inclined to

* No. 32.

think that they are in the main just with respect to the former as well as the latter. And under this impression I shall lay it down as a rule that the state courts will *retain* the jurisdiction they now have, unless it appears to be taken away in one of the enumerated modes.

Number 83 by Hamilton
(excerpt)

Having now seen that the maxims relied upon will not bear the use made of them, let us endeavor to ascertain their proper use and true meaning. This will be best done by examples. The plan of the convention declares that the power of congress or in other words of the *national legislature,* shall extend to certain enumerated cases. This specification of particulars evidently excludes all pretension to a general legislative authority; because an affirmative grant of special powers would be absurd as well as useless, if a general authority was intended.

In like manner, the judicial authority of the federal judicatures, is declared by the constitution to comprehend certain cases particularly specified. The expression of those cases marks the precise limits beyond which the federal courts cannot extend their jurisdiction; because the objects of their cognizance being enumerated, the specification would be nugatory if it did not exclude all ideas of more extensive authority.

Number 22 by Hamilton
(excerpt)

A circumstance, which crowns the defects of the confederation, remains yet to be mentioned—the want of a judiciary power. Laws are a dead letter without courts to expound and define their true meaning and operation. The treaties of the United States, to have any force at all, must be considered as part of the law of the land. Their true import, as far as respects individuals, must, like all other laws, be ascertained by judicial determinations. To produce uniformity in these determinations, they ought to be submitted in the last resort, to one SUPREME TRIBUNAL. And this tribunal ought to be instituted under the same authority which forms the treaties themselves. These ingredients are both indispensable. If there is in each State a court of final jurisdiction, there may be as many different final determinations on the same point, as there are courts. There are endless diversities in the opinions of men. We often see not only different courts, but the judges of the same courts differing from each other. To avoid the confusion which would unavoidably result from the contradictory decisions of a number of independent judicatories, all nations have found it necessary to establish one court paramount to the rest, possessing a general superintendence, and authorized to settle and declare in the last resort an uniform rule of civil justice.

This is the more necessary where the frame of the government is so compounded, that the laws of the whole are in danger of being contravened by the laws of the parts. In this case, if the particular tribunals are invested with a right of ultimate jurisdiction, besides the contradictions to be expected from difference of opinion, there will be much to fear from the bias of local views and prejudices, and from the interference of local regulations.

Number 33 by Hamilton
(excerpt)

But it may be again asked, who is to judge of the *necessity* and *propriety* of the laws to be passed for executing the powers of the union? I answer first that this question arises as well and as fully upon the simple grant of those powers, as upon the declaratory clause; and I answer in the second place, that the national government, like every other, must judge in the first instance of the proper exercise of its powers, and its constituents in the last. If the federal government should overpass the just bounds of its authority, and make a tyrannical use of its powers; the people whose creature it is must appeal to the standard they have formed, and take such measures to redress the injury done to the constitution, as the exigency may suggest and prudence justify. The propriety of a law in a constitutional light, must always be determined by the nature of the powers upon which it is founded. . . .

But it is said, that the laws of the union are to be the *supreme law* of the land. What inference can be drawn from this, or what would they amount to, if they were not to be supreme? It is evident they would amount to nothing. A LAW by the very meaning of the term includes supremacy. It is a rule which those to whom it is prescribed are bound to observe. This results from every political association. If individuals enter into a state of society, the laws of that society must be the supreme regulator of their conduct. If a number of political societies enter into a larger political society, the laws which the latter may enact, pursuant to the powers entrusted to it by its constitution, must necessarily be supreme over those societies, and the individuals of whom they are composed. It would otherwise be a mere treaty, dependent on the good faith of the parties, and not a government; which is only another word for POLITICAL POWER AND SUPREMACY. But it will not follow from this doctrine that acts of the larger society which are *not pursuant* to its constitutional powers, but which are invasions of the residuary authorities of the smaller societies, will become the supreme law of the land. These will be merely acts of usurpation, and will deserve to be treated as such. Hence we perceive that the clause which declares the supremacy of the laws of the union, like the one we have just before considered, only declares a truth, which flows immediately and necessarily from the institution of a federal government. It will not, I presume, have escaped observation, that it *expressly* confines this supremacy to laws made *pursuant to the constitution;* which I mention merely as an instance of caution in the convention; since that limitation would have been to be understood, though it had not been expressed.

Number 39 by Madison
(excerpt)

But if the government be national with regard to the *operation* of its powers, it changes its aspect again when we contemplate it in relation to the *extent* of its powers. The idea of a national government involves in it, not only an authority over the individual citizens, but an indefinite supremacy over all persons and things, so far as they are objects of lawful government. Among a people consolidated into one nation, this supremacy is compleatly vested in the national legislature. Among communities united for particular purposes, it is vested partly in the general, and partly in the municipal legislatures. In the former case, all local authorities are subordinate to the supreme; and may be controuled, directed, or abolished by it at pleasure. In the latter, the local or municipal authorities form distinct and independent portions of the supremacy, no more subject within their respective spheres to the general authority, than the general authority is subject to them within its own sphere. In this relation then, the proposed government cannot be deemed a *national* one; since its jurisdiction extends to certain enumerated objects only, and leaves to the several states a residuary and inviolable sovereignty over all other objects. It is true that in controversies relating to the boundary between the two jurisdictions, the tribunal which is ultimately to decide, is to be established under the general government. But this does not change the principle of the case. The decision is to be impartially made, according to the rules of the constitution; and all the usual and most effectual precautions are taken to secure this impartiality. Some such tribunal is clearly essential to prevent an appeal to the sword, and a dissolution of the compact; and that it ought to be established under the general, rather than under the local governments; or to speak more properly, that it could be safely established under the first alone, is a position not likely to be combated.

Number 44 by Madison
(excerpt)

If it be asked, what is to be the consequence, in case the congress shall misconstrue this part of the constitution, and exercise powers not warranted by its true meaning? I answer the same as if they should misconstrue or enlarge any other power vested in them, as if the general power had been reduced to particulars, and any one of these were to be violated; the same in short, as if the state legislatures should violate their respective constitutional authorities. In the first instance, the success of the usurpation will depend on the executive and judiciary departments, which are to expound and give effect to the legislative acts; and in the last resort, a remedy must be obtained from the people, who can by the election of more faithful representatives, annul the acts of the usurpers. The truth is, that this ultimate redress may be more confided in against unconstitutional acts of the federal than of the state legislatures, for this plain reason, that as every such act of the former, will be an invasion of the rights of the latter, these will be ever ready to mark the innovation, to sound the alarm to the people, and to exert their local influence in effecting a change of federal representatives. There being no such intermediate body between the state legislatures and the people, interested in watching the conduct of the former, violations of the state constitutions are more likely to remain unnoticed and unredressed.

VIRGINIA RESOLUTIONS OF 1798 AND 1799

(as adopted by the House of Delegates of Virginia—per
text in Madison's *Writings,* Hunt edition, VI, 326 *et seq.*)

Explanatory Note

This supplements the discussion of these resolutions in the main
text (pages 16-17, 143-145, *ante*) in connection with the 1825 resolution of the Board of Visitors of the University of Virginia.

After the adoption of the *Virginia Resolutions* of 1798, criticism
induced the adoption in the following January of the companion
resolutions of 1799 in order to make expressly clear the points
covered, so as to dispel any misunderstanding in this regard. This
pertains especially to the repudiation, in the first of the "Resolves"
adopted in 1799, of the idea that "there is a party in this Commonwealth under the influence of any foreign Power"—meaning the
Jefferson "party" (political followers). The "intrigues" of foreign
Powers, also referred to there, were those of the French government
mainly—through its agents in the United States involved in activities
which the Administration of President John Adams considered to be
subversive, as well as the contemptuous and hostile conduct in general
in this period of the French government toward the United States.
The famous "XYZ" affair is an example. It was Jefferson's long and
well known sympathy for the French people, in their struggle toward
Liberty commencing with the French Revolution in 1789, which
caused the widespread misunderstanding—chiefly in New England
and mainly among the followers of his political opponents: Hamilton
and President John Adams.

The foregoing explains why it is sound to consider that the mention,
in the 1825 University resolution mentioned above, of the resolutions
of 1799 as being one of the sources of correct information concerning
the fundamental American principles, was intended by Jefferson and
Madison to embrace also, by implied reference, the more famous
Virginia Resolutions of 1798.

The text of the two sets of resolutions, of 1798 and 1799, are
as follows:

RESOLUTIONS OF 1798

[1.] *Resolved,* That the General Assembly of Virginia doth un-equivocally express a firm resolution to maintain and defend the Constitution of the United States, and the Constitution of this State, against every aggression either foreign or domestic; and that they will support the Government of the United States in all measures warranted by the former.

[2.] That this Assembly most solemnly declares a warm attachment to the Union of the States, to maintain which it pledges all its powers; and that, for this end, it is their duty to watch over and oppose every infraction of those principles which constitute the only basis of that Union, because a faithful observance of them can alone secure its existence and the public happiness.

[3.] That this Assembly doth explicitly and peremptorily declare that it views the powers of the Federal Government as resulting from the compact to which the States are parties, as limited by the plain sense and intention of the instrument constituting that compact; as no further valid than they are authorized by the grants enumerated in that compact; and that, in case of a deliberate, palpable, and dangerous exercise of other powers not granted by the said compact, the States, who are parties thereto, have the right and are in duty bound to interpose for arresting the progress of the evil, and for maintaining within their respective limits the authorities, rights, and liberties appertaining to them.

[4.] That the General Assembly doth also express its deep regret, that a spirit has in sundry instances been manifested by the Federal Government to enlarge its powers by forced constructions of the constitutional charter which defines them; and that indications have appeared of a design to expound certain general phrases (which, having been copied from the very limited grant of powers in the former Articles of Confederation, were the less liable to be mis-construed) so as to destroy the meaning and effect of the particular enumeration which necessarily explains and limits the general phrases; and so as to consolidate the States, by degrees, into one sovereignty, the obvious tendency and inevitable result of which would be to transform the present republican system of the United States into an absolute, or, at best, a mixed monarchy.

[5.] That the General Assembly doth particularly protest against the palpable and alarming infractions of the Constitution in the two late cases of the "Alien and Sedition Acts," passed at the last session of Congress; the first of which exercises a power nowhere delegated to the Federal Government and which, by uniting legislative and judicial powers to those of [the] executive, subvert the general principles of free government, as well as the particular organization and positive provisions of the Federal Constitution; and the other of which acts exercises, in like manner, a power not delegated by the Constitution, but, on the contrary, expressly and positively forbidden by one of the amendments thereto,—a power which more than any other, ought to produce universal alarm, because it is levelled against the right of freely examining public characters and measures, and of free communication among the people thereon, which has ever been justly deemed the only effectual guardian of every other right.

[6.] That this State having by its Convention which ratified the Federal Constitution expressly declared that, among other essential rights, "the liberty of conscience and of the press cannot be cancelled, abridged, restrained or modified by any authority of the United States," and from its extreme anxiety to guard these rights from every possible attack of sophistry or ambition, having, with other States, recommended an amendment for that purpose, which amendment was in due time annexed to the Constitution,—it would mark a reproachful inconsistency and criminal degeneracy, if an indifference were now shown to the palpable violation of one of the rights thus declared and secured, and to the establishment of a precedent which may be fatal to the other.

[7.] That the good people of this Commonwealth, having ever felt and continuing to feel the most sincere affection for their brethren of the other States, the truest anxiety for establishing and perpetuating the union of all and the most scrupulous fidelity to that Constitution, which is the pledge of mutual friendship, and the instrument of mutual happiness, the General Assembly doth solemnly appeal to the like dispositions of the other States, in confidence that they will concur with this Commonwealth in declaring, as it does hereby declare, that the acts aforesaid are unconstitutional; and that the necessary and proper measures will be taken by each for co-operating with this State, in maintaining unimpaired the authorities, rights, and liberties reserved to the States respectively, or to the people.

[8.] That the Governor be desired to transmit a copy of the foregoing resolutions to the Executive authority of each of the other States, with a request that the same may be communicated to the Legislature thereof; and that a copy be furnished to each of the Senators and Representatives representing this State in the Congress of the United States.

RESOLUTIONS OF 1799

IN THE HOUSE OF DELEGATES,
Friday, January 4, 1799.

Resolved, That the General Assembly of Virginia will cooperate with the authorities of the United States in maintaining the independence, Union, and Constitution thereof, against the hostilities or intrigues of all foreign Powers whatsoever; and that although differences of opinion do exist in relation to internal and domestic measures, yet a charge that there is a party in this Commonwealth under the influence of any foreign Power is unfounded and calumnious.

Resolved, That the General Assembly do, and will always, behold with indignation, depredations on our commerce, insults on our citizens, impressments of our seamen, or any other injuries committed on the people or Government of the United States by foreign nations.

Resolved, Nevertheless, that our security from invasion and the force of our militia render a standing army unnecessary; that the policy of the United States forbids a war of aggression; that our whole reliance ought to be on ourselves; and, therefore, that while we will repel invasion at every hazard, we shall deplore and deprecate the evils of war for any other cause.

Resolved, That a copy of the foregoing resolutions be sent to each of the Senators and Representatives of this State in Congress.

THE SUPREME COURT'S RULING
IN THE 1905 SOUTH CAROLINA CASE:
THE ORIGINAL MEANING IS CONTROLLING

The Supreme Court's power is limited with regard to inter-preting the Constitution—ascertaining and defining the intent with which it was framed and ratified (adopted)

(Author's preliminary comment)

The rule is well-settled that the object of interpretation, or construction, of a provision of the Constitution ". . . is to give effect to the intent of its framers, and of the people in adopting it." *Lake County v. Rollins,* 130 U. S. 662, 670 (1889). In this opinion, the Court had earlier made it expressly clear that by the phrase, "the people in adopting it," the meaning was "the people who voted it into existence." This referred to the American people's intent expressed through their duly appointed agents—the members of the State Ratifying Conventions—in 1787-1788; or later, with regard to each amendment, in either the State Ratifying Conventions or the State Legislatures, depending upon which method of ratification was used in any particular instance to approve the amendment.

The basic rule of interpretation is clear and has been repeatedly stated by the Supreme Court, for example in *South Carolina v. United States,* 199 U. S. 437 (1905) at pages 448-449:

> "The Constitution is a written instrument. As such its meaning does not alter. That which it meant when adopted it means now. Being a grant of powers to a government its language is general, and as changes come in social and political life it embraces in its grasp all new conditions which are within the scope of the powers in terms conferred. In other words, while the powers granted do not change, they apply from generation to generation to all things to which they are in their nature applicable. This in no manner abridges the fact of its changeless nature and meaning. Those things which are within its grants of power, *as those grants were understood when made,* are still within them,

291

and those things not within them remain still excluded. As said by Mr. Chief Justice Taney in *Dred Scott v. Sandford,* 19 How. 393, 426:

> " 'It is not only the same in words, but the same in meaning, and delegates the same powers to the Government, and reserves and secures the same rights and privileges to the citizens; and as long as it continues to exist in its present form, it speaks not only in the same words, but *with the same meaning and intent with which it spoke when it came from the hands of its framers, and was voted on and adopted by the people of the United States.* Any other rule of construction would abrogate the judicial character of this court, and make it the mere reflex of the popular opinion or passion of the day.'

"It must also be remembered that the framers of the Constitution were not mere visionaries, toying with speculations or theories, but practical men, dealing with the facts of political life as they understood them, putting into form the government they were creating, and prescribing in language clear and intelligible the powers that government was to take. Mr. Chief Justice Marshall, in *Gibbons v. Ogden,* 9 Wheat. 1, 188, well declared:

> " 'As men whose intentions require no concealment, generally employ the words which most directly and aptly express the ideas they intend to convey, the enlightened patriots who framed our Constitution, and the people who adopted it, must be understood to have employed words in their natural sense, and to have intended what they have said.' "

(Italics added)

Author's further comment

Immediately preceding the above-quoted statement from the opinion in the 1857 *Dred Scott* case—60 U. S. (19 Howard) 393 at 426, the Court had in that opinion made further clarifying remarks about negro slaves in explanation of its refusal to violate the intent of the Constitution—the intent of its Framers and Adopters—merely because of changed popular sentiment about slavery. It stated:

"No one, we presume, supposes that any change in public opinion or feeling, in relation to this unfortunate race, in the civilized nations of Europe or in this country, should induce the court to give to the words of the Constitution a more liberal construction in their favor than they were intended to bear when the instrument was framed and adopted. Such an argument would be altogether inadmissible in any tribunal called on to interpret it. If any of its provisions are deemed unjust, there is a mode prescribed in the instrument itself by which it may be amended; but while it remains unaltered, *it must be construed now as it was understood at the time of its adoption.*" (Italics added)

Author's Note: The above-mentioned *Dred Scott* case concerned the negro slave of that name and this case—in which he sought his freedom—has ever since been famous for political as well as constitutional reasons.

DECLARATION OF INDEPENDENCE

IN CONGRESS, JULY 4, 1776.

The unanimous Declaration of the thirteen united States of America,

When in the Course of human events it becomes necessary for one people to dissolve the political bands which have connected them with another, and to assume among the powers of the earth, the separate and equal station to which the Laws of Nature and of Nature's God entitle them, a decent respect to the opinions of mankind requires that they should declare the causes which impel them to the separation.

We hold these truths to be self-evident, that all men are created equal, that they are endowed by their Creator with certain unalienable Rights, that among these are Life, Liberty and the pursuit of Happiness. That to secure these rights, Governments are instituted among Men, deriving their just powers from the consent of the governed, That whenever any Form of Government becomes destructive of these ends, it is the Right of the People to alter or to abolish it, and to institute new Government, laying its foundation on such principles and organizing its powers in such form, as to them shall seem most likely to effect their Safety and Happiness. Prudence, indeed, will dictate that Governments long established should not be changed for light and transient causes; and accordingly all experience hath shown, that mankind are more disposed to suffer, while evils are sufferable, than to right themselves by abolishing the forms to which they are accustomed. But when a long train of abuses and usurpations, pursuing invariably the same Object evinces a design to reduce them under absolute Despotism, it is their right, it is their duty, to throw off such Government, and to provide new Guards for their future security.— Such has been the patient sufferance of these Colonies; and such is now the necessity which constrains them to alter their former Systems of Government. The history of the present King of Great Britain is a history of repeated injuries and usurpations, all having in direct object the establishment of an absolute Tyranny over these States. To prove this, let Facts be submitted to a candid world.

He has refused his Assent to Laws, the most wholesome and necessary for the public good.

He has forbidden his Governors to pass Laws of immediate and pressing importance, unless suspended in their operation till his Assent should be obtained; and when so suspended, he has utterly neglected to attend to them.

He has refused to pass other Laws for the accommodation of large districts of people, unless those people would relinquish the right of Representation in the Legislature, a right inestimable to them and formidable to tyrants only.

He has called together legislative bodies at places unusual, uncomfortable, and distant from the depository of their public Records, for the sole purpose of fatiguing them into compliance with his measures.

He has dissolved Representative Houses repeatedly, for opposing with manly firmness his invasions on the rights of the people.

He has refused for a long time, after such dissolutions, to cause others to be elected; whereby the Legislative powers, incapable of Annihilation, have returned to the People at large for their exercise; the State remaining in the mean time exposed to all the dangers of invasion from without, and convulsions within.

He has endeavoured to prevent the population of these States; for that purpose obstructing the Laws for Naturalization of Foreigners; refusing to pass others to encourage their migrations hither, and raising the conditions of new Appropriations of Lands.

He has obstructed the Administration of Justice, by refusing his Assent to Laws for establishing Judiciary powers.

He has made Judges dependent on his Will alone, for the tenure of their offices, and the amount and payment of their salaries.

He has erected a multitude of New Offices, and sent hither swarms of Officers to harass our people, and eat out their substance.

He has kept among us, in times of peace, Standing Armies without the Consent of our legislatures.

He has affected to render the Military independent of and superior to the Civil power.

He has combined with others to subject us to a jurisdiction foreign to our constitution, and unacknowledged by our laws; giving his Assent to their Acts of pretended Legislation:

For quartering large bodies of armed troops among us:

For protecting them, by a mock Trial, from punishment for any

Murders which they should commit on the Inhabitants of these States:
For cutting off our Trade with all parts of the world:
For imposing taxes on us without our Consent:
For depriving us in many cases, of the benefits of Trial by Jury:
For transporting us beyond Seas to be tried for pretended offenses:
For abolishing the free System of English Laws in a neighbouring Province, establishing therein an Arbitrary government, and enlarging its Boundaries so as to render it at once an example and fit instrument for introducing the same absolute rule into these Colonies:

For taking away our Charters, abolishing our most valuable Laws and altering fundamentally the Forms of our Governments:

For suspending our own Legislatures, and declaring themselves invested with power to legislate for us in all cases whatsoever.

He has abdicated Government here, by declaring us out of his Protection and waging War against us.

He has plundered our seas, ravaged our Coasts, burnt our towns, and destroyed the lives of our people.

He is at this time transporting large Armies of foreign Mercenaries to compleat the works of death, desolation and tyranny, already begun with circumstances of Cruelty & perfidy scarcely paralleled in the most barbarous ages, and totally unworthy the Head of a civilized nation.

He has constrained our fellow Citizens taken Captive on the high Seas to bear Arms against their Country, to become the executioners of their friends and Brethren, or to fall themselves by their Hands.

He has excited domestic insurrections amongst us, and has endeavoured to bring on the inhabitants of our frontiers, the merciless Indian Savages, whose known rule of warfare, is an undistinguished destruction of all ages, sexes and conditions.

In every stage of these Oppressions We have Petitioned for Redress in the most humble terms: Our repeated Petitions have been answered only by repeated injury. A Prince, whose character is thus marked by every act which may define a Tyrant, is unfit to be the ruler of a free people.

Nor have We been wanting in attentions to our British brethren. We have warned them from time to time of attempts by their legislature to extend an unwarrantable jurisdiction over us. We have reminded them of the circumstances of our emigration and settlement here. We have appealed to their native justice and magnanimity, and we have conjured them by the ties of our common kindred to disavow these usurpations, which would inevitably interrupt our connections and correspondence. They too have been deaf to the voice of justice and of consanguinity. We must, therefore, acquiesce in the necessity, which denounces our Separation, and hold them, as we hold the rest of mankind, Enemies in War, in Peace Friends.

We, therefore, the Representatives of the **united States of America,** in General Congress, Assembled, appealing to the Supreme Judge of the world for the rectitude of our intentions, do, in the Name, and by Authority of the good People of these Colonies, solemnly publish and declare, That these United Colonies are, and of Right ought to be **Free and Independent States;** that they are Absolved from all Allegiance to the British Crown, and that all political connection between them and the State of Great Britain, is and ought to be totally dissolved; and that as Free and Independent States, they have full Power to levy War, conclude Peace, contract Alliances, establish Commerce, and to do all other Acts and Things which Independent States may of right do. And for the support of this Declaration, with a firm reliance on the protection of divine Providence, we mutually pledge to each other our Lives, our Fortunes and our sacred Honor.

John Hancock

(*Connecticut*)

Roger Sherman
Sam'el Huntington
Wm. Williams
Oliver Wolcott

(*Delaware*)

Caesar Rodney
Geo. Read
Tho. M'Kean

(*Georgia*)

Button Gwinnett
Lyman Hall
Geo. Walton

(*Maryland*)

Samuel Chase
Wm. Paca

Thos. Stone
Charles Carroll of Carrollton

(*Massachusetts*)

Saml. Adams
John Adams
Robt. Treat Paine
Elbridge Gerry

(*New Hampshire*)

Josiah Bartlett
Wm. Whipple
Matthew Thornton*

(*New Jersey*)

Richd. Stockton
Jno Witherspoon
Fras. Hopkinson
John Hart
Abra. Clark

Declaration of Independence

(*New York*)

Wm. Floyd
Phil. Livingston
Frans. Lewis
Lewis Morris

(*North Carolina*)

Wm. Hooper
Joseph Hewes
John Penn

(*Pennsylvania*)

Robt. Morris
Benjamin Rush
Benja. Franklin
John Morton
Geo. Clymer
Jas. Smith
Geo. Taylor
James Wilson
Geo. Ross

(*Rhode Island*)

Step. Hopkins
William Ellery

(*South Carolina*)

Edward Rutledge
Thos. Heyward, Junr.
Thomas Lynch, Junr.
Arthur Middleton

(*Virginia*)

George Wythe
Richard Henry **Lee**
Th. Jefferson
Benja. Harrison
Thos. Nelson, jr.
Francis Lightfoot **Lee**
Carter Braxton

* Signature followed Wolcott's.
Signatures grouped by States (names of States omitted), but not alphabetically.

Note: above text is based on the engrossed (handwritten) copy as signed, per facsimile of the original in the National Archives, Washington, D.C. Paragraphing corresponds to the separation by dashes in the original. The first printed copies differ only as to minor capitalization and punctuation. In the original, the words above in bold-face letters were written in large letters.

The signing of the Declaration by all of its signatories required several months because some members of the Congress were absent, at their distant homes, on August 2, 1776 when the document—having been engrossed—was signed by most of the members; and the difficulty of travel and other problems delayed for months the signing by some members.

A NOTE CONCERNING THE CONSTITUTION

RATIFICATION OF THE CONSTITUTION

The proposed Constitution was approved by the Convention on September 17, 1787, and was subsequently ratified by the several States, on the following dates: Delaware, December 7, 1787; Pennsylvania, December 12, 1787; New Jersey, December 18, 1787; Georgia, January 2, 1788; Connecticut, January 9, 1788; Massachusetts, February 6, 1788; Maryland, April 28, 1788; South Carolina, May 23, 1788; New Hampshire, June 21, 1788; Virginia, June 26, 1788; New York, July 26, 1788; North Carolina, November 21, 1789; Rhode Island, May 29, 1790.

(Ratification was effective when ratified by the ninth State—New Hampshire)

DATES OF RATIFICATION OF AMENDMENTS

The first ten amendments were proposed by the First Congress on September 25, 1789 and became effective when ratified by Virginia on December 15, 1791—the last ratification needed to make the required three-fourths. The subsequent amendments became effective on the following dates, respectively: Eleventh, January 8, 1798; Twelfth, September 25, 1804; Thirteenth, December 18, 1865; Fourteenth, July 28, 1868; Fifteenth, March 30, 1870; Sixteenth, February 25, 1913; Seventeenth, May 31, 1913; Eighteenth, January 29, 1919; Nineteenth, August 26, 1920; Twentieth, February 6, 1933; Twenty-First, December 5, 1933; Twenty-Second, March 1, 1951; Twenty-Third, April 3, 1961.

(Note: The foregoing effective dates correspond with those specified in the U. S. Code)

THE TEXT

The following text of the original Constitution conforms to the archetype of September 17, 1787—the engrossed (handwritten) copy signed by members of the Federal (framing) Convention—per facsimile of the original in the National Archives, Washington, D.C. The Amendments are as of November 1, 1963, their text being per the United States Code.

(An excellent index to the Constitution is available in House Document 112; 88th Congress, 1st Session; U.S. Government Printing Office, Washington, D.C.)

CONSTITUTION OF THE UNITED STATES

WE THE PEOPLE of the United States, in Order to form a more perfect Union, establish Justice, insure domestic Tranquility, provide for the common defence, promote the general Welfare, and secure the Blessings of Liberty to ourselves and our Posterity, do ordain and establish this Constitution for the United States of America.

ARTICLE I

SECTION 1. All legislative Powers herein granted shall be vested in a Congress of the United States, which shall consist of a Senate and House of Representatives.

SECTION 2. ¹ The House of Representatives shall be composed of Members chosen every second Year by the People of the several States, and the Electors in each State shall have the Qualifications requisite for Electors of the most numerous Branch of the State Legislature.

² No Person shall be a Representative who shall not have attained to the Age of twenty five Years, and been seven Years a Citizen of the United States, and who shall not, when elected, be an Inhabitant of that State in which he shall be chosen.

³ [Representatives and direct Taxes shall be apportioned among the several States which may be included within this Union, according to their respective Numbers, which shall be determined by adding to the whole Number of free Persons, including those bound to Service for a Term of Years, and excluding Indians not taxed, three fifths of all other Persons.]* The actual Enumeration shall be made within three Years after the first Meeting of the Congress of the United States, and within every subsequent Term of ten Years, in such Manner as they shall by Law direct. The Number of Representatives shall not exceed one for every thirty Thousand, but each State shall have

NOTE.—The superior number preceding the paragraphs designates the number of the clause; not in the original.

* The part included in heavy brackets was changed by section 2 of amendment XIV.

at Least one Representative; and until such enumeration shall be made, the State of New Hampshire shall be entitled to chuse three, Massachusetts eight, Rhode-Island and Providence Plantations one, Connecticut five, New-York six, New Jersey four, Pennsylvania eight, Delaware one, Maryland six, Virginia ten, North Carolina five, South Carolina five, and Georgia three.

⁴ When vacancies happen in the Representation from any State, the Executive Authority thereof shall issue Writs of Election to fill such Vacancies.

⁵ The House of Representatives shall chuse their Speaker and other Officers; and shall have the sole Power of Impeachment.

¹ Section 3. The Senate of the United States shall be composed of two Senators from each State, [chosen by the Legislature thereof,]* for six Years; and each Senator shall have one Vote.

² Immediately after they shall be assembled in Consequence of the first Election, they shall be divided as equally as may be into three Classes. The Seats of the Senators of the first Class shall be vacated at the Expiration of the second Year, of the second Class at the Expiration of the fourth Year, and of the third Class at the Expiration of the sixth Year, so that one third may be chosen every second Year; [and if Vacancies happen by Resignation, or otherwise, during the Recess of the Legislature of any State, the Executive thereof may make temporary Appointments until the next Meeting of the Legislature, which shall then fill such Vacancies]. **

³ No Person shall be a Senator who shall not have attained to the Age of thirty Years, and been nine Years a Citizen of the United States, and who shall not, when elected, be an Inhabitant of that State for which he shall be chosen.

⁴ The Vice President of the United States shall be President of the Senate, but shall have no Vote, unless they be equally divided.

⁵ The Senate shall chuse their other Officers, and also a President pro tempore, in the absence of the Vice President, or when he shall exercise the Office of President of the United States.

⁶ The Senate shall have the sole Power to try all Impeachments. When sitting for that Purpose, they shall be on Oath or Affirmation. When the President of the United States is tried, the Chief Justice

* The part included in heavy brackets was changed by section 1 of amendment XVII.

** The part included in heavy brackets was changed by clause 2 of amendment XVII.

shall preside: And no Person shall be convicted without the Concurrence of two thirds of the Members present.

⁷ Judgment in Cases of Impeachment shall not extend further than to removal from Office, and disqualification to hold and enjoy any Office of honor, Trust or Profit under the United States: but the Party convicted shall nevertheless be liable and subject to Indictment, Trial, Judgment and Punishment, according to Law.

SECTION 4. ¹ The Times, Places and Manner of holding Elections for Senators and Representatives, shall be prescribed in each State by the Legislature thereof; but the Congress may at any time by Law make or alter such Regulations, except as to the Places of chusing Senators.

² The Congress shall assemble at least once in every Year, and such Meeting shall [be on the first Monday in December,] unless they shall by Law appoint a different Day. *

SECTION 5. ¹ Each House shall be the Judge of the Elections, Returns and Qualifications of its own Members, and a Majority of each shall constitute a Quorum to do Business; but a smaller Number may adjourn from day to day, and may be authorized to compel the Attendance of absent Members, in such Manner, and under such Penalties as each House may provide.

² Each House may determine the Rules of its Proceedings, punish its Members for disorderly Behaviour, and, with the Concurrence of two thirds, expel a Member.

³ Each House shall keep a Journal of its Proceedings, and from time to time publish the same, excepting such Parts as may in their Judgment require Secrecy; and the Yeas and Nays of the Members of either House on any question shall, at the Desire of one fifth of those Present, be entered on the Journal.

⁴ Neither House, during the Session of Congress, shall, without the Consent of the other, adjourn for more than three days, nor to any other Place than that in which the two Houses shall be sitting.

SECTION 6. ¹ The Senators and Representatives shall receive a Compensation for their Services, to be ascertained by Law, and paid out of the Treasury of the United States. They shall in all Cases, except Treason, Felony and Breach of the Peace, be privileged from Arrest during their Attendance at the Session of their respective Houses, and

* The part included in heavy brackets was changed by section 2 of amendment XX.

303

in going to and returning from the same; and for any Speech or Debate in either House, they shall not be questioned in any other Place.

[2] No Senator or Representative shall, during the Time for which he was elected, be appointed to any civil Office under the Authority of the United States, which shall have been created, or the Emoluments whereof shall have been encreased during such time; and no Person holding any Office under the United States, shall be a Member of either House during his Continuance in Office.

SECTION 7. [1] All Bills for raising Revenue shall originate in the House of Representatives; but the Senate may propose or concur with Amendments as on other Bills.

[2] Every Bill which shall have passed the House of Representatives and the Senate, shall, before it become a Law, be presented to the President of the United States; If he approve he shall sign it, but if not he shall return it, with his Objections to that House in which it shall have originated, who shall enter the Objections at large on their Journal, and proceed to reconsider it. If after such Reconsideration two thirds of that House shall agree to pass the Bill, it shall be sent, together with the Objections, to the other House, by which it shall likewise be reconsidered, and if approved by two thirds of that House, it shall become a Law. But in all such Cases the Votes of both Houses shall be determined by yeas and Nays, and the Names of the Persons voting for and against the Bill shall be entered on the Journal of each House respectively. If any Bill shall not be returned by the President within ten Days (Sundays excepted) after it shall have been presented to him, the Same shall be a Law, in like Manner as if he had signed it, unless the Congress by their Adjournment prevent its Return, in which Case it shall not be a Law.

[3] Every Order, Resolution, or Vote to which the Concurrence of the Senate and House of Representatives may be necessary (except on a question of Adjournment) shall be presented to the President of the United States; and before the Same shall take Effect, shall be approved by him, or being disapproved by him, shall be repassed by two thirds of the Senate and House of Representatives, according to the Rules and Limitations prescribed in the Case of a Bill.

SECTION 8. The Congress shall have Power To lay and collect Taxes, Duties, Imposts and Excises, to pay the Debts and provide for the common Defence and general Welfare of the United States; but all Duties, Imposts and Excises shall be uniform throughout the United States;

[2] To borrow Money on the credit of the United States;

[3] To regulate Commerce with foreign Nations, and among the several States, and with the Indian Tribes;

[4] To establish an uniform Rule of Naturalization, and uniform Laws on the subject of Bankruptcies throughout the United States;

[5] To coin Money, regulate the Value thereof, and of foreign Coin, and fix the Standard of Weights and Measures;

[6] To provide for the Punishment of counterfeiting the Securities and current Coin of the United States;

[7] To Establish Post Offices and post Roads;

[8] To promote the Progress of Science and useful Arts, by securing for limited Times to Authors and Inventors the exclusive Right to their respective Writings and Discoveries;

[9] To constitute Tribunals inferior to the supreme Court;

[10] To define and punish Piracies and Felonies committed on the high Seas, and Offences against the Law of Nations;

[11] To declare War, grant Letters of Marque and Reprisal, and make Rules concerning Captures on Land and Water;

[12] To raise and support Armies, but no Appropriation of Money to that Use shall be for a longer Term than two Years;

[13] To provide and maintain a Navy;

[14] To make Rules for the Government and Regulation of the land and naval Forces;

[15] To provide for calling forth the Militia to execute the Laws of the Union, suppress Insurrections and repel Invasions;

[16] To provide for organizing, arming, and disciplining, the Militia, and for governing such Part of them as may be employed in the Service of the United States, reserving to the States respectively, the Appointment of the Officers, and the Authority of training the Militia according to the discipline prescribed by Congress;

[17] To exercise exclusive Legislation in all Cases whatsoever, over such District (not exceeding ten Miles square) as may, by Cession of particular States, and the Acceptance of Congress, become the Seat of the Government of the United States, and to exercise like Authority over all Places purchased by the Consent of the Legislature of the State in which the Same shall be, for the Erection of Forts, Magazines, Arsenals, dock-Yards, and other needful Buildings;—And

[18] To make all Laws which shall be necessary and proper for carrying into Execution the foregoing Powers, and all other Powers vested

by this Constitution in the Government of the United States, or in any Department or Officer thereof.

SECTION 9. ¹ The Migration or Importation of such Persons as any of the States now existing shall think proper to admit, shall not be prohibited by the Congress prior to the Year one thousand eight hundred and eight, but a Tax or duty may be imposed on such Importation, not exceeding ten dollars for each Person.

² The privilege of the Writ of Habeas Corpus shall not be suspended, unless when in Cases of Rebellion or Invasion the public Safety may require it.

³ No Bill of Attainder or ex post facto Law shall be passed.

*⁴ No Capitation, or other direct, Tax shall be laid, unless in Proportion to the Census or Enumeration herein before directed to be taken.

⁵ No Tax or Duty shall be laid on Articles exported from any State.

⁶ No Preference shall be given by any Regulation of Commerce or Revenue to the Ports of one State over those of another: nor shall Vessels bound to, or from, one State be obliged to enter, clear, or pay Duties in another.

⁷ No money shall be drawn from the Treasury, but in Consequence of Appropriations made by Law; and a regular Statement and Account of the Receipts and Expenditures of all public Money shall be published from time to time.

⁸ No Title of Nobility shall be granted by the United States: And no Person holding any Office of Profit or Trust under them, shall, without the Consent of the Congress, accept of any present, Emolument, Office, or Title, of any kind whatever, from any King, Prince, or foreign State.

SECTION 10. ¹ No State shall enter into any Treaty, Alliance, or Confederation; grant Letters of Marque and Reprisal; coin Money; emit Bills of Credit; make any Thing but gold and silver Coin a Tender in Payment of Debts; pass any Bill of Attainder, ex post facto Law, or Law impairing the Obligation of Contracts, or grant any Title of Nobility.

² No State shall, without the Consent of the Congress, lay any Imposts or Duties on Imports or Exports, except what may be absolutely necessary for executing it's inspection Laws: and the net Produce of all Duties and Imposts, laid by any State on Imports or Exports, shall be for the Use of the Treasury of the United States; and

Note: 3rd line above, appears "it's" but means "its"
* See also amendment XVI.

all such Laws shall be subject to the Revision and Controul of the Congress.

³ No State shall, without the Consent of Congress, lay any Duty of Tonnage, keep Troops, or Ships of War in time of Peace, enter into any Agreement or Compact with another State, or with a foreign Power, or engage in War, unless actually invaded, or in such imminent Danger as will not admit of delay.

ARTICLE II

SECTION 1. ¹ The executive Power shall be vested in a President of the United States of America. He shall hold his Office during the Term of four Years, and, together with the Vice President, chosen for the same Term, be elected, as follows

² Each State shall appoint, in such Manner as the Legislature thereof may direct, a Number of Electors, equal to the whole Number of Senators and Representatives to which the State may be entitled in the Congress: but no Senator or Representative, or Person holding an Office of Trust or Profit under the United States, shall be appointed an Elector.

*[The Electors shall meet in their respective States, and vote by Ballot for two Persons, of whom one at least shall not be an Inhabitant of the same State with themselves. And they shall make a List of all the Persons voted for, and of the Number of Votes for each; which List they shall sign and certify, and transmit sealed to the Seat of the Government of the United States, directed to the President of the Senate. The President of the Senate shall, in the Presence of the Senate and House of Representatives, open all the Certificates, and the Votes shall then be counted. The Person having the greatest Number of Votes shall be the President, if such Number be a Majority of the whole Number of Electors appointed; and if there be more than one who have such Majority, and have an equal Number of Votes, then the House of Representatives shall immediately chuse by Ballot one of them for President; and if no Person have a Majority, then from the five highest on the List the said House shall in like Manner chuse the President. But in chusing the President, the Votes shall be taken by States, the Representation from each State having one Vote; A quorum for this Purpose shall consist of a Member or Members from two thirds of the States, and a Majority of all the States shall be

* This paragraph has been superseded by amendment XII.

necessary to a Choice. In every Case, after the Choice of the President, the Person having the greatest Number of Votes of the Electors shall be the Vice President. But if there should remain two or more who have equal Votes, the Senate shall chuse from them by Ballot the Vice President.**]**

³ The Congress may determine the Time of chusing the Electors, and the Day on which they shall give their Votes; which Day shall be the same throughout the United States.

⁴ No person except a natural born Citizen, or a Citizen of the United States, at the time of the Adoption of this Constitution, shall be eligible to the Office of President; neither shall any Person be eligible to that Office who shall not have attained to the Age of thirty five Years, and been fourteen Years a Resident within the United States.

⁵ In case of the Removal of the President from Office, or of his Death, Resignation, or Inability to discharge the Powers and Duties of the said Office, the Same shall devolve on the Vice President, and the Congress may by Law provide for the Case of Removal, Death, Resignation or Inability, both of the President and Vice President, declaring what Officer shall then act as President, and such Officer shall act accordingly, until the Disability be removed, or a President shall be elected.

⁶ The President shall, at stated Times, receive for his Services, a Compensation, which shall neither be encreased nor diminished during the Period for which he shall have been elected, and he shall not receive within that Period any other Emolument from the United States, or any of them.

⁷ Before he enter on the Execution of his Office, he shall take the following Oath or Affirmation:—"I do solemnly swear (or affirm) that I will faithfully execute the Office of President of the United States, and will to the best of my Ability, preserve, protect and defend the Constitution of the United States."

SECTION 2. **¹** The President shall be Commander in Chief of the Army and Navy of the United States, and of the Militia of the several States, when called into the actual Service of the United States; he may require the Opinion, in writing, of the principal Officer in each of the executive Departments, upon any Subject relating to the Duties of their respective Offices, and he shall have Power to grant Reprieves and Pardons for Offences against the United States, except in Cases of Impeachment.

² He shall have Power, by and with the Advice and Consent of the

Senate, to make Treaties, provided two thirds of the Senators present concur; and he shall nominate, and by and with the Advice and Consent of the Senate, shall appoint Ambassadors, other public Ministers and Consuls, Judges of the supreme Court, and all other Officers of the United States, whose Appointments are not herein otherwise provided for, and which shall be established by Law: but the Congress may by Law vest the Appointment of such inferior Officers, as they think proper, in the President alone, in the Courts of Law, or in the Heads of Departments.

³ The President shall have Power to fill up all Vacancies that may happen during the Recess of the Senate, by granting Commissions which shall expire at the End of their next Session.

SECTION 3. He shall from time to time give to the Congress Information of the State of the Union, and recommend to their Consideration such Measures as he shall judge necessary and expedient; he may, on extraordinary Occasions, convene both Houses, or either of them, and in Case of Disagreement between them, with Respect to the Time of Adjournment, he may adjourn them to such Time as he shall think proper; he shall receive Ambassadors and other public Ministers; he shall take Care that the Laws be faithfully executed, and shall Commission all the Officers of the United States.

SECTION 4. The President, Vice President and all civil Officers of the United States, shall be removed from Office on Impeachment for, and Conviction of, Treason, Bribery, or other high Crimes and Misdemeanors.

ARTICLE III

SECTION 1. The judicial Power of the United States, shall be vested in one supreme Court, and in such inferior Courts as the Congress may from time to time ordain and establish. The Judges, both of the supreme and inferior Courts, shall hold their Offices during good Behaviour, and shall, at stated Times, receive for their Services, a Compensation, which shall not be diminished during their Continuance in Office.

SECTION 2. ¹ The judicial Power shall extend to all Cases, in Law and Equity, arising under this Constitution, the Laws of the United States, and Treaties made, or which shall be made, under their Authority;—to all Cases affecting Ambassadors, other public Ministers and Consuls;—to all Cases of admiralty and maritime Jurisdiction;—to Controversies to which the United States shall be a Party;—to

Controversies between two or more States;—between a State and Citizens of another State;*—between Citizens of different States,—between Citizens of the same State claiming Lands under Grants of different States, and between a State, or the Citizens thereof, and foreign States, Citizens or Subjects.

² In all Cases affecting Ambassadors, other public Ministers and Consuls, and those in which a State shall be Party, the supreme Court shall have original Jurisdiction. In all the other Cases before mentioned, the supreme Court shall have appellate Jurisdiction, both as to Law and Fact, with such Exceptions, and under such Regulations as the Congress shall make.

³ The Trial of all Crimes, except in Cases of Impeachment, shall be by Jury; and such Trial shall be held in the State where the said Crimes shall have been committed; but when not committed within any State, the Trial shall be at such Place or Places as the Congress may by Law have directed.

SECTION 3. ¹ Treason against the United States, shall consist only in levying War against them, or in adhering to their Enemies, giving them Aid and Comfort. No Person shall be convicted of Treason unless on the Testimony of two Witnesses to the same overt Act, or on Confession in open Court.

² The Congress shall have power to declare the Punishment of Treason, but no Attainder of Treason shall work Corruption of Blood, or Forfeiture except during the Life of the Person attainted.

ARTICLE IV

SECTION 1. Full Faith and Credit shall be given in each State to the public Acts, Records, and judicial Proceedings of every other State. And the Congress may by general Laws prescribe the Manner in which such Acts, Records and Proceedings shall be proved, and the Effect thereof.

SECTION 2. ¹ The Citizens of each State shall be entitled to all Privileges and Immunities of Citizens in the several States.

² A Person charged in any State with Treason, Felony, or other Crime, who shall flee from Justice, and be found in another State, shall on Demand of the executive Authority of the State from which he fled, be delivered up, to be removed to the State having Jurisdiction of the Crime.

³ [No Person held to Service or Labour in one State, under the Laws thereof, escaping into another, shall, in Consequence of any Law

* This clause has been affected by amendment XI.

or Regulation therein, be discharged from such Service or Labour, but shall be delivered up on Claim of the Party to whom such Service or Labour may be due.]*

SECTION 3. [1] New States may be admitted by the Congress into this Union; but no new State shall be formed or erected within the Jurisdiction of any other State; nor any State be formed by the Junction of two or more States, or Parts of States, without the Consent of the Legislatures of the States concerned as well as of the Congress.

[2] The Congress shall have Power to dispose of and make all needful Rules and Regulations respecting the Territory or other Property belonging to the United States; and nothing in this Constitution shall be so construed as to Prejudice any Claims of the United States, or of any particular State.

SECTION 4. The United States shall guarantee to every State in this Union a Republican Form of Government, and shall protect each of them against Invasion; and on Application of the Legislature, or of the Executive (when the Legislature cannot be convened) against domestic Violence.

ARTICLE V

The Congress, whenever two thirds of both Houses shall deem it necessary, shall propose Amendments to this Constitution, or, on the Application of the Legislatures of two thirds of the several States, shall call a Convention for proposing Amendments, which, in either Case, shall be valid to all Intents and Purposes, as Part of this Constitution, when ratified by the Legislatures of three fourths of the several States, or by Conventions in three fourths thereof, as the one or the other Mode of Ratification may be proposed by the Congress: Provided that no Amendment which may be made prior to the Year One thousand eight hundred and eight shall in any Manner affect the first and fourth Clauses in the Ninth Section of the first Article; and that no State, without its Consent, shall be deprived of its equal Suffrage in the Senate.

ARTICLE VI

[1] All Debts contracted and Engagements entered into, before the Adoption of this Constitution, shall be as valid against the United States under this Constitution, as under the Confederation.

[2] This Constitution, and the Laws of the United States which shall be made in Pursuance thereof; and all Treaties made, or which shall be

* This paragraph has been superseded by amendment XIII.

made, under the Authority of the United States, shall be the supreme Law of the Land; and the Judges in every State shall be bound thereby, any Thing in the Constitution or Laws of any State to the Contrary notwithstanding.

[3] The Senators and Representatives before mentioned, and the Members of the several State Legislatures, and all executive and judicial Officers, both of the United States and of the several States, shall be bound by Oath or Affirmation, to support this Constitution; but no religious Test shall ever be required as a Qualification to any Office or public Trust under the United States.

ARTICLE VII

The Ratification of the Conventions of nine States, shall be sufficient for the Establishment of this Constitution between the States so ratifying the Same.

DONE in Convention by the Unanimous Consent of the States present the Seventeenth Day of September in the Year of Our Lord one thousand seven hundred and Eighty seven and of the Independence of the United States of America the Twelfth IN WITNESS whereof We have hereunto subscribed our Names,

Go. WASHINGTON
Presidt and deputy from Virginia
Attest: William Jackson, *Secretary.*

Constitution

Delaware.
GEO: READ
GUNNING BEDFORD jun
JOHN DICKINSON
RICHARD BASSETT
JACO: BROOM

Maryland.
JAMES MCHENRY
DAN: of ST THOS JENIFER
DANL CARROLL

Virginia.
JOHN BLAIR—
JAMES MADISON Jr.

North Carolina.
WM BLOUNT
RICHD DOBBS SPAIGHT,
HU WILLIAMSON

South Carolina.
J. RUTLEDGE
CHARLES COTESWORTH PINCKNEY
CHARLES PINCKNEY
PIERCE BUTLER.

Georgia.
WILLIAM FEW
ABR BALDWIN

New Hampshire.
JOHN LANGDON
NICHOLAS GILMAN

Massachusetts.
NATHANIEL GORHAM
RUFUS KING

Connecticut.
WM SAML JOHNSON
ROGER SHERMAN

New York.
ALEXANDER HAMILTON

New Jersey.
WIL: LIVINGSTON
DAVID BREARLEY.
WM PATTERSON
JONA: DAYTON

Pennsylvania.
B. FRANKLIN
THOMAS MIFFLIN
ROBT. MORRIS
GEO. CLYMER
THOS. FITZSIMONS
JARED INGERSOLL
JAMES WILSON
GOUV MORRIS

(Note: the above is the order of the signatures, under Washington's signature, as they appear in the original—the right hand column being directly under Washington's signature and the other column to the left.

Except for inconsequential differences in capitalization and punctuation, the only difference between the foregoing text—based on facsimile of original— and the text of the printed copies prepared by the Continental Congress and sent to the States for consideration as to ratification is the use in the latter of the singular "Court" instead of "Courts" in the second sentence of Article III—obviously due to typographical error which could have misled no one.)

ARTICLES IN ADDITION TO, AND AMENDMENT OF, THE CONSTITUTION OF THE UNITED STATES OF AMERICA, PROPOSED BY CONGRESS, AND RATIFIED BY THE LEGISLATURES OF THE SEVERAL STATES PURSUANT TO THE FIFTH ARTICLE OF THE ORIGINAL CONSTITUTION

AMENDMENT I

Congress shall make no law respecting an establishment of religion, or prohibiting the free exercise thereof; or abridging the freedom of speech, or of the press; or the right of the people peaceably to assemble, and to petition the Government for a redress of grievances.

AMENDMENT II

A well regulated Militia, being necessary to the security of a free State, the right of the people to keep and bear Arms, shall not be infringed.

AMENDMENT III

No Soldier shall, in time of peace be quartered in any house, without the consent of the Owner, nor in time of war, but in a manner to be prescribed by law.

AMENDMENT IV

The right of the people to be secure in their persons, houses, papers, and effects, against unreasonable searches and seizures, shall not be violated, and no Warrants shall issue, but upon probable cause, supported by Oath or affirmation, and particularly describing the place to be searched, and the persons or things to be seized.

AMENDMENT V

No person shall be held to answer for a capital, or otherwise infamous crime, unless on a presentment or indictment of a Grand Jury, except in cases arising in the land or naval forces, or in the Militia, when in actual service in time of War or public danger; nor shall any person be subject for the same offence to be twice put in jeopardy of life or limb; nor shall be compelled in any criminal case to be a witness against himself, nor be deprived of life, liberty, or property, without due process of law; nor shall private property be taken for public use, without just compensation.

AMENDMENT VI

In all criminal prosecutions, the accused shall enjoy the right to a speedy and public trial, by an impartial jury of the State and district wherein the crime shall have been committed, which district shall have been previously ascertained by law, and to be informed of the nature and cause of the accusation; to be confronted with the witnesses against him; to have compulsory process for obtaining Witnesses in his favor, and to have the Assistance of Counsel for his defence.

AMENDMENT VII

In Suits at common law, where the value in controversy shall exceed twenty dollars, the right of trial by jury shall be preserved, and no fact tried by a jury, shall be otherwise reexamined in any Court of the United States, than according to the rules of the common law.

AMENDMENT VIII

Excessive bail shall not be required, nor excessive fines imposed, nor cruel and unusual punishments inflicted.

AMENDMENT IX

The enumeration in the Constitution, of certain rights, shall not be construed to deny or disparage others retained by the people.

AMENDMENT X

The powers not delegated to the United States by the Constitution, nor prohibited by it to the States, are reserved to the States respectively, or to the people.

AMENDMENT XI

The Judicial power of the United States shall not be construed to extend to any suit in law or equity, commenced or prosecuted against one of the United States by Citizens of another State, or by Citizens or Subjects of any Foreign State.

AMENDMENT XII

The electors shall meet in their respective states and vote by ballot for President and Vice-President, one of whom, at least, shall not be

an inhabitant of the same state with themselves; they sháll name in
their ballots the person voted for as President, and in distinct ballots
the person voted for as Vice-President, and they shall make distinct
lists of all persons voted for as President, and of all persons voted for
as Vice-President, and of the number of votes for each, which lists
they shall sign and certify, and transmit sealed to the seat of the government of the United States, directed to the President of the Senate;
—The President of the Senate shall, in presence of the Senate and
House of Representatives, open all the certificates and the votes shall
then be counted;—The person having the greatest number of votes for
President, shall be the President, if such number be a majority of the
whole number of Electors appointed; and if no person have such
majority, then from the persons having the highest numbers not exceeding three on the list of those voted for as President, the House of
Representatives shall choose immediately, by ballot, the President.
But in choosing the President, the votes shall be taken by states, the
representation from each state having one vote; a quorum for this
purpose shall consist of a member or members from two-thirds of the
states, and a majority of all the states shall be necessary to a choice.
[And if the House of Representatives shall not choose a President
whenever the right of choice shall devolve upon them, before the
fourth day of March next following, then the Vice-President shall act
as President, as in the case of the death or other constitutional disability of the President.]* The person having the greatest number
of votes as Vice-President, shall be the Vice-President, if such number be a majority of the whole number of Electors appointed, and if
no person have a majority, then from the two highest numbers on the
list, the Senate shall choose the Vice-President; a quorum for the purpose shall consist of two-thirds of the whole number of Senators, and
a majority of the whole number shall be necessary to a choice. But
no person constitutionally ineligible to the office of President shall be
eligible to that of Vice-President of the United States.

AMENDMENT XIII

SECTION 1. Neither slavery nor involuntary servitude, except as a
punishment for crime whereof the party shall have been duly convicted, shall exist within the United States, or any place subject to
their jurisdiction.

* The part included in heavy brackets has been superseded by section 3 of
amendment XX.

Section 2. Congress shall have power to enforce this article by appropriate legislation.

Section 1. All persons born or naturalized in the United States, and subject to the jurisdiction thereof, are citizens of the United States and of the State wherein they reside. No State shall make or enforce any law which shall abridge the privileges or immunities of citizens of the United States; nor shall any State deprive any person of life, liberty, or property, without due process of law; nor deny to any person within its jurisdiction the equal protection of the laws.

Section 2. Representatives shall be apportioned among the several States according to their respective numbers, counting the whole number of persons in each State, excluding Indians not taxed. But when the right to vote at any election for the choice of electors for President and Vice President of the United States, Representatives in Congress, the Executive and Judicial officers of a State, or the members of the Legislature thereof, is denied to any of the male inhabitants of such State, being twenty-one years of age, and citizens of the United States, or in any way abridged, except for participation in rebellion, or other crime, the basis of representation therein shall be reduced in the proportion which the number of such male citizens shall bear to the whole number of male citizens twenty-one years of age in such State.

Section 3. No person shall be a Senator or Representative in Congress, or elector of President and Vice President, or hold any office, civil or military, under the United States, or under any State, who, having previously taken an oath, as a member of Congress, or as an officer of the United States, or as a member of any State legislature, or as an executive or judicial officer of any State, to support the Constitution of the United States, shall have engaged in insurrection or rebellion against the same, or given aid or comfort to the enemies thereof. But Congress may by a vote of two-thirds of each House, remove such disability.

Section 4. The validity of the public debt of the United States, authorized by law, including debts incurred for payment of pensions and bounties for services in suppressing insurrection or rebellion, shall not be questioned. But neither the United States nor any State shall assume or pay any debt or obligation incurred in aid of insurrection or rebellion against the United States, or any claim for the loss or emancipation of any slave; but all such debts, obligations and claims shall be held illegal and void.

SECTION 5. The Congress shall have power to enforce, by appropriate legislation, the provisions of this article.

AMENDMENT XV

SECTION 1. The right of citizens of the United States to vote shall not be denied or abridged by the United States or by any State on account of race, color, or previous condition of servitude.

SECTION 2. The Congress shall have power to enforce this article by appropriate legislation.

AMENDMENT XVI

The Congress shall have power to lay and collect taxes on incomes, from whatever source derived, without apportionment among the several States, and without regard to any census or enumeration.

AMENDMENT XVII

The Senate of the United States shall be composed of two Senators from each state, elected by the people thereof, for six years; and each Senator shall have one vote. The electors in each State shall have the qualifications requisite for electors of the most numerous branch of the State legislatures.

When vacancies happen in the representation of any State in the Senate, the executive authority of such State shall issue writs of election to fill such vacancies: *Provided,* That the legislature of any State may empower the executive thereof to make temporary appointments until the people fill the vacancies by election as the legislature may direct.

This amendment shall not be so construed as to affect the election or term of any Senator chosen before it becomes valid as part of the Constitution.

AMENDMENT XVIII

[SECTION 1. After one year from the ratification of this article the manufacture, sale, or transportation of intoxicating liquors within, the importation thereof into, or the exportation thereof from the United States and all territory subject to the jurisdiction thereof for beverage purposes is hereby prohibited.

Section 2. The Congress and the several States shall have concurrent power to enforce this article by appropriate legislation.]*

AMENDMENT XIX

The right of citizens of the United States to vote shall not be denied or abridged by the United States or by any State on account of sex. Congress shall have power to enforce this article by appropriate legislation.

AMENDMENT XX

Section 1. The terms of the President and Vice President shall end at noon on the 20th day of January, and the terms of Senators and Representatives at noon on the 3d day of January, of the years in which such terms would have ended if this article had not been ratified; and the terms of their successors shall then begin.

Section 2. The Congress shall assemble at least once in every year, and such meeting shall begin at noon on the 3d day of January, unless they shall by law appoint a different day.

Section 3. If, at the time fixed for the beginning of the term of the President, the President elect shall have died, the Vice President elect shall become President. If a President shall not have been chosen before the time fixed for the beginning of his term, or if the President elect shall have failed to qualify, then the Vice President elect shall act as President until a President shall have qualified; and the Congress may by law provide for the case wherein neither a President elect nor a Vice President elect shall have qualified, declaring who shall then act as President, or the manner in which one who is to act shall be selected, and such person shall act accordingly until a President or Vice President shall have qualified.

Section 4. The Congress may by law provide for the case of the death of any of the persons from whom the House of Representatives may choose a President whenever the right of choice shall have devolved upon them, and for the case of the death of any of the persons from whom the Senate may choose a Vice President whenever the right of choice shall have devolved upon them.

Section 5. Sections 1 and 2 shall take effect on the 15th day of October following the ratification of this article.

* Repealed by section 1 of amendment XXI.

AMENDMENT XXI

SECTION 1. The eighteenth article of amendment to the Constitution of the United States is hereby repealed.

SECTION 2. The transportation or importation into any State, Territory, or possession of the United States for delivery or use therein of intoxicating liquors, in violation of the laws thereof, is hereby prohibited.

AMENDMENT XXII

No person shall be elected to the office of the President more than twice, and no person who has held the office of President, or acted as President, for more than two years of a term to which some other person was elected President shall be elected to the office of the President more than once. But this Article shall not apply to any person holding the office of President when this Article was proposed by the Congress, and shall not prevent any person who may be holding the office of President, or acting as President, during the term within which this Article becomes operative from holding the office of President or acting as President during the remainder of such term.

AMENDMENT XXIII

SECTION 1. The District constituting the seat of Government of the United States shall appoint in such manner as the Congress may direct:

A number of electors of President and Vice President equal to the whole number of Senators and Representatives in Congress to which the District would be entitled if it were a State, but in no event more than the least populous State; they shall be in addition to those appointed by the States, but they shall be considered, for the purposes of the election of President and Vice President, to be electors appointed by a State; and they shall meet in the District and perform such duties as provided by the twelfth article of amendment.

SECTION 2. The Congress shall have power to enforce this article by appropriate legislation.

———

(Author's note: The enacting proviso, or clause, has been deleted from numbers xviii, xx, xxi and xxii. In the original, each Amendment is captioned "Article.")

(*continued on p. 322 lower part*)

321

Acknowledgments

(see also page xxx)

Quotations in this study-guide are, in the main, from writings of The Founders of the general period 1750-1800 which are in the public domain and need no permission to quote. This applies also to various additional quotations other than those indicated below. The few exceptions are as follows; and acknowledgment, with thanks, is made of the grant of permission to quote the copyrighted material (page references being to the pages of this study-guide where the quotations involved occur):

Thos. Y. Crowell Co., New York; *Flags of the U.S.A.,* 1959, by David Eggenberger: "Culpeper Minutemen" flag, page vi

G. P. Putnam's Sons, New York; Bryce book quotation, page 136

Belknap Press of Harvard University Press, Cambridge, Mass.; Holmes quotation, page 237

McKinley Publishing Co., Philadelphia, Pa.; Corwin quotation, p. 236

Little, Brown Co., Boston; Holmes quotation, page 237

Princeton University Press, Princeton, N. J.; Brown book quotation, page 236

The Macmillan Co., New York; quoting Beard p. 346, Dicey p. 136

University of Kentucky Press, Lexington, Ky.; Beale book quotation, pages 345-347

Grateful acknowledgment is made of the extensive cooperation of various members of the staffs of the following libraries especially: Library of Congress; New York Public Library; Newberry Library of Chicago; Library of Association of the Bar of the City of N.Y.

The Author

(*continued from p. 321*)

BRIEF BIOGRAPHICAL NOTES

Regarding Those Quoted Who Are Not So Well Known As the Former Presi-dents and Benjamin Franklin and Alexander Hamilton, Concerning Some Main Details of Their Careers

Adams, Samuel; 1722-1803; lawyer, business man, statesman; pre-1776 leader in Boston for "Liberty and Independence," notably as early as 1764 in opposing the Stamp Act; a leader of Mass. legislature 1765-1774, then a member (until 1781) of the Continental Congress, in which he continued to be a leader for "Liberty and Independence;" author and co-author of many famous "Liberty" writings, including documents of the Mass. legislature and Resolutions of Town of Boston; signer of Declaration of Independence; member of Mass. Constitutional Convention 1779-1780 which framed history's first true Constitution; member for years of Mass. Senate and Council; member of Mass. Convention which ratified U.S. Constitution, 1788; Lt. Governor 1789-1793, then Governor until 1797.

Allen, Rev. Thomas; 1743-1810; first clergyman in Pittsfield, Berkshire County, Mass., 1764—served 46 years in that then frontier region; for years prior to 1776 a leader in the fight for Liberty—partly as head of "The Berkshire Constitutionalists" in the forefront of the movement for written Constitutions to safeguard Liberty; always active in town-meetings in this connection, helping to draft and get adopted appropriate resolutions; active as a Chaplain in the Revolutionary forces; typified New England clergy's leadership in working and fighting for "Liberty and Independence."

Barlow, Joel; 1754-1812; poet, teacher and statesman; while a college student, 1776, fought in Battle of Long Island; author of epic poem: "The Vision of Columbus" envisioning a majestic future for America; made U.S. Minister to France by President Monroe.

de Crévecoeur, Michel-Guillaume Jean (pen name: J. Hector St. John); 1735-1813; farmer, traveller, writer; native of France, pioneer to French Canada, 1754; came to New York 1759, travelled extensively in America and, becoming an American citizen in 1765, settled as a farmer in New York and wrote his famous *Letters From An American Farmer* (1782) under name of J. Hector St. John de Crévecoeur, extolling freedom and life in America.

Dickinson, John; 1732-1808; lawyer, writer and statesman; from time to time member of legislatures of both Delaware (as part of Pa.) and Pennsylvania—also at times President of governments of both Delaware and Pennsylvania; wrote the famous and widely influential "Letters From A Farmer in Pennsylvania" (1767) espousing the cause of American liberties as opposed to British tyranny; member of 1st and 2nd Continental Congresses (did not sign the Declaration of Independence, as being premature); Colonel of first battalion raised in

323

Philadelphia 1775-1776; elected President of Supreme Executive Council of Delaware in 1781 and thereafter held same office in Pennsylvania; in 1787 a member of the Federal Convention which framed the Constitution and one of its signers.

Eliot, Rev. Andrew; 1718-1778; a prominent clergyman in Boston—upheld the Congregational Church in opposition to the Episcopalian Church; in the pre-1776 period a strong supporter of the American cause of "Liberty and Independence;" for example, in Election Sermon on May 29, 1765 (the same day Patrick Henry introduced his famous Resolutions in the Virginia legislature against the Stamp Act) delivered before the Royal Governor and the legislature of Massachusetts, he upheld the right of resistance against usurpers and tyranny.

Ellsworth, Oliver; 1745-1807; lawyer, statesman, judge; member of Continental Congress 1777-1783; member of Governor's Council of Conn., 1780; member of Federal Convention, 1787, which framed the Constitution and in 1788 member of the Conn. Ratifying Convention—writing "Letters of a Landholder" in favor of ratification; member of U.S. Senate 1789-1796; appointed Chief Justice of the U.S., 1796; U.S. Commissioner to France 1799-1800.

Gadsden, Christopher; 1724-1805; merchant, Revolutionary leader, statesman; member of Assembly of S.C. from 1757 onward over a period of 30 years; a leader in pre-1776 period for protection of American rights against British tyranny; member of Stamp Act Congress, 1765—a leader for union of the colonies; member of 1st and 2nd Continental Congress—left latter in Jan. 1776 to become active as Colonel of S.C. forces, after membership in S.C. Provincial Congress advocating American independence in Feb. 1776; Brig. General in Continental Army Sept., 1776; in S.C. Convention which ratified the U.S. Constitution, 1788 and in S.C. Convention, 1790, regarding the State Constitution.

Gerry, Elbridge; 1744-1814; Revolutionary leader and statesman; in pre-1776, a fiery supporter in Mass. of the cause of "Liberty and Independence;" member of Mass. legislature 1772-1773 and thereafter of 1st and 2nd Provincial Congresses of Mass.; member of 2nd Continental Congress 1775-1776 and a signer of the Declaration of Independence; member of the Federal Convention which framed the U.S. Constitution, 1787 but did not sign it, thereafter opposing ratification and wrote "Observations on the New Constitution . . ." stating his views; elected to Congress 1789; Vice President under President Madison, 1812.

Hancock, John; 1736/7-1793; merchant and statesman; member of Mass. legislature 1769; President Mass. Provincial Congress, 1774-1775; member and President of Continental Congress, 1775-1776, being first signer of the Declaration of Independence; member of Mass. Convention which adopted history's first genuine Constitution, 1780; elected first Governor of Mass. and re-elected intermittently for total of nine terms, dying in office in 1793; in 1788 presided over the Mass. Convention which ratified the U.S. Constitution.

Henry, Patrick; 1736-1799; lawyer, statesman, Revolutionary leader; member of Va. legislature 1765, when he introduced famous Resolutions, and made celebrated address, against Stamp Act; member of 1st Va. Convention and of 1st Continental Congress, 1774; in 2nd Va. Convention, 1775, made his famous "Give me liberty or give me death" address; member of 2nd Continental Congress, 1775, and of 3rd Va. Convention, 1776—helped draft first Va. "Constitution" and declaration favoring Independence, May, 1776; Governor of Va. several terms; opposed ratification of U.S. Constitution—fearing danger of usurpation and abuse of power by Federal government and demanding amendments to limit its power more strictly.

Iredell, James; 1751-1799; lawyer, judge, statesman; active in support of American rights prior to 1776; member of N.C. Council and a supporter of ratification of U.S. Constitution in 1788 N.C. Convention; appointed to U.S. Supreme Court in 1790 where, as early as 1792, he upheld "judicial review"—judges' enforcing the Constitution against violations by other Branches of government.

Jay, John; 1745-1829; judge and statesman; member of 1st and 2nd Continental Congresses, also N.Y. Provincial Congress; chief draftsman of "Constitution" of N.Y., 1776; Chief Justice of N.Y. 1776-1779; member and President of Continental Congress, 1778; Minister to Spain, 1779; member of Commission to negotiate treaty with Great Britain, 1782; in charge of foreign affairs for the Confederation government, 1784-1790; co-author with Madison and Hamilton of *The Federalist,* 1787-1788, written in support of ratification of the Constitution (he wrote 5 essays on foreign affairs); appointed first Chief Justice of the U.S., 1789; negotiated "Jay's Treaty" with Great Britain in 1794; elected Governor of N.Y. in 1795, served until 1800 and, as such, signed into law the Act abolishing slavery in N.Y.

Lee, Richard Henry; Revolutionary leader and statesman; entered Va. legislature 1758; a leader in opposing Stamp Act, 1764—closely allied with Patrick Henry in fight for "Liberty and Independence;" member 1st and 2nd Continental Congresses, 1774-1776; a leader in Va. Convention, May, 1776 calling for

declaration of Independence by Congress—in the latter offering "Independence" Resolution, June 7, 1776; returned to Va. to help form its new government; later member of Congress—its President, 1784—and helped in the adoption, 1787, of Northwest Ordinance; opposed ratification of U.S. Constitution due to fear of usurpation and abuse of power by Federal government—urged amendments to limit its power more strictly and expressed his views in the widely read "Letters From the Federal Farmer;" as a member of U.S. Senate, 1789, helped in framing of first amendments ("Bill of Rights") to the Constitution.

Livingston, William; 1723-1790; lawyer and statesman; a political leader of popular causes in New York State but removed to his N.J. estate after political defeat in N.Y. in 1779; delegate from N.J. to 1st and 2nd Continental Congress; commanded N.J. Militia in 1776; elected first Governor of State of N.J. and served for 14 years; in 1787 was a member of the Federal Convention which framed the Constitution and was a signer.

Marshall, John; 1755-1835; judge and statesman; officer in Revolutionary army—at Valley Forge; member of Va. Bar and then Assembly 1782-1784, again in 1787; member of Va. Convention in 1788 which ratified the U.S. Constitution—stating then that courts would declare void any legislative Act violating the Constitution; U.S. Commissioner to France, 1797; member of Congress 1799; Secretary of State, 1800; appointed Chief Justice of the U.S., 1801 and served until his death.

Mason, George; 1725-1792; judge and statesman; member Va. legislature, 1759 and a leader in the cause of American rights in opposition to British tyranny; author "Fairfax Resolves," 1774; member Va. Convention, 1775 and 1776—when he drafted Va. Declaration of Rights and a good part of Va. "Constitution;" in Va. legislature 1776-1780 and later; active in work leading up to 1787 Convention which framed U.S. Constitution, also as a member; did not sign Constitution and opposed ratification due to fear of inadequate limits on Federal power to prevent its becoming tyrannical; urged addition of "Bill of Rights;" was one of principal slave-owners (including Washington and Jefferson) who deplored existence of slavery and favored abolition, with compensation by government to owners of freed slaves.

Mayhew, Rev. Jonathan; 1720-1776; a leading New England clergyman; served West Church in Boston from 1747 to death; famous, in part, for his 1750 and 1754 Election Sermons espousing American rights —the cause of Liberty and the right and duty to resist tyranny; other famous sermons included "The Snare Broken," 1766. His sermons and writings were a powerful influence in the development of the movement for "Liberty and Independence," exemplifying in exceptional degree the leadership of the New England clergy in this connection.

Morris, Gouverneur; 1752-1816; lawyer and statesman; member of N.Y. Provincial Congress, 1775 and N.Y. Convention in 1776 which framed this State's "Constitution;" member of Continental Congress 1778-1779; assisted Robert Morris 1781-1785 as Superintendent of Finance for the Confederation government; member (from Pa.) of 1787 Convention which framed U.S. Constitution, of which he was a signer; U.S. Minister to France, 1792-1794.

Pinckney, Charles; 1757-1824; member of S.C. legislature, 1779-1780; member of Confederation Congress, 1784-1787; member of 1787 Convention which framed U.S. Constitution and proposed a number of suggestions which were

incorporated in it; Governor of S.C. several terms; elected to U.S. Senate, 1798; U.S. Minister to Spain, under President Jefferson.

Otis, James; 1725-1783; lawyer, political writer and early leader, firebrand defender of American Rights in opposition to British tyranny; resigned royal office to fight in court the infamous Writs of Assistance Act in 1761; elected to Mass. legislature, 1761 and a political leader of the Colony until 1769; an organizer of Sons of Liberty—ardent supporters of cause of "Liberty"; wrote his famous "The Rights of the British Colonies—Asserted and Proved," 1764—adopted by Mass. legislature as own document; member of Stamp Act Congress; he and Sam. Adams, as members of Mass. legislature, largely instrumental in drafting many "State Papers" in support of American rights against British tyranny; a head injury in 1771 virtually ended his usefulness.

Parsons, Theophilus; 1750-1813; judge and statesman; a leader in Essex County Convention which opposed 1778 draft of Constitution for Mass. —per its "Essex Result" report, written by him; a leader in 1779 Convention regarding new Mass. Constitution; in 1788 member of Mass. Convention which ratified U.S. Constitution—wrote address of its presiding officer, John Hancock; member of Mass. legislature 1787-1791, also 1805; became Chief Justice of Mass. in 1806.

Rush, Benjamin; 1745-1813; physician, educator, humanitarian, patriot leader, writer; a physician in Philadelphia; Professor of Chemistry, College of Phila.; in 1774 helped organize society favoring abolition of slavery and its president, 1803; member Pa. Provincial Convention, 1776—a leader for Independence; member of Continental Congress, 1776, and a signer of Declaration of Independence; Surgeon General of part of army, 1777; lecturer at Pa. State College, 1778 and helped found Dickinson College, 1783—one of its trustees; member of Pa. Convention which ratified U.S. Constitution—a leader for ratification; in 1789 helped adopt improved State Constitution; a vigorous supporter of prison reform, better education, and other social progress.

Story, Joseph; 1779-1845; law professor, jurist, statesman; member of Mass. legislature, 1805 and in 1811 —Speaker of the House; member of Congress 1808-1809; member of U.S. Supreme Court 1811 to his death; simultaneously member of Law Faculty of Harvard University, 1829 to death; author of celebrated *Commentaries on the Constitution of the U.S.,* 1833.

Warren, Joseph; 1741-1775; educator, physician, soldier, patriot leader; in pre-1776 period, extremely active in the cause of "Liberty and Independence" in association with Samuel and John Adams, John Hancock and others in Boston; drafted the famous "Suffolk Resolves" sent to the Continental Congress; engaged in a multitude of public duties; President of Mass. Provincial Congress, 1775; appointed by Continental Congress to be a Major General, 1775; fought and killed at battle of Bunker Hill, June 17, 1775.

West, Rev. Samuel; 1730-1807; served church in Dartmouth, Mass. from 1761 to 1803 (later re-named New Bedford); deciphered for General Washington the treasonous letter of Benjamin Church; delivered Sermon in 1776 before the Mass. Council; a member of a committee which framed the Constitution of Mass.; a member of the Mass. Convention which ratified the U.S. Constitution, 1788.

Williams, Rev. Elisha; 1694-1755; educator, clergyman, soldier, statesman; in 1717 and for 5 sessions member of Conn. legislature; ordained a clergyman 1722 and served Wethersfield church until 1726; then made Rector of Yale College, served for 13 years; member of Conn. legislature 1740-1749; in 1744 wrote "A Seasonable Plea for the Liberty of Conscience and the Right of Private Judgment in Matters of Religion Without any Controul from Human Authority;" also a Colonel of Militia; a delegate to the Albany Congress, 1754.

Wilson, James; 1742-1798; educator, statesman and jurist; arrived in America from Scotland 1765; admitted to the Bar 1767 after study in office of John Dickinson; instructor College of Philadelphia; member of Pa. Provincial Convention, 1774; wrote a widely distributed essay showing why Parliament lacked authority over the American Colonies; member of 2nd Continental Congress, voted for Independence and a signer of Declaration of Independence; also in Congress repeatedly in period 1777-1787; member of the Federal Convention, 1787, which framed the Constitution—of which he was a signer; member of Pa. Ratifying Convention, Oct.-Dec., 1787; became member of U.S. Supreme Court 1789; lectured on law 1790-1791 at College of Philadelphia.

Wise, Rev. John; 1652-1725; a leading churchman and a strong supporter of Liberty; served Congregational church in parish of Ipswich, Mass. from ordination to his death; led fellow townsmen in 1687 in revolt against tax levied by the royal Governor Andros without consent of legislative body—was jailed in the course of the dispute; in 1717 wrote *A Vindication of the Government of New England Churches,* in which he stressed the main principles to be proclaimed in 1776 in the Declaration of Independence; exemplified the early leadership of the American people by the New England clergy in support of the cause of Liberty.

Witherspoon, Rev. John; 1723-1794; educator, statesman, church leader; came to America from Scotland in

1768 by invitation to be head of Princeton College, then a Presbyterian institution; an outspoken advocate of cause of "Liberty and Independence;" member of the 2nd Continental Congress, 1776, and signed Declaration of Independence; served in Congress until 1782; at Princeton 1782-1794; member of legislature of N.J., 1783, and of 1787 Convention in N.J. which ratified U.S. Constitution; in 1789 became Moderator of first General Assembly of Presbyterian Church.

(General Reference: Dictionary of American Biography)

REFERENCES

A Note Concerning the References

In the following pages, references are listed by page and by author of writing quoted or cited.

A few of the writings, repeatedly quoted in the text, are listed on the next following page for the reader's convenient reference. In the detailed references which follow, these writings are cited in abbreviated form.

Two editions of the writings of Benjamin Franklin are referred to—the Smyth and the Sparks editions. References to the Sparks edition are expressly noted; unless Sparks is noted, the reference is to the Smyth edition.

For Jefferson also, two editions of his writings are referred to—the Ford edition and the H. A. Washington edition. Unless the latter is expressly noted, any reference is to the Ford edition. Both were published in the 19th century and are probably the sets of his writings most widely distributed among the libraries of the country; and they are the references used in *The Jeffersonian Cyclopedia* (1900) referred to in the Introduction to this study-guide.

All of the numerous editions of *The Federalist,* in reproducing the original text as published in two volumes in 1788, follow the same paragraphing used then; so, in the following pages, references to quotations from *The Federalist* are in each instance to the paragraph where found—identified by its opening words. This makes location of any reference simpler and quicker.

Regarding references to Samuel Adams' writings, involving resolutions of the Town of Boston or of the Legislature of Massachusetts prior to 1776, it should be kept in mind that they were often drafted by a committee of which he was a member; and the reference to his writings does not necessarily mean he was sole author.

A FEW OF THE WRITINGS REPEATEDLY QUOTED

Adams, John: *The Works of*; C. F. Adams, ed.; 1856, Little, Brown Co., Boston

Adams, Samuel: *The Writings of*; H. A. Cushing, ed.; 1904, G. P. Putnam's Sons, N.Y.

Dickinson, John: *The Political Writings of*, . . . ; 1801, Wilmington, Del.

Franklin, Benjamin: *The Writings of*; A. H. Smyth, ed.; 1905, The Macmillan Co., N.Y.

Franklin, Benjamin: *The Works of*; Jared Sparks, ed.; 1844, Tappan and Whittemore, Boston

Hamilton, Alexander: *The Works of*; H. C. Lodge, ed.; 1904, Putnam's, N.Y.

Jefferson, Thomas: *The Writings of*; P. L. Ford, ed.; 1892-1899, Putnam's, N.Y.

Jefferson, Thomas: *The Writings of*; H. A. Washington, ed.; 1869, J. P. Lippincott Co., Philadelphia

Madison, James: *The Writings of*; G. Hunt, ed.; 1900-1910, Putnam's, N.Y.

Washington, George: *The Writings of*; J. C. Fitzpatrick, ed.; 1931-1944, George Washington Bicentennial Commission, by authority of Congress

Wilson, James: *The Works of*; Bird Wilson, ed.; 1804, Philadelphia

A Compilation of the Messages and Papers of the Presidents; James D. Richardson, ed.; 1897, by authority of Congress

American Archives . . . A Documentary History of the Origin and Progress of the North American Colonies; of the Causes and Accomplishment of the American Revolution; and of the Constitution of Government for the United States, to the Final Ratification Thereof; (In Six Series); Peter Force, ed.; 1848, by authority of Congress

Annals of the Congress of the U.S.—The Debates and Proceedings in the Congress of the U.S. etc.; with running page-head "History of Congress;" 1849, Gales & Seaton, Washington

Documentary History of the Constitution of the United States, 1787-1870; Published 1894 by U.S. Department of State, Washington

Documents of American History; H. S. Commager, ed.; 6th edition; 1958, Appleton-Century-Crofts, Inc., N.Y.

Essays on the Constitution of the U.S. Published During Its Discussion by the People 1787-1788; P. L. Ford, ed.; 1892, Brooklyn, N.Y.

Journals of the Continental Congress; W. C. Ford, ed.; Washington

Pamphlets on The Constitution of the U.S. Published During Its Discussion by the People 1787-1788; P. L. Ford, ed.; 1888, Brooklyn, N.Y.

(P & A): *Principles and Acts of the Revolution In America*; Hezekiah Niles, ed.; 1822; W. O. Niles, Baltimore

The Debates in the Several State Conventions on the Adoption of the Federal Constitution, As Recommended by the General Convention at Philadelphia etc.; Jonathan Elliot, ed.; 1836, 2nd edition, by authority of Congress; 5 vols.

The Federalist—A Collection of Essays Written in Favour of the New Constitution, As Agreed Upon by the Federal Convention, September 17, 1787; by Alexander Hamilton, James Madison and John Jay; in two volumes; 1788, J. and A. M'Lean, N.Y.

The Records of the Federal Convention of 1787; Max Farrand, ed.; 1911, Yale University Press

(See preceding page for full titles etc. of some writings referred to repeatedly; and for full title of "P & A" reference.)

Page v
Jefferson, *Writings;* v. 3, p. 85 at 254; "Notes on the State of Virginia"
Warren, P & A; 24 at 29

vii
Gadsden, *Documentary History of the American Revolution*; R. W. Gibbes, ed.; D. Appleton & Co., N.Y. 1855; v. 1, p. 8
Henry, *Works* of John Adams; v. 2, p. 366-367
Washington, *Writings;* v. 35, p. 219-220
Hamilton, *Works*; v. 10, p. 215 at 217
Crévecoeur, *Letters from An American Farmer*; London, 1782; Library of Congress copy, p. 45 at 51-53

viii
Hancock, P & A; 38 at 40
Otis, *Works* of John Adams; v. 2, p. 521 at 524
Mayhew, Library of Congress copy, p. 12-13

ix
Rush, *Letters of Benjamin Rush*; L. H. Butterfield, ed.; 1951; Princeton University Press; v. 1, p. 83; essay "On Patriotism"
Adams, S., *Writings*; v. 2, p. 149-150

xviii
Adams, J., *Works*; v. 3, p. 445 at 456-457
Jefferson, *Writings;* v. 10, p. 161
Madison, *Writings*; v. 9, p. 103
Washington, *Writings*; v. 30, p. 491 at 493

xix
Jefferson, *Writings*; v. 10, p. 1 at 4
Rush, *The Selected Writings of Benjamin Rush*; D. A. Runes, ed.; 1947, Philosophical Society of New York; p. 97
Madison, *Writings*; v. 6, p. 120

The Federalist, No. 28, par. "The obstacles to . . ."; No. 57, par. "I will add . . ."

xx
Washington, *Writings;* v. 29, p. 479
Hancock, Elliot's *Debates* etc.; v. 2, p. 175
Franklin, Farrand *Records* etc.; v. 2, p. 641 at 642
Jefferson, *Writings*; v. 3, p. 85 at 224-225

xxi
Franklin, *Writings*; v. 3, p. 407 at 418
The Federalist, No. 20, par. "I make no . . ."
Henry, *The Life of Patrick Henry* by Wm. Wirt; McElrath & Bangs, New York, 1831; 4th ed.; p. 138 (per Judge Tucker's report, p. 140fn)
Jefferson, *Writings;* v. 10, p. 37 at 42
Jay, *Pamphlets on the Constitution of the U.S.* . . . (1787-1788); P. L. Ford, ed; 1888, Brooklyn, N.Y.; pamphlet no. 3, p. 71
Washington, *Writings*; v. 35, p. 225-226

xxii
Va. Statute, W. W. Hening, ed.; *Statutes at Large of Va.*; v. 12, p. 84 ff; as cited in *Documents* etc.; Commager, ed.; p. 125 at 126
The Federalist, No. 1, par. "After an unequivocal . . ."
Madison, *Writings*; v. 5, p. 223; also Elliot's *Debates* etc., v. 3, p. 536-537

xxiii
Washington, Farrand *Records* etc.; v. 3, p. 381 at 382
Va. Declaration of Rights, Poore, ed.; *The Federal and State Constitutions*, Part II; p. 1908-1909; as

cited in *Documents* etc.; Commager, ed.; p. 103 at 104

Mass. Bill of Rights, Poore, ed.; *The Federal and State Constitutions,* Part I; p. 956 ff; as cited in *Documents* etc.; Commager, ed.; p. 109

Washington, *Writings;* v. 14, p. 312-313

xxviii

Jefferson, *Writings;* v. 10, p. 342 at 343

Adams, J., *Works;* v. 9, p. 415—letter to Chase
Works; v. 2, p. 512 at 513-514—letter to Pickering

4

Adams, J. Q., Library of Congress copy; p. 26

Wilson, *Works;* v. 1, p. 265

Mass. Bill of Rights, See p. xxiii above; Poore as cited in *Documents* etc.; Commager, ed.; p. 107

Washington, *Writings;* v. 35, p. 229

5

Franklin, Farrand *Records* etc.; v. 1, p. 451; in Federal Convention *Writings* (Sparks ed.); v. 1, p. 103 —Autobiography
Writings (Smyth ed.); v. 3, p. 143 at 144-145—letter to Huey
Writings (Sparks ed); v. 2, p. 1-2, 6, 8—"Articles of Belief . . ."

6

Livingston, P & A, p. 199-200

Adams, S., *Writings;* v. 3, p. 286

7

Wilson, *Works;* v. 1, p. 119-120 regarding Par. 2

12

Adams, S., *Writings;* v. 4, p. 302

The Federalist, No. 25, par. "Reasons have been . . ."; No. 71, par. "There are some . . ."

Jefferson, *Writings;* v. 3, p. 85 at 254

13

Mass. Bill of Rights, See p. xxiii above; Poore as cited in *Documents* etc.; Commager, ed.; p. 110

Marshall, U.S. Supreme Court Reports; v. 5, p. 137 at 163; *Marbury v. Madison*

Mass. House, *Writings* of Samuel Adams; v. 1, p. 342 at 344

Washington, *Writings;* v. 35, p. 221-222

Hamilton, *Works;* v. 6, p. 418 at 419

Adams, S., *Writings;* v. 1, p. 268

14

Lee, *The Letters of Richard Henry Lee;* J. C. Ballagh, ed.; Macmillan Co., N.Y., 1914; v. 2; Letter to Samuel Adams, p. 444 at 445; Letter to George Mason, p. 438

The Federalist, No. 46, par. "Were it admitted . . ."

Hartford Convention, T. Dwight, *History of the Hartford Convention,* p. 376; as cited in *Documents* etc.; Commager, ed.; p. 210

16

Jefferson, *Writings;* v. 2, p. 221—"Diffusion of Knowledge" Bill

Jefferson, *Writings;* v. 7, p. 289; Ky. Resolution, as adopted (page facing 289) and see 303-305

17

Va. Resolutions, 1798, *Writings* of James Madison; v. 6, p. 326 *et seq.*

The Federalist, No. 46, par. "Were it admitted . . ."

Hamilton, *Works;* v. 10, p. 295; letter to Oliver Wolcott, June 29, 1798, regarding first draft of what became the Alien and Sedition Laws

Marshall, *The Life of John Marshall* by Albert J. Beveridge; Houghton Mifflin Co., Boston, 1916; v. 2, p. 388-389, 451

Resolution (1790) Va. Legislature, W. W. Hening, ed.; *Statutes at Large of Va.,* v. 13, p. 237 ff; as cited in *Documents* etc.; Commager, ed.; p. 155

18

Henry, Elliot's *Debates* etc.; v. 3, p. 59

Pittsfield Resolution, *The History of Pittsfield (Berkshire County) Mass.,* etc. (1734-1800); J. E. A. Smith, 1869; Lee & Shepard, Boston; v. 1, p. 353

19

The Federalist, No. 55, par. "Is the danger . . ."

22
Jefferson, *Writings;* v. 3, p. 85 at 267
Hamilton, *Works;* v. 1, p. 53 at 113
Mass. House, *Writings* of Samuel Adams; v. 1, p. 23 at 24
Boston Resolution, *Writings* of Samuel Adams; v. 2, p. 350 at 354-355
23
Adams, J., *Works;* v. 3, p. 445 at 456-457
Braintree Resolution, *Massachusetts Archives,* CCLXXVII, 63; Resolution June 5, 1780, concerning qualified approval of the proposed new Constitution of the State
Lexington Resolution, *History of the Town of Lexington* etc. (Mass.), by Charles Hudson; revised by Lexington Historical Society, 1913; Houghton Mifflin Co., Boston; v. 1, p. 233
"Essex Result" Report, 1778, Library of Congress bound copy, p. 13-14; reprinted in *Memoir of Theophilus Parsons,* by his son of same name, Boston, 1859; p. 365-366; the fuller title of the Report being: "Result of the Convention of Delegates Holden at Ipswich in the County of Essex . . . (to consider) . . . the Constitution . . . Proposed . . . (for Mass.) . . . 1778"
24
Jefferson, *Writings;* v. 1, p. 427 at 447
Pittsfield Resolution, *The History of Pittsfield* (see above, under p. 18); v. 1, p. 366
Petition of Mass. Churches, *The New England Clergy and The American Revolution,* by Alice M. Baldwin; Duke University Press, 1928, and Frederick Ungar Publishing Co., N.Y., 1958; p. 78, footnote; and references there cited
Williams, *A Seasonable Plea for the Liberty of Conscience and the Right of Private Judgment in Matters of Religion Without Any Controul from Human Authority;* Boston, 1744; Library of Congress copy,
p. 2-3; also quoted in the Baldwin book cited above, p. 176-177 and see 65-68
26
Jefferson, *Writings;* v. 7, p. 56 at 57
26-7
The Federalist, No. 84, par. "There remains but . . ." and see the preceding 4 paragraphs
29
Washington, Farrand *Records* etc.; v. 2, p. 666-667
32
Henry, Elliot's *Debates* etc.; v. 3, p. 324
Va. Declaration of Rights, See xxiii above, Poore, as cited in *Documents* etc.; Commager, ed.; p. 103
Wilson, *Works;* v. 1, p. 426
Boston Resolution, *Writings* of Samuel Adams; v. 2, p. 350 at 354
Adams, S., *Writings;* v. 2, p. 142 at 150
Franklin, Farrand *Records* etc.; v. 2, p. 120
33
Gerry, "Observations on the New Constitution . . ." by "A Columbian Patriot"—1788; Library of Congress copy, p. 6; attributed by some to Mercy Warren, but to Gerry by the Dictionary of American Biography (and by others)
Mayhew, Library of Congress copy, p. 18
Jefferson, *Writings;* v. 10, p. 22 at 24
Madison, *Writings;* v. 6, p. 102-103
34
Va. Declaration of Rights, See p. xxiii above, Poore, as cited in *Documents* etc.; Commager, ed.; p. 103
Jefferson, Richardson's *Messages and Papers of the Presidents;* v. 1, p. 311—First Inaugural Address; also *Writings,* H. A. Washington, ed.; v. 8, p. 1 at 3-4
Jefferson, *Writings;* v. 3, p. 85 at 264— "Notes on the State of Virginia"
40
Adams, J., *Works;* 5, p. 490
Wilson, *Works;* v. 1, p. 407 (1st quotation); v. 1, p. 439-440 (2nd quotation)

References

Madison, *Writings;* v. 2, p. 183 at 185-186

41

Jefferson, *Writings*; v. 10, p. 246 at 248

The Federalist, No. 78, par. "Whoever attentively considers . . ." and the next succeeding paragraph

N.Y. Ratifying Convention, *Documentary History of the Constitution of the U.S., 1787-1870;* v. 2, p. 190 at 194

Madison, *Writings*; v. 9, p. 55 at 58

Dickinson, *Political Writings*; v. 2, p. 291

42

Washington, *Writings*; v. 35—1st quotation, p. 224; 2nd quotation, p. 229; 3rd quotation, p. 228-229

44

The Federalist, No. 51, par. "First. In a . . ." as well as the preceding paragraph; and see use of term "balances and checks" in No. 9 in paragraph commencing "But it is . . ."; also note No. 47 regarding importance of division of powers

45

The Federalist, No. 51, par. "First, in a . . ."

46

The Federalist, No. 45, par. "The powers delegated . . ."

47

The Federalist, No. 83, par. "Having now seen . . ."

Hamilton, *Works*; v. 3, p. 445 at 484-485—"Opinion" regarding Bank

The Federalist, No. 41, par. "Some who have . . .", rest of essay

Hamilton, *Works*; v. 4, p. 70 at 150-152—Report on "Manufactures"

47-48

Carter case, U.S. Supreme Court Reports; v. 298, p. 238 at 291-292, *Carter v. Carter Coal Co.;* (citing *U.S. v. Butler,* 297 U.S. 1, 64)

48

The Federalist, No. 17, par. "But let it . . ."

No. 28, par. "The obstacles to . . ." and adjoining paragraphs

No. 33, par. "But suspicion may . . ." and the following 2 paragraphs

No. 78, par. "But in regard . . ." and following 4 paragraphs

No. 44, par. "If it be . . ."

No. 46, par. "Were it admitted . . ." and succeeding paragraphs

Hamilton, *Works*; v. 4, p. 230 at 280

Washington, *Writings*; v. 35, p. 229

49

Franklin, *American Archives,* 5th Ser., Peter Force, ed; v. 1, cols. 943-4; also *Familiar Letters of John Adams and His Wife,* Charles F. Adams, ed.; 1876; Hurd and Houghton, Boston; p. 210-211; Letter J. A. to his wife Aug. 14, 1776 (See also John Bartlett's *Familiar Quotations,* p. 260 and 945-946, referring to Ezra Stiles' quotation in connection with the judges who presided at the trial of King Charles I)

Adams, S., *Writings*; v. 2, p. 250 at 256

49-50

Va. Convention, *Documentary History of the Constitution of the U.S., 1787-1870*; v. 2, p. 377

52

Otis, Library of Congress copy, p. 32

Williams, Library of Congress copy, p. 29 (see full title etc. under p. 24 above)

West, Library of Congress copy, p. 14; and see *The Pulpit of the American Revolution—Or, The Political Sermons of the Period of 1776*; John W. Thornton, ed.; Boston, 1860; p. 257 at 274; also see *The New England Clergy and the American Revolution* by Alice M. Baldwin (cited under p. 24, above) p. 181

Mayhew, Library of Congress copy, p. 45-46 footnote; also see *The Pulpit of the American Revolution—Or, The Political Sermons of the Period of 1776*; John W. Thornton, ed.; Boston, 1860; p. 94-95 footnote

N.C. Convention, *Documentary History of the Constitution of the U.S., 1787-1870*; v. 2, p. 266-267

53

Washington, *Writings*; v. 2, p. 500 at 501

The Federalist, No. 28, par. "If the representatives . . ." and continued

The Federalist, No. 46, par. "But ambitious encroachments . . ."

54

Marshall, U.S. Supreme Court Reports; v. 17, p. 316 at 403; *McCulloch v. Maryland*

Jefferson, *Writings* (H. A. Washington edition); v. 7, p. 215 at 216

Adams, S., *Writings*; v. 2, p. 250 at 255-256

55

The Federalist, No. 51; par. "First. In a . . ."

56

The Federalist, No. 45; par. "The powers delegated . . ."

58

Hamilton, *Works;* v. 2, p. 45

The Federalist, No. 17, par. "But let it . . ."

No. 28, par. "If the representatives . . ." and following 3 paragraphs

No. 45, par. "The State governments . . ." and following 4 paragraphs

No. 46, par. "Were it admitted . . ." and remainder of the essay

Jefferson, Richardson's *Messages and Papers of the Presidents*; v. 1, p. 311—First Inaugural Address; and *Writings*; H. A. Washington, ed.; v. 8, p. 1 at 4

Jefferson, *Writings*; v. 9, p. 308-309—letter to Tracy

Jefferson, *Writings*; v. 8, p. 108 at 123—Annual Message 1801

59

The Federalist, No. 46, par. "Were it admitted . . ."

60

The Federalist, No. 28, par. "The obstacles to . . ." and remainder of essay

No. 46, par. "But ambitious encroachments . . ." and the following paragraph

Va. Declaration of Rights, See p. xxiii above, Poore, as cited in *Documents* etc.; Commager, ed.; p. 104

64

Va. Declaration of Rights, See p. xxiii above, Poore, as cited in *Documents* etc.; Commager, ed.; p. 103

The Federalist, No. 10, par. "The second expedient . . ."

Adams, S., *Writings*; v. 4, p. 353 at 356-358

65

Pa. Evening Post, Library of Congress copy; March 14, 1776; p. 2, col. 2

Franklin, *Writings*; v. 10, p. 59-60

Pinckney, Farrand *Records* etc.; v. 1, p. 398

Adams, S., *Writings*; v. 2, p. 151

66

Jefferson, Richardson's *Messages and Papers of the Presidents*; v. 1, p. 309 at 311; and *Writings* (H. A. Washington edition); v. 8, p. 1 at 4; First Inaugural Address

The Federalist, No. 10, "From this view . . ."

Jefferson, *Writings;* v. 9, p. 424 at 425; letter to Adams

Washington, *Writings;* v. 28, p. 407 at 408

Jefferson, *Writings;* v. 1, p. 427 at 440; "A Summary View of the Rights of British America" etc.

68

Jefferson, *Writings;* v. 1, p. 427 at 440; "A Summary View of the Rights of British America" etc.

Jefferson, *Writings*; v. 1, p. 34-35—first draft of Declaration of Independence

Northwest Ordinance, *Federal and State Constitutions*; F. N. Thorpe, ed.; v. 2, p. 957 ff; as cited in *Documents* etc.; Commager, ed.; p. 128 at 132 (Art. VI)

Wilson, *Works*; v. 2, p. 488 regarding slavery repugnant to Natural Law

74

Wilson, *Works*; v. 2, p. 473

Adams, J. Q., Library of Congress copy, p. 13

Dickinson, *Political Writings*; v. 1, p. 329 at 395; "An Essay etc."

Wilson, *Works*; v. 3, p. 299 at 309-310

75

Iredell, *Life and Correspondence of James Iredell*; D. Appleton & Co., N.Y., 1857; G. J. McRee, ed.; v. 1, p. 245

Warren, P & A; p. 20 at 21

Mass. Bill of Rights, See p. xxiii above, Poore, as cited in *Documents* etc., Commager, ed.; p. 107

Dickinson, *Political Writings*; v. 1, p. 97 at 111-112; "An Address to the Committee on Correspondence in Barbadoes"

Jefferson, *Writings*; v. 3, p. 85 at 253

76

Va. Declaration of Rights, See p. xxiii above, Poore, as cited in *Documents* etc.; Commager, ed.; p. 103

Pinckney, Farrand *Records* etc.; v. 1, p. 402

Mayhew, Library of Congress copy; p. 9

Wilson, *Works*; v. 3, p. 206

84

Henry, *The Life of Patrick Henry*, p. 141 (see details under p. xxi above)

Washington, *Writings*; v. 35, p. 226

Dickinson, *Political Writings*; v. 1, p. 203 at 212

The Federalist, No. 37, par. "Among the difficulties . . ."

85

Madison, *Letters and Other Writings*; J. P. Lippincott and Co., 1865; v. 2, p. 140-141

The Federalist, No. 10, par. "It could never . . ."

Boston Resolution, *Writings* of Samuel Adams; v. 2, p. 350 at 351

Franklin, *Writings*; v. 10, p. 130

86

Jefferson, *Writings*; v. 2, p. 92 at 98-99

Va. Declaration of Rights, See p. xxiii above, Poore, as cited in *Documents* etc.; Commager, ed.; p. 103 at 104

Va. Statute, See p. xxii above, Hening as cited in *Documents* etc.; Commager, ed.; p. 125 at 126

"Essex Result," Library of Congress copy; p. 14; reprinted in *Memoir of Theophilus Parsons*, p. 366 (see under p. 23, above)

89

The Federalist, No. 79, par. "Next to permanency . . ."

Butler case, U.S. Supreme Court Reports; v. 297, p. 1 at 71

90

Henry, *The Life of Patrick Henry*, p. 141 (see details under p. xxi, above)

Franklin, *Familiar Quotations*; John Bartlett, ed.; Little, Brown Co., Boston; 13th edition; p. 331; citing Historical Review of Pa., 1759

91

Washington, *Writings*; v. 30, p. 291 at 294-295

94

Mass. Bill of Rights, See xxiii above, Poore, as cited in *Documents* etc.; Commager, ed.; p. 107

Witherspoon, Library of Congress copy; p. 40-41

Va. Declaration of Rights, See p. xxiii above, Poore, as cited in *Documents* etc.; Commager, ed.; p. 103

Cont'l Congress Resolution, *Journals of the Continental Congress*, 1776; W. C. Ford, ed.; v. 4, p. 357 at 358

Mass. House, *Writings* of Samuel Adams; v. 1, p. 152 at 156-157

95

Adams, J., *Works*; v. 6, p. 280

Jefferson, *Writings* (H. A. Washington edition); v. 8, p. 40 at 44-45

Madison, *Annals*—History of Congress; v. 1, columns 433 at 434; also see Madison's *Writings*, v. 5, p. 376

Mayhew, Library of Congress copy; p. 6-7

Williams, Library of Congress copy; p. 3 (see full title, p. 24 above)

96

Madison, *Writings*; v. 6, p. 101 at 103

The Federalist, No. 10, par. "The influence of . . ."

Mass. House, *Writings* of Samuel Adams; v. 1, p. 134 at 137

Otis, Library of Congress copy; p. 7-10

98

The Federalist, No. 79, par. "Next to permanency . . ."

99

Cont'l Congress Resolution, *Journals of the Continental Congress*, 1774; W. C. Ford, ed.; p. 63 at 67

"The Body of Liberties," *The Liberties of the Massachusetts Colonie in New England, 1641*; in Old South Leaflets, No. 164, Library of Congress copy; p. 1

101

Warren, P & A; p. 24-25

104

The Federalist, No. 31, par. "A government ought . . ."

Braintree Instructions, *Works* of John Adams; v. 3, p. 465 at 468

Madison, *Writings;* v. 6, p. 101 at 103

Jefferson, *writings;* H. A. Washington, ed.; v. 6, p. 570 at 574-575

105

Dickinson, *Political Writings;* 1st quotation—v. 1, p. 329-330; in Pa. Provincial Convention, 1774; 2nd quotation—v. 1, p. 271 at 275-278; "Letters From a Farmer," No. 12

The Federalist, No. 21, par. "It is a . . ."

106

Madison, *Writings;* v. 6, p. 10 at 11, footnote

Washington, *Writings;* v. 35, p. 214 at 230

Jefferson, *Writings;* v. 9, p. 388 at 389

Hamilton, *Works;* v. 2, p. 227 at 283; Report to House of Representatives dated January 9, 1790

109

The Federalist, No. 17, par. "An objection of . . ."

Mass. House, *Writings* of Samuel Adams; v. 1, p. 137 (see fuller quotation on page 96, *ante*)

The Federalist, No. 10, par. "The influence of . . ."

Jefferson, *Writings* (H. A. Washington edition); v. 6, p. 570 at 574-575 (see fuller quotation on page 104, *ante*)

The Federalist, No. 83, par. "Having now seen . . ."

111

The Federalist, No. 31, par. "As theory and . . ."

112

The Federalist, No. 45, par. "The powers delegated . . ."

113

Franklin, *Writings;* v. 3, p. 407 at 409—"The Way to Wealth—Preface to Poor Richard Improved: 1758"

1913 Income Tax Law, Maximum rates: on Individuals' income—basic rate 1 per cent, surtax 6 per cent; on Corporations' income, rate of 1 per cent

116

Madison, *Writings;* 1st quotation: v. 5, p. 269 at 272; 2nd quotation: v. 5, p. 126 (and Elliot's *Debates* etc.; v. 3, p. 87)

The Federalist, No. 51, par. "Second. It is . . ."

117

Wise, *A Vindication of the Government of New England Churches*, 1717; Library of Congress copy, reprinted in 1772; p. 48

The Federalist, No. 10, par. "Among the numerous . . ."

Wilson, Elliot's *Debates* etc.; v. 2, p. 432; *Works*, v. 3, p. 292

Adams, J., *Works;* 1st quotation: v. 6, p. 8

2nd quotation: v. 6, p. 48

3rd quotation: v. 5, p. 490

118

Jefferson, *Writings;* 1st quotation: v. 10, p. 22 at 24

2nd quotation: v. 9, p. 28 at 29

3rd quotation: v. 3, p. 85 at 223-224

119

Jefferson, Richardson's *Messages and Papers of the Presidents*, v. 1, p. 310; and *Writings* (H. A. Washington edition); v. 8, p. 1 at 2

120

The Federalist, No. 53, par. "In searching for . . ."

122

Jefferson, *Writings;* v. 3, p. 85 at 224 (see fuller quotation on page 118, *ante*)

129

Adams, J., *Works;* v. 3, p. 465 at 467

References

130
Adams, J., *Works*; v. 10, p. 172
Wilson, Elliot's *Debates* etc.; v. 2, p. 457
Adams, J. Q., Library of Congress copy; p. 11-12; "The Jubilee of the Constitution," April 30, 1839
131
Wilson, *Selected Political Essays of;* R. G. Adams, ed.; 1930, A. A. Knopf, N.Y.; p. 121
132
Wilson, Elliot's *Debates* etc.; v. 2, p. 432; *Works*, v. 3, p. 271 at 292
Ky. Constitution, *The Federal and State Constitutions etc;* F. N. Thorpe, ed.; Govt. Printing Office, 1909; v. 3, p. 1312
133
Cont'l Congress Declaration, *Journals of the Continental Congress*, 1775; W. C. Ford, ed.; v. 2, p. 128 at 155-156; as cited in *Documents* etc.; Commager, ed.; p. 92 at 95
134
Wilson, *Works;* v. 3, 299 at 310
Rush, P & A; 1st part, p. 234; 2nd part, p. 236
135
Adams, J. Q., Library of Congress copy, p. 40-41
Blackstone, *Commentaries;* 9th ed., 1783; *v.* 1, p. 49, 162
136
The Federalist, No. 53, par. "In searching for . . ."
Dicey, *Introduction . . . Constitution*; Macmillan Co., N.Y. 1924, 8th ed.; p. xviii, 37 as to Parliament's supremacy; p. 122-123 as to "Constitution" etc.
Bryce, *The American Commonwealth*; 1959 abridged edition, G. P. Putnam's Sons, N.Y.; v. 1, Chap. 5, p. 51-52
The Federalist, No. 84, par. "It has been . . ."
137
Adams, J. Q., Library of Congress copy; p. 5-6, 8-9
138
Jefferson, *Writings*; v. 10, p. 342 at

343—letter to Lee; v. 10, p. 346— letter to Mease
138-9
Adams, J., *Works*; v. 2, p. 512 at 514—1822 letter to Pickering
139
Adams, J., *Works*; v. 9, p. 415— letter to Chase
139-40
Wise, *A Vindication* etc.; Library of Congress copy (see details p. 117, above); p. 23-24, 26-30, 41-42, 45; and p. 36-7 regarding "the prince . . . is the rebel"
140
Wise and Andros tax, *Ipswich In the Massachusetts Bay Colony*, by Thomas F. Waters; The Ipswich Historical Society, 1905, Ipswich, Mass.—p. 238-242
Barlow, P & A; p. 145 at 150
141-2
Univ. of Va. Resolution 1825, *Writings* of Thos. Jefferson; A. A. Lipscomb, editor in chief, 1904-1905; v. 19, p. 459 at 460-461 (the wording used in the text is based upon photo-copy of original record of Univ. of Va.)
143
Madison, *Writings;* v. 9, p. 218-219 —letter to Jefferson
144
Adams, J., *Works;* v. 5, p. 490
Va. Resolutions 1798 and 1799, *Writings* of James Madison; v. 6, p. 331, Resolutions of 1799; p. 341 *et seq.* regarding Report
145
Resolution (1790) Va. Legislature, (See p. 17 above. Hening, etc.)
Laws (1798) repealed, *Writings* of James Madison; v. 9, p. 383 at 397—letter to Edward Everett, Aug. 28, 1830, regarding Va. Resolutions of 1798 and 1799 being conducive to their repeal
Mass. Legislature Resolution; *Acts & Resolves*, 1858, Chapter 44, p. 170
146
Wisc. Legislature Resolution of 1859, *General Laws*, 1859, p. 247-248
Madison, *Writings;* v. 9, p. 573 *et seq.*

—"Notes on Nullification"; v. 9, p. 383 *et seq.*, footnote—letter to Everett; v. 9, p. 489 *et seq.*— letter to Trist
The Federalist, No. 78, par. "There is no . . ." and following 5 pars.
No. 33, par. "But it may . . ." and the following paragraph
No. 34, par. "In the case . . ."
No. 46, par. "Were it admitted . . ."

147
Madison, *Writings;* v. 9, p. 573 at 584—"Notes on Nullification"
Adams, J. Q., Library of Congress copy; p. 21-22
147-8
Univ. of Va. Res. (See 141-2 above)
148
Madison, *Writings*; v. 9, p. 218 at 219
Jefferson, *Writings;* v. 5, p. 52 at 53
148-9
Washington, *Writings*; v. 30, p. 66
151
Washington, *Writings;* v. 29, p. 402— to Madison Feb. 5, 1788
p. 308—to Hamilton
p. 323—to Stuart
p. 331—to Madison Dec. 7, 1787
Hamilton, *Works;* v. 9, p. 432 at 434 —letter to Madison June 8, 1788, regarding copies sent to Randolph
152
Madison, *Annals*; History of Congress; v. 5, column 776—April 6, 1796
Madison, *Writings*; v. 9, p. 471 at 477 —letter to Trist
Marshall, U.S. Supreme Court Reports; v. 17, p. 316 at 403; *McCulloch v. Maryland*
Madison about *The Federalist*, See page 148 above
153
The Federalist, no. 39, par. "On examining the . . ."
Marshall, U.S. Supreme Court Reports: v. 17, p. 316—*McCulloch v. Maryland;* v. 19, p. 264—*Cohens v. Virginia;* v. 158, p. 601—*Pollock v. Farmers' Loan & Trust Co.*
154
The Federalist, No. 43, par. "8. 'To provide for . . ."

155
The Federalist, Various numbers regarding the enduring need of the Constitution's safeguards against the never-changing weaknesses of human nature—for example:
No. 6, par. "From this summary . . ."
No. 10, par. "The latent causes . . ." and par. "If a faction . . ." and the following paragraph
No. 48. par. "In a government . . ." and remainder of the essay
No. 51, par. "But the great . . ."
No. 62, par. "First. It is . . ." and following paragraph
No. 63, par. "Thus far I . . ."
No. 71, par. "There are some . . ."
No. 73, par. "But this observation . . ."
No. 78, par. "This independence of . . ."
The Federalist, No. 33, par. "But it is . . ."
No. 78, par. "The complete independence . . ."
156-7
Jefferson, *Writings;* v. 5, p. 171 at 173 —letter to Randolph; v. 9, p. 71-72 —letter to Norvell
159
Jefferson, *Writings;* v. 3, p. 85 at 223-224, "Notes on the State of Va."
160
Jefferson, *Writings*; v. 5, p. 80 at 83, letter to Madison
Madison, *Writings*; v. 5, p. 269 at 272, letter to Jefferson Oct. 17, 1788 (and see Gov. Randolph's illustration in Va. Ratifying Convention; Elliot's *Debates* etc., v. 3, p. 66-67, 70)
161
The Federalist, No. 10, par. "From this view . . ."
162
Adams, J., *Works*; v. 3, p. 20
"Essex Result" Library of Congress copy; p. 8; reprinted in *Memoir of Theophilus Parsons*, p. 362 (see under p. 23 above)

163

The Federalist, No. 55, par. "Is the danger . . ."
No. 10, par. "A republic, by . . ."
No. 39, par. "If we resort . . ."
Adams J., *Works;* v. 4, p. 189 at 194 and 204-205

164

Malden Instructions, P & A; p. 132
"Essex Result" Library of Congress copy; p. 12; reprinted in *Memoir of Theophilus Parsons,* p. 365 (see details under p. 23 above)
Adams, J., *Works;* v. 9, p. 414
Hamilton, *Works;* v. 1, p. 277 at 286-287
Wilson, Farrand *Records* etc.; v. 1, p. 66 and 74—in Framing Convention

165

Wilson, Elliot's *Debates* etc.; v. 2, p. 421, 428—Pa. Ratifying Convention; *Works,* v. 3, p. 277, 286-287
Hamilton, *Works;* v. 2, p. 40; also see Elliot's *Debates* etc.; v. 2, p. 301
The Federalist, No. 39, par. "The last paper . . ."
No. 37, par. "Among the difficulties . . ."
No. 51, par. "First. In a . . ." and "Second. It is . . ."

165-6

The Federalist, No. 45, par. "The powers delegated . . ."

166

Wilson, U.S. Supreme Court Reports; v. 2, p. 454; *Chisholm v. Ga.*

167

Mass. Legislature, P & A; p. 125
Wilson (see entries under, p. 132)

168

The Federalist, No. 17, par. "An objection of . . ."
No. 32, par. "An entire consolidation . . ."
No. 33, par. "These two clauses . . ." and par. "But it is . . ."
No. 83, par. "Having now seen . . ." and the next succeeding par.
No. 39, par. "On examining the . . ." and the next succeeding par.
No. 40, par. "The truth is . . ."

and the preceding sentence, also the remainder of the essay
No. 41, par. "Some who have . . ." and the remainder of the essay
No. 45, par. "The powers delegated . . ." and the remainder of the essay
Butler case, U.S. Supreme Court Reports; v. 297, p. 1 at 63; *U.S. v. Butler*

169

Madison, *Writings;* v. 5, p. 17 at 25

170

The Federalist, No. 14, par. "Such a fallacy . . ."
No. 56, par. "The experience of . . ."
No. 57, Entire essay
No. 58, Entire essay
Wilson, *Works;* v. 1, p. 429-430

170-1

Madison, *Annals;* History of Congress; v. 1, column 738; Aug. 15, 1789

171

The Federalist, No. 63, par. "Thus far I . . ."
No. 71, par. "There are some . . ."

171-2

The Federalist, No 78, par. "This independence of . . ."

172

The Federalist, No. 84, par. "It has been . . ." and following 4 pars.

173

The Federalist, No. 26, par. "From the same . . ."
No. 84 (see p. 172 above)
Madison, *Writings;* v. 5, p. 269 at 271; letter to Jefferson
Madison, *Annals;* History of Congress; v. 1, columns 449-450 and 453-457
Wilson, *Selected Political Essays of James Wilson;* R. G. Adams, ed.; Alfred A. Knopf, N.Y., 1930; p. 153 at 154
Wilson, Elliot's *Debates* etc.; v. 2, p. 435-437, 453-454
Washington, *Writings;* v. 29, p. 475 at 478

174
Bartkus case, U.S. Supreme Court Reports; v. 359, p. 121 at 124; *Bartkus v. Illinois*
175
U.S. House of Representatives, *Annals*; History of Congress; v. 1, columns 749 at 755, Aug. 17, 1789, and column 913 as to final action Sept. 24, 1789
175-6
The Federalist, No. 45, par. "The powers delegated . . ."
176
The Federalist, No. 17, par. "An objection of . . ."
176-7
Jefferson, *Writings*; v. 8, p. 341 at 343-344; Second Inaugural Address
177
Jefferson, *Writings*; v. 8, p. 482 at 494; sixth annual Message to Congress
173
The Federalist, No. 79, par. "Next to permanency . . ."
Hamilton, *Works*; v. 3, p. 445 at 485 —"Opinion" (regarding Bank of U.S.). v. 4, p. 70 at 152—Report on "Manufactures"
178-9
The Federalist, No. 83, par. "Having now seen . . ."
179
Butler case, U.S. Supreme Court Reports; v. 297, p. 1 at 70-74; *U.S. v. Butler*
Wickard case, U.S. Supreme Court Reports; v. 317, p. 111 at 131; *Wickard v. Filburn*
181
Roosevelt, *The Public Papers and Addresses of Franklin D. Roosevelt*; Random House, N.Y., 1938; v. 1, p. 569
Hamilton, *The Federalist* No. 17, regarding agriculture (see p. 176 above)
Butler case, See p. 179 above
182
The Federalist, No. 78, par. "This independence of . . ."
Washington, *Writings*; v. 35, p. 214 at 229

183
Madison—Framing Convention, Farrand *Records* etc.; v. 2, p. 417
184
Hamilton, *Works*; v. 5, p. 476 footnote; v. 6, p. 171 at 174; and as to authorship see v. 5, p. 476 footnote and v. 6, p. 140
The Federalist, No. 33, par. "But it is . . ."
Henry, Elliot's *Debates* etc.; v. 3, p. 512-514
Madison, Elliot's *Debates* etc.; v. 3, p. 514
184-5
Nicholas, Elliot's *Debates* etc.; v. 3, p. 507
185
Madison, *Writings*; v. 6, p. 262 at 272; also see *Annals*, History of Congress; v. 5, columns 776-777
Jefferson, *Writings* (H. A. Washington edition); v. 9, p. 5 at 80-81
186
Reid case, U.S. Supreme Court Reports; v. 354, p. 1; *Reid v. Covert*
The Federalist, No. 33 (see p. 184 above)
186-7
The Federalist, No. 75, par. "However proper or . . ."
187
Madison, *Letters and Other Writings*; J. P. Lippincott and Co., 1865; v. 2, p. 140-141
Washington, *Writings*; v. 35, p. 233
189
The Federalist, No. 83 (see p. 178-179 above)
189-90
American Daily Advertiser, Library of Congress copy; page 3, column 2
190
Phila. Gazette, Library of Congress copy; page 2, column 4
Annals, History of Congress; v. 4, columns 170-171
190-1
Story, *Commentaries on the Constitution of the United States*, by Joseph Story; Hilliard Gray & Co., Philadelphia, 1833; v. 2, Sec. 919

References

192

Madison, *Writings*; v. 9, p. 471 at 477

193

Adams, J., *Works;* v. 3, p. 445 at 454

Marshall, C. J.; U.S. Supreme Court Reports; v. 22, p. 1 at 188; *Gibbons v. Ogden*

Ellsworth, *Essays on the Constitution of the U.S., 1787-1788*; P. L. Ford, ed.; "The Letters of A Landholder" by Oliver Ellsworth; Dec. 3, 1787; p. 135 at 156; Nov. 1787-March, 1788; No. 5

194

The Federalist, No. 33, par. "But it is . . ."

No. 78, par. "There is no . . ." and following 5 paragraphs

No. 53, par. "In searching for . . ."

Wilson, *Works*; v. 1, p. 462-463 regarding Point 1

South Carolina case, U.S. Supreme Court Reports; v. 199, p. 437 at 448-449

195

The Federalist, No. 78, par. "It can be . . ." and par. "There is yet . . ."

No. 39, par. "But if the . . ."

No. 81, par. "But perhaps . . ."

196

Dimick case, U.S. Supreme Court Reports; v. 293, p. 474 at 487

The Federalist, No. 81, par. "In the first . . ."

No. 33, par. "But it is . . ."

No. 39, par. "But if the . . ."

No. 78, par. "There is no . . ."

No. 80, par. "The first point . . ."

Framing Convention, Farrand *Records* etc.; v. 1, p. 97 as to Gerry and p. 109 as to King; v. 2, p. 78 as to Mason, p. 93 as to Madison

State Ratifying Conventions, Elliot's *Debates* etc.; v. 2, p. 131 as to Samuel Adams (Mass.) p. 196 as to Ellsworth, and p. 445-446 as to Wilson, v. 3, p. 553 as to Marshall, p. 532 as to Madison, p. 324-325 as to Patrick Henry, p. 567 as to Grayson (Va.), p. 548 as to Pendleton (Va.)

197

Otis, *Works* of John Adams; v. 2, p. 523 at 525—as to Otis' argument in Court; also *The Rights of the British Colonies*, 1764; Library of Congress copy, p. 47

The Federalist, No. 83, par. "In like manner . . ."

199

Hamilton, *Works;* v. 4, p. 230 at 280 —"Letters of Phocion," No. 2

Adams, J. Q., Richardson's *Messages and Papers of the Presidents*; v. 2, p. 865 at 877

200

The Federalist, Nos. 26 and 46, for example (regarding usurpation) using the word "traitor" with respect to one aspect of usurpation of power to subvert the people's liberties: No. 26, par. "Schemes to subvert . . ."; No. 46, par. "The only refuge . . ."

Wilson, *Works*; v. 1, p. 408

202-3

Jefferson, *Writings* (H. A. Washington edition); v. 1, p. 45

203

Tripoli Treaty, *Treaties and Other International Acts of the United States of America;* Hunter Miller, ed.; U.S. Gov't Printing Office, 1931; v. 2 (1776-1818), p. 364 at 365, Art. 11.

204

Jefferson, *Writings;* v. 8, p. 341 at 344

205

Federal Gazette, Library of Congress copy; p. 2; signed "K" (the author Benjamin Franklin, per Library of Congress information)

Franklin in Framing Convention, Farrand *Records* etc; v. 1, p. 450-451

205-6

Pinckney, Farrand *Records* etc.; v. 3, p. 301—Letter in State Gazette of S.C., Charleston, May 2, 1788

206

Hamilton, *Essays on the Constitution of the U.S., 1787-1788*; P. L. Ford, ed.; p. 286 at 288—"The Letters of Caesar," No. 2, Oct. 17, 1787

The Federalist, No. 37, par. "Would it be . . ."
U.S. House Resolution, *Annals;* History of Congress; v. 1, column 914
206-7
Adams J. Q., Library of Congress copy; p. 62
208
Witherspoon, Sermon, 1776; Library of Congress copy; p. 40-41
Adams, S., *Writings;* v. 2, p. 332 at 336
Hamilton, *Works;* v. 1, p. 3 at 37— "A Full Vindication in Support of Measures of the Continental Congress . . ."
Madison, *Writings;* v. 2, p. 183 at 190
Conn. Ministers, *American Archives,* 4th Series, 1774-1775, Peter Force, ed.; v. 1, column 442
209
Jefferson, *Writings;* v. 8, p. 108 at 123
210
Franklin, *Writings;* v. 4, p. 467 at 469-470
220
Eliot, A., Library of Congress copy, p. 42-43; also see *The New England Clergy and the American Revolution* (see under p. 24 above); p. 90
Pitt, P & A, p. 455 at 459
221
Pitt (continued), P & A, 457 (first part of quotation); 458 (as to latter part)
Declaration of Causes, *Journals of the Continental Congress,* W. C. Ford, ed.; v. 2, p. 140 at 154-155; as cited in *Documents* etc.; Commager, ed.; p. 92 at 95
221-2
Hancock, P & A, p. 39, col. 2
222
Jefferson, *Writings;* v. 10, p. 390 at 391-392
Adams, J., *Works;* v. 9, p. 417 at 420
222-3
Gladstone, *Familiar Quotations,* by John Bartlett; 13th edition; Little, Brown and Co., Boston; p. 534
223
Jefferson, *Writings* (H. A. Washington edition); v. 2, p. 257 at 260

Madison, Elliot's *Debates* etc.; v. 3, p. 94
Wilson, *Works;* v. 3, p. 279 (1st quotation); p. 293 (2nd quotation); see also Elliot's *Debates* etc.; v, 2, p. 432-433
224
The Federalist, No. 40, Entire essay
Madison, *Annals;* History of Congress; v. 1, column 102; (and see, for example, Wilson in Pa. Ratifying Convention, *Works,* v. 3, p. 271 at 290, also Elliot's *Debates* etc., v. 2, p. 431; Gov. Randolph in Va. Ratifying Convention, Elliot's *Debates* etc., v. 3, p. 82-84)
224-5
Mason, Farrand *Records* etc.; v. 4, p. 75-76
225
The Federalist No. 30, par. "In the Ottoman . . ."
Madison, Elliot's *Debates* etc.; v. 3, p. 399
Washington, *Writings;* v. 29, p. 409 at 411—letter to Lafayette
Washington, Farrand *Records* etc.; v. 2, p. 666-667—letter to Congress
Washington, *Writings;* v. 29, p. 217 at 224—letter to Jefferson
Adams, J. Q., Library of Congress copy; p. 11
226-7
Madison, *Writings;* v. 2, p. 361 at 363; and list of topics 361-366
227
Coup d'état defined, *Webster's New Practical Dictionary* (1951); G&C Merriam Co., Worcester, Mass.; fuller definition in *Webster's New International Dictionary;* 2nd edition; 1943; unabridged: "A sudden decisive exercise of force whereby the existing government is subverted; an unexpected measure of state, more or less violent; a stroke of policy."
228
The Federalist, No. 22, par. "It has not . . ."
Framing Convention Resolutions, Farrand *Records* etc.; v. 1, p. 232— Resolution of June 13; v. 2, p. 665

References

—Resolution of Sept. 17
228-9
Washington, Farrand *Records* etc.; v. 2, p. 666-667—letter to Congress
230
Morris, Farrand *Records* etc.; v. 3, p. 381 at 382
Congress Resolution, *Documentary History of the Constitution of the U.S., 1787-1870;* v. 2, p. 22
232-3
Madison, *Writings;* v. 6, p. 101
235
The Federalist, No. 10, par. "The second expedient . . ." and the following paragraph
A writing (1937), Identified at page 239, below
Beard, *An Economic Interpretation of the Constitution of the United States;* 1913, Macmillan Co., N.Y.; for example, see especially pages: 6 fn, 7, 12, 14-15, 15 fn, 16, 17-18, 50-51, 153, 188, 290, 291, 324 and Chapters 5 and 6 in particular; also 218—quoting with approval another book (John W. Burgess' *Political Science and Comparative Constitutional Law*) which accuses The Framers of perpetrating a *coup d'état.*
236
Corwin, History Teachers Magazine, Feb. 1914; p. 65 at 66
Brown, book quoted, at p. 111
237
Beard's 1935 2nd edition, 1935 reprint of book cited under p. 235 above, with new Introduction by Beard, p. xvi

Holmes, *Holmes-Pollock Letters;* Mark de Wolfe Howe, ed.; 1941, Harvard University Press; Letter July 12, 1916 to Pollock—v. 1, p. 237; Letter June 20, 1928 to Pollock—v. 2, p. 222-223
Holmes, *The Mind and Faith of Justice Holmes;* Max Lerner, ed.; 1943, Little, Brown and Co., Boston; letter to John C. H. Wu, June 21, 1928; p. 434-435
238
Beale book about Beard; Univ. of Ky. Press, 1954 (see comments pages 345-347, *post*)
239
Earle, 1937 Introduction to *The Federalist,* Modern Library Edition
240
Dickinson, *Political Writings;* v. 1, p. 312
Washington, *Writings;* v. 30, p. 291 at 294-295 (and see, as to a model for other peoples, Wilson in Pa. Ratifying Convention, Elliot's *Debates* etc., v. 2, p. 529)
241
Adams, S., *Writings;* v. 2, p. 256 at 263
Adams, J. Q., Richardson's *Messages and Papers of the Presidents;* v. 2, p. 861
242
Adams, S., *Writings;* v. 2, p. 287-288
243-5
Adams, J., *Works;* v. 3, p. 445 at 461-464—"A Dissertation . . ."
245-6
Warren, P & A; p. 24 at 29

Author's Additional Comment Regarding
Charles A. Beard's 1913 Book
(See pages 235-239 of main text)

The topic mentioned at pages 237-238, *ante:* the motive of Dr. Beard in writing his 1913 book (title p. 235)—attacking, in effect, the motives and integrity of The Framers and therefore their handiwork, the Constitution—will be discussed briefly in the light mainly of the posthumous volume of essays about him by some of those who knew him intimately, including educators: *Charles A. Beard—An Appraisal,* edited by Howard K. Beale and published in 1954 by the University of Kentucky Press. (See also other pertinent writings, especially *The Autobiography of James T. Shotwell;* 1961, page 43, regarding the strongly Socialistic bias of Dr. Beard and his wife.)

Note first that the extent to which Dr. Beard was Socialistic in his thinking in the period of 1913 helps greatly to explain his hostility to the Constitution and its Framers. This is true because this basic law's limits on the Federal government's power—according to the controlling intent of those who framed and adopted the initial instrument and later each of its amendments, to the present time—were designed to bar from America (unless and until the people should change the Constitution by appropriate amendment) centralized control by government of the national economy, of the basic economic activities of the people of the nation. Such centralized control, also called Collectivism (synonymous with Socialism in its economic aspect especially), is of the essence of the philosophy of Socialism, underlying the philosophy of fully developed Socialism called Communism as advocated, for example, by Karl Marx and by Friedrich Engels, his benefactor, collaborator and co-author with Marx of *The Communist Manifesto* (1848). The Marx theory of Socialism-Communism, or Communist Socialism, (called Marxism) includes, as one of its main tenets, the idea of economic determinism. This means the economic factor, The Material, controls Man and his development, controls history and the development of social and political institutions. This spells, in effect, Materialism: the atheistic school of thought which denies Man's creation by God, denies the existence of God and puts Man on a par in this respect with things physical, like a clod of dirt.

This is the very antithesis of the basic tenets of the traditional American philosophy expressed in the Declaration of Independence—including the idea of God-given rights—which the Constitution sought to make effective and secure governmentally and was firmly believed in by the Signers of these two documents and their fellow Americans in general: ". . . all men are created . . . endowed by their Creator with certain unalienable rights . . ." (unalienable *because* God-given). So to believe is, of course, to reject the godless concept of Materialism; and, by the same token, to believe in the economic determinism of Marxist Socialism is to reject the American philosophy of Man's creation by God and endowment with God-given rights: Natural Rights.

The foregoing highlights the significance, in the 1913 Beard book, of his express espousal in effect of economic determinism (for example, p. 7): "The theory of economic determinism has not been tried out in American history, and until it is tried out, it cannot be found wanting." His repeated references to economic determinism made it evident that, in this book, he was in substance (though not with sufficient candidness, perhaps, to alert the general reader) advocating economic determinism, though perhaps not Marx's full thesis.

345

It is noteworthy that in his book (p. 6 fn) Beard also cited three books of "Socialist" writers "that deserve study . . ." (quoting his own words). As to another work, E.R.A. Seligman's *The Economic Interpretation of History,* Beard quotes (from page 3) at his own page 15n:

> "The theory of the economic interpretation of history as stated by Professor Seligman seems as nearly axiomatic as any proposition in social science can be . . . [quoting Seligman, in part] . . . 'To economic causes, therefore, must be traced in the last instance those transformations in the structure of society which themselves condition the relations of social classes and the various manifestations of social life.' "

Beard approved; "axiomatic" means self-evident, as a truth.

Beard was introduced to *The Communist Manifesto* by one of his professors while he was a young student at Depauw University (per article in The American Political Science Review, Dec. 1949, p. 1166) and it is evident that he was greatly and favorably impressed by it, judged by later developments. Of special interest, in this connection, is the statement (Beale book, p. 236-7) by Dr. George S. Counts of Teachers College, Columbia University (retired in 1955)—a long-time associate and close friend of Dr. Beard—that while Beard was in England at the turn of the century he:

> "probed deeply into the thought of international revolutionary Socialism and was profoundly influenced by it. Though never a Marxian, after re-reading Marx and Engels in the middle thirties in the German edition of their collected works, he remarked that their total achievement stands over all other comparable efforts in history as a 'mountain stands over the surrounding foothills.' "

Yet in July, 1948, just before his death, Beard told Counts "that he had been mistaken in his general interpretation of Marxist Socialism"—disillusioned by the developments in the Union of Soviet Socialist Republics: Soviet Russia. (Counts, in the Beale book, p. 237.)

At the turn of the century, Beard spent several years in England—at first as a student and then as a militant worker for the Socialist-Labor movement. Meanwhile he helped to found Ruskin Hall at Oxford University as a "Labor" school, where he lectured for a time. In this period, Beard—always of a fiery disposition—was a crusader for Socialistic developments in England; as he was later in America, though often more subtly.

One further observation by Counts in his essay (Beale book, p. 250) is of special interest at this point: that Beard was asked in 1941 whether he was satisfied with his 1913 book (the one under consideration here) and he replied in the negative. Counts states (his own emphasis):

> "When Beard was asked in 1941 whether he was satisfied with his *Economic Interpretation* . . . [meaning the 1913 book] . . . he replied at once in the negative. He said that it had been written without sufficient attention to historical perspective. Had he been rewriting it he probably would have emphasized not so much that the framers were not democrats as that they *were* republicans in a world where republicanism was forward-looking."

(Here "republicans" means advocates of a republic for America. Regarding the comment about "not democrats," note discussion at pages 159-160 of this study-guide.)

How tragic for America that Dr. Beard's recantation—regarding his 1913 book which defamed The Framers—came only after decades of the resulting damage, through teaching and writings, to the minds of American Youth, of educators, of the public and to the cause of Education as well as to sound, constitutional government (as intended by the Framers and Adopters in 1787-1788) which depends, in last analysis, upon public respect for it and indoctrinating the Young accordingly. Moreover, Dr. Beard went to his grave without publicly acknowledging his profound errors.

It is clearly indicative of Beard's motive, in writing his 1913 book, that in his teachings as a Professor at Columbia University in this period he was so militantly and controversially critical of, indeed hostile toward, the Constitution and governmental institutions in America that, according to Counts, Beard was grilled for an hour in 1916 by Columbia's President and a committee of trustees about his fostering disrespect among students toward American institutions; and he was, Counts states: "ordered to warn all other men in his department against teachings 'likely to inculcate disrespect for American institutions.' " (Beale book, p. 243.)

In concluding this brief comment—about Dr. Beard's motives in writing his 1913 book attacking The Framers and the Constitution—in relation to the text of this study-guide (pages 235-239), it merits mention that Dr. Beard's published writings in the period of the 1930's, especially during and after the "Great Depression" of 1929-1932, evidenced unmistakably his strong belief in centralized control by government of the national economy—an essential part of any well-developed system of Socialism—and his hostility to America's traditional system of individual, competitive, private enterprise. His writings in this period especially also evidenced his desire to see America develop governmentally into a Socialistic (Collectivistic) nation, in part through the influence of Socialistic teachings in the schools and colleges.

Yet he was always careful, and skillful enough with words, to cloak his real meaning in euphemisms—the subtly disguised terms designed to make his meaning clear to the knowledgeable but too obscure to the general reader to permit them to get the point; as illustrated by his calculated, consistent use of the term Collectivism instead of Socialism, though meaning in truth a Socialistic system, essentially. (See, for example, with regard to such use of terms by Beard, an article by Professor Franklin Bobbitt of the University of Chicago in "School and Society," August 18, 1934; also an article by the late, celebrated Socialist: Professor Harold J. Laski of the London School of Economics, in "The New Republic," July 29, 1936; and see article by Professor Harry D. Gideonse of the University of Chicago in "The Journal of Political Economy," December, 1935. The Laski article labels as a "blueprint for Socialism" the 1934 volume: recommendations for restructuring schools' curricula, written by Beard for the American Historical Association. The Beale book, of essays about Beard, throws further light on the above points: his Socialist bent.

In conclusion, it needs re-emphasizing that Beard and his 1913 book—his baseless, destructive defamation of The Framers and the Constitution—set a trend in educational and intellectual circles for decades with infinite and continuing harm to the minds of Youth and the people at large and to American governmental institutions—consequently to Posterity's just heritage. The great, harmful and continuing influence of Beard's book, in the educational world especially, is discussed by Professor Douglass Adair in a devastatingly critical article in William and Mary Quarterly (being its Managing Editor) in 1951, v. VIII, p. 48: "The Tenth Federalist Revisited;" in which he exposes Beard's flagrant violations of sound scholarship and historical truth with political motives in his book—indicating also Beard's Socialistic bent.

(End of comment about the Beard book)

347

QUOTATIONS INDEX-DIGEST
(topic and author)

Academic Freedom (precedent for inculcating American principles and barring any inculcation of principles "incompatible" with Constitutions of U.S. and Va.)—University of Va. Board, Jefferson, Madison (and see Madison 143-144) 142

Agriculture (power over, and other intra-State concerns prohibited to Federal government by Constitution)—*The Federalist*, Hamilton, 176; (among fields of power prohibited to Federal government by Constitution)—F. D. Roosevelt, 181; (most thriving when left most free to Individual Enterprise)—Jefferson, 58, 209

Aid, foreign (see Foreign aid)

Alarm (instant at first sign of danger to liberty, first duty)—Madison, 40

Amendment (is the only proper way to change powers under Constitution—not by usurpation)—Washington's *Farewell Address*, 42, 182

America (the empire of reason in an age of philosophy, 1787)—Barlow, 140

American (significance)—Gadsden; Henry; Washington; Hamilton; de Crévecoeur, vii

Americans (a religious people)—Adams, J. Q., 4; (as trustees regarding fate of Liberty and republican model of government)—Washington, 91, 240; (must understand, proclaim—study and pass on to the Young—knowledge of their heritage of Liberty)—Adams, J., 243-245; (must act worthy of themselves—the country being endangered)—Warren, v, 246; (praised for their peaceable change of governmental arrangements)—Wilson, 223; (self-

governing, role)—*The Federalist*, xxii

Ancestors (defended against criticism by detractors) Adams, S., 241

Appropriation (of money by Congress under Constitution is a limited power)—Hamilton, 178

Aristocracy (natural)—Jefferson, 66

Authority, legislative (of Congress under Constitution is limited—not general)—*The Federalist*, 178-179

Beard, Charles A. (unsoundness of his 1913 book about The Farmers)—Brown, 236; Holmes (in text), 237; (comment about Beard)—Counts, 346-347

Bill of Rights (reason, omitted from Constitution stated)—Wilson, 173; (not made by 14th Amendment applicable against States)—Supreme Court, 174

Birthright (defense of, of freedom which we ever enjoyed is cause of taking up arms)—Declaration of Causes . . . 1775 (and see 221), 133

Business (among fields of power prohibited to Federal government by Constitution)—F. D. Roosevelt, 181

Charity (is no part of the legislative duty of the Federal government under the Constitution—applicable also to foreign aid)—Madison, in Congress, 189-190; Story *Commentaries*, 191

Checks and balances (needed to safeguard Liberty)—Adams, J., 40

Commerce (arrives at prices best in private hands free from government interference)—Franklin, 210; (most thriving when left free to Individual Enterprise)—Jefferson, 58, 209

Confidence in officials (the parent of

348

defended against "lawless" usurpers)—Adams, S., 54; (defense of, ever enjoyed is cause of taking up arms)—Declaration of Causes . . . , (1775) 133, 221

Life (and Liberty inseparable)—Jefferson, 24; (the gift of heaven and no proof needed as to Man's right to Life)—Wilson; (the limited conditions permitting the taking of a life)—Adams, J. Q., 74; (a Natural Right)—Boston Res., "The Rights of the Colonists," 85

Livelihood, earning (no right to obstruct)—Jefferson; Madison, 33

Magna Carta (philosophy of, that of Government-over-Man: that of king-granted rights)—Adams, J. Q., 137

Majority (fatally dangerous to Liberty if omnipotent)—Madison; *The Federalist*, 116; Adams, J., 117; Jefferson, 118; ("Bill of Rights" in Va. violated by the, at its pleasure)—Madison (and see 160), 116; Jefferson, 118; (unlimited rule by the, has been history's most frequent producer of despotism)—Madison, 116; (history proves the, has often oppressed the Minority)—Adams, J., 117; (vote by count of at least half-plus-one)—Wise, 117; (designed to be checked by the Constitution to prevent tyrannical rule)—*The Federalist*, 117; (oppressing the Minority, "guilty of a crime" and breaks up society's foundations)—Jefferson, 118; (in Connecticut, has oppressed the Minority—as in most States similarly situated)—Jefferson, 118; (subject to "this sacred principle" that rights of Minority must be respected, else it is despotism)—Jefferson, 119; (even largest, has no arbitrary power over freemen's liberties, etc. in a republic)—1850 Kentucky Constitution, 132

Manufactures (most thriving when left most free to Individual Enterprise)—Jefferson, 58, 209

Military Establishment (dangerous, if excessive)—Washington's *Farewell Address*, 13

Military power (despised if insolent)—Adams, S., 13

Minority (rights of, protected by "this sacred principle" that their rights must be respected by Majority)—Jefferson, 119

Money (power of Congress to appropriate, limited)—Hamilton, 178

Morality (first elements may be taught in public schools)—Jefferson, 75; (basis of government)—Mass. and Va. Bill of Rights, xxiii. Jefferson, 26

Nature, human (better qualities of, are presupposed in a Republic)—Madison, 163; (a degree of depravity in)—Madison, 163

Navigation (most thriving when left most free to Individual Enterprise)—Jefferson, 58, 209

Non-resistance to tyranny (is absurd, slavish, etc.)—Va. Ratifying Convention's assertion, 50; Otis; Rev. Williams; Rev. Mayhew; N.C. Ratifying Convention's assertion, 52

Oath of office (prescribed by Constitution is in keeping with Declaration of Independence and adds religious faith as a support of this basic law)—Adams, J. Q., 206-207; (to support the Constitution, only)—U.S. Constitution, Art. VI, 40

Officials (are public servants, of the people as their masters)—Henry; Va. Declaration of Rights; Wilson; Boston Res.: "The Rights of the Colonists;" Adams, S.; Franklin, 32

Patriotism (meaning; demands)—Hancock; Otis; Mayhew; Rush; Adams, S., viii, ix

People (source of all power and supreme over public servants)—Gerry; Mayhew, 33; (in America, superior to their Constitutions and legislatures)—Wilson, 132; (the, source of all authority of government)—*The Federalist*; Hamilton, 228

Political Economy, by Jean-Baptiste Say (opinion of)—Jefferson, 157

Posterity (duty toward, on the part of each generation)—Dickinson, 240

Power (trust not, of government but guard against by chains of Constitution)—Jefferson; Ky. Resolutions, 16-17; (legislative, executive and judicial power concentrated in same hands is the definition of despotic government such as the "elective despotism" in Va. with legislature dominant—and similarly in other States)—Jefferson, 118, 159; (arbitrary, over liberties etc. of freemen exists nowhere in a republic—not even in largest majority)—1850 Ky. Constitution, 132; (sovereign, does not exist governmentally under the U.S. Constitution or in America while sovereign, exists politically only in the people)—Wilson and Mass. Legislature, 166-167

Powers (of Federal government under Constitution do not include specified fields)—Hamilton, 176; Jefferson, 177; Roosevelt, 181

Prayer (motion for, in Framing Convention seeking Divine guidance)—Franklin, 205

President (not given sole power to make treaties because too dangerous a power for one person)—*The Federalist,* 186-187

Prices (commercial, best arrived at by Individuals and not government)—Franklin, 210

Principle (this sacred, that Majority must respect Minority's rights)—Jefferson, First Inaugural, 119

Principles (American—as defined in Declaration of Independence and Constitutions of U.S. and Va.—should be taught students)—Board of University of Va.; Jefferson; Madison, 142, 143-144; (a return to fundamental,)—xxiii

Property (God-given right to be happy and free [partly] through security of,)—Dickinson, 75; (right to, one of basic rights)—"Bill of Rights" of Va. and Mass., 94; Madison, in first Congress, 95; (right to, considered a Natural Right)—Boston Res., "The Rights of the Colonists," 85; Mass. House, 94; Rev. Williams, 95; (protection of right to, a main end of government)—Mass. House, 94; Madison; Mayhew, 95; Otis, 96; (call to protect,

with Life and Liberty)—Continental Congress, 94; (right to, and Liberty including religious liberty, and government, stand or fall together)—Mass. House; Rev. Witherspoon, 94; Adams, J., 95; (equal or unequal, of every person, to be protected)—Jefferson, 2nd Inaugural, 95; (includes, in rights as well as rights of,)—Madison, 96; (right to, a derivative right—derived from Natural Right to freedom)—Warren, 101; (an essay concerning, as to its nature and value etc.)—Madison, 232-233

Prosperity (four pillars of: agriculture, commerce, manufactures and navigation—most thriving when left most free to Individual Enterprise)—Jefferson, 58, 209

Public utilities (a field of power prohibited to Federal government by Constitution)—F. D. Roosevelt, 181

Reason, capacity to (God-given and the basis of right to knowledge)—Adams, J., 23

Religion (characteristic of the American people)—Adams, J. Q., 4; (most important; conscience not subject to laws)—Livingston. 6; (decline of, and virtue means decline of Liberty and Happiness)—Adams, S., 6; (Congress' lack of power concerning, confirmed)—1st Amendment; (Individual's freedom of choice defines religious liberty)—Jefferson; (freedom of choice and exercise of, guaranteed)—Va. Declaration of Rights, and Va. Statute of Religious Liberty, 86; (is one of fields of power prohibited to the Federal government by the Constitution—reserved to the respective States)—Jefferson, 204

Religions (of every sect and denomination included in protection by Va. Statute of Religious Liberty)—Jefferson, 202-203

Religious liberty (and civil liberty stand or fall together)—Rev. Witherspoon; Adams, S.; Hamilton; Madison; Conn. Ministers, 208

Remedies of States (against Federal

States Rights (include all powers not
granted to the Federal government)—F. D. Roosevelt, 181; (reserved under the Constitution excluded from U.S. Treaty power)—
Jefferson, 185
Students (should be taught American
principles and nothing in conflict
with Constitutions of U.S. and Va.)
—Board of University of Va., Jefferson, Madison, 142, 143-144
Supremacy Clause (of Constitution
makes U.S. Laws supreme only if
conforming to the Constitution)—
The Federalist, 184
Supreme Court (criticism and defiance
of decision by, concerning slavery)
—Legislatures of Mass. and Wisc.,
1858-1859, in text, 145-146; (danger of usurpation by)—Jefferson;
The Federalist; N.Y. Ratifying Convention; Madison, 41
Taxes (taking from some to give to
others is oppression and violates
fundamental principles)—Madison;
Jefferson (and see "leveling", 96),
104; (for unconstitutional purposes
must be avoided)—Braintree Res.;
(arbitrary, oppressive, victimize
Liberty and Property)—Madison,
104; (confiscatory, in effect make
the people a property)—Dickinson;
(confiscatory, make virtual slaves
of the people—violate right to property, freedom, happiness, etc.)—
Dickinson, 105
Taxing power (limited to support of
constitutional duties and responsibilities)—*The Federalist,* 104; (of
Congress for common defense and
general welfare is a limited power)
—Hamilton, 178; Story, 191
Thanksgiving (Resolution by first
Congress recommending President
issue Proclamation for,)—U.S.
House of Rep., 206
Trade (see Commerce)
Treaty Clause (of Constitution
worded so as to include future
and past treaties)—Madison, 183
Treaty power (of U.S. under Constitu-
tion not unlimited—confined to
regulation of foreign relations and
does not authorize infringement of

any essential right)—Madison, 184;
(confined to matters usually covered by treaty and cannot otherwise be regulated—excludes powers
reserved to the States by the Constitution)—Jefferson, 185; (too dangerous to entrust to only one person: the President)—*The Federalist,* 186-187
Trust in government (dangerous to
Liberty, if human weaknesses disregarded)—Adams, S.; *The Federalist;* Jefferson, 12
Truth (prevails over error if left free)
Va. Statute of Religious Liberty,
1786, xxii; (can stand alone; error
alone needs support by government)—Jefferson, 34
Tyranny (may prevail, though forms
of Constitution remain)—Dickinson, 41; (eternal enmity to, declared)—Hancock, 222
Tyrant-ruler ("unkings" himself by
acting against people's rights and
his oath)—Rev. Mayhew, 52
Tyrant's acts (void—tyranny violates
Natural Law)—Rev. West, 52
Unalienable rights (unalienable because God-given)—Jefferson; Hamilton; (cannot be taken away by
Man, by law)—Hamilton; Mass.
House Resolution; (cannot be alienated, renounced)—Boston Res.:
"The Rights of the Colonists," 22
University of Va. (Board Resolution
regarding teaching students basic
American principles)—Jefferson,
Madison, 142, 143-144
Usurpation (tyranny may prevail
while the forms of a constitution
remain)—Dickinson, 41; (danger
of, by Supreme Court)—Jefferson;
The Federalist; N.Y. Ratifying Convention; Madison, 41; (by Federal
government expected to be prevented by Constitution's political
checks)—Madison, 169; (is customary weapon by which free governments are destroyed and not
proper way to make change in
powers under the Constitution)—
Washington's *Farewell Address,* 42,
182
Utilities, public (among fields of

power prohibited to Federal government by Constitution)—F. D. Roosevelt, 181

Virtue (Liberty's safeguard)— Madison, xxii

Washington (urged the Framing Convention to set a lofty standard), xxiii, 230; (letter to Congress from, conveying draft of proposed Constitution), 229; (extolled for high principles at his death)—Morris, 230; Americans as trustees of Liberty and republican model of government 91, 240

Weaknesses of human nature (only safeguard against, is a constitution)—Pittsfield Res., 18; (requiring some distrust balanced by better qualities meriting some confidence)—Madison, *The Federalist*, 163

Wealth of Nations by Adam Smith (opinion of)—Jefferson, 156-157

Welfare, social (among fields of power prohibited to Federal government by Constitution)—F. D. Roosevelt, 181

Work, right to (no one has right to obstruct)—Jefferson; Madison, 33; Madison, 233

Worship God (right, duty)—Mass. Bill of Rights; Washington's *Farewell Address,* 4

AUTHOR "FINDER"

INDEX-DIGEST
(to main text)

In this Index-Digest the comma is used to refer to the main heading in bold-face type under which the entry occurs. In an indented entry such as "glory and promise of—" under "Declaration of Independence" (which is under the main heading "Adams, John") below, the dash refers to the entry "Declaration of Independence" under which the indented entry appears. Repetition of some important references under different headings is used to permit quicker and more certain finding of topic sought.

359

361

gress 46-48, 108-109, 178, 190, 191, 252
God's existence recognized in, 206-207
Government lacks power to alter the, as the people's fundamental law 44, 112, 154-155, 191, 194
Guarantees a Republic as form of government for each State 45, 165
Hamilton's opinion that General Welfare clause created no Federal power to *control* agreed with Jefferson's and Madison's 47, 108-109, 178-179
History provided no model for, 223
Influence of, in other countries 91, 240-241
Intent of Convention which framed, controlled (per *The Federalist*) against Hamilton's later conflicting argument in Supreme Court 153-154
understood and adopted by State Ratifying Conventions 150-151
Interpretation of, by courts subject to limits on their authority and to principles defined 192-201
Judicial Branch's role and limited power under, 192-201
"Judicial Review" concerning, 196-197
Law of the Land (Supreme) 44, 50, 155, 182-183, 194, 196-197
Letter of Washington conveying draft of, to the Continental Congress 228-229
"Liberty" in Preamble of, 87, 153, 201
Limited-power government created by, 16, 43-61, 107-113, 165-209
Meaning of,
comprehensible with common sense and by study 193
per original intent is controlling 43-44, 112, 148, 150-152, 155, 172, 191, 194-198, 293
per report in *The Federalist* of original intent also understood by Ratifying Conventions 150-152
Mystery as to meaning entirely lacking 193
Military officials (sworn to support the,) must refuse to obey orders conflicting with, 61

Need of safeguards provided by the, as enduring as their objects: the never-changing weaknesses of human nature 155
Oath of office
basically religious but not a prohibited religious test 206-207
to support the, 50, 61, 183, 194, 199-200, 244
People of each State assured of sole ratification role and authority as to the 1787 draft of, 228-230
Peoples of other countries served by the, as a guidelight 91, 240
Preamble of,
connecting link with Declaration of Independence 87, 153, 201
"general Welfare" in—merely states a goal and a limit on powers granted in the body of, 46
word "Liberty" in—87, 153, 201
"We the People" in—refers to people of each State separately 153
Praised by William E. Gladstone 222-223
Ratification of, by people of separate States 45, 152, 153, 168, 224, 227-230
Ratifying Conventions understood Framing Convention's intent 150-151
Reconciliation of Man's need of Government with longing for Liberty effected by, 130
Religion a field of power
prohibited to the Federal government by, and reserved to States 201-202, 204
reserved to the States under, 201-202, 204
Religious nature of the, as a document wholly lacking 203-204, 207
Republic's essential foundation is a written, 45, 157, 161
"Right" is a word not in original, 26
Rights protected by, 26-28, 35-36, 43, 99, 120, 161, 163, 201, 211
Sovereign power of government barred from America by, 35, 46, 166-169, 186
States' reserved powers ("rights") broad and undefined under, 46, 55-56, 58, 144-145, 166, 176-177, 180-181, 249

367

371

belief in—as basis of morality and in the latter as the foundation of self-government was characteristic of, 7, 205-206, 208

Sentiments of, similar to Warren's plea 245-246

Fourteenth Amendment

Not intended to make Bill of Rights amendments applicable against the States 174-175

Not intended to give judges blank-check power 175, 199

Framers, The

(See Founders; also Framing—Federal—Convention)

Framing (Federal) Convention

Bill of Rights omission from original Constitution by, explained 26-27, 172-174

Crisis which confronted, due to Confederation's breakdown 224-229

Democracy

as a *form* (not type) of government criticized by, 122-123, 158-160

excesses of—as discussed in, explained 122-123, 158-160

Experiment of America in government due to work of, unparalleled in history 223

False charges against, refuted 224-239

Gladstone praised handiwork of, 222-223

Intent of,

expressed in plain words in Constitution to be given natural meaning 193

important as to Constitution's meaning 43-44, 112, 148, 150-152, 155, 191, 194-198

known to Ratifying Conventions in the main and accepted as Constitution's meaning 150-151

Jefferson's praise of members of, 223

Model to go by lacking in all recorded history 223

People of separate States assured (through steps prescribed by,) of control over Constitution's being made effective 228-229

Records of, a main source of knowledge as to American philosophy and system 155-156, 193

Secrecy of proceedings of, explained 151

Usurpation by Federal government expected by, to be resisted effectively by States 49-50, 60

Washington's plea to, regarding need of setting a lofty standard 229-230

Franklin, Benjamin

Commerce recommended be left to Individual Enterprise free from government interference 210

Divine inspiration of Framers believed in 205-206

Liberty preferred to security 90

Prayer for Divine guidance urged in Framing Convention 205

Quotations by, (on page 5) referred to 205

Resistance to tyranny considered to be a moral duty 49

Standard for judging as to excessive taxes suggested ·113

Free Enterprise

(See also: Individual Enterprise)

Alternative and recommended term: "Individual Enterprise" 214-215

Inaccurate and disapproved term 214-215

Free Man

Self-factors of,

self-discipline 90

self-reliance 89

self-respect 89

Freedom, Academic

(See Academic Freedom)

Freedom (of)

Association

right to, not violated by law-defined "guilt by association" of *persons* (not of ideas) 70, 88

right to work a part of, 37, 70, 88

Choice 27, 37, 57, 68, 70-72, 88, 210

Conscience (see Religious Liberty)

Enjoyment of rights 70-72

Opportunity 68, 71

Religion (see Religious Liberty)

Free-Market Economy

(See: Economy, Free-Market; Individual Enterprise)

French Revolution (1789)

American Revolution entirely different from, 134-135

Liberty (Religious)

Bill for—in Va. (1786) embraced all faiths 202-203

protected by Constitution against Federal interference; governmental authority concerning—reserved to State governments 204

Limits on Federal power under Constitution must be enforced strictly 16-17, 48, 57-58

Madison's letter to, about political checks on Federal government 169; letter to, about Bill of Rights 173

Majority in power must respect Minority's rights 119

Manufactures most thriving when left to Individual Enterprise 58, 209

Militia of States to be used in last resort in resisting Federal usurpers 58-59

Navigation most thriving when left to Individual Enterprise 58, 209

Political Economy writings praised by, 156-157

Powers (Some) prohibited to Federal government 176-177

Property Right supported by, 100

Rector of University of Va. 141

Religion ⎱ see above: Liberty
Religious liberty ⎰ (Religious)

Republican Party founded and led by, 150

Resistance to tyranny is moral duty (inscription on Seal of,) 49

"Rights of British America" (1774) by, 68

Rights of Man declared by, (1826) to be in the ascendancy 222

Slave trade's abolition urged by, (as early as 1774) 68

Students at University of Va. required by its Board including, to be inculcated (indoctrinated) with American Principles and not any conflicting ones 141-142

States' powers surest bulwark of Liberty 58

States' Militia designed to be used in last resort in defense against Federal usurpers 58-59

Subsidies by Federal government to achieve indirectly unauthorized control would have been disapproved by, 180

Treaty clause's scope limited 185

Usurpation by Federal government expected to be resisted by States by force in last resort 58-59

Washington's letter to, about Confederation's breakdown and need of a remedy 225

Writings of, consulted extensively in preparation of this study-guide xxviii-xxix, 143

Jeffersonian Cyclopedia, The: book of quotations from Jefferson's writings xxviii

Jesus Christ

Mentioned in connection with Va. Statute of Religious Liberty 202

John, King

(See King John)

Journal

Of Congress—very sketchy at first xxix-xxx

"Jubilee" Address

Adams (John Quincy), on April 30, 1839 17, 130, 135, 206, 225

Judges

Bound by Constitution's principles and oath of office in interpreting and enforcing this basic law 194-200

Culpability for breach of oath of office and Constitution is individual and personal 198-199

Importance of not usurping power so as to intrude into field of governmental policy 200-201

Oath of office is individual and personal to support Constitution only 194, 198-199

Judicial Branch

Mystery about role and authority of, is non-existent 193

Role and duty of, to respect Consti-

safeguards of Constitution designed to prevent—from being dangerous 184

special language of—explained 183

Usurpation

incapable of altering power of Congress 192

remedies against—by Federal government include for example protests by legislatures 17, 59; use by States of force in last resort 50, 60

Washington's *Farewell Address* prepared in part by, 147-148

Writings of, consulted extensively in preparation of this study-guide 143

Magna Carta

Philosophy of, antithesis of American philosophy 136-137

Majority, The

Democracy does not limit, 120-121, 157-161

Individual (The) and The Minority safeguarded against oppression by, 36, 70-71, 80, 119, 157, 161-163

Jefferson: "sacred principle" that, must respect rights of The Minority 119

Limitations on, 36, 119-123

"Limited for Liberty" a main American Principle 119-123

Republic limits, 120, 157, 161, 163

Rule by, Omnipotent barred from America 163

Majority Vote

Rule by, a necessary mechanic of government 119, 158

Malden, Mass.

Demand for a Republic (1776) 164-165

Man

Capacity to reason 26, 97-98, 140

Divine creation of, 7, 9

Imperfectible nature of, 15

Mixture of good and evil 15, 19

Man-Over-Government

Constitution's system of, 154

Economic Liberty in relation to, 56, 97-98, 209-211

Equality in keeping with, precludes government's providing things material etc. 68-69, 71-72

Federalist (The) explained system of, under Constitution 154

Government-provided security is antithetical to, 81

Happiness under, requires officials' obedience to the Constitution 81

Liberty against Government-over-Man is meaning of, 81, 87, 90

Oppression of The Individual or The Minority barred under, 36, 70-71, 80, 119

Public officials

servants of the people 37-38

act without authority when outside scope of office 49-50

Rights of The Individual may not be sacrificed under, 36, 70-71, 80, 119

Tax tyranny barred under, 107, 111-112

Twin Revolution's goal (1776) was, 131, 133

Manufactures

A field of power prohibited to Federal government 177

Hamilton's report (1791) on, 47, 178

Jefferson's statement that, best left to Individual Enterprise 58, 209

Marshall, John

Constitution's plain language expresses controlling intent of Framers and Adopters and to be given natural meaning 193

Federalist (The) authoritative as to Framers' intent and Constitution's meaning 153-154

"Judicial Review" (courts deciding constitutionality of laws) a part of the constitutional system per, in Va. Ratifying Convention 1788) 196

Ratifying Conventions' understanding controls as to meaning of Constitution 152

Sedition Act (1798) opposed by, as member of Congress 17

Marxist Socialism-Communism

Economic determinism a part of philosophy of, 236

Mason, George

Confederation's breakdown 224-225

"Judicial Review" (courts deciding constitutionality of laws) a part of the constitutional system per,

ruling that:

Fourteenth Amendment did not make Bill of Rights amendments apply against States 174-175

its own power limited 172, 291-293

power to control benefits is power to coerce or destroy 89, 179

subsidy-control of agriculture (*Butler* case) is a power prohibited to Federal government 179,181-182

U.S. law (Act of Congress) in conflict with Constitution is made instantly null and void by latter 181-182

Dred Scott decision (1857) protested by Mass. and Wisc. legislatures 145-146 (see opinion 292-293)

Federalist (The)

authoritative as to Framers' intent and Constitution's meaning according to the, 153-154

text quoted at length concerning, 271-286

upheld by, as to Constitution's meaning in opposition to Hamilton's conflicting argument in 1796 case 153-154

Fourteenth Amendment's wording was not intended to give the, any blank-check power regarding Bill of Rights amendments 174-175

General Welfare clause defined by, as limited and limiting 47-48

Respect in practice by, for constitutional system's limits on its authority essential to Liberty 192

Role of, under Constitutional system not mysterious 193

State versus Federal powers defined in general by, 168-169

Treaty clause ruled by, to be limited by whole Constitution 186

Usurpation by,

justifies "positive defiance" of, according to Wisc. Legislature (1859) 145-146

of policy-making power in governmental (political) area most dangerous to Liberty 200-201

protested by State legislatures 16-18, 59, 144-147, 287-290

through Constitution's misinterpretation prohibₗₜₑ ₁54-155, 194-

200; also pertinent passages of portions of *The Federalist* quoted pages 271-286 *post*

Supreme Law of the Land

Defined as including

Constitution (in its original meaning) 44, 50, 155, 182-183, 194, 196-197, 199

Laws (Acts of Congress) conforming to the Constitution 183, 197

Treaties conforming to the Constitution 183-186, 197

Supreme Court decisions not, 197

Taxes

American Revolution induced in part by royal abuse of power of levying, 107, 112

Confiscatory, forbidden by principles of Declaration of Independence 111-112

Consumption, automatically limited 111

Death (inheritance), 112

Estate (inheritance), 112

Federal rate (maximum) for income, under first law (1913) 113

Federal power to levy,

Hamilton on—47, 108, 178-179

limited by the "general Welfare" clause 46-48, 108, 178, 191, (and Roosevelt address 1930) 252; for Liberty 107-108, 111-112; to suit limited duties and responsibilities authorized by the Constitution 108

on income limited by basic American Principles 111-112

on inheritance limited by basic American Principles 112

Prohibited uses of—:

benevolence (aid) at home 110; or abroad 110, 188-191

control indirectly where not directly authorized 108

examples 108-111

General Welfare in Congress' discretion 47-48, 109

governmental change not directly authorized 108, 179

Individual Enterprise system's injury 109

"leveling" (tax some to give to others) 109

prevent criticism of officials by the Press 108-109

Judges guilty of, through violating the Constitution flout Rule-by-Law and in effect substitute Rule-by-Man (Par. 12) 199-200

Oath of office of all officials Civil and Military requires resistance against, 50, 61

Resistance by States by force in last resort against Federal, 50, 58-61

Rule-by-Man replaces Rule-by-Law in case of, 49-50, 133, 140, 199-200

State legislatures protested Federal, 16-18, 59, 144-146, 287-290

Taxing-power not authorized to be used to support activities furthering, 108, 110-111, 190-191

Treasonable offense against the people (Hamilton) 48, 199

Warnings by Founders against, 48-49, 154, 182, 190, 199-201; (Washington's *Farewell Address*) 263

Usurpers

(See also: Remedies; Usurpation of power)

Constitution voids all things governmental perpetrated by, 61, 146, 183-184, 194, 196-198

Culpability of, is personal and individual under oath of office as in the case of a usurper-judge 198-200

Judges as, intruding in field of governmental (political) policy are deadly foes of Liberty 200-201

Violate limits on their authority and act outside of Law: as "out-laws" 49, 133, 140, 199-200

"Vices" etc. (Madison)

"Vices of the Political System of the U.S." by Madison (1787) under the Confederation 226-227

———

Vindication of the Government of New-England Churches, A—book by Rev. John Wise (1717) 139-140

———

Virginia

Bill to establish religious freedom 202-203

Declaration of Rights quoted concerning standing armies 60

Legislature of,

excesses (after 1776) 122, 159-160

protested debt assumption (1790) 17, 144-145

protested Federal usurpation (1798-1799) 16-18, 59, 143-147, 287-290

"Memorial and Remonstrance Against Religious Assessments, A" (1785) 208

Ratifying Convention (1788) of,

Patrick Henry in—18

proposed amendments 49-50

The Federalist used in, 151

University of, Board of Visitors' resolution (1825):

students to be inculcated (indoctrinated) with American Principles and source books recommended 141-144

The Federalist cited in—as authoritative source regarding Constitution's meaning 148

Jefferson Rector of University of, 141

Vermont

Represented in Hartford Convention 145

Voluntariness

American philosophy features, 27, 57, 69, 70-72, 78-80, 88, 210-213

Freedom of choice based on, 27, 57, 70-72, 88, 210-213

Individual Enterprise system based on, 210-213

Key factor in enjoyment of right to Life and pursuit of Happiness 78-80

"Wall Street"

Mentioned incidentally 211

Ward, Nathaniel

Compiler of Mass. Laws (1641) 99

Warren, Joseph

Plea by, to Americans to act worthily in face of danger v, 245-246

Property Right a derivative right 101

Washington, George

Bill of Rights needless in original Constitution 173

Character of, as a patriot and his motives in Framing Convention supported against attackers 238-239